GABRIEL N. FINDER AND
ALEXANDER V. PRUSIN

Justice behind
the Iron Curtain

Nazis on Trial in Communist Poland

UNIVERSITY OF TORONTO PRESS
Toronto Buffalo London

© University of Toronto Press 2018
Toronto Buffalo London
utorontopress.com
Printed in Canada

ISBN 978-1-4426-3745-0 (cloth)   ISBN 978-1-4875-2268-1 (paper)

(German and European Studies)

Library and Archives Canada Cataloguing in Publication

Finder, Gabriel N., author
Justice behind the Iron Curtain : Nazis on trial in communist Poland /
Gabriel N. Finder and Alexander V. Prusin.

(German and European studies ; 32)
Includes bibliographical references and index.

ISBN 978-1-4426-3745-0 (hardcover)   ISBN 978-1-4875-2268-1 (paper)

1. War crime trials – Poland – History – 20th century.   2. War criminals – Poland –
History – 20th century.   3. Nazis – Poland – History – 20th century.   4. Holocaust,
Jewish (1939-1945).   5. Communism – Poland – History – 20th century.   I. Prusin,
Alexander Victor, author   II. Title.   III. Series: German and European studies ; 32.

KZ1174.5.F56 2018   341.6'90268   C2018-902035-0

This book has been published with the help of a grant from the Federation
for the Humanities and Social Sciences, through the Awards to Scholarly
Publications Program, using funds provided by the Social Sciences
and Humanities Research Council of Canada.

University of Toronto Press acknowledges the financial assistance
to its publishing program of the Canada Council for the Arts and
the Ontario Arts Council, an agency of the Government of Ontario.

Canada Council   Conseil des Arts
for the Arts   du Canada

ONTARIO ARTS COUNCIL
CONSEIL DES ARTS DE L'ONTARIO
an Ontario government agency
un organisme du gouvernement de l'Ontario

Funded by the   Financé par le
Government   gouvernement
of Canada   du Canada

Canadä

JUSTICE BEHIND THE IRON CURTAIN

Nazis on Trial in Communist Poland

In *Justice behind the Iron Curtain*, Gabriel N. Finder and Alexander V. Prusin examine Poland's role in prosecuting Nazi German criminals during the first decade and a half of the postwar era. Finder and Prusin contend that the Polish trials of Nazi war criminals were a pragmatic political response to postwar Polish society and its desire for vengeance against German Nazis. Although characterized by numerous inconsistencies, Poland's prosecutions of Nazis exhibited a reasonable degree of due process and were not unlike similar proceedings in Western democratic countries.

The authors examine reactions to the trials among Poles and Jews. Although Polish-Jewish relations were quite tense in the wake of the extremely brutal German wartime occupation of Poland, postwar Polish prosecutions of German Nazis placed emphasis on the fate of Jews during the Holocaust.

Justice behind the Iron Curtain is the first work to approach communist Poland's judicial postwar confrontation with the legacy of the Nazi occupation.

(German and European Studies)

GABRIEL N. FINDER is an associate professor in the Department of Germanic Languages and Literatures and Ida and Nathan Kolodiz Director of Jewish Studies at the University of Virginia.

ALEXANDER V. PRUSIN is a professor of history at the New Mexico Institute of Mining and Technology.

GERMAN AND EUROPEAN STUDIES
General Editor: Jennifer J. Jenkins

Contents

Illustrations

Acknowledgments

The idea for this book began to germinate a decade ago. After several years of discussion and collaborative research and writing, that idea has come to fruition in *Justice behind the Iron Curtain*.

Trial records held in the archives of the United States Holocaust Memorial Museum (USHMM) in Washington, DC, and in the Institute of National Remembrance–Commission for the Prosecution of Crimes against the Polish Nation (Instytut Pamięci Narodowej–Komisja Ścigania Zbrodni przeciwko Narodowi Polskiemu, IPN) in Warsaw form the backbone of our book. We wish to thank librarians Vincent Slatt and Megan Lewis for their generous help in identifying pertinent records among the USHMM's extensive archival holdings. We are particularly indebted to Tomasz Frydel, Katarzyna Person, Marcin Urynowicz, and Barbara Engelking for their magnanimous assistance in helping us obtain files from the IPN that are crucial to our study.

We also wish to express our thanks to Bożena Szaynok, Jakub Tyszkiewicz, and Łukasz Kamiński from the University of Wrocław, who each checked our manuscript with a fine-tooth comb and made invaluable suggestions for improving it at the Fifteenth Annual Conference of "Recovering Forgotten History: The Image of East-Central Europe in English-Language Academic Books and Textbooks," which was held in Poland in June 2017. We are grateful to Professor Andrzej S. Kamiński and the other coordinators of the conference for inviting us to participate.

We owe a deep debt of gratitude to Stephen Shapiro, Frances Mundy, and Richard Ratzlaff, our editors, who have so expertly and graciously shepherded our manuscript from its initial editorial stages to the finished product. It has been a pleasure to work with them and their colleagues at the University of Toronto Press. We would also like to thank Matthew Kudelka, our copy editor, and Noeline Bridge, our indexer, for their indispensible contributions to this text.

We would be remiss if we did not thank each other. This book has been a joint endeavour from start to finish. We were close friends before we started writing this book together. We're even closer friends now upon its completion.

We dedicate our book to Herbert Finder and to the late Victor Prusin, our fathers, men of courage and integrity.

Postscript: As this book was going to press, Alexander Prusin, my very dear friend and colleague, passed away suddenly and unexpectedly, his life cut short much too soon. I'm heartbroken. Alex was like a brother to me. We met more than twenty years ago when we were both graduate students, just a few years after he had left the Soviet Union in search of breathing space in the United States. He delighted in his newfound personal and academic freedom. I was his first close friend in America and our friendship was cemented when we coauthored two articles early in our parallel careers. Academic writing in our field is generally a solitary enterprise. To write with another scholar is demanding: it requires mutual respect for each other's viewpoints, openness to the strength of each other's arguments, and willingness to find middle ground. So it was between Alex and me. Then we decided to write this book, which, over the course of a decade, demanded much, not least emotionally, of both of us, the children and grandchildren of Holocaust survivors and victims. It was, however, a labour of love. And now Alex won't be here to see our book appear in print; he should have been.

We dedicated our book to our respective fathers, Herbert Finder and the late Victor Prusin. Each of them survived the Second World War and the Holocaust, and they both rebuilt their lives in truly remarkable and admirable ways. Like our fathers, Alex was a man of courage and integrity, a good man, who learned from the pasts of men like our fathers to forge his own truly remarkable and admirable path in life. Now Alex is gone. I will sorely miss him. Our book is a tribute to his life.

Gabriel Finder
August 2018

Abbreviations

AAN	(Archiwum Akt Nowych) – Archive of New Files, Warsaw
AK	(Armia Krajowa) – Home Army, the main Polish underground organization, subordinate to the government-in-exile in London
BAL	(Bundesarchiv Ludwigsburg) – Central Office for the Investigation of National Socialist Crimes, Ludwigsburg, Germany
CKŻP	(Centralny Komitet Żydów w Polsce) – Central Committee of Jews in Poland
CŻKH	(Centralna Żydowska Komisja Historyczna) – Central Jewish Historical Commission
GKBZN	(Główna Komisja Badania Zbrodni Niemieckich w Polsce) – Main Commission for the Investigation of German Crimes in Poland (in 1949 renamed Główna Komisja Badania Zbrodni Hitlerowskich w Polsce – Main Commission for the Investigation of Hitlerite Crimes in Poland, GKBZH)
GL	(Gwardia Ludowa) – People's Guard, the communist underground organization, subordinate to the Polish Workers' Party (PPR). In January 1944 renamed Armia Ludowa (People's Army, AL)
HSSPF	(Höherer SS- und Polizeiführer) – Supreme SS and Police Leader
IMT	International Military Tribunal
IPN	(Instytut Pamięci Narodowej-Komisja Ścigania Zbrodni przeciwko Narodowi Polskiemu) – Institute of National Remembrance–Commission for the Prosecution of Crimes against the Polish Nation, Warsaw

KdS   (Kommandeur der Sicherheitspolizei) – regional (German)
          Command of the Security Police, which included the Secret
          State Police (Gestapo), the SD, and the Kripo
Kripo   (Kriminalpolizei) – (German) Criminal Police
KRN   (Krajowa Rada Narodowa) – State National Council
MBP   (Ministerstwo Bezpieczeństwa Publicznego) – Ministry of
          Public Security; between July and December 1944, known
          as Department of Public Security (Resort Bezpieczeństwa
          Publicznego)
NKVD   (Narodnyi Kommissariat Vnutrennikh Del) – People's
          Commissariat for Internal Affairs, Soviet Union
NSDAP   (Nationalsozialistische Deutsche Arbeiterpartei, NSDAP) –
          National Socialist German Workers' Party or Nazi Party
NTN   (Najwyższy Trybunał Narodowy) – Supreme National
          Tribunal
PKWN   (Polski Komitet Wyzwolenia Narodowego) – Polish
          Committee of National Liberation
PPR   (Polska Partia Robotnicza) – Polish Workers' Party
          (communist)
PPS   (Polska Partia Socjalistyczna) – Polish Socialist Party
PSL   (Polskie Stronnictwo Ludowe) – Polish People's Party
PZPR   (Polska Zjednoczona Partia Robotnicza) – Polish United
          Workers' Party (communist), created in 1948 from the
          merger of PPR and PPS
TRJN   (Tymczasowy Rząd Jedności Narodowej) – Provisional
          Government of National Unity
RSHA   (Reichssicherheitshauptamt) – (German) Reich Main
          Security Office
SA   (Sturmabteilung) – (German) Storm Detachment (Storm
          Troopers)
SD   (Sicherheitsdienst) – (German) Security Service
Sipo   (Sicherheitspolizei) – (German) Security Police (included
          the Gestapo and the Kripo)
SS   (Schutzstaffel) – (German) Protective Squadron
SSPF   (SS- und Polizeiführer) – SS and Police Leader
TSKŻ   (Towarzystwo Społeczno-Kulturalne Żydów w Polsce) –
          Social and Cultural Association of Jews in Poland
UB   (Urząd Bezpieczeństwa) – regional (Polish) branches of
          MBP
UNWCC   United Nations War Crimes Commission

USHMM　United States Holocaust Memorial Museum, Washington, DC

ZPP　(Związek Patriotów Polskich) – Union of Polish Patriots in the USSR

ŻIH　(Żydowski Instytut Historyczny) – Jewish Historical Institute, Warsaw

ŻOB　(Żydowska Organizacja Bojowa) – Jewish Combat Organization

ŻZW　(Żydowski Związek Wojskowy) – Jewish Military Union

Map of Poland in 1939–45

1 Adapted from "Territories of Poland occupied by the Third Reich,"
by Lonio17, Wikimedia Commons. Used under a CC BY-SA-4.0 licence.

Map of Poland in 1945

2 Adapted from "A map presenting Poland [according to] the Curzon Line"
by radek.s, Wikimedia Commons. Used under a CC BY-SA-3.0 licence.

JUSTICE BEHIND THE IRON CURTAIN

Nazis on Trial in Communist Poland

Introduction

The overarching subject of this book, which is reflected in its title, is Poland's postwar confrontation in its courts of law with the legacy of its occupation by Nazi Germany during the Second World War. The country's occupation by German forces was oppressive, violent, and murderous. To be sure, in the wake of the war, all Allied nations wanted to prosecute war crimes and humanitarian atrocities committed by the Axis powers on their soil, but the Polish case was exceptional by any standard. In the course of six years Poland was subjected to three foreign occupations: between 1939 and 1941 it was divided between Nazi Germany and the Soviet Union, from 1941 to 1944 it was occupied solely by German forces, and progressively from mid-1944 through the spring of 1945, while the Germans were in retreat, it again fell under Soviet domination, remaining so after the war's end. Both occupiers subjected Poland to extensive social engineering, which involved the elimination of that country's national elites and the mass relocation of its population, not to mention mass murder. Among all of the European countries affected by the war, it was Poland that suffered the highest death rate – six million, or about 17 per cent of its prewar population. German terror alone claimed the lives of approximately 5.5 million Polish citizens, including 3 million Jews.[1]

Most Poles quite understandably wanted the Germans (and Austrians) who had been active in Poland during the occupation and who were responsible for this horrific carnage to be brought to justice. At the same time, however, the political circumstances in postwar Poland were extremely volatile. Under the protection of the Soviet army, Polish communists, formed into the Polish Workers' Party (Polska Partia

Robotnicza, PPR),[2] manoeuvred first to seize power and then to consolidate it, even though most Poles viewed them as stooges imposed by a hostile foreign entity. In the immediate postwar years, the non-communist armed underground had controlled much of the countryside and non-communist political parties had still been represented in the government. But after Polish communists consolidated power in the late 1940s, culminating in the merger of the PPR with the left-wing Polish Socialist Party (Polska Partia Socjalistyczna, PPS) and the subsequent establishment of the Polish United Workers' Party (Polska Zjednoczona Partia Robotnicza, PZPR), in December 1948, they imposed a repressive, Stalinist form of communism on the country. Until the end of Stalinism (the Soviet dictator died in 1953) and the consequent political "thaw" (odwilż) in 1956, the communists were preoccupied with repressing political opposition, and many members of the non-communist parties were imprisoned or executed on trumped-up charges. Accordingly, trials of German (and Austrian) Nazis played a less important role in Poland's official reckoning with the past. Nevertheless, reflecting the desires of the average person on the street, the upper echelons in the PPR (later the PZPR), in order to demonstrate the impartiality of Polish law, which had been reconstituted in the postwar era under communist rule, supported a concerted effort by the Polish legal system to bring Nazi criminals to justice. In an article published in the Polish press during the trial of the commandant of Auschwitz, Rudolf Höss, a prominent prosecutor, Tadeusz Cyprian, referred to "historical justice" as a task well suited to the new judicial system – in this instance, "the court itself would write the history of the crime."[3]

Since in postwar Poland the prosecution of Soviet crimes was out of the question, the trials of Nazi criminals became the sole avenue for postwar retribution and as well as the sole venue in which all segments of Polish society, regardless of political affiliation, could come to some consensus. Given that they functioned in the politically and ideologically loaded postwar context, the war crimes trials in Poland raise many legal and moral questions of historical importance, especially when one considers that law in Soviet-dominated Eastern Europe was subordinated to political expediency and that questions of individual guilt were often irrelevant. Because the communist regime was preoccupied with eliminating political opposition, both real and imagined, thousands of Polish citizens were convicted of war crimes for ostensibly aiding or "collaborating" with the Nazi occupation regime. Between 1944 and 1956, Polish courts convicted about 17,000 individuals for war crimes;

only one-third of these people – some 5,500 – were German or Austrian nationals or ethnic Germans (*Volksdeutsche*).[4] (As of 1954, 84,200 political prisoners were incarcerated in Poland, having been sentenced under various charges.)[5] In the Lublin District between 1944 and 1954, the courts convicted 12,000 members of opposition and resistance groups (515 of whom were sentenced to death), but they tried only 141 Nazi criminals (17 of whom received the death penalty).[6] To add insult to injury, Polish authorities often incarcerated members of the wartime Polish non-communist resistance to Nazism in the same prison cells as senior Nazis: Kazimierz Moczarski, an officer in the Home Army (Armia Krajowa, AK), the underground military organization of the Polish government-in-exile,[7] which was headquartered in London, shared a prison cell for 225 days with SS-Gruppenführer (Lieutenant General) Jürgen Stroop, who had been in charge of the German forces that liquidated the Warsaw Ghetto and suppressed the Warsaw Ghetto Uprising in April–May 1943; August Emil Fieldorf, alias "Nil," a Polish brigadier general and commander-in-chief of the AK after the failure of the 1944 Warsaw Uprising, spent time in the same cell as Jakob Sporrenberg, SS and Police Leader (SS- und Polizeiführer, SSPF) of the Lublin District; and Stanisława Rachwał, a member of the Polish resistance in Kraków, encountered Maria Mandel, the vicious supervisor of the women's camp in Auschwitz, in Kraków's Montelupich prison, which the Gestapo had used during the war to imprison Poles.[8] It is beyond doubt that the communist regime was more concerned with the political opposition than with Nazi culprits and that it misused the Polish legal system to persecute Polish citizens whom it viewed as political opponents, even tarring some of them with the same brush as they applied to the Nazis. All of this raises the question: Was Polish officials' professed commitment to punish Nazi criminals merely a smokescreen to appease popular sentiments? In our opinion, the answer is no.

Poland was more persistent than any of the other Soviet satellites in pursuing Nazi criminals and investigating Nazi crimes. Around 5,500 German Nazis were put on trial in Polish courts in the first decade or so of the postwar era – a not inconsiderable number in its own right – and in addition to this, from 1944 to 1985, Polish authorities investigated between 80,000 and 100,000 cases.[9] Truth be told, the Allies were less responsive to the extradition efforts of other Eastern European countries than they were to those made by Poland.[10] Even so, the Allies were supportive of Polish efforts only to a degree. Many if not most Nazis wound up in Allied-occupied western Germany, and with the onset of the Cold War the Americans and the British grew increasingly reluctant to extradite alleged war criminals in their custody to Eastern Europe. By 1947, Polish authorities had handed the Western Allies the names of between 12,000 and 15,000 individuals accused of committing atrocities in Poland, but only some 1,800 had been extradited to Warsaw by 1949, when the extraditions were suspended.[11]

After the war, the Polish authorities vigorously pursued Nazi war criminals, yet only a few scholars in or outside Poland have investigated this.[12] No monograph on this topic has been written in any language. This book aims to fill this lacuna in studies of Poland under communist rule and to expand the treatment of the postwar trials of Nazi criminals to include countries behind the Iron Curtain. However, this book is *not* a study of Polish postwar justice in general. Hence, the trials of political opponents and native collaborators are beyond its scope.

In this book we advance two intertwined arguments. First, we contend that the postwar trials of Nazis in communist Poland, ending with the trial of Erich Koch in 1959, were not Stalinist-type show trials. On the contrary, although they were not immune from inconsistencies, Polish trials for Nazi crimes exhibited a fair degree of due process and resembled similar proceedings in Western democratic countries (which displayed their own share of distortions and contradictions). Furthermore, the trials had an integrative social function: after six years of brutal German occupation, they constituted a pragmatic and popular political response to postwar Polish society's strong yearning for justice – and vengeance. Thus, although the communist authorities had every intention of exploiting the postwar legal system in order to eliminate the political opposition, they left the prosecution of Nazi criminals – which in their minds was secondary to the judicial neutralization of political opponents – more or less alone. At a time when the repression of real and alleged opponents of the regime was reaching its peak, Polish judges, prosecutors, and defence counsel active in war crimes trials were afforded significant latitude to try these cases applying conventional legal and moral standards comparable to those found in contemporary trials of Nazis in the West, including the Nuremberg trials; and since many had received their legal training in the interwar period, they took advantage of this unique opportunity to follow their inclinations to conduct these particular trials in the spirit of the rule of law. By the same token, the trials of Nazis, which resonated in Polish political circles and Polish society alike, afforded average Poles an opportunity to gain more or less unvarnished insight into the criminal liability of individual Nazi perpetrators of mass terror, destruction, enslavement, and genocide. Indeed, the Polish trials of Nazi war criminals legitimized the communist regime to some degree, both within and outside Poland.

Second, we argue that, as much as it was possible in postwar Eastern Europe in general and in postwar Poland in particular, in an atmosphere permeated by antisemitism to varying degrees even "after Auschwitz,"[13] the Polish trials of Nazi culprits addressed the Nazi genocide of the Jews – that is to say, the Holocaust – in a relatively open and even-handed manner. Every country that had been subjected to German occupation was confronted with two interwoven and vexed issues: the tragedy of its ethnic majority, and the tragedy of its Jewish minority. Across Europe, the governments of the countries that Germany had occupied took pains to shoehorn the fate of their Jewish populations into a context adapted to their distinctive permutations of collective national memory.[14] The communist regime in Poland was no different in this regard. As part of an effort to soften the strong popular aversion to the Soviet-installed regime, official discourse in Poland set out to shape collective memory by highlighting the horrific losses of the nation without making distinctions between ethnic Poles and Jewish Poles. According to official propaganda, therefore, the suffering of Poland's Jews flowed from and was a by-product of Nazi Germany's war aims, which were to conquer, exploit, enslave, and murder the Poles and other Slavic peoples.[15]

But in Poland the communist monopoly on memory was never ironclad, and despite official efforts to dictate memory, Polish and Jewish memories were dynamic rather than static. So it was in particular in the Polish trials of Nazi criminals. Thus, during the Polish trials of Nazis, Polish courts and legal personnel generally acknowledged the distinctiveness of the Nazi genocide of Poland's Jews. Indeed, this became a central issue in several trials. The trial of Rudolf Höss, the commandant of Auschwitz, is the best-known in this regard, but it was not the only one: the trials of Jürgen Stroop, Amon Göth, the commandant of the Płaszów concentration camp, and Hans Biebow, the Nazi official in charge of the Łódź Ghetto, could, well before the 1961 Eichmann trial in Jerusalem, justifiably be regarded as Holocaust trials, since they dealt specifically with the genocide of Jews. Importantly, the participation of Jewish eyewitnesses and historians in these trials – which Polish legal officials, to their credit, welcomed – helped offset the tendency in Poland and in the rest of Eastern (and Western) Europe to erase the distinction between Jewish and non-Jewish victims of Nazism. For their part, Jews in Poland (and elsewhere) considered it their solemn duty to help bring Nazi perpetrators to justice. The professional and amateur historians from within the surviving remnant of Polish Jewry formed the Central Jewish Historical Commission (Centralna Żydowska Komisja Historyczna, CŻKH), succeeded by the Jewish Historical Institute (Żydowski Instytut Historyczny, ŻIH), in large part to gather evidence of Nazi crimes against Jews for use at trials. To this end, they interviewed thousands of survivors and collected and analysed thousands of German documents. Many Jewish historians would eventually prepare reports and testify in court in their capacity as expert witnesses for the prosecution. Thus the Polish trials of Nazis became, in one way, a site of what literary scholar Michael Rothberg would call "multidirectional" memories – Rothberg's term for the productive, intercultural, and often unexpected interaction of memories in an open and contested public sphere.[16] But the trials were not immune from what Rothberg calls "competitive memory." Wanting to remain relevant and to be asked by Polish legal officials to return to testify in future trials, Jewish historians were reluctant to press the distinctive quality of Jewish suffering too far. Thus, to the chagrin of many of Nachman Blumental's colleagues in the CŻKH, who wanted him to be a forceful advocate for the Jewish people as an expert witness for the prosecution in the trial of Rudolf Höss, he testified that Poles and Jews shared a "common enemy."[17] Even so, the Polish trials of Nazis went a long way towards bridging the long-standing gap between ethnic Poles and Polish Jews – a gap made wider during the war years and by postwar antisemitism – but they did not close that gap.

The format of this study is predominantly chronological and thematic. Chapter 1 describes the immediate postwar prosecution of Nazis in Poland from 1944 to 1947. The pursuit of Nazi criminals was a high priority in the minds of Polish leaders during the Second World War. Both the Polish government-in-exile, based in London, and after 1944 the Soviet-sponsored Polish Committee for National Liberation (Polski Komitet Wyzwolenia Narodowego, PKWN), declared their intent to punish war criminals and their accomplices after the war. This chapter thus explores the competing efforts of communists and London-based Poles to promote postwar justice, as well as the communists' plans for war crimes trials once they had been installed in power during the Red Army offensive in the summer of 1944 and their vision of these trials' intended function in a future communist state. In this context, we trace the promulgation of new laws to confront Nazi criminality and the establishment of special penal courts to administer postwar justice, a process propelled by pervasive hatred of Germans. We also consider the role that the Nazis' mass murder of Jews played in Polish leaders' political calculations.

Chapter 2 examines the role of the Polish delegation to the Nuremberg Trial. In August 1945 the United States, Great Britain, France, and the Soviet Union signed the London Agreement, which declared their intention to try the most prominent German war criminals. Appended to the agreement was a charter for the International Military Tribunal (IMT), to be held in Nuremberg. Under the terms of the charter, each signatory was permitted to appoint a chief prosecutor and a staff of prosecutors under him, but it made no provisions for permanent delegations from other countries. In the name of the Republic of Poland, prosecutors from Poland's Ministry of Justice were given permission to prepare and submit reports and documents to Allied prosecutors. Polish prosecutors were not allowed to participate directly in the court proceedings, but they did receive permission to interrogate witnesses suspected of having committed war crimes in Poland. The chapter pays special attention to the "Polish indictment," a comprehensive report on crimes the Nazis perpetrated in Poland that the Polish delegation submitted in December 1945 to Allied prosecutors and that Soviet prosecutors presented to the tribunal as evidence. We further examine the testimony of the trial's only two witnesses from Poland, who, sponsored by the Polish delegation, described the ordeal of Jews at Auschwitz and Treblinka. We also explore the role of the Holocaust in the minds of the lawyers who represented Poland at the IMT.

Chapter 3 examines the establishment and *modus operandi* of Poland's Supreme National Tribunal (Najwyższy Trybunał Narodowy, NTN), which was designed specifically to prosecute major Nazi criminals and collaborators. It functioned between 1946 and 1948 amid a ferocious struggle for power in postwar Poland, during which the communist-dominated government focused its efforts on eliminating political opponents. Nevertheless, in its proceedings the NTN applied conventional legal and moral standards comparable to those used in Western courts and investigated each case comprehensively within the broad framework of Nazi policies in Poland. This chapter concentrates on the proceedings, the legal and political contexts, and the outcomes of the NTN's trials of both the top brass of the Nazi administration in Poland – including Arthur Greiser, the governor of the so-called Warthegau (the area of western Poland annexed to Germany); Albert Forster, *Gauleiter* (regional leader) of the Nazi Party in Gdańsk; and Josef Bühler, the deputy of Hans Frank, Governor General of occupied Poland, the so-called General Government – and those who directly carried out the Nazis' genocidal policies – Amon Göth, Rudolf Höss, and forty Auschwitz guards and functionaries.

Chapter 4 explores the prosecutions of Nazi criminals conducted during the Stalinist purges in Poland between 1948 and 1952, when a vicious campaign against "national communists," set against the background of the intensifying Cold War, greatly overshadowed the trials for Nazi crimes. Yet even during this period, Polish provincial courts tried several figures who had played a particularly sinister role in the mass murder of Poles and Jews: Waldemar Macholl, a Gestapo functionary in Białystok; Josef Grzimek, a notorious commandant of several Jewish ghettos and camps; and Jürgen Stroop. A prominent theme in this chapter is the attempts by the courts to explain what compelled the defendants to commit their heinous crimes.

Chapter 5 examines the Jewish stake in bringing Nazi criminals to justice in Poland and the constraints under which Jewish historians were compelled to operate if they wanted to play a role in the prosecution of Nazi criminals. Jews' and Poles' memories of the war diverged sharply, yet they shared a strong interest in the prosecution of Nazi criminals. During the war, Polish Jews had painstakingly recorded the Germans' crimes in ghetto chronicles and individual diaries. The first contingent of Jewish survivors to arrive in liberated Lublin in the fall of 1944 organized an *ad hoc* historical commission whose mandate was to document the fate of Polish Jewry under German occupation; in 1947, that body's permanent successor, the CŻKH, was reorganized as the ŻIH, which was more ideologically attuned to the spirit of the times. In turn, the state-sponsored Main Commission for the Investigation of German Crimes in Poland (Główna Komisja Badania Zbrodni Niemieckich w Polsce, GKBZN), in 1950 renamed the Main Commission for the Investigation of Hitlerite Crimes in Poland (Główna Komisja Badania Zbrodni Hitlerowskich w Polsce, GKBZH), encouraged and welcomed cooperation with the Jewish historical commissions at the central and local levels, and the Polish Ministry of Justice solicited the expert testimony of Jewish historians for trials of Nazi criminals. But Jewish historians had to toe a fine line. In the fluid and volatile political climate of postwar Poland, they had to avoid provoking official disapproval by appearing too aggressive in pressing the distinctive fate of Jews under Nazism.

By the late 1940s the prosecution of Nazi criminals had lost its political significance and the numbers of trials rapidly dwindled. Chapter 6 examines two trials – the 1954 trial of Paul Otto Geibel, SSPF of the Warsaw District; and the 1958–9 trial of Erich Koch, *Reichskommissar* of Ukraine and the chief of the Białystok administration – in the context of the interplay of politics and memory. The transcripts of Geibel's trial help re-create the history of the single largest massacre of an urban population during the Second World War – the Nazi destruction of the Polish capital in the summer and fall of 1944. Since an open trial of Geibel might well have undercut the state-approved version of the Warsaw Uprising, it was conducted in a restrained and inconspicuous manner. In contrast, the trial of Erich Koch – the last high-level Nazi tried in Poland – became a Cold War *cause célèbre* and a powerful platform for publicly condemning the "imperialist powers" for apparently granting immunity to Nazi criminals in the West.

A few remarks on terms and sources are in order. Under the German occupation, Poland was divided into several administrative zones, where, in line with the Nazi racial program, Germans pursued their policies of colonization, enslavement, and mass murder. Western Poland, which included the Gdańsk (Danzig in German) region, Pomerania (the so-called Polish Corridor), Poznań province (Posen in German), and most of Upper Silesia, was incorporated into the Third Reich. The Ciechanów District of the Warsaw province was integrated into East Prussia; the Białystok province, which was governed by Erich Koch,[18] the Gauleiter of East Prussia, was a separate administrative entity; and most of central Poland became the so-called General Government, which also included the district of East Galicia, under the rule of Hans Frank. Poland's eastern provinces – the *Kresy Wschodnie* – became parts of the Reichskommissariat (Reich Commissariat) Ostland and Reichskommisariat Ukraine (see map). From 1939 to 1941 and then from 1944 on, the *Kresy Wschodnie* and East Galicia were incorporated into the Soviet Union, absorbed by the Soviet republics of Lithuania, Byelorussia, and Ukraine.

We have retained the native spellings of contemporary German or Polish geographical names, except when those names have joined the English vernacular (for example, "Warsaw"). The Polish term *województwo* (voivodship) roughly corresponds to a province and *okręg* to a region or district. Hence, we refer to provincial (*wojewódski*) and district (*okręgowy*) courts. We correlate German military ranks with their US Army equivalents.

As Devin Pendas observes, "war crimes trial" is a flawed term. It is a highly politicized and historically inaccurate term of reference; furthermore, it has exculpatory undertones, for it implies that Nazi crimes were, *in potentia*, the equivalent of criminal acts committed by the Allies in the course of fighting and that all Nazi crimes were committed in the prosecution of conventional war. In fact, the Nazi crimes were distinguished by their unprecedented scale and brutality, and the aim of those crimes was not to help win the war, but to dehumanize and enslave civilian populations and to carry out a genocide against them.[19] We do our best to minimize use of the term "war crimes trials" in favour of admittedly more cumbersome phrases such as "trials of Nazi criminals," "trials for Nazi crimes," and the like. However, the term's wide contemporary usage after the Second World War makes periodic resort to it in this book unavoidable.

Trial records of Nazi criminals in Poland from the archives of the United States Holocaust Memorial Museum (USHMM) in Washington, D.C., and the Institute of National Remembrance–Commission for the Prosecution of Crimes against the Polish Nation (Instytut Pamięci Narodowej–Komisja Ścigania Zbrodni przeciwko Narodowi Polskiemu, IPN) in Warsaw lay the foundation for this study. The files of these trials in the USHMM and the IPN's unparalleled archival collections contain not only transcripts of the proceedings but also detailed investigative descriptions of Nazi crimes in Poland and an abundance of sundry documents that afford insight into the *modus operandi* of Poland's courts and its judicial system's approach to the trials of Nazis. Unfortunately, many records lack pagination, dates, or document titles. In such cases, sources will be cited in English in accordance, wherever possible, with their contents and provenance, or, if available, by microfilm frame numbers.

Chapter One

A Restive Society Demands Swift Justice

Over the course of the Second World War, the London-based Polish government-in-exile – which was the legally constituted government of Poland during the country's occupation by Nazi Germany – and, after 1944, the Polish communists in Moscow formulated separate policies to punish the German perpetrators of war crimes. That said, the prospective prosecution of Nazi war criminals played a secondary role in the long-term plans of both the exile government and the communists. The overriding concern for both (albeit their objectives were divergent) was to win the war and, after that, to reorganize postwar Poland; this would include re-establishing its borders, which had been significantly altered in 1939. These two opposing camps anticipated that they would be struggling for supremacy in postwar Poland, and both saw the benefit in declaring their intent to punish German war criminals and their accomplices after the war. These intentions had two corresponding aims: to act in unison with the Allied powers, which had declared their determination to prosecute Nazi war criminals, and to win popular support in Poland. Since Poles' loathing of the German occupation was so intense, and did not soften after the war, no Polish political party needed to expend much effort to exploit it; and since popular demands for justice were so vociferous, both the government-in-exile and the communists calculated that they stood only to gain from the prosecution of the most notorious Nazi culprits. To ensure those gains, they each issued a series of decrees for the postwar punishment of war criminals and their accomplices. In the wake of the Soviet summer offensive of 1944, the communists arrived in Poland; the decrees they promulgated at that time laid the foundation for a series of war crimes trials immediately after the war that would help legitimize the PPR's ambition to assume the reins of power. The exile government, relegated to the political wilderness, could only watch these and subsequent trials unfold from afar.

The Government-in-Exile and War Crimes Legislation

During the interwar period, Poles had articulated a deterrent war crimes policy; indeed, Polish jurists had played a prominent role in developing more precise definitions of the Geneva and Hague Conventions, which regulated warfare. For example, Emil Rappaport, a jurist of Jewish origin, helped found the International Association of Criminal Law, under whose auspices he advocated for international laws to punish aggressive war. He and other Polish jurists also contributed to research on the Soviet and Nazi legal systems.

A trailblazer in the field of international criminal law was Raphael Lemkin.[1] A Polish Jew who had studied philosophy at the University of Heidelberg and law at the University of Jan Casimir in Lwów (today L'viv University in Ukraine), he became deputy prosecutor at a Warsaw district court. He later took part in the codification of the 1932 Polish penal code. At the Fifth International Conference for the Unification of Penal Law, held in Madrid in 1933, he proposed that two new international crimes be established: "barbarity," defined as "oppressive and destructive actions directed against individuals as members of a national, religious, or racial group"; and "vandalism," defined as "the destruction of works of art and culture." While these offences were punishable by other names in the criminal codes of many countries, Lemkin sought to have them proscribed by a unitary international law on the grounds that they not only threatened the existence of entire groups but also possessed destructive transnational potential. The Madrid Conference did not adopt his resolutions. In 1937, Lemkin was appointed to the Polish mission to the Fourth Congress on Criminal Law in Paris, where he introduced the possibility of defending peace through criminal law.[2] When he joined the proposed crimes of "barbarity" and "vandalism" under the heading of "genocide" – the first appearance of that word in print – in *Axis Rule in Occupied Europe* (1944), he rued, as Berel Lang observes, "that the earlier proposals would have provided legal instruments for judging the actions of the Nazis in the years since."[3]

The Polish government-in-exile was a tenacious advocate of postwar retribution for German atrocities and was a leader among the exile governments of countries under German occupation in urging Great Britain and the United States to condemn Nazi war crimes, punish their perpetrators, and formulate a policy to try war criminals after the war.[4] The government-in-exile made several public statements promising postwar justice for German crimes. For example, on 1 September 1942, the president of Poland, Władysław Raczkiewicz, addressing his countrymen in a speech that was broadcast to Poland by the BBC, proclaimed that "not a single German, whether he gave or executed a criminal order, will escape the punishing hand of justice. The Polish government in London has been compiling the list of culprits ... This list has been growing every day and will be complete when victory is achieved."[5] On 5–21 November 1941, the government-in-exile and representatives of eight other German-occupied countries (Belgium, Czechoslovakia, Greece, Luxembourg, the Netherlands, Norway, and Yugoslavia, along with the French National Committee) agreed to formulate common legal grounds for the postwar prosecution of war criminals and to collect evidence of war crimes committed on their respective territories.[6]

On 13 January 1942, the representatives of these nine nations convened an international conference in London dedicated to the prosecution of Nazi crimes. Poland's role in initiating the conference (alongside the Czechoslovak government) was reflected in the fact that its chairman was Polish Prime Minister Władysław Sikorski. With the approval of Great Britain, the United States, and the Soviet Union (the "Big Three"), they signed the St James Declaration (named after the palace in London where the signatories met), which stipulated that individuals who issued or executed criminal orders, or participated in their implementation, would be punished. The declaration's terms prepared the ground for the postwar Allied prosecution of war criminals. The signatories organized themselves into the Inter-Allied Commission on War Crimes and committed themselves to "the punishment, through the channel of organized justice," of war criminals.[7] Since the spring of 1942, a steady stream of reports detailing unprecedented atrocities in Nazi-occupied Europe, including the systematic massacre of European Jews, had been reaching Western capitals, and as a consequence, the British and American governments found themselves under increasing pressure to act. In October 1943 the British and the Americans announced the establishment of the London-based United Nations War Crimes Commission (UNWCC); Poland and the other exile governments joined this body, together with Australia, China, India, New Zealand, and South Africa. Scholar Dan Plesch explains the UNWCC's remit: "Member nations of the commission presented cases to it for consideration in the form of dossiers – charge files – summarizing the case. If the cases were approved, the individuals and units were listed as accused war criminals and the nations concerned sought to apprehend them and bring them to trial in national courts."[8] This meant, in effect, that criminal prosecutions in national courts ensuing from cases approved by the UNWCC were being supported by the international community. However, the UNWCC had been formed without Moscow's participation. Instead, the Soviets established their own Extraordinary State Commission to investigate Nazi crimes on Soviet territory and to lay the foundations for Soviet war crimes trials, which commenced in 1943.[9]

The Polish exile government and its representatives did not limit themselves to crimes committed by Germans. In April 1940 the government-in-exile ordered the formation of "hood courts" (sądy kapturowe) to punish enemy agents – Polish, Ukrainian, and Russian as well as German – informants, deserters, and bandits. In May, the command of the Związek Walki Zbrojnej (ZWZ, the forerunner of the AK) issued a penal code for these courts, which stipulated that the crimes of high treason, espionage, provocation, denunciation, inhuman abuse (zbrodnie nieludzkiego prześladowania), and mistreatment of the Polish population were to be investigated and punished. This code's guidelines were based on the prewar Polish criminal and military penal codes. In the context of the extreme conditions precipitated by the German occupation, its centrepiece was the implementation of summary justice – once the sentence was confirmed by the ZWZ commander, it was final and not subject to appeal.[10] During the German occupation of Poland, the ZWZ and AK hood courts sentenced to death between 3,000 and 3,500 people – most of them Poles, but with some ethnic Germans among them – for collaboration with the enemy and other crimes.[11]

Since early 1942, Polish jurists had been drafting a special decree to define and punish war crimes. A conference devoted to this decree took place in London on 27–30 April 1942. Participants included Wacław Komarnicki, chairman of the Commission on Legislation (which acted on behalf of the government-in-exile with regard to all legislative issues), representatives of several ministries, and prominent jurists, including professors of law Stefan Glaser, Tadeusz Cyprian, and Bohdan Winiarski. The main task of the conference was to make Polish prewar legislation a more effective instrument for dealing with German war crimes and compatible with international legal standards, particularly the retroactive application of law (lex retro non agit).[12]

The draft of the decree was sent to the exile government's cabinet of ministers, which approved its general contents in July. Nevertheless, discussions on the formulation of the decree continued until October, when the cabinet signed the final version, which was then approved by the National Council. On 30 March 1943, President Raczkiewicz, Minister of Justice Komarnicki, and Prime Minister Władysław Sikorski signed the decree, which targeted German and other nationals who, acting on behalf of the Third Reich, violated international norms, regardless of where their crimes had been committed. Articles 2 and 3 of the decree stipulated imprisonment or the death penalty for violations of international law and crimes committed against the Polish state, Polish officials, or Polish citizens. Article 4 provided the death penalty or imprisonment for acts detrimental to life or human health, applicable to crimes committed in places of detention or concentration camps. Article 7 imposed the same punishment for violations of international laws pertaining to robbery, theft, destruction, or damage of public or private property, if such property was of national value. Article 10 specified that those who gave criminal orders and those who implemented them were equally liable.[13] The decree was the first Allied legislation to deal specifically with the prosecution of war criminals.[14]

In November 1943, Poland joined the Moscow Declaration, signed by US President Franklin D. Roosevelt, British Prime Minister Winston Churchill, and Soviet leader Josef Stalin on 1 November. The Allies emphasized the extradition of "German officers and men and members of the Nazi Party" for trial in liberated countries in which they had committed their "abominable deeds." (The Big Three – the US, the UK, and the USSR – simultaneously permitted themselves to decide in the future the appropriate process for punishing "major criminals whose offences have no particular geographical location." This proviso set the stage for the establishment of the IMT at Nuremberg in 1945–6.) Among German crimes mentioned in the declaration were "slaughters inflicted on the people of Poland." The declaration directed German-occupied countries to compile lists of German criminals and their deeds.[15]

To this end, the Polish government in London formed a special bureau for collecting information on German war crimes in Poland, including a special section devoted to developing charges for crimes against Jews. In February 1944 it submitted its first charge file to the UNWCC; named in it were SS-Gruppenführer (Lieutenant General) Ludolf von Alvensleben, accused of responsibility for mass executions in Pomerania, and Ernst Zörner, the mayor of Kraków and the governor of the Lublin District of occupied Poland. By August 1944 the government-in-exile had submitted charges against 267 individuals to the UNWCC.[16] Included in the

London government's charge sheets were cases for the persecution and murder of Jews. In April 1944 the exile government brought charges against eight Nazi officials implicated in the extermination of Jews at Treblinka; in June it submitted a charge file against twenty-one Nazi officials involved in crimes against Jews in various concentration camps located in Poland; in September it filed charges against ninety-five Nazis and prisoners implicated in the persecution and extermination of Jews at Auschwitz. All told, the Polish exile government brought to the UNWCC 1,535 cases against Germans and other Axis nationals for war crimes. (Only France filed more.)

August Decree (*Sierpniówka*)

Meanwhile, determined to defy the government-in-exile and preparing for the struggle for power, on 1 January 1944 the PPR formed the State National Council (Krajowa Rada Narodowa, KRN), which claimed to represent the "anti-fascist democratic movements" in Polish society. The KRN's political platform rejected the legitimacy of the "London Poles," renounced claims on eastern Poland, which had been annexed by the Soviet Union, and stipulated the formation of a provisional government allied with Moscow. In March 1944 and again in November, the communists issued declarations pertaining to war crimes that warned of retribution not only against war criminals but also against "traitors and enemies of the Polish people." The latter category alluded to the inevitable non-communist political opposition in postwar Poland.[17]

On 31 May 1944 the Military Council of the Polish Armed Forces in the USSR, which acted under the auspices of the Union of Polish Patriots in the USSR (Związek Patriotów Polskich, ZPP),[18] issued a long-winded decree titled "The Punishment of War Criminals Guilty of Murder and the Mistreatment of the Civilian Population and POWs." It closely mirrored the Soviet decree of 19 April 1943, which stipulated harsh punishment for Axis war criminals and their native collaborators but did not define what constituted a war crime, using instead the suggestive but imprecise term "atrocities."[19]

Since the Polish government-in-exile was the legal heir to Poland's prewar government, was recognized by the Western Allies, and was supported by the majority of Polish political parties, the communist leadership felt it had to act quickly. On 22 July 1944, in the Soviet-liberated city of Chełm, representatives of the KRN and the ZPP issued a manifesto announcing the creation of the PKWN, which was to function as the provisional government of Poland and the sole legitimate representative of the Polish nation. In fact, preparations for a takeover had begun much earlier, when the leading communist activists in the Soviet Union contemplated establishing the Polish National Committee, which would steer the war of national liberation towards one of social revolution. Under Moscow's auspices, the PKWN was to appear as a coalition body, though in reality the PPR would hold a monopoly in all spheres of politics and public life. Leftists and socialist parties were to be drawn or forced into an alliance with the PPR; independent and non-communist parties were marked for eventual elimination. With the support of Stalin and backed by Soviet military and security forces, the communists immediately began forming a new political and judicial system based on the Soviet model.[20]

The manifesto contained several important provisions. It recognized that Poland had lost its eastern provinces to the Soviet Union (in accordance with the decisions made by the Allies at the Tehran Conference in 1943).[21] It declared illegal the Polish government-in-exile and the interwar constitution of 1935, and it promised that independent Polish courts would "ensure the swift administration of justice," whereby "no fascist war criminal or traitor to the Polish nation would escape punishment." Particularly foreboding was the promise that all "fascist organizations [would] be suppressed by the fullest force of law as anti-national."[22] On 15 August the KRN and PKWN issued a statute granting the temporary – that is, communist-dominated – organs of power the right to issue decrees that had the force of law. For all intents and purposes, the statute rendered invalid all rulings of the government-in-exile. Put simply, with the support of the Soviet army and having wrested control over the most important levers of power – Polish troops, the security and police forces, law, and censorship – the KRN and PKWN had effectively elevated themselves to the top political position in Poland, while rejecting the government-in-exile as the legitimate representative of the Polish people.[23]

On 31 August 1944, using its previous decrees as a blueprint, the PKWN issued what came to be known in common parlance in Poland as the "August Decree" (*sierpniówka*). This would become the principal legal tool for the prosecution of war crimes in Poland. Article 1 of the decree stated that

anyone who, assisting the German occupation authorities, (a) took or will take part in the commission of murder of civilians or prisoners of war, in their mistreatment or persecution, [or] (b) acts or acted to the detriment of individuals pursued or sought by German occupation authorities for any reason (except for the commission of a common crime) by denouncing, capturing, or deporting them, is subject to the death penalty.

Article 2 stipulated that anyone who attempted to profit from black-mailing individuals sought by the Germans would be sentenced to a maximum of life in prison. Article 3 rejected the defence of following a superior's orders or acting under duress a mitigating circumstance, while Article 4 held instigators, their accomplices, and those who car-ried out criminal orders equally responsible.[24]

Mindful that the Western Allies were suspicious of the communists' intentions (and, quite likely, at Moscow's insistence), the PKWN felt com-pelled to exercise restraint and to demonstrate that it had obtained power legally; thus it temporarily embraced the 1921 constitution and laws of the Second Polish Republic.[25] Reflecting this, Article 6 of the August Decree stipulated that it should be used in conjunction with the corresponding articles of the 1932 Polish Criminal Code, which covered such criminal acts as murder (Article 225.1), bodily injury (Article 235.1), robbery (Articles 258–9), and spoliation of property (Article 257.1). Articles 100 to 103 of the Criminal Code specifically addressed collaboration with the enemy, which in wartime carried a long prison sentence (from ten years to life) or the death penalty.[26]

The August Decree was applicable retroactively from 1 September 1939 (the day the Germans invaded Poland), and in emulation of simi-lar Soviet decrees, it was formulated to serve as a universal and flex-ible tool of political justice. Thus, although the decree referred to the punishment of "fascist-Hitlerite criminals" and "traitors to the Polish nation," the phrase "assisting the German occupation authorities" provided the courts with wide latitude when it came to prosecuting broad categories of alleged culprits and interpreting the degree of guilt; in effect, the authorities were given leeway to target members of the political opposition. At a meeting of the PKWN on 4 October 1944, the chief of its Security Department (the precursor of postwar Poland's Security Service, the Urząd Bezpieczeństwa or UB) endorsed making the August Decree applicable to members of the AK. On 30 October a special decree, "For the Protection of the State," was an-nounced specifically for this purpose. In years to come both decrees would be used to sentence thousands of real and potential political opponents of the communist regime to death or long prison terms in

Stalinist-type trials.[27] Some Polish defence attorneys, acting on behalf of Germans tried in Polish courts for Nazi crimes, would later argue that the August Decree was applicable only to Polish citizens and did not authorize Polish courts to exercise jurisdiction over German nationals.

The August Decree was an extraordinary wartime measure: all crimes adjudicated under its Article 1 were punishable by death, and judges would not have to differentiate between murder, manslaughter, and accessory to murder. In contrast to the decree of 30 March 1943, which carried imprisonment for criminal offences not connected with murder, Article 1 (parts "a" and "b") of the August Decree imposed the death penalty for such acts, without specifying what sort of "assistance" (to the German occupation authorities) was involved. Furthermore, the decree covered the offence of "renunciation of nationality" (*odstępstwo od narodowości*), which applied to individuals who during the war had declared themselves to be of German stock.

With the exception of the crime of collaboration, the August Decree covered in essence what the IMT at Nuremberg later defined as war crimes (violations of the rules of warfare) and crimes against humanity (against POWs and civilians). The decree was amended five times between 1945 and 1949 to introduce several important amendments: its jurisdiction was expanded, and more severe punishment was to be imposed for the murder, mistreatment, and persecution of civilians and POWs. In its original version, Article 1(b) had referred solely to crimes committed "on the territory of the Polish State," but in February 1945 that clause was removed so that the August Decree could be applied to crimes committed outside Poland – in particular, to crimes perpetrated against Poles on German soil (contrary to Article 28 of the Criminal Code, which left the punishment of perpetrators of crimes against Poles outside Poland to the laws of their respective countries). Article 1 was expanded, moreover, to include culprits who "acted ... in any way, not [already] stipulated in [Article] 1, to the detriment of the Polish State, or to civilians or prisoners of war," imposing a punishment of three to fifteen years in prison, in addition to the death penalty. This amendment provided the courts with wide latitude to interpret criminal activities.[28] Apparently to avoid any potential reference to the Soviet occupation of eastern Poland between 1939 and 1941, the amendment of December 1946 changed the phrase in Article 1 "assisting the German occupation authorities" to "assisting the authorities of the German state or its allies."[29] Simultaneously, Article 4, part 1, of the December 1946 decree introduced a punishment (imprisonment of no less than three years, life imprisonment, or the death penalty) solely for membership in a criminal organization. Clause 2 of Article 4 listed as criminal any group or organization that aimed to commit crimes against peace, war crimes, or crimes against humanity. The determination of such intent was left to the courts. Furthermore, Clause 3 listed as criminal the leadership of the Nazi Party, the SS, the Gestapo, the German Security Service (SD), and political associations acting on behalf of the German state. Moreover, while Article 5 confirmed that acting under a superior's orders and acting under duress were not mitigating circumstances, it allowed the courts to apply leniency, depending on the personality of the perpetrator or the circumstances of the offence or both.[30]

Central to the effort to bring Nazis to justice in Poland was the KRN's creation in March 1945 of the GKBZN, whose appointed tasks were to gather evidence of German crimes on Polish soil under the auspices of the Polish Ministry of Justice[31] in its pursuit of Nazi criminals and to provide Polish and Allied courts with evidence of war crimes. The Ministry of Justice established fifteen district field offices, along with one field office of the commission in the capital, and vested these with sweeping powers to investigate German crimes, including collecting documentary, medical, and forensic evidence and questioning witnesses and survivors. The UB and the People's Militia were authorized to work closely with and fulfil the requests and instructions of the commission, whose expert opinions and protocols carried legal weight in court.[32] The information collected by the commission would serve as crucial source material about German (and, after 1989, Soviet) crimes in occupied Poland.

Given the magnitude of the German crimes in Poland, the UNWCC granted the commission favoured status. The Polish government-in-exile dispatched special envoys (Dr Stefan Glaser and Dr Tadeusz Cyprian) to the UNWCC. However, after the Allies recognized the Provisional Government of National Unity (Tymczasowy Rząd Jedności Narodowej, TRJN) – ostensibly a coalition of postwar parties, dominated however by the communists[33] – the government-in-exile withdrew from the commission in July 1945. In its place, the TRJN's Ministry of Justice appointed its own representative, Dr Mieczysław Szerer, with Cyprian as his deputy.[34]

To expedite the extradition of war criminals to Poland, in January 1946 the Ministry of Defence in Warsaw created the Polish Military Mission of the Investigation of War Crimes and Restitution and War Reparations for Occupation Zones in Germany (Misja Wojskowa do

1.1 Josef Bühler, deputy to Hans Frank, is brought in handcuffs to the airport
to be flown to Poland for trial as a war criminal, 25 May 1946.
United States Holocaust Memorial Museum, courtesy of Colleen A. Picchi.

Badania Zbrodni Wojennych i Biuro Rewindykacji i Odszkodowań Wojennych dla Stref Okupacyjnych w Niemczech). Faced as it was with financial constraints, the mission requested the extradition of only the most notorious culprits. Most of these requests were granted.[35] The Warsaw government submitted its last two charge files to the UNWCC in March 1948, just prior to the commission's closure later that month.[36]

Still, whereas in January 1947 the UNWCC possessed about 10,000 names of alleged Nazi criminals, Poland's extradition lists initially contained only 800 names, reflecting the new government's preoccupation with other (mostly political) priorities. Given the scope of Nazi crimes in Poland, this low number of extradition requests tended to downplay Poland's suffering under Nazi rule and had the potential to buttress claims made by German lawyers that the magnitude of Nazi crimes in Poland had been greatly exaggerated. To counter this, the Polish leadership urged the Ministry of Justice, the Ministry of State Security, and the GKBZN to redouble their efforts to submit longer lists of names to the UNWCC. At Poland's request, the UNWCC granted the Polish delegate the right to submit the names of alleged war criminals without having to provide detailed evidence of the crimes alleged or the transcripts of trials held in Poland at which information about the crimes in question was presented as evidence. Consequently, by late 1947 the Polish delegation was able to request the extradition of entire staffs of concentration camps and of the offices of the German Security Police (Sipo). For example, 437 names were submitted for Auschwitz, 249 for Majdanek, and 185 for the Sipo in Katowice, even though by June 1947 Poland had submitted to the UNWCC the transcript from only one trial – that of Arthur Greiser.[37] In total, the Polish representatives to the UNWCC submitted the names of 7,405 war criminals; about 1,800 of these were actually extradited to Poland.[38]

"Each German Is an Enemy"

The fact that the mandate of the GKBZN – reflected unambiguously in its name – was to pursue "German" crimes indicates that the Polish leadership did not differentiate between Germans and Nazis. Nor did ordinary Poles, who, as Polish historian Marcin Zaremba observes, in the years immediately following the occupation were consumed with hatred for Germans and with the desire for vengeance. In an effort to legitimate their own authority and deflect popular criticism, the communist authorities exploited these profoundly anti-German feelings in

Polish society in their propaganda efforts, touting the Soviet Union as the defender of Poland and the victor over Germany.[39]

Indeed, the negative stereotype of "the German" permeated all segments of Polish society to the point that anger towards Germans was the only thing that Poles of different political persuasions had in common.[40] As early as the fall of 1940 the underground paper *Poland Lives!* asserted that the "old German nation – the nation of Beethoven and Goethe – does not exist anymore. The Germans have as little right to invoke their names as modern Italians could call themselves the heirs to ancient Rome."[41] As the war progressed, the terms "German" and "Nazi" became interchangeable and anti-German vitriol became more vicious. On 30 July 1944, shortly before the Warsaw Uprising, the AK's organ *Biuletyn Informacyjny* stressed that "there are no good Germans, and there are no decent Germans. Some are robbers and murderers, while others have supported the robbers and murderers. Each German is an enemy and each should face the ruthless retribution of Polish justice." A day later, the *Biuletyn Informacyjny* promised to find those who had escaped justice, "even if they hid at the bottom of hell ... even if we have to track them for years on end."[42]

Polish military personnel stationed in the Soviet Union had been thoroughly indoctrinated to hate Germans through lectures, films, and photographs of German crimes. In September 1943 the chairwoman of the ZPP in the USSR, Wanda Wasilewska, appealed to her countrymen to show no mercy towards the "bloody German henchmen." Leaflets published after the liberation of Polish cities called on Poles to shed "much German blood to satisfy [the Polish] thirst for revenge."[43] Going into combat, the soldiers of the 1st Tadeusz Kościuszko Division (formed in the Soviet Union) swore to "hate the German enemy to the last drop of blood, to the last breath." And they carried out their pledge: their executions of German captives became so frequent that the NKVD plenipotentiary at the Byelorussian Front, Ivan Sierov (a chief executor of Stalin's repressive policies), reported the "extremely brutal treatment of the Germans" by the personnel of the 1st Polish Army. According to his report, in one instance the soldiers of the Kościuszko captured eighty German soldiers but delivered only two to the collection point.[44]

The fall of the Third Reich did not soften the anti-German hate campaign. Although PPR propaganda initially attempted to differentiate between "bad" and "good" Germans, applying the "class" approach and stressing that those Germans who had joined the anti-Nazi effort could be considered allies in the common struggle,[45] in February 1945 the PPR plenum issued a directive stipulating that "all of [Polish] society is engulfed by hatred for Germans. Such a situation creates a great opportunity to unite this society in a single uniform national front." The potential resurgence of militaristic Germany, therefore, was to be used as a pretext to unify the Polish nation under communist leadership.[46] In late May 1945, Jakub Berman, a leading member of the Central Committee of the PPR, instructed functionaries from agencies responsible for control of the press: "Since the war is over, should we allay our [anti-German] hatred and arouse mercy? No reason for that. Our reckoning with the Germans is not finished. We must strengthen vigilance against the German danger."[47] The non-communist political groups were of the same opinion; thus, the Catholic and agrarian Christian democratic press called for the punishment of German society as a whole. In January 1946, at a conference of the Polish People's Party (Polskie Stronnictwo Ludowe, PSL), its leader Stanisław Mikołajczyk called the Germans the "eternal enemy of Poland and Slavdom." Some non-communist publications called for the wholesale execution of all NSDAP members, while others tried to convince their readers that the Germans had mutated into a "biologically degenerate" nation and as such did not belong to the common family of European nations. By June 1945 the first deportations of Germans from Poland were being carried out in accordance with the decisions of the Allied Control Commission.[48] The major difference between the non-communist and communist views of Germany and Germans was that the latter insisted on the "class character" of fascism and National Socialism. In other words, it was the German and international "bourgeoisie" and "imperialism" that had made the Nazi takeover possible.[49] But this difference aside, the fact that Germany and Germans were the targets of intense public hostility and odium in immediate postwar Poland was instrumental in laying the foundation for the trials of Nazis in Polish courts.

Special Penal Courts

According to Article 7 of the August Decree, war crimes and crimes against humanity were under the jurisdiction of "special penal courts" (*specjalne sądy karne*). This practice was not new; on 3 May 1944 the AK had announced that "special penal courts" would dispense justice in a summary manner after the liberation of Poland.[50] On 12 September 1944 the PKWN decreed the establishment of the special penal courts and set out their format and jurisdiction. In October the first three special penal courts were established in Lublin, Kraków, and Siedlce. (In 1945, six more courts would be formed in other districts.) Special penal courts consisted of one judge and two assessors; the power of judges in the special penal courts equalled that of judges in regular courts, while assessors acted much like a jury.[51]

The Polish judicial system had suffered staggering losses during the war: out of 7,980 practising lawyers, more than half had perished at the hands of the Nazis and the Soviets. Because the Ministry of Justice was unable to fill so many vacancies with qualified candidates, on 22 February 1946 the Council of Ministers issued a decree requiring that all individuals possessing the qualifications of judges register with the courts.[52] But at the same time, the new authorities were suspicious of the remaining jurists, who had received their education in "bourgeois" Poland or abroad and who were mostly lukewarm towards the new regime. Accordingly, by the end of the year, out of 3,500 available lawyers, only 1,300 were readmitted to the bar. (Many trained lawyers who were anti-communist remained abroad in exile.) As a result, many unqualified but politically reliable individuals were admitted to practice in the judicial system.[53]

From the outset, the special penal courts were envisioned as pliable tools of political justice. In this vein, the first chairman of the Supreme Court, Wacław Barcikowski, admitted that the government did not trust the regular courts to purge "unreliable" elements from Polish society. Until the formation of the NTN in January 1946, the special penal courts were not subject to any jurisdictional control; rather, they were directly subordinated to the Department of Justice and the Department of Public Security.[54] Thus, whereas judges and prosecutors for penal (and regular) courts were selected from available qualified individuals, assessors were drawn from the national councils. On 11 September the chairman of the PKWN, Edward Osóbka-Morawski, and the chairman of the KRN, Bolesław Bierut, signed a special statute that empowered national councils to function as temporary legislative and administrative organs of power. The cadres for the councils were to be selected from the members of "democratic-independent organizations that supported the constitution of March 1921" (!) and the representatives of Polish organizations abroad that had subordinated themselves to the KRN. Those who had collaborated with the Germans or who had participated "in the fratricidal fight against the democratic-independent organizations" (i.e., against communists writ large) were banned from the councils.[55] In prewar Poland, assessors were important members of the judicial system, although they played a secondary role in the proceedings. The decree of 11 September effectively elevated their status in the decision-making process. The PKWN leadership counted on loyal assessors, or at least those sympathetic to the communist cause, to provide a counterbalance to less reliable judges.[56]

In fulfilment of their political role, the special penal courts were expected to collaborate closely with the UB, which was destined to become a key instrument in the communist takeover. Article 8 of the special penal courts decree specified that the investigative stage was not mandatory. A prosecutor who thought it necessary could conduct an investigation or authorize the UB to do it. Once the court received a case (from the UB), it could place a suspect in custody and have his property seized. In accordance with Article 12, an indictment was to be delivered within fourteen days after arrest; justification for the indictment – one of the most important aspects of the Polish judicial process – was not required. The trial could take place forty-eight hours after the defendant had received the indictment. The presence of defence counsel was mandatory; however, sentences of the special penal courts were not subject to appeal.[57]

Peremptory proceedings and harsh sentences by special penal courts in the trials of Nazi war criminals were designed in part to satisfy the popular sense of justice in a country that had been devastated by war. According to an eminent Polish jurist, Jerzy Sawicki, who would lead the prosecution in many trials of Nazi criminals, the special penal courts, first and foremost, had to satisfy popular demands for justice – "only reprisals in the form of pure vengeance could pacify a restive [Polish] society." Accordingly, "the format and proceedings of the special courts emanated from emotional needs of the moment and the new democratic trends of the [Polish] judiciary."[58] In this emotionally charged environment, some trials held in the special penal courts turned into huge public spectacles. Between 25 April and 31 May 1946, a trial of concentration camp staff took place in the special penal court in Gdańsk, where fifteen defendants (including five women) were charged with atrocities committed at the Stutthoff (Sztutowo) concentration camp. Stutthof was the first Nazi concentration camp erected outside prewar German borders and the last camp liberated by Allied (Soviet) forces, on 9 May 1945. The proceedings revealed the six-year reign of terror in the camp, which, in the words of the prosecution, represented an inseparable part of the Nazi system and of German culture. The court sentenced eleven defendants to death, including the monstrous chief of the women's camp (*Oberaufseherin*), Gerda Steinhoff, and four other female defendants. The president of the KRN, Boleslaw Bierut, denied requests for clemency. On 4 July 1946, as many as 50,000 people watched as the culprits were led to the gallows. The brutality of the war just ended and the thirst for revenge on Germans had numbed many Poles to the suffering of others, and as a consequence, open-air executions became spectacles, a form of public entertainment. The regional newspaper announced the date and time of the execution at Stutthoff; indeed, some factories and institutions shortened their work hours and even organized transport so that their employees could attend, and among the spectators were women with children. The warm sunny day and the consumption of beer lent the proceedings a picnic-like atmosphere. When the trucks with the defendants arrived, the crowd began to shout. The executioners were volunteers – former camp inmates and family members of those who had perished in the camp. As the defendants dangled in the nooses, the crowd rushed forward so that the guards had to fire in the air to stop the human wave. Even so, the crowd pulled the boots from the corpses and later cut them down to get a piece of a noose, as popular tradition held that such a souvenir brought luck.[59]

The Majdanek Trial

Even before the promulgation of the decree of 12 September 1944, several trials of German offenders were held in the liberated Polish territories on the pattern of the special penal courts. But the most heavily publicized trial conducted under the authority of the August Decree (the thirteenth such trial up to that point), while the war still raged, started on 27 November 1944, in Lublin, where an SS officer, four SS non-commissioned officers and guards, and two prisoner-functionaries (*kapos*) were charged with atrocities committed at the Lublin concentration camp, widely known by its local name, Majdanek.

The construction of Majdanek, three miles southeast of Lublin, began in the summer of 1941 on the orders of Heinrich Himmler. The purpose of the camp was to provide forced labour for the construction of SS and police facilities in and near Lublin. The forced labour detachment comprised Jews temporarily spared from the Nazis' murder campaign. Majdanek was also a detention camp for Poles suspected of underground activities, as well as a transit camp for Poles and Soviet citizens being deported to forced labour in Germany and for Poles being resettled to make room for German resettlement of their areas. Between

April 1942 and November 1943, between 74,000 and 90,000 Jewish prisoners were registered at Majdanek; at least 56,500 were Polish Jews. Non-Jewish Poles were the largest minority of prisoners in the camp during this period, forming between 20 and 25 per cent of the inmate population, which also included Germans, Austrians, Ukrainians, and Soviet POWs. After the autumn of 1943, Majdanek acquired several sub-camps in the Lublin area with Jewish labour detachments.

Majdanek claimed tens of thousands of Jewish victims. The majority of them were forced labourers, who either died from exhaustion, disease, and starvation – a consequence of inhumane conditions – or random shootings, or who were killed in gas chambers erected in the camp after the Germans determined that they were no longer capable of work. Some Jews were sent straight to the gas chambers upon arrival, but surviving documentation does not permit an estimate of their numbers. The SS also used Majdanek to kill members of the Polish resistance as well as hostages held in the Sipo prison in Lublin. On 3 November 1943, in Operation *Erntefest* (Harvest Festival), special SS and police units shot 18,000 Jews just outside the camp. At least 8,000 of these victims were prisoners at Majdanek; the remainder were forced labourers from other camps or prisons in Lublin. After the *Erntefest* killing, only a small number of Jews remained at Majdanek. According to current estimates, some 70,000 Jews and 20,000 non-Jews, mostly Poles, were killed at Majdanek. However, contemporary estimates of the number of victims were much higher. In the spring of 1944, as the Red Army advanced, the Germans evacuated most of the remaining prisoners to concentration camps farther west. Soviet forces liberated Lublin and Majdanek on 24 July 1944.[60]

The Majdanek trial attracted wide publicity in the press. There were several reasons for this. Majdanek was the first large concentration and death camp liberated by Allied forces in Europe. Although by the summer of 1944 the Soviet army had discovered numerous traces of Nazi atrocities in places like Babi Yar and Slavuta[61] in Ukraine and Maly Trostenets near Minsk, and in many other localities, Majdanek, before the liberation of Auschwitz, was viewed as the pinnacle of Nazi industrial killing. When Soviet troops entered Majdanek on 24 July 1944, traces of the horror were everywhere, despite the Germans' evacuation of prisoners and their attempts (including the destruction of a crematorium) to eliminate evidence of their crimes. One day before their departure, the Germans shot 700 Polish inmates from the city prison, alongside Jewish artisans who had been temporarily spared, and hastily buried them on the grounds of the camp. When Soviet and Polish soldiers of the 1st Byelorussian Front, accompanied by Soviet and foreign journalists, first entered the gates of Majdanek, they were shocked to find huge piles of shoes, as well as ashes in the cremato- rium. What they saw seemed so unbelievable that the *Times* (London) refused to publish the communiqués of its correspondent, Alexander Werth; the editors thought he was the victim of a Soviet propaganda ruse. Only after Allied troops entered Bergen-Belsen and Buchenwald would the reports from Majdanek and Auschwitz be accepted as incon- trovertible truth.[62]

The Soviet government as well as the Polish communists understood the propaganda potential of Majdanek. On 1 August 1944, Warsaw, un- der the leadership of the AK, rose in revolt, and the PKWN in particular saw an opportunity to declare itself the new legitimate government – in contrast to the "adventurist clique" that had ordered the uprising. To this end, Soviet and Polish propaganda emphasized Lublin's jubilant re- ception of the troops of the 1st Polish Army, which had been organized in the Soviet Union; at the same time, film crews shot footage of desper- ate residents seeking their relatives among the corpses in the Gestapo dungeons in the Lublin castle. Film crews also filmed Majdanek and the exhumation of corpses carried out by members of the Soviet and Polish special commissions. The PKWN dispatched communiqués about the camp and invited about thirty journalists accredited in the Soviet Union to see Majdanek with their own eyes.[63] A prominent Soviet writ- er, Konstantin Simonov, published a pamphlet titled *An Extermination Camp* that was translated into English and French and disseminated by Moscow's foreign-languages publisher. Simonov described Majdanek as "too horrible to comprehend" and compared it to Bełżec, Sobibór, Auschwitz, and Slavuta. Simonov's arguments bore a clear trace of the Soviet government's bidding, for he insinuated that in order to conceal the murder of Polish officers at Katyn (Katyń in Polish), the Germans had incinerated their bodies in Majdanek's crematoria.[64] The grim reali- ty of Majdanek provided the PKWN with an opportunity to assert its le- gitimacy by staging (with Moscow's approval) a public war crimes trial that would have national and international resonance. In light of the scale and brutality of German crimes in Poland, official propaganda did not have to try too hard to convince the population that harsh and swift retribution was necessary. Communist functionary Jerzy Putrament ad- mitted that a speedy trial was imperative to "render some partial albeit fast satisfaction to the people who for five years had been oppressed by a merciless and brutal occupier."[65] The political value of an open and highly publicized trial was obvious: it would satisfy the popular sense of justice and, at the same time, demonstrate the PKWN's adherence to international and national legal norms. The PKWN's competence in judicial affairs would send an implicit message to international observers as well as to Poles that the victors sought not revenge but justice. The preparations for the trial began in early August, when Soviet and Polish authorities formed a joint "Extraordinary Commission for the Investigation of German Crimes Committed at the Majdanek Camp" (Polsko-Radziecka Komisja Nadzwyczajna do Zbadania Zbrodni Niemieckich Dokonanych w Obozie na Majdanku). Its membership was impressive. It was headed by Andrzej Witos, the chief of the PKWN's agriculture department. (Since Witos was largely absent from Lublin, he was represented there by Dmitrii Kudriavtsev, the Soviet state counsellor of justice and a member of the Soviet Extraordinary Commission for the Investigation of German Crimes.)[66] Other members included Soviet and Polish forensic and medical experts; the former rector of the Catholic University of Lublin, Professor Józef Kruszyński; the chairman of the Polish Red Cross, Ludwik Christians; and the chairman of the Bureau of Aid for the Jewish Population (Referat do Spraw Pomocy Ludności Żydowskiej), Emil Sommerstein.[67] Although Soviet and Polish authorities would consistently try to subsume the genocide of Jews under the rubric of the "murder of Polish citizens," the appointment of Sommerstein indicated that they acknowledged the magnitude of distinctively Jewish suffering at Majdanek at the hands of the Nazis.[68]

The commission possessed no documents from the German camp administration and had to base its findings primarily on witness testimonies and on the interrogations of captured SS functionaries and camp guards. In addition, its team of experts exhumed several hundred corpses in the camp and its vicinity and counted 820,000 pairs of shoes from a number of European cities.[69] Having calculated the amount of ashes and the estimated capacity of the crematoria, the commission estimated the death toll at Majdanek to be a staggering 1.5 million. (As previously mentioned, recent research has estimated the death toll downward to tens of thousands.)[70] The commission's findings, which were reported widely, became the main evidentiary source for the Majdanek trial; the Soviet prosecution team at the International Military Tribunal at Nuremberg later relied on them. By the fall of 1944 it had been decided to turn Majdanek into a site of national martyrdom. Ironically, at the same time the NKVD turned the camp into a "filtration" station – that

1.2 Former SS-Obersturmführer (1st Lieutenant) Anton Thernes testifies
to the Polish–Soviet joint commission investigating crimes in Majdanek.
United States Holocaust Memorial Museum,
courtesy of unknown Russian archive.

is, a place to search for war criminals and political opponents among
German and Polish captives.[71]

Putrament would later muse that "our newly created administration,
lacking experience and imagination, mishandled [the trial] from the beginning." When the defendants were escorted on foot to the building
where the trial took place – a walk most likely arranged for the purpose of heightening popular emotions – they were attacked by a mob,
which screamed, whistled, and spat into their faces.[72] The newspaper
Głos Ludu, an organ of the PPR, reported "salvos of automatic weapons
as the escort officers shoot in the air, protecting the convicts. The agi-
tated crowd strides in front and behind the murderers. In a moment the
people of Lublin will tear the criminals apart. In a moment, justice will

be done here on the streets of martyred Lublin. From all sides arms flail in anger in the direction of the murderers … In windows, on balconies, thousands of people, everywhere shout 'death to them, death!'"[73]

In an atmosphere of utmost haste, the trial opened on 27 November 1944 in the Lublin special penal court; Bohdan Zembrzuski, who before the war had been a prosecutor at the Tarnów district court, was the presiding judge. The prosecution was represented by Jerzy Sawicki, who had defended individuals charged with political offences before the war and who was active in left-wing underground organizations during the war,[74] and Henryk Cieśluk, who represented the PPR but had no legal background. Six defendants stood in the dock: the deputy chief of the camp Gestapo office, SS-Obersturmführer (First Lieutenant) Anton Thernes; SS-Haupscharführer (Sergeant 1st Class) Wilhelm Gerstenmeier, a member of the camp administration; SS guards Hermann Vogel and Theodor Schöllen; and *kapos* Heinz Stalp and Edmund Pohlmann. They were charged under Article 1 of the August Decree with participating in the torture, mistreatment, and murder of camp inmates; the two *kapos* faced additional charges of raping women, often in the presence of their families.[75]

Polish defence attorneys were reluctant to participate in war crimes trials; doing so generated negative popular reactions in war-devastated Poland, and the defence of an individual who was undoubtedly guilty of committing horrible crimes seemed a lost cause. Hence, the Majdanek trial began with the defence attorneys' requesting to be removed from the case. In an eloquent speech, Wojciech Jarosławski quoted Article 67 of the Statute of the Bar, which stipulated that a lawyer's task was "to protect law and justice." Jarosławski stressed that, as a Pole and a defence lawyer, he was willing "to protect law and justice, but not a crime," thus effectively acknowledging that his clients were guilty. The court, however, quoted Article 15 of the decree on penal courts, which stipulated that defendants must have defence attorneys, and turned down the requests of Jarosławski and his colleagues.[76]

Having accepted the court's ruling, the defence raised a crucial issue that would become a bone of contention between the prosecution and the defence in subsequent trials. Jarosławski and his colleague Kazimierz Krzymowski questioned the jurisdiction of the special penal court in adjudicating the case of the defendants, who according to the Hague and the Geneva Conventions were POWs and, therefore, subject to trial by a military tribunal. In response, prosecutor Sawicki argued that, although these international conventions specified the rights of

1.3 Majdanek trial. Public domain:
http://www.iwm.org.uk/collections/item/object/205401868.

POWs, the common law enshrined the "'principle of material truth,'
which would be revealed by the basic facts of the case." In other words,
the defendants were not POWs, but members of a criminal formation
(the SS "Death Head" units) "created for the extermination of the civilian population," and therefore without the rights of combatants.[77] In
Sawicki's words,

> whoever acts according to the rules of warfare [as stipulated by the inter-
> national conventions] is subject to the aforementioned conventions even if
> one is not a member of the regular armed forces. Conversely, whoever is
> just dressed in a military uniform, but does not act according to the most
> elementary rules of international law, loses the right of combatant and
> should be treated as a common criminal.[78]

In support of his argument, Sawicki referred for precedent to the case
of Henry Wirtz, the commandant of the Confederate POW camp at
Andersonville, Georgia, who after the American Civil War was tried and
hanged for violating the rules of warfare. In addition, he pointed out
that the St James Declaration empowered formerly German-occupied

countries to try war criminals on their territories and in their courts.[79] Upon consultation, the court ruled that according to Article 11 of the Criminal Code and Article 6 of the decree on special penal courts (which empowered special penal courts to function in accordance with criminal law), the court in Lublin was a proper legal body to adjudicate the case. In the same vein, the court adopted Sawicki's argument and ruled that due to their functions in the SS Death Head formations, the defendants were neither combatants nor POWs, but common criminals.[80]

From the beginning, the trial appeared as a sort of blueprint for special penal court proceedings in that each participant fulfilled what seemed to be a carefully orchestrated function. Since the German camp administration had destroyed its documents, the trial proceedings were based solely on the testimonies of the defendants and eyewitnesses. In accordance with European judicial traditions, the judges acted in an inquisitorial fashion, highlighting the most horrific episodes of the German occupation, while the prosecution attempted to show that although they were of low rank, all of the defendants possessed the same ideological motivations as their superiors and, therefore, the will to commit their crimes. Conversely, while admitting that they had "heard" or "known" about the camp's horrors, the defendants denied they had ever participated in atrocities.

Questioned about the camp's regimen, Stalp testified that prisoners worked from six o'clock in the morning until six o'clock in the evening and that an extremely poor diet and hard labour resulted in the prison population's extremely high death rate. He admitted being "present" at gassings and witnessing a new contingent of inmates being pushed into the gas chamber, right on top of the already existing piles of corpses. Similarly, Gerstenmeier claimed that although he had witnessed the mass executions of prisoners, he never took part in them. Thernes insisted that he was merely the camp's bookkeeper and only "heard" about the mass extermination of prisoners. He did admit, however, that the camp administration constantly sent "huge sums" of money and valuables back to Berlin.[81]

The prosecution presented several witnesses who testified about the atrocities committed by the camp functionaries and guards. Tadeusz Budzyń recalled that the camp's chief prisoner-functionary (*Lagerkapo*), Pohlmann, was master over life and death and brutally beat prisoners with clubs, killing many. Budzyń also described in detail the gassing process: The gas chamber was filled with carbon monoxide from a diesel engine, or "Zyklon B" was tossed in. Since the murderers were initially inexperienced, people took a long time to die of suffocation.[82] Witness Dora Mintz had seen infants torn from the arms of their mothers and tossed into the gas chamber. She had also witnessed inmates being forced to hang their own relatives.[83] Romuald Olszański testified that every camp functionary and *kapo* beat and tormented inmates; those who did not display particular brutality were considered "nice." He identified Pohlmann as one of the most sadistic *kapos*, whose "specialty" was murdering emaciated prisoners (called *"Muselmänner"* in Nazi slang); on the day of his arrival (he had been transferred from Germany), Pohlmann murdered eighteen people.[84]

Survivors testified further that although there were about 100 "official" executions at the camp, the SS guards, the *kapos*, and other camp functionaries routinely murdered inmates for the slightest transgression or without any pretext. In line with the Nazis' euphemisms for murder, such instances were registered in the camp records as "death from natural causes"; those who were sent to gas chambers were recorded as "transferred" (*überstellt*). Several witnesses testified that in the wake of large-scale operations (*Aktionen*), the crematoria were overloaded and corpses were burned in the open, between 500 and 1,000 a day.[85]

A crucial aspect of the Majdanek trial and subsequent trials was the Holocaust. Although the court had not set out to emphasize Jewish suffering, it was systematically exposed by the defendants' and survivors' testimonies. Stalp described for the court how Jewish mothers had led their children into the gas chamber while telling them fairy tales.[86] Vogel testified that during Operation Erntefest on 3 November 1943, 8,400 inmates from Majdanek and its satellites, mostly Jews, were shot, while witness Bronisław Baran recalled that on that day the camp loudspeakers played loud music in order to suppress the sound of machineguns when Jews were being shot.[87]

The prosecution summoned a member of the Soviet–Polish commission, Piotr Sobolewski, who testified that judging by the amount of clothing and goods found in the camp, a million and a half people were murdered there, a number that was accepted at face value by the court and disseminated by Soviet and Polish propaganda. Sobolewski also testified that the quantity of Zyklon B found in the camp was enough to gas four million people.[88]

In line with Soviet court practices, the prosecution turned the courtroom into a platform for a vitriolic propaganda campaign. In his final peroration, prosecutor Cieśluk barely mentioned the crimes of the defendants even while demanding the death penalty for all of them. He called Majdanek a "death factory" (*fabryka śmierci*) – this phrase would become common currency in Polish trials of Nazi criminals and in Polish media accounts of their deeds – whose beginnings could be traced to early German history, and he warned that Poland's security was rooted in the new political system in Eastern Europe:

> Germans are responsible for Hitler. Crimes in Majdanek emanated from the history of the pagan German hordes, from the anti-Slavic Crusades, and from the "Iron Chancellor" Bismarck, culminating in the rise of Hitler – the symbol of [German] hatred of Poles and of Slavic peoples ... The guarantee [against renewed German aggression] must be the permanent borders on the Oder and Neisse Rivers, which would create a defensive wall of the Slavic people, allied to the Western democracies.[89]

Even more emotional was the closing statement of prosecutor Sawicki:

> Words are created by humans, but what happened in the camp is inhuman. Words are comprehensible, but what happened here is incomprehensible. Words have their own logic, but what happened here defies logic ... I could demand punishment for the defendants solely on the basis of their membership in a criminal association. If there weren't any evidence [of their guilt], I could demand punishment since the defendants were a part and parcel of the "system of evil." Imagine a husband who powerlessly watches as his wife is raped. This is Majdanek! Imagine the powerlessness of mothers, who went to their deaths along with their children. This is Majdanek! [90]

In an atmosphere of lingering economic misery and hunger – the war was still raging – popular expectations of revenge were running high. In November the film *Vernichtungslager Majdanek – Cmentarzysko Europy* (The Majdanek Extermination Camp – Europe's Cemetery), directed by Alexander Ford, was shown in Lublin's cinemas, further fuelling popular rage against the Germans.[91] During the trial, megaphones were set up outside the courtroom, where crowds stood in the cold, listening to the proceedings.[92]

In light of the highly emotional testimony of survivors, the defence attorneys stood little chance of saving their clients, even if they tried. Indeed, all of the defence attorneys seemed to grasp that their efforts would be futile and offered only brief statements. Jarosławski at least attempted to argue that only one witness saw his client Thernes beating a man and a woman, whereas attorney Krzymowski effectively abandoned his clients Gerstenmeier and Vogel. He referred to the former as a "true Satan of death" but pointed out that he had been "drawn into a horrible machinery of destruction" and asked the court to impose an "appropriate" punishment on him and Vogel.[93] Attorney Kunicki mentioned that Stalp himself had been a prisoner and was not an NSDAP member, but he did not elaborate on the potential ramifications of these facts.[94]

In their final statements, all of the defendants contended that they were not guilty. On 2 December 1944, the judges sentenced five defendants to death under Article 1a of the August Decree; Vogel was convicted under Article 1b.[95] (Pohlmann, who realized what the inevitable outcome would be, committed suicide on 30 November.) In obvious emulation of Soviet war crimes trials, the Ministry of Justice issued a decree one day before the verdict was handed down stipulating that most notorious war criminals would be publicly executed.[96]

On 3 December about 25,000 people gathered in Lublin to watch as the five defendants were led to the gallows constructed near the camp crematoria. One witness to the execution of the Majdanek defendants wrote to his friend: "Yesterday they hanged those 'Fritzes' who ran Majdanek and killed people. You could imagine what was happening there. Ten thousand people, the screaming and crying of those who had lost their families; [the crowd] literally attempted to tear them to pieces."[97]

But according to the prominent essayist Zbigniew Załuski, popular satisfaction was subdued: "The same crowd, which a few days ago on the street almost tore to pieces both the defendants and their small escort and whose wrath could be stopped in the name of justice and order only by tanks, now was silent, probably unsure why the execution did not bring expected satisfaction. Perhaps it was the disproportion between the crime and the punishment, but possibly it was the awareness – not yet fully realized – that during the war something morally irreversible happened ... and a moral threshold that humanity had crossed cannot be crossed back."[98] Putrament concurred that in contrast to the mob frenzy of several days earlier, the crowd remained silent as the defendants dangled from their nooses. People felt "confused why the execution did not satisfy their thirst for revenge." After the crowd dispersed, the popular mood remained gloomy, "for everybody understood that it [the execution] solved nothing. In the evening, many people got drunk; everyone felt worse."[99]

The Majdanek trial both shaped and closely reflected popular perceptions about what war crimes trials were supposed to entail – swift and harsh retribution – and contributed to the ongoing hate campaign, which gained momentum as the war wound down. Filmed under the title *The Swastika and the Gallows* by a prominent Polish director, Kazimierz Czyński, the trial was shown in movie theatres.[100] In the winter of 1945, special "rallies of hate" were organized under the slogan "For Majdanek, Auschwitz, and Warsaw" near notorious execution sites, where state propagandists preached inevitable retribution for German crimes. A key element of these rallies was the accusation that the Germans were a nation of criminals. On 7 March 1945 the newspaper *Głos Ludu* stressed that "every German is guilty, for [each] German male or female took part in the diabolic acts of destruction, in each apartment there was an SS-man or another [dressed] in a green or black uniform ... who lived off our blood." On 22 March 1945 the commander-in-chief of the Polish army issued an order that stated that alongside "the German army, the Nazi Party, and the civilian administration, all Germans are responsible for war crimes."[101]

Some Polish jurists joined the anti-German tirade. In November 1945, Emil Rappaport published a book titled *The Criminal Nation*, which was inspired by the theories of Italian criminologist Cesare Lombroso (1835–1909), who had posited the existence of the "born criminal" whose criminal behaviour is inherited. Rappaport expanded Lombroso's theory beyond the individual to include nations. If a predisposition to criminality is innate in certain individuals, reasoned Rappaport, so it is in certain nations. Germany was one such nation – indeed, perhaps the most criminal nation in history. Rappaport argued that the criminal character of the German nation, evidenced throughout German history, had set the stage for the rise of Hitler and the Third Reich.[102]

At the request of the Ministry of Justice, district courts collected information about mass executions, concentration camps, and ghettos in their districts as well as the names, ranks, and functions of alleged war criminals. Photographs from such places and reports from war crimes trials were disseminated and displayed in public places. Transcripts of the Majdanek trial were published in Polish and Russian. Echoing the words of prosecutor Cieśluk in his closing argument, state propaganda presented Majdanek, Auschwitz, and other camps as "death factories" (*fabryki śmierci*) – sites of immeasurable suffering, which dictated meting out the harshest possible punishments to war criminals.[103]

Trials in District and Provincial Courts

In November 1946 the special penal courts were abolished and their functions transferred to district and provincial courts. The state media stressed that the special penal courts had fulfilled their functions, especially while the war was still raging, providing the popular demand for justice within a legal context. However, the special penal courts left a lingering legacy, as the regular courts often acted in similar fashion, clearly underscoring the peremptory character of state justice in the first years after the war. Indeed, many trials were conducted according to the format of the special penal courts: the charges were based solely on eyewitness testimonies (newspapers often published the culprits' names and asked potential eyewitnesses to come forward), and a number of culprits were tried in groups, connected only by the fact that they had been extradited together to Poland by the Allied authorities.[104] In contrast to the Majdanek and Gdańsk trials, these trials were conducted with much less publicity and sometimes lasted only a few hours.

On 15 October 1947 the Warsaw district court heard allegations of war crimes five members of the German police. Even though during the war they had served in different localities (three in Germany and two in East Galicia), they were tried as a group, reflecting the hasty organization of the trial. Indeed, the judges acknowledged that they found it difficult to try five unconnected cases together and that the evidence consisted solely of eyewitness testimonies and affidavits collected by the Allied authorities.[105]

Accordingly, since there were only a few testimonies against the defendant August Wasserfuhr, the court decided that he had not displayed particular brutality in carrying out his duties and sentenced him to seven years in prison. In contrast, a dozen testimonies against Karl Shöpel convinced the judges of his zeal in beating and abusing Polish labourers. The court interpreted these acts as "marked by extreme brutality" (bestialstwo) and sentenced him to life imprisonment under Article 1 of the August Decree.[106]

The court found especially damning the evidence against Eustachy Prindyn, a member of the Ukrainian police in Drohobycz (Drohobych in Ukrainian). Several Jewish witnesses testified that he had directly participated in the round-ups and executions of Jews. An additional witness in the court – who happened to be the vice-prosecutor of the district court in Grudziąz – lived in Drohobycz during the war and corroborated that the Ukrainian police had taken active part in the genocide of Jews.[107] Although the witness did not recognize Prindyn, the court ruled that Prindyn's participation in the murder of Jews and membership in two criminal organizations – the SD (to which his unit was subordinated) and the SS (after his police service, Prindyn enlisted in the SS-Division "Galizien" and his court file contained his photo in the SS uniform) – merited the death penalty under Articles 1, 2, and 4 of the December 1946 amendment of the August Decree.[108]

Similarly, on 17 November 1947, in a brief session, the Warsaw provincial court convicted a group of Gestapo functionaries who were apparently tried together because three of them had committed crimes in East Galicia. According to testimonies collected by the Allied and Polish authorities, Peter Leideritz had headed the Border Police Commissariat (Grenzpolizeikommisariat) in Kołomyja (Kolomyia in Ukrainian),[109] where he organized and participated in the mass executions of Jews and Poles. Erich Buder and Franz Schauer had taken part in executions of Polish citizens in Lwów (L'viv), while Philip Spang and Paul Simon had served as prison wardens in Germany and were charged with the mistreatment of Polish inmates.[110]

In the courtroom, several former ghetto inhabitants in Kołomyja testified that Leideritz had organized deportations to the Bełżec death camp and had himself shot several Jews. Buder and Schauer confirmed the testimonies they gave to American authorities that they had taken part in the executions of civilians in Lwów, but argued that they had acted under orders.[111] Attorney Juliusz Ryteń had to defend all five defendants and made a rather feeble attempt to find mitigating circumstances for them. He argued that Leideritz was a "victim" of the Nazi system, that Buder and Schauer only assisted in crimes, and that Simon and Spang had been "drafted" into the Gestapo against their will.[112]

The court ruled that the defendants' membership in two criminal organizations – the Gestapo and the SS – sufficed for the imposition of the death penalty under Article 4 of the August Decree (in its December 1946 reading) and that their guilt was aggravated by the manifold crimes they committed. Accordingly, the court sentenced Leideritz, Schauer, and Buder to death. However, it placed stock in Spang's plea that he had been drafted into the Gestapo relatively late (in July 1943) and took into account that he did had not committed crimes on Polish soil.[113] Hence, it sentenced him to seven years' imprisonment. At the same time, although

Simon's wartime activities appeared similar, the court sentenced him to life in prison solely for his membership in the Gestapo.[114]

The Trial of Hans Biebow

The April 1947 trial of Hans Biebow (1902–1947), former head of the ghetto administration (*Ghettoverwaltung*) in the Łódź Ghetto, in the Łódź District Court was one of the most publicized and comprehensive trials of a Nazi criminal ever held in postwar Poland. Łódź, seventy-five miles southwest of Warsaw, was the centre of the Polish textile industry. After conquering Poland, the Nazis took steps to Germanize the city, which they renamed Litzmannstadt, and to segregate, oppress, plunder, exploit, and eventually liquidate its large and vibrant Jewish community, which numbered more than 230,000, the second-largest in Poland before the war. The Łódź Ghetto, which held roughly 160,000 Jews at any one time (some 75,000 Jews left Łódź in the first six months of the German occupation), was "sealed" on 30 April 1940; it was the second-largest ghetto established by the Germans, after Warsaw. Thanks to the deportation of foreign Jews, mostly from Germany, to Łódź, 200,000 Jews or more lived in the ghetto over the course of its almost four-and-a-half-year existence. All but a few perished before the end of the war. More than 45,000, or almost one-quarter, of the ghetto's inhabitants died as a result of the unspeakable conditions that prevailed in the ghetto. Almost 78,000 were deported to the death camp of Chełmno (Kulmhof in German) between January 1942 and July 1944. The Łódź Ghetto lasted longer than any other ghetto because its manufacturing capacity was such that Nazi officials temporarily spared a significant percentage of its Jewish labourers from death in the gas chambers. As a result, this ghetto lasted until the summer of 1944, when the Germans liquidated it, deporting the 72,000 Jewish inhabitants who were left to Auschwitz–Birkenau. When the Soviets liberated Łódź on 19 January 1945, only some 900 Jews remained, most of them in hiding. An estimated 20,000 Jews from Łódź survived the Holocaust.[115]

Hans Biebow, a coffee merchant from Bremen, was named chief of the Nazis' Office of Nourishment and Economy (Ernährungs- und Wirtschaftsstelle) in the Łódź Ghetto in May 1940; then in October he was elevated to head of the Ghetto Administration, a special department within the municipal administration. Operating in this capacity until the summer of 1944, Biebow was the key figure in the exploitation of the ghetto's labour force, the plundering and starving of the ghetto population, and the deportation of thousands of its Jewish inhabitants to Chełmno and Auschwitz–Birkenau. He was a vigorous champion of the use of Jewish forced labour, but in 1944, after the killing of all Jews (even Jewish forced labourers) was given precedence over the exploitation of Jewish labour in Nazi policy, he adapted. Indeed, Biebow was no mere "desk murderer" operating from a distance. He issued orders to Mordechai Chaim Rumkowski, the chairman of the Jewish Council, expecting him to execute them, and after the autumn of 1942, he more and more often went over Rumkowski's head and issued orders directly to factory managers, punishing them or threatening them with punishment if they failed to meet quotas or trim their workforces. Revolver in hand, Biebow took part in brutal selections of Jews during the liquidation of small Jewish ghettos in the vicinity of Łódź, condemning those deemed unfit for labour in ghetto industries to death in the camps. He also directed Nazi police forces and was on the ground during the final liquidation of the Łódź Ghetto in 1944.[116] The Polish mission at the UNWCC identified Biebow as a key culprit, and in May 1946 the British extradited him to Poland in the first transport of war criminals.[117]

Biebow's trial was significant for a number of reasons. In contrast to similar proceedings of the period, he was tried as a single defendant. However, he was regarded as symbolizing the upper echelons of the Nazi regime in Poland, whom Poles wanted to see held accountable after the war for their misdeeds. Also, the pretrial investigation provided a comprehensive body of evidence, mostly in the form of witness testimonies, but in addition, some documents had been found pertaining to the ghetto's functioning. And finally, the nature of Biebow's criminal activities and the evidence thereof as presented in the courtroom constituted a clear signal that the Polish political establishment had consented to place the Holocaust at the centre of the trial.

The indictment included criminal activities under Articles 1, 2, and 4 of the August Decree. According to the indictment, between May 1940 and the summer of 1944 Biebow had been the chief Nazi administrator of the Łódź ghetto, during which time the numbers of inhabitants varied between 200,000 and 70,000, including small children, until its final liquidation. The ghetto was ravaged by cold and disease, and its inhabitants' daily caloric intake averaged between 700 and 1,000, well below the acceptable daily rate of at least 3,000 for a labourer. As a consequence, the death rate in the ghetto rose precipitously, from 8,474 in 1940 to 11,456 in 1941 and 18,000 in 1942. The ghetto administration regularly selected and sent to their deaths those inhabitants who were no longer capable of work; between January and June 1942, 66 transports with 55,145 people were sent to the Chełmno death camp. All in all, Biebow participated in the "systematic extermination" of 300,000 Jews from the Warthegau.[118]

During the pretrial investigation, Biebow denied most of the charges, admitting only that he had killed one Jewish woman while "carelessly handling" his gun. He insisted that he was not the chief of the ghetto administration, but was responsible solely for food supplies for the city. He argued that the chief of the ghetto was the Sipo and SD chief, SS-Obersturmbannführer (Lieutenant-Colonel) Otto Bradfisch, who was responsible for deportations. Biebow claimed that he did not know that Jews were being deported to their deaths and that he had tried to make deportations as "humane" as possible.[119]

The trial began on 23 April 1947. In his opening statement, the presiding judge Jerzy Walewski called the trial particularly important since it concerned the "genocide of the Jewish people."[120] The court called upon experts. Historian Artur Eisenbach of the CŻKH related the Nazis' plans for the extermination of the Jews of Europe, the unfolding of those plans specifically in the Warthegau, and the destruction of the Łódź Ghetto. According to Eisenbach, 45,708 people died in the ghetto, while about 80,000 were deported to the death camps. Thus, he declared, the ghetto was a "criminal association" whose specific task was the murder of Jews. Expert witness Władysław Bednarz, who investigated the Nazi crimes at Chełmno on behalf of the GKBZN, explained to the court its dual function as a concentration and death camp.[121]

The prosecution possessed several original German documents pertaining to the running of Łódź Ghetto. For example, on 20 October 1941, Biebow composed a circular in which he stressed that the ghetto administration "[would] solve the Jewish question in cooperation with other [German] authorities and this affair must be held in utmost secret. We will carry out this task, according to the Führer's will."[122] The court also summoned thirty-seven prosecution witnesses, most of them Łódź Ghetto survivors, who described the horrible conditions there. Julian Wajnberg testified that Biebow held power over life and death in the ghetto and that he deliberately lied to the Jews, promising that deportations would be directed at the "resettlement" of Jews to sites where they would live and work in better conditions. Leon Szykier told the court that, in contrast to other ghettos, the Łódź Ghetto was completely isolated since all houses between the ghetto and the city had been razed. This "dead zone" made it extremely difficult to smuggle food into the ghetto, and Biebow deliberately minimized food rations so that under his supervision 40,000 Jews died of hunger.[123] Other witnesses testified that Biebow himself had shot a Jew, and that in September 1942 the SS liquidated patients in the Jewish hospital.[124]

The prosecution presented Biebow with two documents that bore his signature: one was his appeal to ghetto inhabitants to return to labour after the first deportation in October 1942; the other was his request to the city administration for a financial bonus for the German unit that had participated in the deportation. Biebow admitted that he had shot two Jews who were alleged thieves, but he denied that he had exploited the ghetto's inhabitants and that he ever participated in deportations, claiming that these were solely the prerogatives of the Sipo and SD and the mayor of Łódź – he, Biebow, was merely obeying orders. He also blamed the Jewish ghetto council and its chairman, Mordechai Rumkowski, for helping the Nazis run the ghetto and claimed that he did not know or did not fully understand Hitler's plans for the extermination of the Jews.[125]

Prosecutor Jerzy Lewiński began his closing argument by stating that the trial of Biebow was also the trial of the German people and of a particular world view, known as Nazism. Germany had fallen victim to a mass psychosis – Hitlerism – and the murder of the Jews had been but part of the traditional German war of extermination against the Slavic people. In the words of the prosecutor, Biebow was merely a cog in the German destruction machine and, much like Rudolf Höss, the commandant of Auschwitz, a "typical executor of his superiors' ideas." As a member of the NSDAP, Biebow "knew or must have known" of Hitler's exterminatory policies towards Jews, and he had energetically implemented those policies by confiscating property and commodities and by deliberately inflicting starvation, cold, and disease – in other words, by creating particular conditions in which the death rate in the ghetto would soar. In these ways, he had violated specific international conventions. Thus, Biebow was guilty of stealing from the occupied population, violating the national honour and religious practices of the ghetto population, carrying out mass executions and illegal confiscations, and destroying national, religious, and historical monuments and artefacts. In sum, under Biebow's supervision, the ghetto administration had continuously violated a principal clause of the Hague Convention – namely, that "war is fought between states and armies, not against the civilian population."[126]

The court summoned only 8 out of 122 witnesses requested by Biebow, and they did not add anything that could mitigate the charges against him. Thus Biebow's attorney, Zygmunt Deczyński, focused on the psychological and political environment in which Biebow had functioned, arguing that obedience to authority was engrained in the German mentality. Biebow, he continued, had been "victimized" by the Nazi system; he had not initially displayed any particular anti-Semitic proclivities. Compared to key war criminals like Arthur Greiser, Ludwig Fischer, and Rudolf Höss, Biebow was merely a cog in the Nazi killing machine, a completely "normal man," who in any other position would have been an "ordinary employee" of the Third Reich. In addition, Deczyński pointed out that the ultimate objective of the ghetto administration had been to contain and exploit Jews, not to murder them. Hence, that administration could not be classified as a "criminal organization" in the sense of Article 4 of the August Decree. Biebow's correspondence with the city administration, in which he complained that meagre food supplies were causing a high death rate in the ghetto, supposedly showed that he had attempted to mitigate the conditions in the ghetto. Finally, Deczyński observed that the testimonies of the ghetto survivors should not be accepted at face value, since for the survivors Biebow symbolized the horrors they had lived through. In the end, Deczyński asked for a just sentence that would reflect the "conscience of the court and [the fair] mentality of the Polish people."[127]

The eyewitnesses' testimonies, Biebow's attempts to defend himself, and the atrocities described in the courtroom were transmitted to the public through the press, which continuously referred to the defendant as a "coward," a "sadist," and a "true son of a criminal nation." Megaphones were set up outside the courtroom, where crowds gathered every day to listen to the proceedings. The media thus reflected the psychological atmosphere of the trial, whereby Biebow embodied the evil that emanated from Germany and from the German people as a whole.[128]

On 30 April 1947, the Łódź district court found Biebow guilty under Articles 1 and 2 of the August Decree (in its December 1946 version) and corresponding articles of the Criminal Code pertaining to instigation and serving as an accessory to crime, and sentenced him to death.[129]

The justification for the ruling began with a lengthy invective against Germany and the Germans, explaining Biebow's criminal activities as rooted in the criminal mentality of the German people and mirrored by German literature, science, and philosophy ... Egoism is ingrained in the German mentality and perpetuated by the philosophies of Max Stirner and Friedrich Nietzsche. Traditional [German] amorality laid the foundation for German imperialism and eventually for Hitler's ascendance to power. In turn, Hitlerism was but a new form of the German mentality, which entails the destruction of everything non-German.[130]

The second central point in the court's ruling related to the Nazis' deliberate efforts to systematically carry out the "biological destruction of the Jewish nation" (*niszczenie biologiczne narodu żydowskiego*), which was a fundamental principle of the Nazi system. Since Biebow had joined the NSDAP in 1937, the court reasoned that he must have known that Hitler's key objective was to persecute and eradicate the Jewish people.[131]

The justification for the verdict then described, on the basis of the testimony of witnesses for the prosecution, the defendant's specific criminal activities. It referred to the Łódź Ghetto as an instrument of murder. Alongside the NSDAP, the SS, the SD, and the Gestapo, the ghetto administration was a "criminal association," and as the head of that association Biebow was subject to the death penalty. The Chełmno camp was the main "death factory" for the Jews in the Wartheland, and Biebow not only knew about the camp's main purpose but also energetically participated in the deportations of Jews to their final destination. Biebow and his co-workers enjoyed unlimited power over the ghetto's inhabitants, frequently acted on their own initiative, and used their power for personal aggrandizement, stealing from the ghetto's inhabitants at will; they sold furniture, linen, furs, and *bijouterie* to their German colleagues and acquaintances at reduced prices, thus accumulating massive fortunes and violating even the Nazis' own regulations in such matters. [132]

In what looked like a gesture towards the official Soviet policy of subsuming the Holocaust under the rubric of "murder of peaceful citizens," the judgment stressed that "Jews were destined by the Nazis for utter annihilation, and after them Poles were to meet the very same fate."[133] But one should distinguish between Soviet policy, which didn't differentiate between Jewish victims and other victims, placing them all in the same boat, without regard to the Nazis' priorities in their targeting of victims, and the general practice in Polish trials of Nazis, which acknowledged Jews as the uppermost victim group, among Nazism's various victim groups – Slavs in general and Poles in particular being in second place – in the framework of Nazi ideology and policies.

The court concluded that condemning Biebow to death was the only proper way to eliminate from human society the "gangrene of Hitlerism and of individuals who became its carriers."[134] President Bierut rejected Biebow's appeal of the sentence, and he was hanged on 23 June 1947.[135]

Conclusion

The definition and implementation of justice in postwar Europe was deeply intertwined with politics, and Poland was no exception. To re-build a viable justice system in a country ravaged by the war was an ex-tremely difficult task, exacerbated tenfold by the ongoing struggle for power in immediate postwar Poland and by popular demands for swift and merciless retribution. The Polish government-in-exile vigorously advocated postwar punishment for Nazi criminals, but even before the cessation of hostilities, it was forced to watch from the sidelines as the Soviet-installed provisional communist government started to function on Polish territory. The issuance of the August Decree, whose wording emulated Soviet decrees on war crimes, reflected the political goals of Polish communists while satisfying popular sentiments. In this reality, miscarriages of justice and legal inconsistencies were all but inevitable, especially when accompanied by the massive forcible resettlement of ethnic Germans from Poland between 1945 and 1947, after the Big Three demarcated Poland's postwar borders at the Potsdam Conference of July–August 1945. This political and psychological environment could not but affect the rulings and judgments of, first, the special penal courts and then district and provincial courts, which became the main instruments of retributive justice in the immediate aftermath of the war. By the end of the war, Poland was an emotionally overwrought society, living in a state of – to borrow from the title of Marcin Zaremba's book – "great fear," and overpowered by a deep sense of helplessness, despair, and rage – all caused by fresh memories of the German and Soviet oc-cupations, during which family ties were severed, traditional cultural and moral values were violated, and relatives and friends were lost to combat, executions, and deportations. At least 60,000 Poles lost their sanity as a result of the war or suffered severe psychological impacts from it.[136] Against their will, most Poles found themselves citizens of an alien state, and they tried to hide inside their own rapidly diminishing private world; meanwhile, the breakdown of the state apparatus and of the traditional social and economic order escalated mutual suspicions, frustrations, and fears of the "other" – Jews, communists, Germans, Soviet soldiers, bandits, speculators, and new settlers.[137] In such an atmosphere, trials of Nazi war criminals were often the only venue through which one could unleash personal grievances and frustrations.

The trials also served as a steady reminder to the public of a danger emanating from Poland's western neighbour, Germany. In the summer of 1945 the Polish administration of Wrocław (Breslau) ordered the German population to wear white armbands as a symbol of its new subordinate status. Soon, however, the order was cancelled, for the appearance of thousands of white armbands was a clear indication that the German population was much larger than the Polish one.[138] In some localities, Polish activists organized "marches of Adolf Hitler" to "remind" local Germans of their guilt in that they had supported Hitler. Polish settlers forced residents of entire German villages – predominantly women, children, the sick, and the elderly – out of their houses and made them march under a mounted escort.[139]

By warning the population of the potential resurgence of militarist Germany, official propaganda thus exacerbated hatred of Germans and heightened the sense of uncertainty and fear, which could easily be triggered by the sight of German POWs or the sound of spoken German on the streets. Any instance of benevolent treatment of POWs or ethnic Germans caused a wave of popular protests and demands that "Hitlerites" be punished more harshly. Random executions and the lynching of German civilians were not rare, and the expulsion of the Germans from Poland was approved by most Poles, whatever their political persuasion.[140]

In many cases, the courts passed sentences solely on the basis of defendants' membership in Nazi criminal organizations as defined by the IMT, or they applied the term "criminal association" as developed by Poland's own NTN. As a rule, the courts also turned down defendants' requests to summon witnesses from Germany. Still, to the extent that it was politically and psychologically feasible in postwar Poland, not all judgments were incorrect or biased. By November 1946, when the special penal courts were abolished after operating for two years, they had investigated more than 40,000 cases but convicted only 9,949 individuals. The difference between cases filed for consideration and convictions indicates that despite the special penal courts' extraordinary nature, they were not simply a blunt instrument of postwar justice. The courts in the immediate postwar years were simply overwhelmed by the number of cases they had to process, especially those pertaining to the charge of renunciation of nationality (which fell under the jurisdiction of Article 2 of the August Decree, in its February 1945 version); so it seems that they summarily dismissed a large number of cases for which there was little or no incriminating evidence.[141]

Recent research by scholars of the Second World War has largely corroborated the testimonies of witnesses for the prosecution in this first phase of trials of Nazi criminals in Poland. For example, a recent study has demonstrated that Peter Leideritz organized the massacres and deportations of Jews in Kołomyja.[142] In the case of Hans Biebow, modern research has shown that his exploitation of Łódź Ghetto inhabitants was driven less by ideological considerations than by the desire to enrich himself personally. That is, his main goal was to make as much profit from the exploitation of the Jews as possible, as indicated by the testimonies for the prosecution at his trial. When Jews were deported to the Chełmno death camp and when Jewish ghettos in the Łódź district were liquidated, Biebow attempted to monopolize control over the goods left behind by the victims.[143]

Finally, in contrast to official Soviet policies, which either passed over the Holocaust in silence or subsumed it under the category of the Nazi murder of "peaceful Soviet citizens," even during the first phase of Polish trials of Nazis the Holocaust was a central issue, from major trials like Biebow's to the trials of rank-and-file Nazis. To be sure, at the same time, Polish lawyers and judges, like Polish politicians, maintained that the Holocaust had been but the beginning of a large-scale genocidal campaign against the Slavs. This means that Polish judicial personnel generally acknowledged the centrality of the Holocaust within the Nazi terror system, but that they were constrained to place it in the context of new political realities. Thus, already in this first phase of Polish trials of Nazis, the courts were calling upon experts associated with the CŻKH, among assessors there were representatives of the local Jewish communities, and judges and prosecutors unequivocally referred to the mass murder of the Jews as a distinctive element of the Nazi genocidal campaign. Although such candor could have been generated by a variety of motives, the judicial system felt compelled to acknowledge that Poland had been a primary site of the Nazi "Final Solution," a fact integral to a large number of war crimes trials conducted on Polish soil.

Chapter Two

The Poles at Nuremberg

On 8 August 1945 the Four Powers – the United States, Great Britain, France, and the Soviet Union – signed an agreement – the London Agreement – "for the prosecution and punishment of the major war criminals of the European Axis" and appended to it a charter for an International Military Tribunal. As Laura Jockusch observes, the IMT was "the first and only Nazi war-crime trial held jointly by the four victorious Allies."[1] Nineteen countries, including Poland, adhered to the agreement and the charter. Article 1 of the agreement authorized the tribunal to try war criminals "whose offenses have no geographical location whether they be accused individually or in their capacity as members of organizations or groups or in both capacities."[2] Under Article 6 the IMT was "to have power to try and punish persons who, acting in the interests of the European Axis countries," were implicated in "planning, preparation, initiation or waging of a war of aggression." Article 6 further empowered the tribunal to try the perpetrators of "war crimes" or "violations of the laws or customs of war," which included "murder, ill-treatment or deportation to slave labor" of civilians, "murder or ill-treatment of prisoners of war ... killing of hostages, plunder of public or private property, wanton destruction of cities, towns, or villages, or devastation not justified by military necessity." Finally, Article 6 granted the tribunal the power to try perpetrators of "crimes against humanity"; this introduced a novel concept into international law that was applicable to atrocities committed against individual civilians.[3] Subsumed under crimes against humanity were "murder, extermination, enslavement, deportation, and other inhumane acts committed against any civilian population, before or during the war, or persecutions on political, racial, or religious grounds." "Leaders, organizers, instigators, and accomplices" participating in a plan or conspiracy to commit any of these crimes were to be held "responsible for all acts performed by any persons in execution of such plan."[4]

The indictment, signed by representatives of each of the Four Powers on 6 October 1945 and lodged with the IMT on 17 October, named twenty-three defendants, all high-ranking Nazis from a cross-section of the Third Reich's political, military, diplomatic, and economic elite. Nineteen defendants were found guilty. Twelve of them were hanged, three sentenced to life in prison, two to twenty years in prison, one to fifteen years, and one to ten years. Three were acquitted on all charges. The trial lasted from 14 November 1945 to 1 October 1946.[5]

In accordance with Article 14 of the charter, each of the Four Powers was permitted to appoint a chief prosecutor and a staff of prosecuting attorneys under him, but the charter made no provisions for permanent prosecutorial delegations from other countries.[6] After adhering to the London Agreement and the charter on 8 August, the Polish delegation to the London negotiations requested permission from the Four Powers to send a credentialed delegation to the IMT. Poland's stake in the IMT was incontrovertible. It had suffered inordinately under Nazi occupation, and in the opinion of Poles, Poland's ordeal gave it a right to participate in the trial. Moreover, Poles had been preparing for this day since the war, when the Polish exile government in London and its representatives in the underground "secret state" in Nazi-occupied Poland collected evidence of Nazi crimes in anticipation of postwar trials of Nazis.[7] The Poles were particularly interested in taking part in defendant Hans Frank's prosecution. Frank had been the Governor General of the General Government, responsible for the civil administration of the greater part of Nazi-occupied Poland. In support of their request for a credentialed delegation, the Poles had supplied Allied prosecutors with valuable evidence supplied by the GKBZN with the cooperation of the justice and foreign affairs ministries. British prosecutors, however, objected to the inclusion of the Eastern Europeans lest too many prosecutors from various countries pursue competing interests and stall the trial. Furthermore, as historians Ann Tusa and John Tusa note, the British "felt that since the whole idea of an International Military Tribunal had been to try those whose crimes had no particular geographical location, there was no point in mounting a prosecution based on a multitude of individual national accusations."[8]

However, Lieutenant-General Roman A. Rudenko, the chief prosecutor for the Soviet Union, endorsed the participation of prosecutors from

Poland, Czechoslovakia, and Yugoslavia so that they could present evidence of Nazi crimes that had been committed in their countries. He even expressed his willingness to attach Eastern Europeans to his legal staff, reasoning that their familiarity with the Nazi occupation in their respective countries would no doubt be invaluable to the Soviet prosecution's efforts to provide proof of German crimes in Eastern Europe, especially on Soviet territory. The Americans and British initially opposed the Soviet initiative.[9] But the Poles' persistence eventually met with partial success. American and British opposition softened, and in November 1945 a Polish delegation was accredited, albeit with a restricted remit. (Others, such as the Czechs, Yugoslavs, Danes, and Norwegians, followed Poland's lead and also received limited accreditation.) The Poles were assigned an office in the Palace of Justice in Nuremberg, the site of the IMT, and would be entitled, in the name of the Polish government in Warsaw, to submit memoranda, requests, and documents to Allied prosecutors and to consult case files relevant to Poland. Allied prosecutors solicited the advice of the Polish delegation's members, and the Polish lawyers explicated and construed documents that were to be presented to the tribunal. The Poles would not be permitted, however, to take part in trial proceedings. US Supreme Court Justice Robert H. Jackson, the US chief of counsel at Nuremberg, did grant Jerzy Sawicki, a member of the Polish delegation, the authority to conduct interrogations of German generals and officials in the former General Government who were suspected of having committed crimes in Poland and who were in Allied custody awaiting summonses to testify before the IMT.[10] For its part, the Soviet prosecution, acting on behalf of Poland – it also acted on behalf of Czechoslovakia, Yugoslavia, and Greece – would introduce evidence of crimes committed in Poland, including an official Polish government report. The "Polish indictment" (*polski akt oskarżenia*), prepared by the Polish delegation, with accompanying documents, was in essence a written summary of facts and legal points supporting Polish allegations of German crimes committed in Poland, prepared by an interested party with no formal status in the proceedings, which is what the Polish delegation in effect was.[11]

The understaffed Polish delegation comprised four lawyers: Stefan Kurowski, head of the delegation; Stanisław Piotrowski; Tadeusz Cyprian; and Sawicki. All four were in Nuremberg through April 1946; then from May 1946 until the tribunal read its verdict in the courtroom on 30 September and 1 October 1946, Piotrowski would be the delegation's sole representative there.[12] Kurowski, Piotrowski, and

Sawicki occupied important posts in the Polish Ministry of Justice; Cyprian was a prosecutor attached to Poland's Supreme Court and a Polish representative on the UNWCC.[13] Kurowski and Sawicki were of Jewish origin.[14] Sawicki was no stranger to German war crimes trials, since he had already prosecuted personnel from Majdanek. After the Nuremberg Trial, Kurowski, Cyprian, and Sawicki would go on to prosecute several accused Nazis in Poland's NTN. Cyprian and Sawicki would eventually become law professors and co-author several books about the Nuremberg Trial. Kurowski would become a judge on Poland's Supreme Court and eventually its president.[15] All four jurists were evidently acceptable to and trusted by the authorities of the Soviet-installed provisional government in Warsaw – indeed, Sawicki was a delegate to the KRN. But if the books by Cyprian and Sawicki are any indication, they were not doctrinaire communists and were, above all, professional lawyers.[16]

That said, they were sensitive to Western criticisms of Poland, and Kurowski, Piotrowski, and Sawicki reported these in their meeting with Zygmunt Modzelewski, Poland's Deputy Minister of Foreign Affairs, in late October 1945 after the three lawyers had returned to Warsaw from a trip to London. Some English observers, the lawyers related, had challenged Poland's victim status and wondered whether it was now a victimizer. Postwar Polish antisemitism and antisemitic violence, exemplified by an anti-Jewish riot that had reportedly claimed five lives in Kraków in August 1945 and by Polish decrees that placed an onerous burden of proof on Jewish survivors who laid claim to the property of their relatives murdered by the Germans, elicited considerable concern in England. The British had also raised concerns about Poland's expulsion of ethnic Germans after the war and the fairness of its judicial system. Sawicki believed that Poland was only the indirect target of these attacks, a stand-in for the Soviet Union, but English and American Jews and left-wingers were all opposed to both Poland and the Soviet Union. Sawicki argued that in response, "Poles ought to assume the defense of Jews at Nuremberg, naturally within the borders of present-day Poland."[17] Indeed, the lawyers in the Polish delegation to the IMT did just that, perhaps even beyond their original intentions.

If this criticism of Poland was any indication, the Polish delegation had a tough row to hoe. For the delegation's members, however, it was all worth the effort because they, not to mention the government and the Polish public, were sceptical that Allied prosecutors would adequately represent the scale of the harm done by the Nazis to Poland and its people without the intervention of Polish lawyers. But did the delegation's labour bear fruit? To what extent did the efforts of the Polish delegation contribute to the prosecution's cases? Can one discern traces of Polish efforts in the closing arguments or the judgment? What did the Polish delegation accomplish within the limits of its remit? What initiatives did it undertake? Did it affect the prosecution's case? Can one discern any effects of its advocacy on the IMT's judgment? This chapter addresses these questions.

The Polish Indictment

The Polish indictment, a draft of which the Polish delegation had submitted to Allied prosecutors in December 1945, was perhaps its most notable achievement. Article 21 of the IMT's charter authorized the tribunal to accept official government reports and documents produced by Allied countries. In his opening address before the IMT on 8 February, Rudenko, after enumerating evidence to be presented of Nazi crimes in the Soviet and Czechoslovakia, explained the significance of Polish indictment:

> The Soviet Prosecution will likewise present evidence regarding the crimes perpetrated by the [Nazi] conspirators in Poland. The basic document to be presented on this subject by the Soviet Prosecution will be the report of the Polish Government dated 22 January 1946. The official documents of the Polish Government were the primary source of the report of the Polish Government on the German crimes committed in Poland. Both the official report of the Polish Government and the documents appended thereto ... represent unquestionable evidence.[18]

According to Cyprian and Sawicki, writing after the Nuremberg Trial, the Polish delegation filed the Polish indictment because of the Allied indictment's curt treatment of Polish grievances regarding a multitude of German crimes committed in Poland. (The first draft of the Polish indictment had been prepared in London by Manfred Lachs with the help of Aleksander Bramson even before the delegation arrived in Nuremberg.)[19] Dissatisfaction with the Allied indictment was reflected in the Polish press in the fall and winter of 1945. Cyprian and Sawicki attributed the Allies' insufficient attention to the Nazis' anti-Polish crimes to the absence of a Polish representative on the UNWCC in the summer of 1945, when the Four Powers were determining which Nazi officials to indict and what to charge them with.[20] Withdrawal of official recognition of the Polish government-in-exile by the United States and Great Britain in July 1945 left Poland temporarily with no representative on the UNWCC in London until Cyprian, representing the provisional government in Warsaw, went to London in the autumn of the same year.[21]

To what extent did Nazi crimes committed in Poland and against its citizens figure in the Allied indictment? Count 1 of the indictment charged the defendants with participation in a criminal conspiracy to attack Poland on 1 September 1939 and to wage aggressive war against it in violation of the laws and customs of war.[22] According to Count 3, the defendants "conducted deliberate and systematic genocide, viz., the extermination of racial and national groups, against the civilian populations of certain occupied territories in order to destroy particular races and classes of people and national, racial, or religious groups, particularly Jews, Poles, and ... others."[23] Among the many crimes specified in this count were "murders and ill treatments at concentration camps and similar establishments set up by the Germans in the Eastern Countries ... including those set up at Maidanek [sic, Majdanek] and Auschwitz ... About 1,500,000 persons were exterminated in Maidnanek [sic, Majdanek] and about 4,000,000 persons were exterminated in Auschwitz, among whom were citizens of Poland ... and other countries."[24]

On the face of it, then, the Allied indictment paid considerable attention to crimes the Nazis had committed in Poland, but relative to Nazi war crimes and crimes against humanity committed in several other countries, particularly in France and the Soviet Union, similar crimes perpetrated in Poland received short shrift. For example, Count 3 recited the Nazis' deportations of civilians from various occupied countries for the purposes of slave or forced labour, but Poles were not mentioned in that count even though the Germans deported at least 1,250,000 ethnic Poles to German territory for forced labour, especially as farm labour, and at least 130,000 Polish workers died in Germany from mistreatment.[25] There was no reference in the indictment to the Nazis' "AB Action" (*Ausserordentliche Befriedigungsaktion*, or *AB-Aktion*) – the "pacification," in other words, mass executions, of the Polish intelligentsia and elite; nor was there mention of the Nazis' plundering of public and private property in Poland and of Polish cultural treasures. In the context of the Nazis' destruction of cities, their brutal suppression of the 1944 Warsaw Uprising was not mentioned, nor was their razing of Warsaw. In the section of the indictment that referred to the Nazis' efforts to Germanize certain territories under German control, the Warthegau in Western Poland received no mention. The Polish indictment was intended to address these lacunae.[26]

To be sure, in their opening speeches before the IMT, Allied prosecutors addressed Nazi crimes in Poland. In his famous opening address for the United States before the tribunal on 21 November 1945, the second day of the trial, Jackson referred to Poland a few times. He held forth on the Nazi leadership's plans to attack Poland and subdue it through aggression. In the context of Nazi antisemitic policies, Jackson said: "Jewish property was the first to be expropriated, but the custom grew and included similar measures against anti-Nazi Germans, Poles, Czechs, Frenchmen, and Belgians. Extermination of the Jews enabled the Nazis to bring a practiced hand to similar measures against Poles, Serbs, and Greeks." Jackson addressed Frank's culpability, associating him with both the deportation of Poles for slave labour and the Nazis' anti-Jewish crimes.[27] On 4 December 1945, for his part, Sir Hartley Shawcross, Great Britain's attorney general and leader of the British prosecution, devoted a large part of his opening speech to the attack on Poland in 1939, which had set the stage for Nazi acts of aggression across Europe.[28] In his opening address on 8 February 1946, Rudenko referred several times to the aggressive attack on Poland and to Nazi crimes committed in Poland. He had Poland in mind when he condemned the Nazis' reign of terror in countries under Nazi occupation: "The population of these countries, and of the Slav countries above all others – especially Russians, Ukrainians, Bielorussians, Poles, Czechs, Serbians, Slovenes, Jews – were subjected to merciless persecution and mass extermination." "The Polish people," asserted Rudenko, "were subjected to mass extermination and their cities and villages were mercilessly destroyed." He also mentioned the deportation of Poles, along with other conquered people in Eastern Europe, to perform slave labour in Germany, as well as Nazi plans to eliminate the Polish intelligentsia.[29] But even after the American, British, and Soviet prosecutors' opening addresses (the French prosecutor barely mentioned Poland), which may have somewhat mollified the Polish delegation, the Poles still felt obliged to press Poland's case through the intervention of Soviet prosecutors. They did so largely on the strength of the Polish indictment.

Justification for the Polish indictment was articulated in its prolegomena. The Allies' indictment had been lodged with the IMT by the Four Powers, which themselves had borne immeasurable burdens, sacrifices, and suffering at the hands of the Nazis throughout the war. In this vein, the prolegomena stated that "Poland has the painful privilege of being THE COUNTRY against which THE INDICTED launched the first, most bitter attack; on the territory of which the most gruesome crimes had been committed; which records the greatest number of victims."[30] The Polish indictment presented extensive evidence of German crimes against peace, war crimes, and crimes against humanity committed specifically against Poland and Poles. It described the German military's systematic use of terror during the invasion of Poland in 1939, including widespread wanton executions of civilians, ethnic Poles and Polish Jews alike; the population transfers of ethnic Poles; the maltreatment and murder of Poland's intellectual elite and clergy; the German takeover of Polish cultural institutions and media; the expropriation and plunder of public and private property, including Jewish property; the mistreatment and murder of Polish prisoners of war; the deportation of the civilian population for forced labour in Germany; the imprisonment of ethnic Polish civilians in concentration camps in Poland and Germany; and the mass murder of ethnic Polish civilians throughout the period of the Nazi occupation. Also addressed in the Polish indictment were the Nazis' plundering of public and private property in Poland; the destruction, pillaging, and looting of artworks, libraries, archives, and scientific laboratories; the demolition of national monuments; the deportation of Polish civilians for forced labour; and the mistreatment of Polish prisoners of war. The Polish indictment discussed many of these topics at length.

However, the Polish indictment did not condemn the Germans for brutally crushing the 1944 Warsaw Uprising or for the destruction of Warsaw. A plausible explanation for this omission is that the communist-dominated provisional government that the Polish delegation represented was loath to suggest approval of the uprising because it had been led by the non-communist AK, with the support of the non-communist Polish exile government in London. It may seem incongruous, then, that Sawicki would later avail himself of the opportunity at Nuremberg to interrogate Erich von dem Bach-Zelewski, the SS general who had spearheaded the suppression of the Warsaw Uprising, and Ernst Rode (sometimes spelled Rhode), Bach's chief of staff. The interrogation of Bach-Zelewski, in particular, was meant to gather evidence of his crimes in preparation, in the event of his extradition, for a trial in Poland, at which the prosecutors would have been able, if they so chose, to establish a narrative that pinned blame for the failure of the Warsaw Uprising on the AK. As fate would have it, Bach-Zelewski never faced charges in Poland.

The Polish indictment devoted significant attention to the Nazis' concerted plan for the "Germanisation of Poland" in areas of western Poland incorporated into Nazi Germany – the so-called Warthegau. According to the Polish indictment, this policy included the usurpation of Polish sovereignty through the imposition of a German administration in place of a Polish one; the abrogation of Polish laws and, in turn, the imposition of a German judicial system and the enactment of German law; the population transfer of hundreds of thousands of Polish civilians from these areas and their colonization by ethnic Germans; the abduction of Polish children to Germany; the imposition of a German administration in Polish schools and universities; and the takeover of Polish cultural institutions. This policy was to be implemented ruthlessly, and force would not be spared if required. The Polish indictment described each one of these measures and others in detail. For example, it listed by name twenty towns in Poland from which the Polish population had been expelled and described the plight of the expellees, who were not only ordered to leave but also prohibited from taking their belongings with them. In the words of the Polish indictment, "the place of those Poles deported from their homes, shops, and estated [sic, estates] was taken by the German newcomers. *By January 1941 more than 450,000 Germans had thus been re-settled.*" It continues: "*The German plan envisaged the expulsion of at least 5,000,000 Poles.* This was one of the greates [sic, greatest] forced migrations in history, carried out in most unhuman [sic] conditions, with the complete disregard of life, health, dignity, private property and – law."[31]

An inventory of German atrocities underpinned the Polish indictment; these included mass reprisals, massacres, hostage-taking, and the maltreatment, abuse, and killing of concentration camp prisoners. "During the whole period of German occupation," read the indictment,

the civilian population was exposed to hardship and cruelties of the occupant [sic, occupier] ... On top of the many restrictions, discriminations and 'legalised' crimes – a wave of crime was sweeping Poland. All this was done with the full knowledge and approval of the highest authorities of the German Government at that time ... In order to give an exact picture of the situation one would have to write the history of occupied Poland between the years 1939–1945, recording daily crimes, barbarities and violence. This will be the task of the historian. But in this legal indictment some of the most atrocious and cruel deeds will be recorded. Only some of them.[32]

One example from the Polish indictment of the abuse and murder of ethnic Poles in Nazi-occupied Poland related to a massacre in the town of Leszno in the wake of the German invasion. In the first days of September 1939, ethnic Germans of Polish nationality attacked their fellow Polish citizens. The attack had been coordinated with the German military to pave its way into Poland, but the local Germans were defeated. "After the occupation of Leszno by the German troops," the indictment continued,

> the German authorities took revenge by starting a massacre of the Polish population which lasted for almost two months. A great number of prominent Poles in the district were arrested, brutally beaten with rifle butts, truncheons and whips. On October 21st, 1939, twenty representatives of the local Polish population were shot at the foot of the Law Courts. Many others were secretly executed while in prison ... The number of victims run [sic, ran] into several hundred persons.[33]

The Polish indictment also described in detail the oppression and killing of Polish citizens in concentration camps located outside Poland. Two examples will be provided here. The first is from the Sachsenhausen concentration camp outside Oranienburg, north of Berlin,

> to which many thousand [sic, thousands] of Polish citizens were deported during the period 1939–1944. The internees were exposed to systematic extermination by means of mass executions, poisoning, injections—to physical torment by continuous flogging, kicking and all sorts of [tormenting] ... While being forced to work under very difficult conditions they received [a] food allotment which was absolutely inadequate ... Owing to undernourishment all kinds of ... diseases ... were rampant ... The most gruesome feature of the camp was the system of punishment adopted by the authorities ... From time to time a thorough purge of the camp was ordered ... The number of Poles in the camp varied. The first transport consisted of University professors ... By the middle of 1944, there were still about 6,000 Poles in this camp, many having died before. Very few left the camp alive. In retaliation for the AK-led Warsaw Uprising, which lasted

from August to October 1944, the Germans expelled most of the Polish population from the city and deported 60,000–80,000 Poles to concentration camps, including 6,000 to Sachsenhausen.[34]

The second example describes the maltreatment of Poles at Mauthausen and Gusen in Upper Austria:

The construction of the camp in Mauthausen began several years before the war. It was completed in 1940 by foreign prisoners[:] Poles, Spaniards, Russians, Czechs, Gypsies and Jews. The first Poles to arrive there came from Buchenwald, Dachau, and [Sachsenhausen near] Oranienburg in March 1940. To accommodate the ever increasing number of foreign prisoners a sub-camp was built in Gusen, about 3 miles away. It was built by Poles, thousands of them brought from Poland and other camps in Germany. All the prisoners detained in those camps were employed in the quarries and the mill attached to the camp. The work was extremely heavy and exhausting even under normal conditions. But under the circumstances prevailing in the camps the prisoners led a life worse than the ancient galley slaves. In the four years of 1940–1944 diseases caused by malnutrition, overwork, ill-treatment as well as direct causes of murder and massacre brought about the death of some 40,000 prisoners in the camp of Gusen alone. Out of this figure 20–25% were Poles. In autumn 1942 a brothel was established there whose female personnel was drawn from other concentration camps … Most of the women recruited to the brothels were from Slav countries.[35]

All in all, the Polish indictment embodied the intention of the lawyers in the Polish delegation, taking their cue from their fellow Poles, to counteract what they perceived was the relative inattention paid by the Allied indictment and Allied prosecutors from the West to the ordeal of ethnic Poles under Nazi rule. But how did Poland's Jews fare in the Polish indictment?

The Polish indictment included detailed descriptions of "the maltreatment, outlawing and extermination of the Jewish people."[36] To be sure, the Allied indictment included several references to Nazi antisemitism and anti-Jewish crimes, but it made minimal reference to Nazi crimes committed against Polish Jews, even though 3,000,000 Polish Jews – about 90 per cent of Poland's prewar Jewish population – were killed at the hands of the Germans and their accomplices. Count 2 of the Allied indictment recounted the killings of 133,000 Jews in the Lwów Ghetto between September 1941 and July 1943.[37] But Count 4, which under the heading of crimes against humanity charged the Nazis with the persecution and extermination of Jews, made no mention of the mass murder of Polish Jews in its list of mass murders of European Jews. In his opening address for the United States, Jackson did describe and in strong language condemn the Nazis' antisemitic program, and their persecution and extermination of Jews, drawing special attention to the notorious report by SS-Brigadeführer Jürgen Stroop chronicling and celebrating the Nazi suppression of the Warsaw Ghetto Uprising in 1943.[38] From Jackson's perspective, the guilt of all of the defendants for Nazi anti-Jewish crimes was unambiguous:

> We charge that all atrocities against Jews were the manifestation and cul-mination of the Nazi plan to which every defendant here was a party … While a few defendants may show efforts to make specific exceptions to the policy of Jewish extermination, I have found no instance in which any defendant opposed the policy itself or sought to revoke or even modify it … Determination to destroy the Jews was a binding force which at all times cemented the elements of this conspiracy. On many internal policies there were differences among the defendants. But there is not one of them who has not echoed the rallying cry of nazism [sic]: "Deutschland er-wache, Juda verrecke!" (Germany awake, Jewry perish!).

But although Jackson showed great sympathy for the plight of Jews, he ultimately misconstrued the Nazis' anti-Jewish world view in that he cast Jews more as political opponents of the regime rather than as a group whose very existence represented a vision of the world that was fatally inimical to Nazi ideology. Thus "the purpose … of getting rid of free labor, the churches, and the Jews," Jackson argued, "was to clear their obstruction to the precipitation of aggressive war."[39]

The degree to which Allied prosecutors and then the tribunal's judg-es paid attention to the Nazi persecution and extermination of Europe's Jews – what we now call "the Holocaust" – is a topic of heated debate among historians. Joshua Rubenstein notes that "contrary to what most people assume about justice at Nuremberg, the mass murder of Jews was not the driving force behind the prosecution, although this was the first time the crime of genocide was included in a criminal indict-ment."[40] Mindful of these limitations, Michael Marrus nevertheless finds much to commend in the approach the Nuremberg prosecutors took to the Jewish tragedy:

> For the first time in a non-Jewish forum, spokesmen for the Allied powers outlined the Nazis' anti-Jewish policy at length, and with ample documentation and evidence, sometimes from eyewitnesses. In detail and conception unknown to all except a handful of Jewish experts, Nuremberg set forth, for the first time, a full account of the massacre of European Jewry. And unlike wartime political leaders, the Nuremberg prosecutors acknowledged the uniqueness of the assault upon the Jews of Europe.[41]

Donald Bloxham contends, in contrast, that the Allies' focus on war crimes and their vision of "aggressive war" as the root of all Nazi criminality prevented them from adequately representing the Nazis' distinctly anti-Jewish murder campaign during the proceedings. The overall effect, according to Bloxham, was to universalize Jewish victimhood, merging Jewish victims into the toll of citizens of the various countries under Nazi rule.[42] Lawrence Douglas steers a middle course. In his view, the Nuremberg Trial was not a "Holocaust trial." "The prosecution was," he argues, "not primarily occupied with trying the defendants for the extermination of the Jews of Europe but instead focused on the accuseds' roles in launching an aggressive war. Still," he continues, "the extermination of the Jews was importantly explored and condemned at Nuremberg, especially as it was filtered through the freshly minted legal category of crimes against humanity."[43]

In light of this debate, it is important to ask what proportion of the Polish indictment was devoted to the Nazi genocide of Polish Jewry and whether it conveyed an appreciation for the scope and character of the Nazis' war against the Jews, in particular Poland's Jewish community. References to Jews appeared in roughly one-quarter of the Polish indictment, two distinct sections of which were devoted to the German expropriation and looting of Jewish-owned property and to the persecution and annihilation of Poland's Jewish community. "3,000,000 JEWS PERISHED IN POLAND," exclaimed the Polish indictment.[44] The Polish indictment described in considerable detail the German brutalization of Jews; the series of German anti-Jewish measures and decrees; the forced resettlement of Jews; their ghettoization; the conscription of Jews into forced labour battalions; and, in five pages, the extermination of Jews in death camps, with an emphasis on Auschwitz (Oświęcim in

Polish), Majdanek, and Treblinka. The Polish indictment's description of the establishment of ghettos was indicative of its treatment of the Nazi genocide of Poland's Jews:

> By orders issued by FRANK Jews were hered [*sic*, herded] into specially erected districts in towns and cities. The outstanding among all those places – called GHETTOES – was the ghetto of WARSAW.
>
> . . . .
>
> About half a million Jews were herded into the Ghetto of Warsaw. All of them had to be accommodated in 1359 houses [,] which meant at the average 393 persons in one house. Thirteen people had to live in one room.
>
> Food allotted to the prisoners of the ghetto was in fact a starvation diet. It was about 1/8 of the pre-war ration in Poland.
>
> Both appalling housing conditions and shortage of food were bound to lead to tremendous growth of diseases. Typhus was raging throughout the time the ghetto was in existence. About 20% of those affected fell victim of [*sic*] it due to lack of adequate medical help.
>
> ... In 1941 ... the birth rate had fallen to almost nil – the death rate however increased from 12/1,000 to about 1% [*sic*].[45] It was steadily growing in later years.
>
> Starved, underfed and tortured the Jews of the ghetto of Warsaw, [*sic*] faced inevitable death, they decided to die with honour and rose against the Germans.
>
> The rising of the ghetto ... lasted for days. The Germans rushed machine-guns and aeroplanes against its population. The ghetto became a heap of ruins, shattered walls: almost all its defenders, including women and children[,] were killed.
>
> Other ghettoes in which the same conditions prevailed were: The ghetto of ŁODZ [*sic*] with 180,000 inhabitants, RADOM – 30,000, LUBLIN, CRACOW – 20,000, KIELCE – 20,000 and several others.[46]

Noteworthy is the Polish indictment's admiration for the Jewish fighters who took part in the 1943 Warsaw Ghetto Uprising. In the antisemitic climate that prevailed in wartime and postwar Poland many Poles insinuated that Jews had been passive victims of Nazism, that they had not done enough to defend themselves against the Nazis, and that honour was not an attribute of even the Jewish resistance in the Warsaw Ghetto.[47] The emphasis on Jewish courage and "honour" reflected an attitude – one that was not universally held in Poland but was promoted by Jews who had stayed in Poland – that Jews, indeed, belonged to the community of brave Polish patriots who fought to free their country from the yoke of Nazism.

Another example of the extent to which the Polish indictment took into account Jewish sensibilities comes from its description of Treblinka, the notorious Nazi death camp, where about 900,000 Jews were killed at the hands of the Nazis and their accomplices. The indictment quoted a passage from Yankiel's Wiernik's book *Rok w Treblince* (A Year in Treblinka). Wiernik, a carpenter by trade, escaped from Treblinka during the prisoner revolt there in August 1943 and reached the outskirts of Warsaw, where the Polish underground gave him shelter and encouraged him to recount his experiences at the notorious death camp. In 1944 the Polish underground clandestinely published and circulated his account, smuggling a copy to the West, where it appeared in 1945 in Yiddish and English. Quoting from the preface of Wiernik's book, the Polish indictment read:

> 'Awake or asleep, I see terrible visions of the thousands calling for help, begging for life and mercy. I have lost my family, I have myself led them to death and I have myself built the death chambers in which they were murdered.
>
> I am afraid of everything. I fear that what I have seen is marked on my face. Old and broken life is a heavy burden but I must carry on and live to tell the world what I have seen of German crimes and barbarism ...' – this is what he says.[48]

For whatever reason, the Polish indictment quoted only one passage from any wartime diary or memoir, although there were many to choose from. It was the diary of a Jew, a gesture of the seriousness with which the Polish delegation approached the Jewish tragedy.

Moreover, the Polish indictment left no doubt that the Nazi genocide of Polish Jewry was premeditated. First, in the context of the expropriation of Jewish property, the indictment read: "One has to remember that steps concerning Jewish property were only preliminaries to the much greater crimes to come. They were meant to settle the Jewish case for the time being ... Having secured the property of the victims; made certain that it would not be lost, the process of extermination was set into motion."[49] Then later in the indictment, in the section devoted to the persecution and mass murder of Polish Jewry, it stated: "The Nazi authorities having more than once declared and made public their attitude to all persons of Jewish origin, put into action a scheme aimed at the outlawing, persecution and finally extermination of all Jews. The scheme was proceeding by stages."[50] Finally, the indictment did not ignore the Nazis' ideological motivation behind the genocide. "In 1942," it asserted, "the policy of the Nazi authorities became openly directed towards the biological extermination of all Jews in Poland."[51] For their part, American, British, French, and Soviet prosecutors may have ranked Jews high on the list of Nazism's victims, but they did not adequately explain why the Nazis were preoccupied with the Jews. In contrast, the Polish indictment did.

Soviet prosecutors read aloud from the Polish indictment into the court record on 9 February and throughout their presentation of the evidence over the course of the proceedings. Soviet colonel Yuri Pokrovsky used it to highlight the Nazis' waging of aggressive war on Poland and the ill-treatment of Polish prisoners-of-war. Chief counsellor Lev Smirnov referred to it in drawing the tribunal's attention to the Nazis' distortion or "Germanization" of Polish law and legal institutions, which resulted in the summary executions of Polish citizens. Colonel Lev Sheinin, assistant prosecutor for the Soviet Union, utilized it to underscore the Nazis' plundering of public and private property in Poland, including the property of Polish Jews. Mark Roginsky, another Soviet assistant prosecutor, drew on it to illuminate the Nazis' destruction of Polish cultural elites, institutions, and treasures. Major General Nikolai Zorya, still another Soviet assistant prosecutor, availed himself of the Polish indictment, along with passages from Frank's diary, to cast light on the Nazis' deportation of Poles to slave labour in Germany and Frank's pivotal role in it. Smirnov referred to it again when he cross-examined Josef Bühler on cultural policies initiated by Frank on the territory of the General Government – specifically, the looting of Polish libraries.[52]

Smirnov further employed the Polish indictment when he presented evidence of Nazi crimes against humanity. In this context he quoted the passage from Wiernik's report on Treblinka that appeared in the Polish indictment. Smirnov described Treblinka as "one of the most terrible centers for the mass extermination of people, created by German fascists." He added:

The persons who came to Treblinka entered ... the antechamber of death. But were they the only victims of this fate? An analysis of probative facts connected with the crimes of the German fascists irrefutably testifies to the

fact that the same fate was shared not only by those who were sent to special extermination camps, but also all those who became victims of these
criminals in the temporarily occupied countries of Eastern Europe.[53]

Smirnov never said, however, that "the persons who came to Treblinka,"
who numbered around 900,000, were killed specifically because they
were Jews. This was in line with Soviet policy, as exemplified in
Rudenko's opening address, which was to claim that all inhabitants
of Eastern Europe fell victim to the Nazis' murderous objectives. As
Marrus puts it: "While prominent in the list of victims ... the Jews were
not held to be the object of a distinctive, obsessive, high-priority Nazi
war aim."[54] Smirnov de-emphasized the Jewish identity of Treblinka's
victims, whereas the Polish indictment made it clear that the camp
"was intended to be a special camp for Jews."[55]

Alfred Seidl, Frank's lawyer, in his closing argument challenged first
the admissibility and then the relevance of the Polish indictment. He
argued that, like the Allied indictment, it contained accusations of only
a general nature. Moreover, as far as Frank was concerned, it offered
no substantive evidence of Frank's personal responsibility. He contended that it was admissible only insofar as its assertions were corroborated by original documents and other incontrovertible statements.[56]
Seidl's attempt to limit the admissibility of the Polish indictment indeed indicates that he recognized its significance.

The Polish indictment ended in dramatic fashion:

The present document ... covers only the most notorious and gruesome
crimes committed during the German occupation and by Germans in
Germany against Polish citizens.

It is of course obvious that in a short legal document like the present not
all the facts and details of five years could possibly be presented.

It is a summary – a very short indictment.

Behind the crimes as proved and submitted here there are thousands of
others overshadowed by the dimension of the murder, mass pillage, and
mass destruction. But they are crimes nevertheless. Both the deeds of the
big and the deeds of the small.

Justice should reach all those guilty. And in this conviction the Polish
government submits the present charge leaving it with full confidence in
the hands of this great Tribunal of the United Nations.

Most of the crimes, most of the damage done to Poland and her people
could not be repared [sic, repaired]. Human lives cannot be restored ...

works of art [cannot be] reconstructed; this is why Poland is still bleeding, the victims of unsaid crimes and suffering.

But when justice will be done – and there is no doubt in us that it will – Poland will proudly look into the future, proud of her part in the struggle for righteousness and freedom.[57]

Drawing attention to the vast scope of Poland's tragic losses, the Polish indictment concluded on a solemn note, but also took a sanguine view of the future.

Before the Polish Prosecutor

Having been granted permission by Jackson to conduct interrogations of German officials in Allied custody who were accused of committing crimes in Poland, Sawicki questioned six men in January and February 1946. SS-Sturmbahnführer (Major) Alfred Naujocks, leading a small German force, had staged an attack on a radio station in Gleiwitz, on the German–Polish border, on 31 August 1939. This incident and others like it, for which the German authorities publicly blamed Poles, had provided the pretext for Germany's invasion of Poland on 1 September. Field Marshal Walther von Brauchitsch, commander-in-chief of the German army, oversaw the invasion of Poland in September 1939. General Heinz Guderian had led the Germans' mobile armoured formations during the Polish campaign; his 19th Army Corps had defeated the Polish army in Pomerania and pushed on to Brest-Litovsk. In 1944 he was appointed the German army's chief of general staff. Josef Bühler was State Secretary and Deputy Governor General of the General Government. SS-Obergruppenführer (General) Erich von dem Bach-Zelewski of the Waffen-SS was the supreme SS and Police Commander (HSSPF) for central Russia, in charge of anti-partisan warfare, before being appointed to command German troops during the 1944 Warsaw Uprising. Ernst Rode was a SS-Brigadeführer (Major General) in the Waffen-SS and Generalmajor (Major General) of the Order Police during the Warsaw Uprising. (Brauchitsch, Bühler, and Bach-Zelewski testified before the IMT, the first two for the defence, Bach-Zelewski for the prosecution.)

Sawicki interrogated Brauchitsch and Guderian for the purpose of clarifying their roles in the Nazi invasion of Poland and in the German military's attacks on Warsaw in September 1939. Brauchitsch went to great lengths to sanitize his part in planning both the invasion and the subsequent attacks on Warsaw and other Polish cities. Sawicki confronted Brauchitsch with the transcript of a high-level meeting in May 1939 that he had attended during which Hitler explained that his demand that the Poles renegotiate the status of the Free City of Danzig was a ploy to isolate Poland from its allies in the West and then attack it. Brauchitsch maintained that he believed that Hitler wanted to avoid armed conflict with Poland. After Hitler decided in August to invade Poland, Brauchitsch claimed that he himself had wanted to spare Warsaw, expecting Polish forces to capitulate; however, he continued, Hitler was intent on bombarding the capital from the air, responsibility for which was placed in Göring's hands. Brauchitsch also denied any responsibility or support for the destruction wrought by SS and police units in Poland. He claimed that in the fall of 1939, before the administration of occupied Poland was entrusted to Frank and civilian authorities, he had advised Hitler to order the SS and police forces to refrain from committing excesses against Jews as long as Poland was under military administration. Irked by Brauchitsch's stonewalling, an exasperated Sawicki asked him whether he understood the foundations of the Nazi system. "Many aspects of German matters were incomprehensible," answered Brauchitsch. "The gas chambers, the crematoria – to this day I've been unable to understand them." Sawicki suggested to Brauchitsch that he and other members of the military exerted themselves to construct a myth that there existed a wide gulf between the military and the Nazi Party and that the party's influence on the military was minimal at best. To the very end, Brauchitsch insisted that there was indeed a sharp division between the military and the Nazi Party and that he and other officers did their utmost to defend the military against the party. He resigned, he claimed, once he realized that he could not prevail against Hitler and the party.[58]

Similarly, Guderian denied any prior knowledge that German leaders were planning to attack Poland when the 19th Army Corps under his command was ordered on 20 August 1939 to station itself in Pomerania, on the Polish border. Guderian's orders were to occupy the Polish Corridor. His troops invaded on 1 September and by 5 September they occupied the Polish Corridor, which had afforded Poland access to the Baltic Sea but divided the greater part of Germany from its province of East Prussia. After leading his troops to Brest-Litovsk, he ceded it to the Red Army in accordance with the agreement reached between Germany and the Soviet Union. His troops then returned to Prussia and never marched on Warsaw. Pressed by Sawicki, Guderian pled ignorance about the annihilation of Polish Jews, though he had heard about the crushing of the Warsaw Ghetto Uprising; he also repudiated Sawicki's insinuation that the general staff of the army took part in the destruction of Polish Jewry. Guderian was elevated to Army Chief of the General Staff in July 1944, just several days prior to the outbreak of the Warsaw Uprising on 1 August. But although Warsaw lay within his field of operations and Hans Frank requested his assistance, as Frank recorded in his diary, which Sawicki read to Guderian, he denied any part in the suppression of the uprising. He further denied that he had received an order from Hitler via Himmler to raze Warsaw, even though Rode had told Sawicki when he was questioned that Himmler had conveyed the order in a telephone conversation. Guderian conceded that SS and police units led by Bach-Zelewski that had been assigned to defeat the uprising may have violated international law and committed crimes against civilians; but he steadfastly rejected Sawicki's accusation that the troops of the 9th Army that participated in the suppression of the uprising could have committed crimes against civilians. Even in the face of incontrovertible proof, Sawicki asked? To which Guderian replied: "And even then I am not responsible. I never would have given my approval for such measures. I never would have issued such an order."[59] Like Brauchitsch, Guderian maintained that the army had done its best to insulate itself from the Nazi Party. He felt no guilt for his part in conduct of the war. He conceded that the destruction of Warsaw was a violation of international law, indeed a crime; but he insisted that Himmler and Bach-Zelewski were responsible for it, not he himself.

Sawicki questioned Bühler for eight days. He pressed Hans Frank's former deputy time and again to acknowledge his administrative role in the AB Action, the persecution of Polish Jews and expropriation of their property, the plundering of Polish cultural treasures, the roundups of Poles for forced labour in Germany, and the establishment of Majdanek. Bühler denied everything, even when Sawicki confronted him with the minutes of meetings in which his complicity was obvious. Bühler minimized his own significance in the administration of the General Government. Like the other former high-ranking officials questioned by Sawicki, he pinned the blame for Nazi crimes on others, in his case on Himmler; on Friedrich-Wilhelm Krüger, SS-Obergruppenführer (General) and Higher SS and Police Leader East (Höherer SS- und Polizeiführer Ost; HSSPF Ost) in the General Government; and, albeit only partly, on Frank, whom he largely defended. Indeed, he claimed that in concert with Frank, he had intervened with Krüger and Odilo Globocnik, SS- and Police Leader of the Lublin

District (SS- und Polizeiführer des Distrikts Lublin), to modify or inter-
rupt various SS and police operations in the General Government, from
the resettlement of Polish farmers from the Zamość region in the winter of 1941–2 to the establishment of Majdanek in 1942. Yet by Bühler's
own account, his principal aim was not to lessen the suffering of ethnic
Poles or Polish Jews. Rather, it was, for example, in the case of Zamość,
to forestall unrest among Poles who felt aggrieved by resettlement measures and by the region's repopulation by ethnic Germans; and in the
case of Majdanek, to minimize the influx of thousands of foreign Jews
to the camp, which was contrary to the General Government's desire
to rid occupied Poland of Jews. Finally, Bühler maintained that he
and Frank had opposed the destruction of Warsaw in the wake of the
Warsaw Uprising, placing responsibility for it squarely on Himmler
and Bach-Zelewski. When Sawicki finally completed his questioning
of Bühler, he informed him that the Polish Republic would be requesting his extradition to stand trial for his part in the elimination of the
Polish people. Bühler's reply: "I, for my part, continuously made an
effort stand in the way of evil."[60]

Sawicki's interrogations of Rode and Bach-Zelewski focused on the
German suppression of the Warsaw Uprising. Rode believed that Hitler
and Guderian had wanted to pass the assignment to suppress the uprising to Bach-Zelewski; they were confident that he would not recoil from
even the harshest measures. Rode pinned the blame for German atrocities on Himmler and especially Guderian. According to Rode, he and
Bach-Zelewski had asked Guderian to intervene directly with Hitler in
an attempt to rescind his order to raze Warsaw because such an order
gave the SS – and especially those SS units composed of criminal elements – licence to abuse and murder civilians, but Guderian refused on
the grounds that an order from Hitler could not be contravened.

Of all the Germans questioned by Sawicki, Bach-Zelewski may have
been the most reviled by Poles. Like all the other Germans whom
Sawicki questioned, Bach-Zelewski went to great lengths to whitewash
his role. When Hitler and Himmler ordered him to report to Warsaw
in early August 1944, his task was to coordinate all German units and
defeat the Polish insurgents who had thwarted the Germans' counter-
attack since the eruption of the uprising two weeks earlier. He admitted
responsibility for the orders he issued, but he resisted taking responsibility for patently illegal excesses his troops perpetrated against insurgents and civilians alike. Sawicki remonstrated: "But you were

their commander. Someone must be responsible for the actions of the troops." To which Bach-Zelewski responded:

> I am responsible for the period that I commanded the troops. I am also responsible for the fact that my people either did not carry out my orders or overrode them. I was of the opinion that it is of significance that I did everything that I could do in my situation to save the population. To my understanding these are mitigating circumstances that have to be taken into account ... I bear full responsibility for that time period that I was in command. Even in cases in which I was unsuccessful in imposing my will on the troops. But these troops to a large extent were not an army but a bunch of swine.[61]

By Bach-Zelewski's own account, when he arrived in Warsaw he learned from Heinz Reinefarth, his subordinate, of Hitler's orders, endorsed by Himmler, not to take any prisoners but to execute all insurgents, to kill all civilians (Reinefarth's men were killing women and children), and to raze Warsaw. He went immediately to see Guderian, since the army had received the same order and Guderian had Hitler's ear, but Guderian did nothing. When his entreaty to Guderian fell on deaf ears, he decided – so he claimed – to take matters into his own hands. His objective was to reach a negotiated political settlement with the Polish leadership of the uprising *before* its final defeat; this would have spared the Polish population and avoided Warsaw's complete destruction. To this end, he asserted, he countermanded Hitler's order while regrouping and even recalling troops under his overall command (starting with the Kaminski Brigade), so as to prevent indiscriminate killing and rampant plundering. But, he contended, his intentions were thwarted, primarily by his rivals, who failed to stem the excesses perpetrated by the troops under their immediate command. In particular, Bach-Zelewski lambasted Guderian, who, he asserted, ignored his urgent request to intervene with Hitler and Himmler even though he may have been the only person with enough stature to persuade Hitler to rescind his order.

At the end of his interrogation of Bach-Zelewski, Sawicki tried one last time to have him admit his guilt. Sawicki: "To conclude I would like to ask you whether you feel guilty toward the Polish civilian population?" Bach-Zelewski: "In the sense in which you presented it, yes. That I was unable ..." Sawicki: We have already spoken about this ..." Bach-Zelewski:

The judgment that will be rendered in connection with my part in combatting the Warsaw Uprising, be it either very good or very bad, depends on the disposition of my judge. I would like to underline that I did everything to mitigate the tough orders that I received from above, or even avert them, insofar as it lay within my authority. I also made an effort to suppress all transgressions of my subordinates. I thought that my mission was to mitigate the evil existing above as well as below. I saw this as my true mission. The extent to which I succeeded in achieving this goal – I leave to the judgment of history.

With this an irked Sawicki had Bach-Zelewski returned to his cell.[62]

The evasiveness of the Germans whom he questioned clearly frustrated Sawicki, who went to great lengths to extract admissions of guilt from the former high-ranking officials, to no avail. Army officers and Bühler blamed the SS, while Bach-Zelewski blamed army and rival SS officers. In his final question to Guderian, the Polish prosecutor returned one last time to the question of guilt. Sawicki: "In conclusion, I ask, after everything that we have clarified here, whether you acknowledge your guilt." Guderian: "I can concede only to the extent that what happened later proves that our actions in this war, seen objectively, in the end brought harm to the German people."

The published version of Sawicki's interrogation of Guderian has an exasperated Sawicki, no longer able to contain himself, speaking directly to Guderian but, in effect, issuing a blanket indictment of all those just like him:

We will never find a common language. Three things doubtless separate us: For me and the world view that I as accuser in the name of the Polish Republic represent, the greatest good remains the human being, while for you race or the idea of the nation, which has been fashioned into a myth, is the highest ideal. This is the first difference. The second is this. We are without a doubt prepared to fight for the ideal of humanity, and we will do a great deal for the victory of this ideal. You fought for your ideals. There are, however, certain means that we do not use under any circumstances, whereas for you and the world view you represent all means are justified if, in your opinion, they validate your myth. Therefore, you did not hesitate to create gas chambers, because of which the smoke of the crematoria did not blind you. There is a third, lying in the same language that we use and that you use. Your language lies. During questioning you often use the term 'Aktion' – we call it ['pogrom']; you said 'combing through' or 'special measures' – we call it ['murder']; you said 'work squad' – we call it 'slavery.' Finally, the word that was created to describe the greatest equality of people around the world, 'socialism,' you used to describe the ruthless rule of one people, one race over others, and, therefore, to describe what is the greatest inequality ... For this reason we will never find a common language, this is why we demand punishment and isolation for you as war criminals and violators of the most fundamental rights of mankind.[63]

It is uncertain whether Sawicki actually said these things to Guderian's face or whether his words were polished for publication with the intent of inspiring approbation among Polish readers. In any event, they reflected how he felt and how many of them must have felt in the face of most Nazi officials' attempts to evade responsibility for their crimes.

Despite Polish requests for the extradition of Bach-Zelewski, Guderian, and Bühler, only one of the men questioned by Sawicki – Bühler – ever stood trial in Poland.[64] Nevertheless, even if Sawicki's efforts led to the trial in Poland of only one of the men, he did not consider his interrogations of high-ranking Nazis to have been wasted effort. In the preface to the first edition of his published interrogations of Nazis in Allied custody at Nuremberg, *Zburzenie Warszawy* (The Destruction of Warsaw), which appeared in 1946, Sawicki attributed two aims to the interrogations. The first was to show that the fascist danger had not passed and that many Germans still defended their crimes and Nazi ideals. "Finally," Sawicki wrote,

the interrogations had one more goal. They went far beyond the defendants and the historical moment. One can easily be convinced and one already hears voices that war crimes trials are primitive revenge of the victors against the vanquished. So the interrogations had the goal of showing the accused – as it turns out, to little effect – and the world that passing judgment on them is not only exploitation of the momentary advantage that the victors have over the vanquished, but also ensues from the necessity of our outlook on life, which must incapacitate and isolate people who shatter the most fundamental principles of communal life.[65]

In other words, the very fact that central figures of the Nazi regime were compelled to answer the questions of a prosecutor from Poland at Nuremberg symbolized, as far as Sawicki was concerned, a triumph over Nazism and a certain measure of historical justice.

Sawicki's questioning of the Germans was not without political overtones. There was a political edge especially in his questioning of Rode and Bach-Zelewski. He asked Rode what the fate was of Polish officers who took part in the Warsaw Uprising after its suppression by German forces. Sawicki expressed particular interest in Brigadier General Tadeusz Bór-Komorowski, commander of the AK during the uprising. According to Rode, Bór-Komorowski and his fellow officers were deemed prisoners-of-war and treated well during their internment in Germany. Indeed, he continued, Bór-Komorowski seemed content to be in German rather than Soviet custody. The point, from Sawicki's perspective and from that of officials of the Soviet-installed government in Warsaw, was to paint Bór-Komorowski and other AK officers who mounted the Warsaw Uprising as traitors rather than as heroes. But his success at portraying Bór-Komorowski in this way was only partial at best, as Bach-Zelewski asserted that Himmler believed he could create a nationalist Polish army under the command of Bór-Komorowski that would oppose the Soviets, but that Bór-Komorowski declined Himmler's invitation to meet with him.[66]

For the most part, however, Sawicki's questioning of former high-ranking Nazis was nonpartisan. From Sawicki's vantage point, his interrogations of the men who played a decisive role in the destruction of Poland, and especially Warsaw, showed that they deserved to be deemed beyond the pale of society. In Sawicki's view, the interrogations alone vindicated Poland's demand for representation at Nuremberg.[67]

Polish Witnesses

Two witnesses from Poland who appeared in court on the basis of a request by the Polish delegation testified before the IMT: Seweryna Szmaglewska (represented as "Severina Shmaglevskaya" in the official transcript), and Samuel Rajzman.[68] Called to the witness stand by Soviet prosecutor Smirnov, they both testified on 27 February 1946.

Szmaglewska was a budding young writer when the Germans arrested her in 1942. She was interned two and a half years at Auschwitz, mostly at Birkenau. Szmaglewska testified that children born to Jewish women who were imprisoned as forced labourers at Birkenau were taken immediately after birth to their deaths, while children born to non-Jewish women were removed, put in special barracks, and then taken from the camp. She testified further that when transports of Jews arrived at Birkenau, mothers and their children were led together to the

gas chambers, but during periods when the number of Jews arriving
on transports was exceedingly high, children were thrown into the cre-
matory ovens or ditches without being asphyxiated by gas. "The children were thrown in alive. Their cries could be heard all over the camp.
It is hard to say how many there were." Szmaglewska and her fellow
inmates estimated the number of children who were killed by count-
ing the baby carriages brought to the warehouse after the Germans'
liquidation of individual transports of Jews. "Sometimes there were
hundreds of these carriages, but sometimes they sent thousands," she
testified. "In one day?," the apparently astonished Soviet prosecutor,
Smirnov, asked. To which she replied, "Not always the same. There
were days when the gas chambers worked from early morning until late
at night." The number of Jewish children killed upon arrival exceeded
Szmaglewska's and her fellow inmates' ability to count them. Non-
Jewish children from Poland, Russia, and Italy who were transported
to the camp suffered from malnutrition and skin diseases and were
often underdressed. Children captured during the Warsaw Uprising
were transported to the camp, and when the Germans commenced deportations from Birkenau to the German interior, these children were
used for heavy labour. They laboured together with the children of
Hungarian Jews who had been sent to Birkenau. When the Germans
evacuated Auschwitz in January 1945, the children were forced to
march to Germany on foot. As Szmaglewska's testimony approached
its conclusion, Smirnov returned to the number of baby carriages: "Tell
me, Witness, do you certify in your testimony, that sometimes the number of carriages remaining after the murder of the children amounted
to a thousand per day?" "Yes," she answered, "sometimes there were
such days."[69]

Of the ninety-four witnesses who testified before the IMT, including thirty-three for the prosecution, only three were Jews. Rajzman, an
agent for a company in Warsaw, was one of them.[70] He may have been
chosen by the Polish delegation because he had travelled to Treblinka the
year before on a joint investigation of the camp led by the government-
sponsored Main Commission for the Investigation of German Crimes
in Poland and the Central Jewish Historical Commission in Poland.
Introducing Rajzman to the tribunal, Smirnov described him as "a
person who returned from 'the other world,'" since the Germans de-
risively called the path leading from the platform at which deported
Jews arrived on trains to the gas chambers "'the Road to Heaven.'"
Before the IMT, Rajzman described the selection process. Transports of

Jews from Germany, Poland, Czechoslovakia, and Greece arrived every day. Immediately after their arrival, men, women, and children were divided and forced to strip, subject to the lashes of the German guards' whips. Workers collected their clothing while they were obliged to walk naked down a path to the gas chambers. Before women entered the gas chambers, their hair was shorn. The entire process, from disembarkation from the trains to being put in the gas chambers, took ten minutes for men, fifteen minutes for women. Every German had a function. Rajzman cited as an example a German officer by the name of Menz whose task was to execute all women, children, elderly people, and ill people, who were led to a fake infirmary (*Lazarett*) because they were too weak to walk to the gas chambers. Rajzman recounted two atrocities committed by Menz. In Rajzman's own words:

> Here is just one example of what was the fate of the children there. A 10-year-old girl was brought to this building from the train with her 2-year-old sister. When the elder girl saw that Menz had taken out a revolver to shoot her 2-year-old sister, she threw herself upon him, crying out, and asking why he wanted to kill her. He did not kill the little sister; he threw her alive into the oven and then killed the elder sister.
>
> Another example: They brought an aged [woman] with her daughter to this building. The latter was in the last stage of pregnancy. She was brought to the 'Lazarett,' was put on a grass plot, and several Germans came to watch the delivery. This spectacle lasted 2 hours. When the child was born, Menz asked the grandmother – that is the mother of this woman – whom she preferred to see killed first. The grandmother preferred to be killed. But, of course, they did the opposite; the newborn baby was killed first, then the child's mother, and finally the grandmother.[71]

Rajzman described further how after disembarking from a train, a woman who claimed to be Sigmund Freud's sister approached Kurt Franz, the notorious deputy to the commander of Treblinka, entreating him to spare her life and allow her to work in an office. After appearing to study her documents, Franz assured her that there must be a mistake and that she would be able to return to Vienna. He instructed her to leave her documents and valuables and go to the bathhouse. When she returned, she would receive her documents and a ticket to Vienna. The bathhouse was actually a gas chamber, and of course she did not return.

Rajzman himself survived thanks to a stroke of luck. He arrived with a transport of 8,000 Jews from Warsaw and was already undressed and walking to the gas chamber when a friend of his from Warsaw who was an overseer of the camp's Jewish labourers spotted him and obtained permission to remove him from those destined to die immediately and put him to work. But he was the only person in his family who survived. He witnessed his mother, sister, and two brothers being led to the gas chambers, unable to help them. Comrades of his found his wife's documents and a photograph of his wife and child. "That is all that I have left of my family, only a photograph."

Rajzman testified that between July 1942 – when killing operations at Treblinka commenced – and December 1942, an average of three transports of sixty freight cars each arrived every day. In 1943 transports arrived with less regularity. He estimated that 10,000 to 12,000 people were killed every day at Treblinka. There were initially three gas chambers, but the Germans had ten additional gas chambers built to accommodate the high volume of victims. According to Rajzman, the Germans had more building materials brought to the camp and intended to increase the number of gas chambers to twenty-five. "I asked, 'Why? There are no more Jews,'" he testified. "They said, 'After you there will be others, and there is still a big job to do.'"[72] On 2 August 1943, Jewish prisoners mounted a revolt. Some three hundred prisoners broke through the perimeter of the camp and fled. Two-thirds were hunted down and killed by German forces. Rajzman was one of the survivors.[73]

The Case against Hans Frank

Defendant Hans Frank (1900–1946) was an early supporter of the NSDAP. A lawyer who was legal adviser to Hitler in the 1930s, he was appointed Governor General of occupied Poland, the so-called General Government, in the wake of the German invasion of Poland. In this capacity he was responsible for the oppression of both ethnic Poles and Polish Jews. As historians have shown, Frank authorized and oversaw, among other things, the deportation of more than one million ethnic Poles from the General Government for forced labour in Germany; the conscription of some one million ethnic Poles for forced labour in armaments factories, construction projects, and agriculture in the General Government; the expulsion of 110,000 ethnic Poles from the Zamość–Lublin region in 1942 and 1943; the expropriation of Polish produce for Germany's population; and the plunder of Polish state property.[74] He further authorized and oversaw the enactment of anti-Jewish legislation, the ghettoization of Jews, and comprehensive logistical support by his administration to SS and police forces for all phases of the deportation of Jews to concentration and death camps. His policies and actions were all animated by a vision to create a Germanized Poland that, through violent means, would be cleansed of Jews and colonized by ethnic Germans, and where Poles would be reduced to a population of serfs or slaves.[75]

The Allied indictment accused Frank in general terms:

> The defendant FRANK between 1932 and 1945 was: A member of the Nazi Party ... Reich Minister without Portfolio ... and Governor General of the occupied Polish territories. The defendant FRANK used the foregoing positions, his personal influence, and his intimate connection with the Führer in such a manner that: He promoted the accession to power of the Nazi conspirators and the consolidation of their control over Germany set forth in Count One of the indictment; he authorized, directed and participated in the War Crimes set forth in Count Three of the Indictment and Crimes against Humanity set forth in Count Four of the Indictment, including particularly the War Crimes and Crimes against Humanity involved in the administration of occupied territories.[76]

In any event, the lawyers in the Polish delegation and Polish government officials could not have been satisfied with the indictment's vague reference to Frank's role in Nazi crimes committed on the territory of the General Government.

The Polish authorities were eager to see the IMT convict Frank. The Polish Minister of Justice, Henryk Świątowski, directed the GKBZN to collect evidence, including witness statements, that could be used against Frank at the IMT.[77] In this vein, the Polish delegation viewed the preparation of incriminating evidence against Frank as vital to its mission at Nuremberg. But Polish authorities had more sweeping plans for Frank after Nuremberg. At his aforementioned meeting with members of the Polish delegation in October 1945, Deputy Minister of Foreign Affairs Zygmunt Modzelewski stressed that "the most important thing is the handing over of Frank, then having him in our hands, we can put him on trial again and then hang him."[78] But Jackson did not keep a promise to the Poles to have Frank extradited to Poland after his conviction by the IMT, and Frank was executed immediately after the trial.

Between October 1939 and April 1945, Frank kept a detailed diary of his daily activities (*Diensttagebuch* in German). Almost all of the entries

2.1 Hans Frank, the former Nazi Governor General of Poland, in the witness box at the International Military Tribunal trial of war criminals at Nuremberg, 19 April 1946. United States Holocaust Memorial Museum, courtesy of National Archives and Records Administration, College Park.

in these thirty-eight volumes focused on his tenure as head of the General Government. The diary's contents, compiled by Frank and his secretaries, included reports from cabinet sessions and Frank's meetings with various Nazi officials, as well as his official pronouncements and speeches. In May 1945, when he was apprehended near his family's home in Neuhaus am Schliersee by Lieutenant Walter Stein of the US 7th Army, Frank handed the diary over to his captor. He did so because he had deluded himself into thinking it would help exonerate him.[79] In fact, it became a key piece of evidence in the Allied prosecution's case *against* him. After the conclusion of the Nuremberg Trial, the American authorities gave Frank's diary to the Polish government, which stored it in the archives of the Main Commission for the Investigation of German Crimes in Poland.[80]

Thomas Dodd, executive trial counsel for the United States, presented to the IMT a compilation of excerpts from Frank's diary prepared by the Americans' legal staff and read aloud from it in open court on 11 December 1945.[81] Allied prosecutors would read excerpts from the diary into the court record numerous times during the trial.[82] The excerpts from Frank's diary read aloud seem to have had a chilling effect on those who heard them.[83] Within the Polish delegation the task of extracting incriminating evidence from Frank's diary was assigned to Piotrowski. On 11 January 1946 he presented a brief to American and Soviet prosecutors for the purpose of cross-examination; in preparing that brief, he had culled passages from the diary in support of Polish arguments for Frank's culpability for Nazi crimes committed on the territory of the General Government.[84]

"I still profess to be a National Socialist and faithful follower of the Führer, Adolf Hitler, whom I have been serving since 1919." This excerpt from Frank's diary from 1942 appeared early in Piotrowski's brief.[85] With this and similar passages Piotrowski strove to show Frank's Nazi pedigree, his political convictions, and his readiness to implement Hitler's policies in occupied Poland. In particular, Piotrowski highlighted the following: Frank's cooperation with the SS in the General Government, his role in the so-called AB Action to eliminate the Polish elite, the Nazis' tactics for instilling terror in the Polish population, the deportation of forced labourers to Germany, the evictions of the population and population transfer, the establishment of concentration camps, the demolition of Poland's cultural institutions and educational system, and the persecution and annihilation of both Polish and foreign Jews. Piotrowski's brief emphasized Frank's acknowledgment of his responsibility. "I bear responsibility and deflect it onto no one else," Piotrowski showed Frank saying in 1940. "Now," wrote Piotrowski in conclusion, "let us allow justice to speak and Dr. Frank to bear the responsibility he desired."[86] The point that Piotrowski clearly wanted to make was that Frank's actions were not arbitrary or made in isolation but were part of a comprehensive plan, in accordance with Nazi general policy, to crush Poland's people and turn the country into a German satrapy.

On the second day of the trial, 21 November 1945, the defendants were asked by Lord Justice Geoffrey Lawrence, the senior British judge, how they pleaded. Like all of his co-defendants, Frank pleaded not guilty. "I declare myself not guilty," he replied.[87] Their pleas were followed by Jackson's famous opening address for the United States. Reading aloud from passages in Frank's diary, Jackson linked Frank directly to the deportation of Poles to slave labour and the murder of Jews. Apropos of the Nazis' anti-Jewish policies, Jackson said: "And the defendant Frank, a lawyer by profession, I say with shame, summarized in his diary in 1944 the Nazi policy thus: 'The Jews are a race which has to be eliminated; whenever we catch one, it is his end ...' And earlier, speaking of his function as governor general of Poland, he confided to his diary this sentiment: 'Of course, I cannot eliminate all lice and Jews in only a year's time ...'"[88] As Philippe Sands observes, "The diaries were a gold mine to be seamed. If Frank had a sense of foreboding as to the use to which his words would be used, he didn't show it."[89]

Frank testified on 18 April 1946. To a question put to him by his defence counsel, Alfred Seidl, regarding his share in events in Poland after 1939, Frank answered, "I bear the responsibility."[90] "I am possessed by a deep sense of guilt," he added, and he attributed that guilt to the insight he had gained during the trial into the atrocities that had been committed.[91] But his acknowledgment of responsibility and expression of remorse rang hollow, in that over the course of the rest of his testimony he repudiated all responsibility for Nazi crimes committed in Poland, shifting it primarily to Himmler and his subordinates in the SS, particularly to Krüger. Frank's testimony beggared belief:

I was never informed about anything. I heard about special action commandos of the SS during this trial. In connection with and immediately following my appointment, special powers were given to Himmler, and my competence in many essential matters was taken away from me. A number of Reich offices governed in matters of economy, social policy, ... food policy, and therefore, all I could do was to lay upon myself the task of seeing to it that amid the conflagration of this war, some sort of order should be built up which would enable men to live ... My aim [as Governor General] was to safeguard justice, without doing harm to our war effort.[92]

"Did you ever participate in the annihilation of Jews?" Seidl eventually asked him. Frank responded: "I say 'yes;' and the reason why I say 'yes' is because after having lived through the 5 months of this trial and having heard the testimony of the witness [Rudolf] Hoess[93] my conscience does not allow me to throw the responsibility solely on these minor people." But he added a caveat:

> I myself have never installed an extermination camp for Jews, or promoted the existence of such camps; but if Adolf Hitler personally has laid that dreadful responsibility on his people, then it is mine too, for we have fought against Jewry for years; and we have indulged in the most horrible utterances – my own diary bears witness against me. Therefore, it is no more than my duty to answer your question in this connection with 'yes.' A thousand years will pass and still this guilt of Germany will not have been erased.[94]

In effect, Frank was linking his own guilt to the guilt of the German people, most of them followers of Hitler. His was not an admission of personal responsibility but one of collective responsibility. In Sands's words, "one step forward, one step back."[95] Of course, Frank had done more that just indulge in blood-curdling antisemitic utterances. He failed to mention his introduction of various decrees and measures to persecute Jews and his administration's support of SS operations to kill Jews. He accepted responsibility for issuing orders to introduce yellow badges to identify Jews and establish ghettos – and that was all. He even claimed that he had no direct knowledge of the killing of Jews, asserting that despite his efforts to discover what was happening to Jews deported from ghettos, Himmler had kept him the dark about the annihilation of Jews in death camps located in the General Government.

Frank was cross-examined by Soviet prosecutor Smirnov and then by American prosecutor Dodd. It appears that Smirnov drew on Piotrowski's brief. Smirnov pressed Frank to admit that the police in the General Government had been under his control, and he accused Frank of playing a pivotal role in the AB Action, points made by Piotrowski. A passage from Frank's diary about the merciless treatment awaiting Poles who were in line to be arrested during the AB campaign that Smirnov quoted appeared in Piotrowski's brief. In contrast, Dodd did not seem to make use of Piotrowski's brief in his perfunctory questioning of Frank.[96] Since Frank had, in Dodd's opinion, practically admitted his guilt on direct examination by his own attorney, extensive cross-examination would have been superfluous.[97]

Closing Arguments

Defence lawyers made their closing arguments in July. When it was his turn to defend his client, Frank's lawyer, Alfred Seidl, minimized Frank's political influence in the NSDAP and argued that Allied prosecutors had failed to connect him to any police and military measures that were taken in the General Government. Unlike Hitler, who was a man of violence, "Frank," Seidl claimed, "considered it his life's work to see the conception of the State founded on law realized in the National Socialist Reich and, above all, to safeguard the independence of the judiciary."[98] He portrayed his client as a defender of the right of the accused to their day in court, as an opponent of the peremptory measures of a police state, and as an opponent of concentration camps. Thus, Seidl asserted, it was unthinkable that Frank would have been part of Hitler's inner circle. Seidl maintained that as governor general in the General Government, Frank's actual authority was curtailed by the police powers vested in Reichsführer SS Himmler, who ignored Frank when he issued orders to his representative in the General Government, Higher SS and Police Leader Krüger. The struggle between Frank's civil administration and the SS in the General Government in effect deprived him of any executive power. It followed, Seidl averred, that Frank played no role in police measures or in the resettlement of ethnic Germans. Seidl downplayed the significance of Frank's diary, from which the prosecution had drawn heavily to make its case. The entries in it, Seidl maintained, did not represent Frank's own words but rather a stenographer's summaries of meetings and Frank's impromptu speeches, in which one could find contradictions. For this reason, its value as evidence was not to be overestimated. The court ought not to overlook Frank's conflicts with Himmler and Krüger as expressed in the diary, which proved his limited administrative latitude. He *had* to cooperate with the police if he wanted to accomplish any administrative goals.

But after disputing the evidentiary value of the diary, Seidl tried to use it to defend Frank. According to Seidl, along with other evidence, entries in the diary showed that Frank "repudiated all measures and tendencies to effect Germanization" in Poland.[99] Frank's lawyer conceded that the resettlement of ethnic Germans caused hardships for Poles who had been expelled to make way for them, but he questioned whether resettlement was a war crime, given that contemporary

Germany was being flooded with ethnic Germans driven from their homes in Eastern Europe.

Frank, argued Seidl, had opposed the deportation of Polish workers to Germany. His hand had been forced, according to Seidl, by over-population, insufficient arable land, and Polish factories' lack of capacity to absorb Polish labourers. "In order to avoid unemployment, and above all in the interest of maintaining public order and security, the administration of the General Government was bound, if only for reasons of state policy, to try to transfer as many workers to Germany as possible."[100] That said, "Defendant Frank had in the very beginning opposed all violent measures in recruiting labor and solely for security reasons and in order not to create new centers of unrest had insisted that no compulsory measures were to be used and only propagandistic methods employed." Seidl added: "The Defendant Frank continuously and repeatedly pleaded for better treatment of the Polish workers in the Reich."[101]

Seidl's portrayal of a benevolent governor general of an occupied territory knew no bounds. In response to the accusation that Frank had directed the requisition of Polish agricultural and industrial production for the benefit of the Reich, Seidl said: "The Defendant Frank, from his first day in office, set himself to integrate the entire economic policy in a manner which one can only term constructive. Certainly he did this partly to strengthen the production capacity of the German nation engaged in a struggle of life and death. But at the same time there can be no doubt that the success of these measures also benefitted the Polish and Ukrainian peoples."[102]

As far as Jews were concerned, Seidl conceded, on the basis of statements in the defendant's diary, that "it shall not be denied that Defendant Frank made no secret of his anti-Semitic views." But he argued that the prosecution had failed "to prove a causal connection between these statements and the measures carried out against the Jews by the Security Police." As witnesses like Bühler, who appeared in the witness box for Frank, had testified, "all the measures concerning Jews in the General Government were carried out exclusively by Reichsführer SS Himmler and his organs. This is true for both the initiation and organization of ghettos and the so-called final solution of the Jewish question." "The administration of the General Government," Seidl added, "had nothing to do with these measures."[103] This was also true in the case of concentration camps. Since Auschwitz was located outside the borders of the General Government (in the province of

Upper Silesia, annexed by Nazi Germany), Frank could not be held responsible for it. But Seidl did his client no favours when he questioned whether the establishment of concentration camps even constituted a war crime or a crime against humanity. In his words,

[s]etting aside the crimes committed in the concentration camps and considering the nature of concentration camps to be that in which people are confined for reasons of state and political security on account of their political opinions and without an opportunity of defending themselves in an ordinary court of law, it appears at least doubtful whether an occupying power should not have the right to take such necessary steps as this in order to maintain public order and security.

In any event, according to Seidl, Frank had "decried the concentration camps as an institution which could in no way be made to harmonize with a state founded on law"; besides, the camps had been under the exclusive command of the SS. "Neither the Governor General nor the general administration of the General Government had anything to do with these camps."[104]

Approaching the end of his closing argument, Seidl made a final pitch on behalf of his client. "My Lords," he said addressing the bench, "I am certainly not going to deny that in the course of the recent war terrible crimes were committed in the territory known as the General Government. Concentration camps had been established in which mass destruction of human beings was carried out. Hostages were shot. Expropriations took place, and so on. The Defendant Frank would be the last to deny this; he himself waged a violent struggle against all such measures." Seidl argued that the evidence showed "that neither the defendant nor the administration of the General Government can be held responsible for the said evils but that the whole responsibility must be borne by ... the Security Police and the SD, or the Higher SS and Police Leader, East."[105] As Sands observes: "Three months earlier, in April, Frank had spoken words that appeared to reflect some degree of collective responsibility, if not personal or individual responsibility. Now his lawyer was adopting a different tack. The other defendants had got to him, impressing upon him the need for solidarity with the group."[106]

Prosecution lawyers made their closing arguments at the end of July. For Jackson, the Nazis' crimes in Poland, from their aggressive attack in September 1939 to their merciless exploitation and oppression of occupied populations, foreshadowed their crimes in other Nazi-occupied countries. Hitler, Jackson maintained, had waged aggressive war in Eastern Europe for the purposes of *Lebensraum*, creating living space for ethnic Germans. Jackson quoted one of Hitler's speeches to his commanders: "'The main objective in Poland is the destruction of the enemy and not the reaching of a certain geographical line.'" He then quoted Frank to show the defendant's agreement with this aim: "'... then, for all I care, mincemeat can be made of the Poles and Ukrainians and all others who run around here – it does not matter what happens.'"[107] Jackson directly attacked Seidl's characterization of Frank's respect for law in scathing terms: "The fanatical Frank," Jackson said, "who solidified Nazi control by establishing the New Order of authority without law, so that the will of the Party was the only test of legality, proceeded to export his lawlessness to Poland, which he governed with the lash of Caesar and whose population he reduced to sorrowing remnants."[108] Jackson ridiculed the defendants' collective defence, adopted also by Frank, of men who "saw no evil, spoke no evil, and none was uttered in their presence." Frank, by his own implausible account, according to Jackson, was a "governor general of Poland who reigned but did not rule."[109]

Shawcross's powerful closing argument for the British broke new ground in its use of the term "genocide" (which had appeared in the indictment once, with little fanfare) to describe Nazi crimes. He drew the judges' attention to the Nazis' aim to remake the world in their image. Hitler and his Nazi minions, including Frank, had hatched a plan to deport Polish labourers to Germany. "The methods employed in their forced deportations are hideous in their brutality and must have been known to every one of these defendants." In this context, Shawcross quoted a speech by Himmler to the officers of the 1st SS Panzer Division "Leibstandarte Adolf Hitler" in which Himmler referred to deportations "'in Poland in weather 40 degrees below zero where we had to haul away thousands, tens of thousands, hundreds of thousands ...'"[110] "That policy was, of course, a short-term policy, the real aim being the elimination of the Eastern peoples," Shawcross argued.[111] Shawcross traced the origins of the Nazis' approach to slave labour to their intent to wage total war, a racial war:

The evidence that these [Nazi-occupied] territories were scenes of murder, slavery, terrorism, and spoliation on a scale without precedent in history, in breach of the most elementary rules as to belligerent occupation, has not really been seriously challenged. These crimes were in no sense sporadic or isolated depending on the sadism of a Koch[112] here or cruelty by a Frank there. They were part of a deliberate and systematic plan of which their action in regard to slave labor was just a symptom. In order to establish the "1,000-year Reich," they set out to accomplish the extermination or permanent weakening of the racial or national groups of Europe or of those sections, such as the intelligentsia, on which the survival of those groups must largely depend.

The origin of this terrible attempt upon the existence of free and ancient nations goes back to the whole Nazi doctrine of total war which rejected war as being merely against states and their armies, as international law provides. Nazi total war was also a war against civilian populations, against whole peoples. Hitler told Keitel[113] at the end of the Polish campaign: "Prudence and severity must be the maxims in this racial struggle in order to spare us from going to battle on account of Poland again.[114]

Shawcross then quoted the conversation from a meeting Hitler, Frank, and defendant Baldur von Schirach held shortly after the invasion of Poland: "'[T]here should be one master only for the Poles – the Germans; two masters side by side cannot and must not exist and therefore all representatives of Polish intelligentsia must be exterminated. This sounds cruel but this is the law of life.'" Shawcross commented on this exchange:

Such were the plans for the Soviet Union, for Poland and for Czechoslovakia. Genocide was not restricted to extermination of the Jewish people or of the Gypsies ... The technique varied from nation to nation, from people to people. The long-term aim was the same in all cases. The methods followed a similar pattern. First a deliberate program of murder, of outright annihilation. This was the method applied to the Polish intelligentsia, to gypsies, and to Jews.[115]

Throughout his closing argument Shawcross addressed the Nazi annihilation of Europe's Jews in powerful terms:

There was one group to which the method of annihilation was applied on a scale so immense that it is my duty to refer separately to the evidence. I mean the extermination of the Jews. If there were no other crime against these men, this one alone, in which all of them were implicated, would suffice. History holds no parallel to these horrors.[116]

Frank, Shawcross averred, was pivotal in the extermination of Jews, especially through his role in the establishment of ghettos in the General Government. "When the order [to deport Jews to their deaths in concentration camps] actually came, the preparatory measures, so far as they affected Poland and Germany, had already been taken." Shawcross referred to the destruction of the Warsaw Ghetto by SS units under the command of Jürgen Stroop. "But the fate of the Jews in Warsaw," Shawcross added, "was only typical of the Jews in every other ghetto in Poland."[117] Frank, Shawcross argued, was a willing accomplice in Nazi crimes: "Frank – if it is not sufficient to convict him that was he responsible for the administration of the General Government and for one of the bloodiest and most brutal chapters in Nazi history – has himself stated: 'One cannot kill all lice and all Jews in one year.' It was no coincidence that this was exactly Hitler's language."[118] Frank, along with the other Nazis in the dock, was complicit not only in the extermination of Jews but also in the other Nazi atrocities, from the internment of millions in concentration camps to the exploitation of millions for slave labour. Shawcross said to the judges:

When they [the defendants] spoke or wrote in support of this horrible policy of genocide, you are asked to accept that their utterances were made in ignorance of the facts, as part of their general duty to support the policy of their government, or finally, should be regarded as merely tactical – that is to say, that only by talking or writing in such a way could they divert Hitler from cruelty or aggression. It is for you to decide.

Shawcross then named all twenty-two defendants, including Frank: "these are the guilty men."[119]

Like the prosecutors whose closing arguments preceded his, Rudenko acclaimed the historical significance of the ITM. "This Trial … is the first of its kind in legal history," he declared in his closing argument for the Soviet Union.[120] The man who immediately preceded him to the podium, French deputy chief prosecutor Charles Dubost, had paid only cursory attention to Nazi crimes in Poland in his closing argument. Referring briefly to Frank, for whom he expressed admiration for his admission of collective responsibility, Dubost said, "[h]is personal activities in Poland contributed to the extermination of numerous Poles."[121] In contrast, Rudenko robustly addressed Nazi crimes in Poland (although, without skipping a beat, he censured the Germans for their invasion of Poland even while brushing the parallel Soviet incursion from the east under the carpet without demur and condemning the Germans for the Katyn massacre of Polish officers, which the overwhelming opinion of the free world attributed to the Soviets). Rudenko situated Frank squarely within the Nazis' overall plan to wage aggressive war and then plunder, exploit, and exterminate the civilians under their occupation. "Frank arrived in Poland," Rudenko asserted, "to realize his entire program for the enslavement and extermination of the people on the territory of a country with an age-old history and with its own culture of high standing."[122] Rudenko made repeated use of Frank's diary to underscore the defendant's commitment to Nazi ideology and his unlawful activities as head of the General Government: from subjugating and terrorizing the Polish people to sending, in Rudenko's estimation, two million Poles to Germany to perform forced labour, ordering the mass murder of the Polish intelligentsia (the AB Action), and sanctioning the summary execution of thousands of Poles for alleged breaches of his regulations. Rudenko drew evidence, moreover, from the report of the Soviet Extraordinary State Commission, in which a French citizen, Ida Vasseau, testified that Hitler Youth (Hitlerjugend) had killed children for shooting practice in Lwów. Although this charge was laid at the feet of defendant Baldur von Schirach, Reich youth leader since 1933, Lwów lay in Frank's territory.[123]

Rudenko availed himself of the diary, furthermore, to underline Frank's role in the annihilation of three and a half million Polish Jews. In sum, "the regime, established by Hans Frank throughout Poland during all the stages of the temporary German domination in this country, was a regime for the inhuman destruction of millions of people by varied, but invariably criminal methods."[124] Regarding the annihilation of Polish Jews, "the criminal activity of this hangman," Rudenko stated, "led to the extermination of millions."[125] Furthermore, Frank was "fully aware of the fact that should war not lead to victory he would have to bear the full responsibility for the crimes committed in Poland, as well as for his participation in the fascist conspiracy."[126] Although Rudenko made only one specific reference to the Polish indictment in his closing argument, one discerns its echoes throughout his analysis of Nazi crimes committed in Poland.

Shawcross, Dubost, and Rudenko all asked the judges to sentence the defendants to "the supreme penalty."[127] Although Jackson had not explicitly asked the judges to impose the death penalty on the defendants, he no doubt concurred. Shawcross framed their request in compelling terms: "This trial must form a milestone in the history of civilization, not only bringing retribution to these guilty men, not only marking that right shall in the end triumph over evil ... The state and the law are made for men ... Ultimately, the rights of men, made as all men are made in the image of God, are fundamental." The judges, Shawcross concluded, should render their decision "not in vengeance – but in a determination that these things shall not occur again."[128]

The prosecutors' closing arguments, especially Shawcross's and Rudenko's forceful speeches, must have pleased not only Piotrowski, the lone member of the Polish delegation who was still in Nuremberg, but also the lawyers in the Polish delegation who had already returned to Poland and Polish officials in Warsaw.

The defendants made brief closing statements on 31 August. When it was his turn, Frank, who had converted to Catholicism the previous October while awaiting trial, invoked God. In April he had attributed his earlier partial admission of guilt, albeit collective guilt, to his newfound faith in God.[129] He now spoke of his and his fellow Nazis' "tremendous spiritual responsibility," since by renouncing God and leading the German people down a godless path they had brought disaster to Germany and had "necessarily become more and more deeply involved in guilt." Ironically, however, Frank the lawyer did not invoke the Nazis' lawlessness, their disregard for legal norms and ethical standards. Moreover, God, not the Allies, was responsible for Germany's defeat. He implored the German people to return from the road of godlessness. But he did not beseech them to renounce their political ideals.

Frank then invoked the war's victims. The trial had been conducted "over the graves of millions" while "the spirits passed accusingly through this room." "Millions had to perish unquestioned and unheard." He did not, however, name the victims.

He then returned to the question of his guilt and the collective guilt of the German people. Four months earlier he had seemed to admit partial, collective responsibility for crimes committed in the name of the Third Reich. Now he did not want to leave any "hidden guilt" unaccounted for. Referring to his testimony in April, he added: "I assumed responsibility on the witness stand for all those things for which I must answer. I have also acknowledged that degree of guilt which attaches to me as a champion of Adolf Hitler, his movement, and his Reich." Frank's ambiguous language, especially his acknowledgment of only a "degree of guilt" and his studied avoidance of the names of his victims – Poles and Jews – could have made observers doubt his commitment to his earlier partial admission of criminal responsibility (not to be confused with a sense of religious guilt) if he had ever indeed made such an admission in the first place.

Finally, Frank wished to "rectify" one statement from his earlier testimony. Since he had appeared on the witness stand he had had a change of heart. Germany was now the victim. He had said that a thousand years would not suffice to erase the guilt of the German people. Now he whistled a different tune. "Every possible guilt incurred by our nation has already been completely wiped out today, not only by the conduct of our war-time enemies toward our nation and its soldiers, which has been carefully kept out of this trial" – Frank might have been alluding, for example, to the Allied bombing of Dresden – "but also by the tremendous mass crimes of the most dreadful sort which – as I have now learned – have been and still are being committed against Germans by Russians, Poles, and Czechs, especially in East Prussia, Silesia, Pomerania, and Sudetenland." Frank was referring to the expulsion of ethnic Germans from those territories. "Who shall ever judge these crimes against the German people?" Thus Frank concluded his closing statement.[130] Even if Frank's previous testimony had contained an actual admission of partial guilt, which is in itself debatable, his closing statement nullified it.

Judgment

"Alas, Poland has been the principal victim," wrote Henri de Donnedieu de Vabres, a French judge on the tribunal, in a letter received by Rafael Lemkin in January 1946.[131] Was Donnedieu's viewpoint reflected in the IMT's judgment? If not, to what extent did the judges address Polish grievances?

The judges pronounced judgment on 30 September and 1 October 1946. Poland occupied a central place in that judgment. It opened with a lengthy analysis of the German invasion of Poland, which in the opinion of the judges constituted a war of aggression and set the stage for a broader world war. In their discussion of war crimes, the judges condemned the establishment of concentration camps, which they deemed "one of the most notorious means of terrorizing the people in occupied territories."[132] "A certain number of concentration camps," the judges stated, "were equipped with gas chambers for the wholesale destruction of the inmates and with furnaces for the burning of the bodies. Some of these were in fact used for the extermination of Jews as part of the 'final solution' of the Jewish problem." The judges probably had

Poland in mind, since the Nazis had constructed the major killing facilities for Jews there. The judges also considered the fate of non-Jewish inmates, of whom most "were used for labor, although the conditions under which they worked made labor and death almost synonymous terms." In light of the murder and ill-treatment of Jews in concentration camps and the mass shootings of Jews and non-Jews by *Einsatzgruppen* (SS mobile killing units) in Soviet territory, the judges noted: "The murder and ill-treatment of civilian populations reached its height in the treatment of the citizens of the Soviet Union and Poland."[133] But the evidence left in the wake of these crimes led the judges to observe that "at any rate in the East, the mass murders and cruelties were not committed solely for the purpose of stamping out opposition or resistance to the German occupying forces. In Poland and the Soviet Union these crimes were part of a plan to get rid of whole native populations by expulsion and annihilation, in order that their territory could be used for colonization by Germans."[134] The judges took note of German plans beginning with the time of the invasion of Poland to exterminate the country's intelligentsia and then move cheap labour to Germany by the hundreds of thousands. In doing so the Nazis hoped to impede the biological propagation of Poles. This policy, administered enthusiastically by Frank, was so successful in Poland "that by the end of the war one third of the population had been killed, and the whole of the country devastated."[135] In their broader discussion of Nazi war crimes, the judges further condemned the Nazis' exploitation of Polish agriculture, which had led to widespread starvation among the Polish people in the General Government, the compulsory and brutal deportation of Polish workers to Germany, and Germanization in Poland.

A separate section of the judgment was titled "Persecution of the Jews." "The persecution of the Jews at the hands of the Nazi government has been proved in the greatest detail before the Tribunal," the judges wrote. "It is a record of consistent and systematic inhumanity on the greatest scale."[136] The fate of Polish Jews figured prominently in this section. The judges underscored the Nazis' brutal liquidation of the Warsaw Ghetto in 1943, evidence of which came from the report compiled by Jürgen Stroop, and the mass murder of Jews at Auschwitz, the subject of Rudolf Höss's testimony before the IMT. "These atrocities were all part and parcel of the policy inaugurated in 1941," the judges noted. "But the methods employed never conformed to a single pattern."[137]

The judges mentioned by name several Nazis responsible for the persecution of the Jews. Adolf Eichmann, a fugitive on the loose in 1946, was one; Hans Frank was another. Frank, they wrote, "spoke the final words of this chapter [in the Nazi persecution of Jews] when he testified in this court." The judges quoted Frank's admission that he and other Nazis had "'fought against Jewry ... for years'" and noted that his diary bore witness to utterances that he and they had made that were "'terrible.'" The judges ended their quotation of Frank's testimony with his partial admission of collective responsibility, the resounding "'[a] thousand years will pass and this guilt of Germany will still not be erased,'"[138] which he retracted in his final statement before the tribunal. His retraction had obviously not impressed the judges.

American judge Francis Biddle pronounced judgment on Frank on 1 October. The tribunal convicted him of war crimes and crimes against humanity. It used his own words to show his intentions. It found that his "occupation policy was based on the complete destruction of Poland as a national entity, and a ruthless exploitation of its human and economic resources for the German war effort." It held him responsible for leading a harsh occupation regime, buttressed by "a reign of terror," whose directives enabled or assisted the SS, the SD, and police units to shoot innocent civilians, take hostages, kill intellectuals, divert agricultural products to Germany, induce starvation in the occupied territory, deport close to one million forced labourers to Germany, and persecute Jews, force them into ghettos, and deport them to concentration and death camps established in the General Government. The tribunal found little credence in Frank's pronouncement that he felt "terrible guilt" for the atrocities committed in the General Government, and it was unmoved by his claim that he was not responsible for them. Although the tribunal acknowledged that Frank's jurisdiction over the police was limited and was subverted by Himmler, that some of the crimes perpetrated in the General Government were committed without his knowledge and even occasionally despite his opposition, and that some of the criminal policies that were put into effect in the General Government did not originate with him but were executed pursuant to orders issued in Germany, the judges ruled that "Frank was a willing and knowing participant in the use of terrorism in Poland; in the economic exploitation of Poland in a way which led to the death by starvation of a large number of people; in the deportation to Germany as slave laborers of almost a million Poles; and in the program involving the murder of at least 3 million Jews."[139]

The tribunal sentenced Frank to death by hanging.[140] Along with the other defendants who received the death penalty (with the exception of

Hermann Göring, who had committed suicide one day earlier), Frank was executed on 16 October 1946.[141] Members of the Polish delegation expressed their satisfaction with Frank's conviction and hanging.[142]

Conclusion

The whole point of the Polish delegation's activity at Nuremberg was to bring what mattered to Poles to the attention of Allied prosecutors and the IMT's judges. Did the delegation's labour bear fruit? To what extent did efforts of the Polish delegation contribute to the prosecution's cases? Can one discern traces of Polish efforts in the closing arguments or the judgment?

A comparison of the Allied indictment, which prosecutors lodged with the IMT before the Polish delegation had even arrived in Nuremberg, and the prosecutors' opening speeches – Jackson and Shawcross delivered their opening speeches before Allied prosecutors ever received the Polish indictment – with the prosecuting attorneys' closing arguments, especially those of Shawcross and Rudenko, shows that as the trial proceeded prosecutors became more and more attuned to crimes that the Nazis committed against Poland and its two major population groups, ethnic Poles and Polish Jews. Soviet prosecutors, for their part, made liberal use of the Polish indictment in presenting evidence, and they put two witnesses supplied by the Poles – Szmaglewska and Rajzman – on the witness stand to describe Nazi atrocities at Auschwitz and Treblinka, respectively. American, British, and French prosecutors never referred to the Polish indictment by name in open court, although they may have consulted it. We don't know. It seems reasonable to infer from Soviet prosecutor Smirnov's cross-examination of Frank that he had consulted Piotrowski's brief in his preparations for his confrontation with the defendant. From American prosecutor Dodd's cursory cross-examination of Frank it is impossible to know whether he read Piotrowski's brief; it's clear at any rate that Dodd did not draw on it during his cross-examination of the defendant.

The IMT received six national reports, including the Polish indictment, but made specific reference to only one, the Czech report, in its judgment. Nazi crimes in Poland committed against ethnic Poles and Polish Jews alike did receive considerable attention in the judgment. All of these crimes were enumerated in the Polish indictment, but it is impossible to know whether the judges drew on the Polish indictment in their discussion of them. For example, the Polish indictment described the mass murder of Jews at Auschwitz and Treblinka and Szmaglewska's and Rajzman's testimony focused on those camps, but it appears that the judges' discussion of Auschwitz in the judgment was influenced primarily by Höss's testimony, while their treatment of Treblinka in the judgment is brief, without any reference to Rajzman's testimony. The judges' discussion of the Nazis' liquidation of the Warsaw Ghetto was clearly shaped by the presentation of Major William F. Walsh, assistant trial counsel for the United States, who produced the report and album that SS general Jürgen Stroop compiled to document and gloat over the Nazis' brutal liquidation of the Warsaw Ghetto and suppression of the Warsaw Ghetto Uprising in April and May 1943. In his preparations Walsh was assisted not by the Poles but by Jacob Robinson of the World Jewish Congress.[143] As far as Frank was concerned, the judges may have considered Smirnov's cross-examination of him, but it is clear that their determination of Frank's guilt was grounded primarily on the incriminating utterances he had made in his diary.

In other words, it is impossible to draw a causal connection between the work product of the lawyers in the Polish delegation on the one hand and the prosecutors' efforts and the judges' opinions in the judgment on the other. What can be said is that much of what the Polish delegation brought to the proceedings appeared in the prosecutors' presentations and arguments and eventually in the judgment. There was much more attention paid to Nazi crimes in Poland and, in turn, to what mattered to Poles, at the end of the trial than at the beginning. It is unclear how much the labour of the Polish delegation contributed to the increasing attention that was paid to Poland.

That said, it's fair to say that the Polish delegation did its best to bring to light Nazi crimes against ethnic Poles and Polish Jews alike. It's to be expected that the Polish delegation, by means of the Polish indictment and the brief Piotrowski prepared against Hans Frank, highlighted Nazi crimes committed against the ethnic Polish majority. The Polish lawyers' emphasis on these things brought home the fact that Poland and its people had suffered grievously at the hands of the Germans and that the Nazi criminals on trial, starting with Hans Frank but not restricted to him, ought to be held accountable for Nazi crimes committed against Poles both in Poland and in Germany.

As far as Polish Jews were concerned, as a result of the Polish indictment, Piotrowski's brief against Frank, Sawicki's persistent questioning of former high-ranking Nazi officials, and the testimony of Szmaglewska and Rajzman, the Polish delegation left no doubt whatsoever as to the central place of the genocide of the Jews in the Nazis' war aims in Poland. The scholarly consensus is that American, British, and French prosecutors generally failed to distinguish Nazi crimes against Jews from Nazi crimes against other peoples and to appreciate the central role that the Nazis' antisemitic ideology played in the annihilation of Jews, while the Soviet prosecutors, for their part, shoehorned the Nazis' extermination of Jews into the merciless persecution and mass annihilation of all inhabitants of Eastern Europe, especially Soviet citizens. As Marrus characterizes the approach of Soviet prosecutors, "mass murder, in their conception, was in the service of conquest."[144] Whereas the deficiency of the American, British, and French prosecutors arguably stemmed from their imperfect understanding of the Nazi mass murder of the Jews, the Soviet prosecutors' approach was driven largely by political calculations, in concert with the Soviet Union's objective to co-opt Eastern Europeans to accept Soviet rule over their countries.

The Polish delegation's handling of the Nazis' persecution and annihilation of Polish Jews stood apart from the approach of Western prosecutors on the one hand and of Soviet prosecutors on the other. Unlike their Western counterparts, Polish lawyers had at their fingertips vast knowledge about the Nazi persecution and mass murder of Jews in Poland, and they deployed that knowledge to place the Holocaust squarely before the IMT. To be sure, Jews played a role in the Polish delegation and in the drafting of the Polish indictment, and their motivations probably played a part in that process. But non-Jewish Poles played a role, too. On the other side of the ledger, it is noteworthy that the Polish delegation's approach was out of sync with the Soviet one, in that Soviet prosecutors insisted that the suffering of Jews was part of a greater tragedy over the course of which all Eastern European peoples suffered. The lawyers in the Polish delegation made the point that the persecution and mass murder of Jews was separate from other Nazi crimes, including Nazi crimes against ethnic Poles, and that the Nazi assault on Jews had a distinct ideological underpinning. This is not to say that the Polish lawyers' approach was not shaped at least partly by political calculations. As indicated by the aforementioned meeting in late October 1945 between Kurowski, Piotrowski, Sawicki, and Zygmunt Modzelewski, Polish Deputy Minister of Foreign Affairs, the regime and the lawyers in the Polish delegation were motivated by foreign criticism of Polish antisemitism to demonstrate the government's disavowal of it through a vigorous effort of its representatives at Nuremberg to shine a light on the Nazis' crimes against Jews as well as ethnic Poles. To be sure, the lawyers who drafted the Polish indictment and who represented the Polish provisional government at Nuremberg would not have contradicted directives from Warsaw. Yet it is noteworthy that although the Nuremberg Trial unfolded at the same time that anti-Jewish animus and violence in postwar Poland were at their peak, the regime abstained from pressuring the delegation to downplay the Nazi genocide of the Jews even though it might have been in its political interest to do so vis-à-vis both the Soviets and the Polish populace. So it seems to us that the lawyers in the Polish delegation took seriously their responsibility to advocate for both ethnic Poles and Polish Jews as "Polish citizens"; note here that the concluding section of the Polish indictment referred to Poland's victims of the Nazi occupation, and did so without sacrificing the distinctiveness of the Jewish tragedy. Given that the Jews were a transnational victim group that was not represented by any single government in an international legal system that was based on state representation, at the IMT the Polish delegation did as much as any other state entity to represent Jews as a distinct group that had suffered at the hands of the Nazis. Unfortunately, however, the implication of the delegation's advocacy at Nuremberg on behalf of the Jewish victims of Nazism that Jews were equal citizens of Poland whose suffering ought to be dignified in the country's collective memory was lost on the great majority of Polish society.

In the opinion of its members, did the Polish delegation's labour bear fruit? In retrospect, Cyprian and Sawicki lamented the delegation's small size and its limited remit. In particular, they regretted that it was not authorized to participate officially in the proceedings. Nevertheless, unlike the Soviet delegation, on balance they regarded the delegation's efforts in a positive light.[145] They wrote:

The work of the Polish delegation was not wasted. Thanks to the collection and provision of necessary Polish documents at the appropriate moment and to the appropriate prosecutors, thanks to the submission of the Polish indictment, drawn up with technical assistance in London, finally thanks to good relations with the press and members of all the delegations of the Great Powers, the Polish delegation played its role in the Nuremberg Trial. It [the delegation] brought to it very many Polish elements and corrected gaps resulting from the two-month absence of Poland at the UNWCC in the period after the withdrawal of recognition of the London [Polish exile] government ... It is possible, therefore, in any event to assert that we were not absent at Nuremberg, as the greatest war crimes trial in world history was taking place there. The experience acquired in turn by the Polish delegates while it lasted was not wasted; publications on and a deepening acquaintance with international criminal law initiated during the Nuremberg Trial testify to this fact. Finally, testifying most convincingly to this fact is the number of places devoted to Polish matters in the tribunal's verdict in comparison to the entire indictment. This [experience] remained applicable as well in trials against war criminals that took place in Poland.[146]

It stands to reason that Cyprian and Sawicki's opinion that the efforts of the Polish delegation to the IMT made an impact on the proceedings and on the judgment is not unreasonable, although that impact was, it seems, modest and indirect. But there is no doubt that the delegation's lawyers put to good use what they learned from the Nuremberg Trial in Poland's own subsequent trials of Nazi criminals.[147]

Chapter Three

The Supreme National Tribunal, 1946–1948[1]

In the early morning of 16 April 1947, Rudolf Höss drank his last cup of coffee at his former commandant's office at Auschwitz. He was then escorted to the notorious "death block," where concentration camp personnel under his command had executed prisoners just a few years earlier. A group of former prisoners and Polish officials watched as Höss, who was quiet and calm, climbed onto a stool and cast a look over the camp where he had ruled over life and death for three and a half years. After the executioner put the noose around his neck, Höss fitted it with a slight head motion. A Catholic priest, whose presence Höss had requested, read a prayer, and a second later the stool was pulled away from under his feet.[2]

The trial and execution of the former commandant of Auschwitz, which riveted Polish public opinion, was the most prominent of a series of public trials held under the auspices of the Polish Supreme National Tribunal (Najwyższy Trybunał Narodowy, NTN). Intended specifically to prosecute major Nazi criminals and collaborators, between 1946 and 1948 the NTN adjudicated seven high-profile cases, in which forty-nine defendants were charged with war crimes and crimes against humanity. The NTN's rulings and decisions were of crucial importance, for they would govern the adjudication of war crimes in Poland for many years to come.

Creation of the NTN

As the IMT began its proceedings at Nuremberg, Polish public opinion was stirred by what seemed on the surface in the eyes of many Poles to be its perfunctory treatment of German crimes in Poland. For example, the Allied indictment presented to the IMT enumerated German crimes such as the massacres at Oradour-sur-Glane in France and Lidice in Czechoslovakia, yet it passed in silence over thousands of destroyed Polish towns and villages. Although the Polish delegation to Nuremberg was fairly satisfied with the trial's outcome, Polish newspapers underscored that the Allied judges at Nuremberg represented countries that had not felt the full brunt of the German occupation and thus could not adequately comprehend the magnitude of Nazi crimes.[3] The acquittals of Hjalmar Schacht and Franz von Papen and the fact that the IMT had not convicted the SA (*Sturmabteilung*, Nazi Storm Troopers), the German High Command, the General Staff, and the German government was met with utter astonishment, and the Polish press called the verdict "shocking," "unheard of," and "unfair."[4] The British and the Americans had viewed the defendants as individuals whose guilt had to be proven, whereas the overwhelming majority of Poles were convinced that their guilt was beyond any doubt. From their perspective, instead of listening to the defendants' lies, questioning witnesses, and perusing thousands of documents, the judges just needed to sentence them all to death.

In response to these sentiments, and anxious for international recognition, the Polish government decided to create its own court both to rectify what Poles perceived as the marginalization of their suffering and to serve domestic political objectives. On 22 January 1946, a decree announced the creation of the NTN, which was authorized to try the most notorious Nazi war criminals extradited by the Allies in accordance with the statute of the Allied Control Council of Germany of 20 December 1945.[5]

Indicative of the regime's intentions, on the same day a decree pertaining to the "responsibility for the September [1939] defeat and the fascistization of national life [*odpowiedzialność za ... faszyzację życia państwowego*]" was promulgated – a clear reference to the members of the elite that had ruled Poland between 1926 and 1939, who were ostensibly responsible for Poland's defeat in September 1939.[6] Clearly, the NTN had been conceived as a "special" court that would impose peremptory justice on the political opposition.[7] Indeed, the NTN was founded at a time when a fierce struggle for power was taking place in Poland. The non-communist parties and the armed underground (which in many regions still controlled the countryside) represented a serious challenge to the communists. Thus the charge of "fascistization of national life" was undoubtedly conceived as a means to neutralize the prewar political establishment by equating it with the Nazi criminals. The NTN was vested with broad powers – its jurisdiction equalled that of the Supreme Court (the chairman of the latter was also the chairman of the former) – including the authority to regulate old or establish new legal norms. In this context, the communist leadership viewed the prosecutions of Nazi criminals as less of a priority than prosecutions of internal enemies; that said, it was well aware that open, heavily publicized, and relatively fair trials of Nazi criminals would enhance the regime's legitimacy. In this regard, the regime hoped that the presence of foreign observers at the NTN trials would bolster its legitimacy abroad, and it recognized that the trials would need to be conducted with moderation and caution.[8]

But finding reliable individuals who combined professionalism with pro-communist affiliations was an extremely daunting task. Many Polish jurists had perished in the war, and others were living abroad; also, the majority of those in Poland had come of age as professionals in "bourgeois" prewar Poland. Therefore, the Ministry of Justice and the Ministry of Public Security, which were authorized to select personnel for the NTN trials, would have to appoint individuals who had not collaborated with the Germans and who "had not been overzealous in persecuting the revolutionary movement and democratic institutions."[9] Consequently, the personnel in NTN courtrooms represented a broad spectrum of personalities and political affiliations. For example, the NTN's chief justice, Wacław Barcikowski, was a member of the Democratic Party (Stronnictwo Demokratyczne); prosecutor Stefan Kurowski was a communist; and defence attorney Antoni Chmurski had in 1918–20 headed the Civil Chancellery under Józef Piłsudski. The latter had been independent Poland's first chief of state (1918–22) and its *de facto* leader from 1926 until his death in 1935, as well as the main public figure blamed by the communists for the "fascistization" of Poland. All of that aside, the NTN's personnel had one vital thing in common – they all had impressive professional credentials. For example, NTN judge Dr Emil Rappaport had defended Polish revolutionaries in Russian imperial courts. As a co-founder of the International Association of the Criminal Law, he had helped draft international laws designed to punish aggressive war, and in 1932 he had co-authored the Polish Criminal Code. Prosecutor Dr Mieczysław Siewierski was an expert in the field of criminal procedure. During the interwar period he had served as a judge and prosecutor in Polish courts; immediately before and after the war, he was appointed chief prosecutor of the

Supreme Court. Like Kurowski, prosecutors Drs Tadeusz Cyprian and Jerzy Sawicki had been members of the Polish delegation to the IMT. Sawicki had held important positions in the Ministry of Justice before embarking on a distinguished academic career. All thirty-seven NTN judges, prosecutors, and defence attorneys had studied and practised law; eighteen held doctorates in law.[10]

Important members of the Polish court system were the assessors (ławnicy) – people's representatives, who played an auxiliary role in the proceedings and in decision-making. Drafted from the State National Council (KRN) and its successor, the Sejm (Parliament),[11] the assessors were selected according to their "high ideological and intellectual level." The Presidium of the KRN dispatched a special instruction regarding the selection of assessors: their "social and political viewpoints were of utmost importance," and they had to be "capable of orienting themselves in frequently complicated cases and resistant to any undesirable influences."[12] Some assessors even represented political parties other than the PPR that were socialist or democratic in character. So however much the communists wished to create a monolithic and obedient tool, the NTN emerged as a relatively diverse body, one that stood apart from the special penal courts, which often delivered summary justice, purging political opponents in numerous show trials. Perhaps for this reason the NTN adjudicated only seven major cases of Nazi war criminals, and as it turned out, not one of those cases pertained to the "fascistization of national life" (perhaps because the communists did not deem the NTN, given its composition, appropriate for such trials).[13]

Between August 1946 and July 1948 the NTN sat in judgment over forty-nine defendants, who had been selected from among individuals extradited by the Allies according to their positions in the Nazi administration in occupied Poland. Apparently these defendants were divided into three categories. The first category comprised the top German brass: SS-Obergruppenführer Arthur Greiser, who had been governor of German-annexed Warthegau (tried June–July 1946); Ludwig Fischer, the governor of the Warsaw District (tried December 1946–February 1947); Albert Forster, the Gauleiter of Gdańsk (Danzig) (tried April 1948); and Jozef Bühler, the deputy of Hans Frank, Governor General of the General Government (tried June–July 1948). Fischer's three co-defendants – Paul Daume, the colonel of the Order Police; Josef Meisinger, the commander of the Security Police and the Security Service (Kommandeur der Sicherheitspolizei, KdS) in Warsaw; and Ludwig Leist, the mayor of occupied Warsaw – comprised the second category, that is, middle-level officials. Amon Göth, the commandant of the Płaszów concentration camp (tried August–September 1946) and the defendants in the two Auschwitz trials – Rudolf Höss, the camp's commandant (tried March 1947) and forty guards and functionaries (tried November–December 1947) – represented the "hands-on" executioners of Hitler's genocidal policies. The indictments against all of the defendants included both general and specific charges – violations of existing international laws, membership in criminal organizations and groups, and individual participation in Nazi crimes.

In the penal courts, evidence often consisted of just a few eyewitness testimonies; by contrast, during the NTN trials each defendant's crimes and respective rank and position in the occupation system were reflected in documentary materials, which had been diligently collected by the GKBZN in Poland and abroad, often with the help of Jewish historical institutions. At Bühler's trial alone, the tribunal had at its disposal more than 100 volumes of documents, including 11,000 pages of Hans Frank's diary, and a collection of German announcements and newspapers. The testimony of witnesses, particularly Jewish survivors, featured heavily in the trials of the concentration camp personnel. For example, 219 individuals testified against Höss and other Auschwitz functionaries, and many others submitted written affidavits about their experiences at Auschwitz.[14]

Indictment

Poland abided by the IMT charter, which declared criminal several Nazi organizations. In accordance with the charter, the criminality of the SS, the SD, and the Gestapo was considered fully established and required no evidence. The NTN followed the guidelines established by the IMT, but it used its position to expand the list of Nazi criminal institutions. In contrast to the IMT, which recognized as criminal only the leadership of the Nazi Party, the NTN decided that mere membership in the NSDAP constituted a crime, since officials at various levels of the party had planned and implemented crimes against peace, war crimes, and crimes against humanity. In addition to the SS, the SA, the Gestapo, and the SD, the NTN declared criminal the top echelons of the General Government. Since the German defendants in Polish courts were members of at least one of the aforementioned organizations, they were subject to conviction simply on the basis of their membership. Just as crucial for the communist reconstruction and ethnic homogenization of Polish society were the NTN rulings that declared criminal entire groups that "had acted in the interests of Nazi Germany" – namely, the Ukrainian-SS formations, the Ukrainian Insurgent Army (the armed wing of the Organization of Ukrainian Nationalists, OUN, that in 1943–5 carried out a brutal ethnic cleansing of Polish settlements in Volhynia and East Galicia), the Selbstschutz (the paramilitary police consisting of Poland's ethnic Germans), and Gestapo personnel, including clerks and interpreters. Such definitions were conveniently broad, providing the courts with numerous tools to indict political opponents.[15]

The NTN trials began with the prosecution's defining of Nazi crimes in the context of international and Polish domestic legislation pertaining to the rules of war. Aware of the arguments in Nuremberg about the retroactivity of war crimes laws, the prosecution called upon experts in Polish and international law. In June 1946, at the first NTN trial against Arthur Greiser, the governor of Poland's western territories (the Warthegau), professors of law Ludwik Ehrlich and Antoni Peretiatkowicz asserted that the claim of *ex post facto* justice was without validity because the Nazis had violated international norms of warfare recognized by the international community (including Germany) before the Second World War. The experts further pointed out that the Allied declarations regarding the prosecution of war criminals and the August Decree had been issued *during* the war; similarly, the prewar Polish Criminal Code qualified the wartime mistreatment of civilians as a criminal act. Peretiatkowicz also stressed that although Poland had been defeated, its army and government continued to function on the territory of an allied state and had fought Germany until its capitulation. Hence, the concept of *debellatio* – the end of a war caused by the complete destruction of the enemy – was not applicable, and the Germans should have treated Poland and the Polish people as combatants rather than as occupied subjects. To this end the experts quoted Article 43 of the Hague Convention, which specified that the "occupying power must use all means at its disposal to reestablish, as far as possible, order and normal civil life" in the occupied country. The NTN fully accepted this notion and convicted Greiser – and, later, Fischer, Forster, and Bühler – for breaching the rules of warfare and military occupation as stipulated by the Hague and Geneva Conventions of 1899 and 1907, for waging aggressive war proscribed by the 1928 Kellogg–Briand Pact (in the courtroom this was termed "criminal invasion"), for violating the German–Polish Non-Aggression Treaty of 1934, and for committing crimes specified by the August Decree and the Polish Criminal Code.[16]

At Forster's trial, expert witness Ehrlich explained that in seizing the city of Gdańsk, the Nazis had violated international conventions, since Articles 100 and 103–4 of the Treaty of Versailles accorded the city the special status of "Free City" under the supervision of the League of Nations. According to Ehrlich, the international conventions did not stipulate an appropriate punishment for such violations. (The IMT had encapsulated those violations as the charge of "waging aggressive war.") Hence, they could be prosecuted according to international regulations and the laws of specific countries that were the victims of Germany's aggression.[17] Similarly, gross violation of the Kellogg–Briand Pact constituted a solid foundation for charging Forster with "waging aggressive war," since, as signatories to the pact, Germany and Poland had renounced war as a tool for solving disputes. Accordingly, the IMT ruled that Germany's unprovoked aggression was part and parcel of an "aggressive war."[18] At the trial of Bühler, the NTN accepted the experts' opinion and ruled that aggression against Poland was illegal since Germany had violated the rules of occupation as defined by Articles 46 and 47 of the Hague International Convention, which stipulated that the occupier had to respect the culture and norms of the occupied country.[19]

At the trial of Greiser, the NTN established a crucial precedent in international law regarding war crimes. It ruled that existing legal regulations were "powerless" – that is to say inadequate – for dealing with Nazi crimes. Consequently, the NTN adopted the term "genocide" (*ludobójstwo*), which had already appeared in the Allied indictment presented to the IMT, and codified it, making it part of Polish law, well before it was codified in international law through the Convention on the Prevention and Punishment of the Crime of Genocide, which was adopted by the United Nations General Assembly in December 1948 and went into force in January 1951. In line with Rafael Lemkin's definition of genocide, the NTN used "genocide" as a descriptive term that incorporated all of the crimes stipulated by the August Decree. In Greiser's case, it was applied to "cultural genocide" (*ludobójstwo kulturalne*), which referred to coordinated efforts to destroy the Polish language, Polish culture and religion, and civil and political institutions.[20]

As the trials went on, the NTN adopted other definitions that expanded the range of the defendants' criminal activities. Thus, at Fischer's trial the tribunal accepted the experts' opinion that after Hitler suspended the German constitution, his regime became unconstitutional and *de facto* illegal. In essence, the tribunal denied Germany the right of national sovereignty, and henceforth, all of the defendants found themselves in a no-win situation, for their very presence in occupied Poland was adjudicated as an illegal act subject to punishment.[21]

As far as specific charges were concerned, Greiser, Fischer, Forster, and Bühler were charged with criminal conspiracy (initiated by the NSDAP) to wage aggressive war, as well as with presiding over mass murder in the territories they governed, mistreatment of civilians, deprivation of freedom, physical abuse, and other actions that caused severe bodily injury, illness, or death, and the systematic destruction of Polish culture. Greiser alone faced fourteen charges, including unlawfully incorporating the Polish territories into the Third Reich, depriving the Polish population of basic civil rights, and waging an assault on Polish religion, culture, and science; he was accused, also, of economic exploitation, forcible resettlement and national degradation of Poles, incarceration of civilians in prisons and camps, mass murder, the extermination of the Jews, the annexation of the Free City of Danzig, and violations of internationally recognized rules of warfare and wartime occupation. Fischer and Bühler were also charged as key officials of the General Government. Reports submitted to the NTN by medical experts testified to the brutality of mass executions and tortures inflicted upon thousands by the Gestapo and concentration camp functionaries within the jurisdiction of the defendants. Hence, Bühler had to account for the atrocities committed in Auschwitz, Greiser in Chełmno, and Fischer in Treblinka.[22]

The prosecution used collected documentary evidence to show not only that Greiser, Forster, Fischer, and Bühler "should have known" or "must have known" about these atrocities, but also that they initiated and energetically implemented Nazi genocidal policies. It presented to the tribunal Greiser's and Forster's orders to implement the "de-polonization" campaign, shut down Polish cultural and educational institutions, confiscate libraries, destroy historical monuments, and Germanize "racially acceptable" Polish children. These crimes constituted the "cultural genocide" of the Polish nation. Greiser and Forster also presided over the deportation of 150,000 Jews (including "Aryan" husbands, as well as wives who refused to divorce their spouses) and 70,000 Poles, especially the intelligentsia, from the Warthegau into the General Government and the transfer of Polish homes, businesses, and estates to ethnic Germans from the Baltic countries and Soviet-controlled Bukovina.[23]

The prosecution read from Frank's diary, in which he described his meetings with Bühler, Fischer, and other Nazi dignitaries at which they discussed in unequivocal terms mass reprisals, the conditions in the concentration camps, and the genocide of Jews. The prosecutors further stated that the role of Bühler and Fischer in the destruction of the Jews was enough in itself to convict them. The former had represented Frank at the Wannsee Conference, while the latter was responsible for the conditions in the Warsaw Ghetto, where between November 1940 and May 1943 tens of thousands of its inhabitants perished from illness, starvation, and executions, not to mention the hundreds of thousands who were deported to death camps. In addition, the defendants' awareness of what happened to the Jews after the deportations to the camps constituted criminal intent.[24]

The NTN also ruled that the degree of a defendant's guilt should be determined not by criminal activities alone, but by the culprit's *intent to do harm* and awareness of the criminality of his actions. For this purpose it elaborated the concept of "criminal association" (*przestępcza wspólnota*) (as distinct from the narrower IMT definition of criminal organization), which folded together concentration camp personnel whether or not they were formally members of the SS, SD, SA, or the Gestapo and connected to one another by common criminal design. Much like the charge of conspiracy to wage aggressive war that was elaborated by American jurists at Nuremberg, the charge of common criminal design could be applied against both individuals and particular Nazi organizations or associations. For example, declaring concentration camp personnel a criminal association guaranteed their conviction either on the basis of their membership in the association or for individual participation in prisoner selections, forced labour, and operating the "machinery of destruction" – gas chambers and crematoria. In effect, all German defendants were subject to punishment either as members of a criminal organization or a criminal association or both, or as individuals "aware" of Nazi crimes. (The courts as a rule rejected the plea of ignorance.)[25]

The charges against Meisinger and Daume consisted of specific crimes to which the defendants had admitted while they were in Allied custody before their extradition to Poland. Meisinger had testified that in May 1940, concurrent with the German invasion of France, the Security Police initiated a mass liquidation campaign against the Polish intelligentsia. Between May and November 1940, the KdS in the Warsaw

District murdered or sent to concentration camps thousands of Polish politicians, priests, students, artists, and athletes. Daume provided the details of a mass reprisal that took place in a Warsaw suburb in December 1939. After common criminals murdered two Germans, Daume presided over a court martial that sentenced to death 107 hostages. In February 1946, Daume admitted to British interrogators that the court martial was but a façade, for the death sentences were predetermined and "the guilt [of the hostages] was not established."[26]

The trials of concentration camp personnel followed a similar pattern: they exposed the roles of individuals who in different capacities – from commandant to SS guard – implemented the Nazis' genocidal policies on a daily basis. The indictment against them consisted of two general charges – membership in a criminal organization, namely the SS (female guards were not formally SS members; however, they were uniformed and paid as SS contractors); and membership in a criminal association, namely concentration camp staff – as well as the specific charge of genocide, wherein the tragedy of European Jews occupied the most prominent place. Much like the Western European courts, the NTN situated the Holocaust within a broader national narrative of German crimes – in this case against "the Polish nation" – but throughout its proceedings the judges, the prosecution, and the defence acknowledged and accentuated the distinct nature of the Jewish tragedy. The prosecution consistently pointed out that the Nazis had singled out Jews for total extermination as a part of the destruction of the entire Polish nation, to which Jews were "closely connected by culture, tradition, and mentality."[27]

At Amon Göth's trial the prosecution described in detail Nazi anti-Jewish policies in Poland, which started in the fall of 1939 with the appropriation of Jewish property, labelling, segregation, and later ghettoization. At the tribunal's request, several experts situated Nazi crimes in the concentration camps within the framework of existing international laws. Experts Ludwik Ehrlich and Nachman Blumental, the chairman of the CŻKH, asserted that the establishment of death camps and the annihilation of defenceless inmates had nothing to do with Germany's military objectives; rather, it was the crucial element of Hitler's racial war against "undesirable" people. The tribunal fully accepted this notion and ruled that Göth was not a POW, but instead a common criminal who in the ranks of criminal organizations and associations (the NSDAP, the SS, and the concentration camp administration) supervised the murder of Jews in the Kraków District.[28]

Numerous witnesses passed through the courtroom revealing to the tribunal the brutal regimen of the Płaszów camp. Hard labour in the quarry near the camp and in road construction served as a killing instrument, and humiliation and beatings were inseparable elements of daily routine. Szalom Leser testified that Amon Göth was personally involved in torturing and murdering inmates. On one occasion, having suspected several prisoners of planning an escape, he smashed their skulls with a hammer. Herman Ladner told the tribunal that in May 1944, during the so-called health *Appell* (health roll call), associations, Göth selected 1,200 children and elderly inmates to be transported to Auschwitz. The camp's brutality repulsed even some Nazis. In April 1944, Hans Frank wrote to the HSSPF in the General Government, SS-Obergruppenführer Wilhelm Koppe, insisting that the camp be moved outside city limits, for it "makes a shattering impression."[29] Göth supervised the liquidation of the Jewish ghettos in Kraków, Tarnów, and Szebnie, where thousands of Jews lost their lives or were sent to Auschwitz. During his "activities," Göth appropriated the valuables of his victims; in September 1944 he was arrested by German authorities for financial fraud.[30]

Similarly, at the core of the indictment against the Auschwitz staff lay the notion that although the defendants represented the whole gamut of military ranks, social classes, and personalities, they amounted to a criminal association, united in its drive to carry out the genocide of Jews and the "Slavic people." Consequently, stressed prosecutor Kurowski, whether or not they escorted the victims to gas chambers, pushed them inside, or dropped Zyklon B pellets into the gas chambers, they all were irreplaceable cogs in the Nazi killing machine that functioned so smoothly only because of their zeal, brutality, and total disregard for human life.[31]

To stress that the defendants were connected by a common criminal design, the prosecution cited their common background and experience as Nazi party and concentration camp functionaries. Höss was a long-time Nazi, having joined the movement in 1922, and had received his SS training under the notorious Theodor Eicke at Dachau. Hans Aumeier, Höss's deputy and the commanding officer of the prison camp (*Lagerführer*), had previously served at the Dachau, Buchenwald, Flossenburg, and Lichtenburg camps. Maria Mandel, the brutal head of the women's camp (*Oberaufseherin*), had served in the camps since 1938, while *Blockführer* Erich Mühsfeldt was a sadist who volunteered for executions and selections. (He was also notorious for being the chief of the crematorium during his service in Majdanek, where he once burned

3.1 Amon Göth while in Polish custody as an accused war criminal, 16 August 1946. United States Holocaust Memorial Museum, courtesy of Instytut Pamięci Narodowej.

a female prisoner alive.) In May 1944, Mühsfeldt "distinguished" himself during the mass murder of Hungarian Jews, personally pushing victims into the gas chamber. Both Mandel and Mühsfeldt were recipients of the Military Cross of Merit Second Class. The prosecution stressed that some camp functionaries such as the chief of the camp Gestapo, Maximilian Grabner, had previous criminal records; others were uneducated police or prison officials. Yet as long as they made up for their lack of special skills through their brutality and obedience, their superiors considered them "fully qualified."[32]

Indeed, Auschwitz survivors, both Poles and Jews, remembered their tormentors well. One after another they imparted to the court stories of continuous degradation, torture, and murder. Aumeier beat prisoners without provocation, Grabner supervised brutal interrogations, and *Lagerführer* Wilhelm Gehring forced "guilty" prisoners to stand still for hours or days between two rows of electrified barbed wire.[33] The

3.2 Auschwitz personnel in the dock. From left to right: T. Brandl, A. Orlowski, L. Danz, H. Lächert. Public domain: httpwww.rmf24.plfaktyswiatnews-cia-zwerbowalo-krwawa-brygide-sadystyczna-nadzorczynie-ss-z-,nId,2275198

prosecution quoted the diary of the camp doctor, Johann Kremer, who callously recorded mass murder as a daily routine:

> 2 September 1942. At 03:00AM for the first time [I] oversaw the "special action." Dante's Inferno is a mere comedy in comparison. Later assisting by the flogging of eight inmates and their execution. [To wash off] I got two pieces of soap ... In the evening again [assisting] in a "special action."
>
> 23 September 1942. Tonight [I] was present at the sixth and seventh "special action." In the evening had dinner in the officers' canteen with SS-Obergruppenführer Pohl. Real feast – fried pikes in large quantities, real coffee, excellent beer, and sandwiches.[34]

The Trial of Rudolf Höss

Without a doubt, the NTN trial that garnered the most public attention both in Poland and abroad was that of Rudolf Höss, Auschwitz's first commandant, who, under Heinrich Himmler, established the camp in 1940, principally for Polish political prisoners, and then directed its expansion into an immense forced labour camp for several hundred thousand prisoners of numerous nationalities as well as an extermination centre – Birkenau or Auschwitz II – for close to one million Jews from across Europe. There was a fundamental difference between the trial of Höss and that of all other Auschwitz personnel.[35] The latter emphasized the Nazi personnel's persecution of registered prisoners. Most Jews deported to Auschwitz were, however, never registered; they were gassed upon arrival. In contrast, the mass murder of Jews was an integral part of the prosecution's case in the Höss trial. Of course, the prosecution's theory of the case, which the tribunal adopted, involved also non-Jews, primarily ethnic Poles and Russians, who, according to the prosecution, were next in line for extermination after the Jews.

The British extradited Höss to Poland in May 1946 to stand trial before the NTN after he had been summoned to testify for the defence at the Nuremberg Trial, where, to the chagrin of defence lawyers, he proved to be a hostile witness and incriminated the Nazi brass sitting in the dock. In Poland, Municipal Court Judge Jan Sehn's extensive pretrial investigation of Höss thoroughly addressed the extermination of Jews. Written in response to Sehn's questions, Höss's autobiography, which Polish authorities published in the *Bulletin of the Central Commission for the Investigation of German Crimes in Poland* in 1951, and then in book form in 1956 (reissued in 1961), included a detailed description of the extermination of Jews in the gas chambers and crematoria at Auschwitz.[36]

According to the indictment, Höss, as commandant of Auschwitz between May 1940 and October 1943 and then as commander of the SS garrison there from June to September 1944,

> deliberately deprived of life ... about 300,000 registered camp inmates ... about 4,000,000 people, mainly Jews, brought to the camp in transports from different European countries with the objective of their immediate extermination [*zagłada*] ... [and] about 12,000 Soviet prisoners of war ... by asphyxiation in gas chambers, shooting ... hanging, lethal injections of phenol and by medical experiments causing death, systematic starvation, by creating conditions in the camp that were causing a high rate of mortality, by excessive work by the inmates, and the bestial treatment of prisoners by the camp's personnel.[37]

The historical section of the indictment accused Höss of being the commandant of a "death factory" (*fabryka śmierci*).[38] This indictment described the Nazi campaign to kill all Jews in Poland and Europe;

3.3 Rudolf Höss on trial. Public domain:
https://en.wikipedia.org/wiki/Rudolf_H%C3%B6ss#/media/
File:Rudolf_H%C3%B6%C3%9F.jpg

Poland was the plan's geographical locus and Auschwitz the central facility for realizing this objective. It divided the existence of Auschwitz into two periods: the first, from the summer of 1940 to the summer of 1942, when it was a concentration camp designed for Poles; the second, until January 1945, when Poles were joined by prisoners from all the conquered countries of Europe. "Among the citizens of so many different countries mentioned here," read the indictment, "the largest group was undoubtedly Polish citizens, Poles and Jews, then Russians … but in general, however, the majority of prisoners in the camp represented nationalities other than Poles, inmates of Jewish origins."[39] The indictment further distinguished between the fate of Jews deported to Auschwitz and the lot of other prisoners there: "For Polish Jews, Auschwitz was, as a rule, an extermination camp, as it was for the Jews of other European countries."[40] According to the indictment, the selection process, the gas chambers, and the crematoria were designed "to solve the massive problem of liquidating large transports of tens of thousands of Jews."[41]

Of course, the indictment was careful not to overlook the fate of Poles under the Nazis. In the words of the indictment, "[t]he realization of the plan for the total extermination of Poles had not yet matured, but the [Germans'] intentions were explicit [and] precise: the complete elimination of Poles in the near future. . . . For the time being, Auschwitz [was the site] for the realization of the plan for the partial extermination of Poles."[42] In other words, first the Jews, then the Poles. Moreover, for all intents and purposes, the essence of the case against Höss, albeit not articulated in this way in the indictment, was genocide.[43]

At trial, replying to questions by prosecutors and the presiding judge, Alfred Eimer, an impassive Höss described the killing of Jews in painstaking detail. But when the prosecutor asked him whether the Germans' plans encompassed the systematic murder of Poles and Russians after the annihilation of Jews, he refused to concede the point.[44] In response, prosecutors put about a hundred former Polish prisoners on the witness stand in the hope that from their elaborate testimony about Polish suffering at Auschwitz, the court would draw the conclusion that Poles and Russians were next in line for annihilation after the Jews.

However, ethnic Polish witnesses did not confine themselves to descriptions of their own ordeals and those of their fellow Poles. Many of them testified about the tragedy that befell the Jews as well. Kazimierz Smoleń, future director of the Auschwitz State Museum, was arrested by the Germans in April 1941 and later incarcerated at Birkenau until January 1945. There, despite his own physical torment, he paid scrupulous attention to the Germans' violent herding of Jews into the gas chambers and to their other methods of killing Jews, including lethal injections. On the witness stand he recalled seeing Höss, haughty and callous, standing there "like God." He testified with precision about the liquidation of Hungarian Jewry in 1944, and his estimate of those killed (400,000) was not far off the mark – a tribute not only to his powers of observation but also to his sensitivity to the plight of the Jews.[45] Eyewitness testimony by Poles was supplemented by the reports and testimony of Polish expert witnesses. Edward Kowalski, a professor at Jagiellonian University in Kraków, testified about the medical experiments that German doctors performed on camp inmates. It was evident from his report and testimony that a large number of the victims of medical experiments were Jews as well as Poles.[46]

Some dozen Jews testified in court, but the evidence provided by three – Henryk Mandelbaum, Szlama Dragan, and Henryk Tauber – overshadowed that of the others. Mandelbaum testified in court; the statements by the other two were read out loud in the courtroom – by the time of the trial they were already residing outside Poland – and became part of the court record.[47] All three had been members of the Jewish *Sonderkommando* at Birkenau, hapless Jewish prisoners whom the Germans selected to hurry terrified and disoriented Jews arriving in transports through the antechambers of gas chambers, and then, after the victims' asphyxiation by gas, to empty the gas chambers, shave the corpses, and pull out their teeth before cremating their bodies in ovens designed for the purpose. Mandelbaum had been deported to Auschwitz in May 1944 and conscripted into the *Sonderkommando* just in time to have to contend with the overflow of bodies from the destruction of Hungarian Jewry. "I thought I was in hell. No one had ever seen anything like it. Corpses, corpses, and still more corpses" – this was Mandelbaum's first impression of the grisly labour the *Sonderkommando* was forced to perform, which he described to the court in excruciating detail.[48] Evidence from the *Sonderkommando* carried considerable weight because of its members' proximity to and involvement – involuntary, to be sure – in the killing process. But the prosecutors may have had another reason in mind for their emphasis on the *Sonderkommando*; evidence provided by Mandelbaum and Tauber indicated that the Germans periodically transported small groups of ethnic Poles, among them partisans, to Birkenau and shot them in the crematoria, where members of the *Sonderkommando* then had to incinerate and dispose of their bodies.[49] Mandelbaum testified, moreover, about the revolt at Birkenau that the *Sonderkommando* mounted in October 1944. Since prosecutors highlighted the camp's underground movement, in which Poles played a leading role, the evidence provided by Mandelbaum called attention to Jewish agency rather than mere passivity at Auschwitz.

The accounts of Jewish eyewitnesses were augmented by the expert testimony of Nachman Blumental, representing the CŻKH. It dealt broadly with Nazi antisemitism and anti-Jewish policies that culminated in the system of extermination at death camps.[50]

The NTN found Höss guilty on all counts and sentenced him to death.[51] In a departure from the indictment, the judgment, taking into account the evidence presented at trial, described Höss's crimes as "participation in the murder" of inmates at Auschwitz rather than, as the indictment put it, "depriving them of life"; it also found that he "acted to the detriment" of prisoners rather than personally mistreating them. The judgment further modified the number of victims cited in the indictment to "an undetermined number of people, at least 2,500,000, mainly Jews."[52] This figure had been asserted by Höss at trial, and the court saw no reason to reject it. The judgment referred specifically to genocide in its description of the extermination process. "In the camp at Birkenau," the judgment read, "was specially perfected the largest genocide [*ludobójstwo*] in the world."[53] After referring to

300,000 registered prisoners who were killed, the judgment considered the fate of the camp's main victims. "The second category of individuals exterminated at Auschwitz includes people, mostly Jews, who were deported to the camp from various countries in Europe with the aim of their immediate annihilation, who without being registered were led to the gas chambers."[54] The judgment made note of Höss's initiative in the destruction of Hungarian Jewry. The judgment, of course, took into account the camp's Polish victims. It described the largest group of inmates at Auschwitz as "Poles and Jews."[55] The third most important category of victims, the court stated, was Soviet POWs, who were killed by gassing.[56] In line with testimony by witnesses from the Jewish *Sonderkommando*, the judgment drew particular attention to thousands of Poles who were killed at Birkenau, whose bodies were disposed of in the crematoria.[57] In this vein, the court invoked Blumental's expert testimony, referring to the German quest for *Lebensraum* (living space) in the East for the proposition that "through the death of millions of Jews and Slavs Hitlerite fascism [would have] secured a new order in Europe" had the Germans prevailed.[58] The NTN noted that "only the victory of the advancing Soviet and Polish forces prevented the Germans from realizing their further plans for genocide."[59]

The Polish press closely followed Höss's trial. The headline in *Dziennik Ludowy* was typical: "There has yet to be a trial like this. Through the person of Rudolf Hoess we are judging the entire German people. The shadows of four million people murdered at Auschwitz accuse."[60] Or in the words of *Głos Ludu*, Höss, "the murderer of millions[,] faces the court."[61] *Dziennik Ludowy* posed the question "whether there is in general a possible balance between the guilt of these people [like Höss] and the punishment that awaits them. The answer is simple: No! And, therefore, the essential point of this type of trial has to be sought elsewhere. The point lies above all else in the very clarification of the truth about [these people] and what occurred [at Auschwitz]."[62] The correspondent for *Życie Warszawy* wrote that "Auschwitz is the capital of Polish martyrdom."[63] In its coverage of the trial, *Życie Warszawy* made sure to acknowledge Auschwitz's Jewish victims. It approvingly cited Blumental's estimates of Jewish victims, including the three million who perished on Polish soil, of whom one and a half million were killed at Auschwitz. At the same time, it stressed his stated view that thirty million Slavs were next in line to lose their lives in the gas chambers, but were saved in the nick of time by the advance of the Red Army, which interrupted Höss's plans.[64]

3.4 Höss hearing his sentence.
Archival Signature 5318/260, Benfes Archives, Yad Vashem.

Höss accepted the NTN's judgment with equanimity. On 16 April 1947, in the presence of many its liberated inmates, he was hanged on the former grounds of the camp where he had only recently stood high and mighty, lording it over his victims "like God."

Defence Arguments and the Verdicts

With the exception of Höss, all of the NTN defendants refused to assume the burden of responsibility and fought tooth and nail to avoid the noose. Greiser asserted that he had always remained a "soldier" who obeyed the orders of his superiors and laboured for the betterment of Germany and the German people. He blamed his superiors, Hitler and Himmler, and without blinking an eye, he had the temerity to claim that he and the entire German nation first learned of these horrible crimes "from the proceedings of the IMT, from the charges against him, and from the witness testimonies" at his trial. Not surprisingly, the trial transcript contains remarks such as "the gallery [at the trial] laughs."[65] His position, however, was undermined by the testimony of Hans Biebow, who, testifying for the prosecution, stated that Greiser was a convinced antisemite who zealously implemented anti-Jewish policies.[66]

Greiser, Forster, and Bühler insisted that after 1939, the Polish state ceased to exist, and that consequently, the international law of occupation did not apply to Poland. They maintained that as civil administrators they had no jurisdiction over the SS, the Sipo, the SD, or the concentration camps and that they were unaware of the crimes committed by those organizations. Greiser compared himself to a "passenger on a plane, who can see wide enough, but had lost any connection with the earth."[67] Fischer claimed to have signed decrees and orders without reading them, while Meisinger contended that his position as the KdS was merely an "honorific" and that all police power rested in the hands of the SSPF of the Warsaw District.[68]

In turn, the concentration camp functionaries denied that they had ever participated in executions and admitted only to "sporadic beating" of the inmates. Göth maintained that he shot only the prisoners who had violated camp regulations and that he flogged some prisoners when he was "too nervous." Höss's successor, Arthur Liebehenschel, and Aumeier justified their actions by reference to orders from their superiors. Grabner had submitted written testimonies implicating his colleagues at Auschwitz and describing them as "exceedingly brutal," but he denied all charges levelled against him personally. Mandel insisted that she had treated prisoners fairly and administered beatings only to those who had violated "discipline." Other defendants blamed Hitler, Himmler, and Höss for "misleading" them into believing that their actions were legal.[69]

In light of the evidence presented in court, in the form of either documentation or eyewitness testimonies, the defence in each trial faced a difficult task. Still, defence counsel diligently tried to challenge the applicability of existing legislation and to minimize the complicity of their clients. Bühler's attorney, Dr Stefan Kosiński, pointed out that Article 3 of the Hague Convention pertaining to the commission of war crimes referred only to the responsibility of a *state*, not of an *individual*. Greiser's lawyers, Drs Stanisław Hejmowski and Jan Kręglewski, argued that the August Decree had no jurisdiction over German nationals, since Article 1 of that decree referred to those who "assisted German authorities." Since the defendant in fact acted as a "German authority," he was outside the decree's jurisdiction. Hejmowski demonstrated his eloquence by arguing that humanity and war were two mutually exclusive concepts, for war by definition is "inhumane." Hence, the accusations of "inhumane occupation" launched at his client held no validity whatsoever. He attempted further to show that Greiser was not responsible for the crimes committed in the Warthegau by the SS and the Security Police, since these organizations were only nominally subordinated to the civil administration and in reality acted on behalf of Heinrich Himmler. At the trials of Bühler and Meisinger, defence counsel asserted that the court had failed to establish the defendants' *intent* to do harm and that the defendants were in no position to prevent the commission of crimes. At times, defence attorneys entered into sharp exchanges with prosecutors about the nuances of the proceedings.[70]

Göth's lawyers, Drs Tadeusz Jakubowski and Brunon Pokorny, attempted to prove that some inmates in Płaszów were killed because they had violated camp regulations and that executions carried out by the Sipo, the SD, and the police on camp grounds were outside Göth's jurisdiction. The defence also made a futile effort to portray concentration camp personnel as victims of Nazi ideological indoctrination who blindly carried out their superiors' orders and would have behaved differently in other circumstances. Several witnesses actually testified to this effect. Thus, Göth's cook, Helena Horowitz, stated that at times he acted like a "normal man." Several Auschwitz inmates confirmed that in contrast to many of his subordinates, Höss did not display excessive brutality. One camp survivor recalled that when he accidentally spilled water on Höss, who was passing by, the commandant just muttered a few words and walked away. A similar encounter with other defendants would certainly have proved fatal. Some former prisoners testified that after Liebehenschel became commandant, he improved camp conditions, prohibiting corporal punishment without his approval, removing the most brutal *kapos*, and reducing the numbers of executions.[71] Mandel's attorney acknowledged her role in the camp but challenged the charge that she had taken part in selections, which, according to documents from the camp and eyewitnesses' testimonies, fell mostly within the domain of SS doctors. Regarding some guards, the defence stressed that they were "simple individuals of limited intelligence" who blindly and obediently carried out their superiors' orders.[72]

The NTN based its verdicts on its evaluation of Nazi policies in Poland and the individual activities of the defendants. (Each decision was explained in a lengthy section reserved for justification for the verdict.) The tribunal ruled that since the German occupation of

Poland was an illegal act, so were the defendants' actions. It accepted prosecutors' argument that although Poland had been defeated in 1939, it enjoyed the protection of international conventions as a sovereign state represented by a legitimate government in London – a rather ironic argument given that the PKWN had refused to recognize the legitimacy of that same government. The tribunal opined that the acts of Greiser, Forster, Fischer, Meisinger, and Bühler were aggravated by their membership in Nazi criminal organizations and associations. Since the Nazi leadership had openly declared its criminal objectives, the defendants could not but have been aware of those objectives and were thus guilty of a common criminal design and its implementation. Although the tribunal acknowledged that the SS, the police, and the administration of the concentration camps each had its own chain of command, it rejected the defence's arguments, stressing that the SS and the police commanders in occupied Poland were formally subordinated to Greiser, Bühler (through Frank), and Fischer and therefore had to coordinate their actions with the German civil administration. Therefore, as with the Nuremberg judgment, the NTN found the top Nazi officials fully responsible for crimes committed within their jurisdictions and sentenced them to death by hanging.[73]

The NTN sentenced Meisinger and Daume to death on account of their hands-on participation in crimes – the former as the organizer of mass reprisals and the latter as a member of drumhead courts martial that, in the tribunal's wording, were "just a tool of suppression, but not institutions of justice."[74] In the case of Leist, the tribunal ruled that his guilt was less egregious, since it was established that he did not display the same zeal and initiative as the other defendants and that he actually saved the lives of several of his Polish employees, interceding with Fischer. Accordingly, the tribunal sentenced him to eight years in prison.[75]

Regarding concentration camp personnel, the tribunal accepted the defence attorneys' contention that the defendants' conduct varied from just following orders to extreme sadism. However, it determined that the occasional instances of "normality" displayed by some functionaries were "dissolved" in the horrors they helped create at Płaszów and Auschwitz. It therefore found Göth for his role at Płaszów, and Höss, Liebehenschel, Aumeier, Grabner, Mandel, Mühsfeldt, and eighteen other particularly brutal Auschwitz functionaries and SS guards, guilty of membership in criminal organizations and associations and of common design to commit mass murder and sentenced them to death by hanging. The tribunal found it possible to spare the lives of defendants whose conduct was judged less notorious – six were sentenced to life and ten to prison terms ranging from three to ten years. One defendant at the Auschwitz trial, Dr Hans Münch, was acquitted because several camp survivors, with the corroboration of an expert witnesss, testified that, unlike other Nazi doctors at Auschwitz, he had not performed harmful medical experiments on prisoners. The survivors testified further that he had, in fact, demonstrated a benevolent attitude towards prisoners and tried to help them.[76]

By a decree of the Ministry of Justice dated 1 December 1944, the most notorious war criminals were to be executed in public.[77] On 21 July 1946, Greiser was hanged before a large crowd at the site of wartime Nazi executions in Poznań. Local newspapers announced the day and time of the execution, and some people arrived early at the execution site to secure a good view. Among the spectators were children, and vendors sold ice cream, sweets, and refreshments.[78] However, by this time there were already protests against public executions. Prominent intellectuals such as Jan Kott, Ewa Szelburg-Zarembina, and Adam Kryński argued that public executions resembled Nazi methods and amounted to public spectacles. As such, they undermined the very purpose of the trials, which was to demonstrate the victory of right and ethics over crime and lawlessness. In early August 1946, Premier Edward Osóbka-Morawski, in a letter to the Ministry of Justice, expressed doubt about the "educational" benefits of public executions.[79] The justice minister, Henryk Świątkowski, responded in writing to the Presidium of the KRN, requesting that it provide its opinion on the matter. Świątkowski noted that many associations such as local councils, unions of former prisoners, and the representatives of political parties were demanding public executions of war criminals. He also pointed out that public executions would serve as a deterrent if they were carried out on German soil in the presence of Germans, whereas public executions in Poland attracted thousands of "unhealthily excited crowds" that were eager for sensation and that included many youths, even children. The executions exposed the crowds to a "horrible psychological shock and sowed the seeds of savagery."[80] Consequently, on 8 September 1946, the justice minister announced that public executions "evoke the lowliest human instincts [among the spectators]" and would no longer be conducted.[81]

Most likely in an effort to impress foreign public opinion, the president of Poland commuted the death sentences handed down to the youngest and the oldest defendants in the second Auschwitz trial. The latter happened to be Doctor Kremer, whose guilt had been proven in court beyond a reasonable doubt. All other death sentences were carried out. Several defendants died while in prison; the rest were released after the amnesty of 1956 stipulated the termination of prison terms for "accomplices" in Nazi war crimes. For reasons that remain unclear, the execution of Forster took place on 28 February 1952, four years after he was sentenced to death and after President Bierut had twice turned down his appeals for mercy.[82]

Some NTN defendants were later tried by German courts. Kremer, who was released in 1958 on account of good behaviour and old age (he was seventy-four), was sentenced to ten years by the Münster district court in 1960. He walked out of the courtroom a free man since the court ruled that he had already served his time in Poland. In 1964 a court in Frankfurt acquitted another Auschwitz defendant, Arthur Breitwieser, due to "lack of evidence." Hildegard Lächert, a female guard at Auschwitz, was less fortunate; in 1975, a court in Düsseldorf sentenced her to twelve years' imprisonment.[83]

Two months after the second Auschwitz trial, Seweryna Szmaglewska, a former inmate at the camp, wrote a letter to the justice minister. Szmaglewska, one of the two Polish witnesses at the Nuremberg Trial, who had moved both the court and the gallery with her stirring testimony, and who had written an autobiographical book, *Dymy nad Birkenau* (Smoke over Birkenau, 1945), questioned whether the presumption of innocence could be applied in the trials of the Nazi criminals. Szmaglewska's letter reflected widespread popular opinion that no punishment was condign to the crimes the Nazis committed in Poland. Hence, even liberal use of the death penalty in these cases did not satisfy public opinion. Prosecutor Stefan Kurowski echoed the public's exasperation during the second Auschwitz trial: "How inadequate are our criminal codes, designed to punish an ordinary, pre-Nazi criminal ... for a single, individual act of violence. Everything we have witnessed in this courtroom is so remote from traditional legal norms that a new legal concept had to be created – genocide."[84] In February 1945, Władysław Gomułka, then deputy premier of the communist-dominated provisional government, asserted that responsibility for the war and atrocities should be borne by the German masses, which had "supported and tolerated Hitler's regime."[85] The communists and their opponents allied with the Polish government-in-exile were united in this regard. Thus Stanisław Mikołajczyk, leader of the PSL, stressed that in order to redress crimes committed against Poland, "no mercy and no weakness are permissible in the punishment of German fascism and Hitlerism."[86]

Such punishment entailed extrajudicial measures, including the redrawing of the German–Polish border along the Oder and Neisse rivers and the expulsion of ethnic Germans from the newly "reacquired territories" (*ziemie odzyskane*). "Only such borders," stressed Gomułka in April 1945, "will compensate the Polish people for their suffering."[87] On 2 August 1945, these plans were set in motion when the Allies signed the Potsdam Declaration, which legitimized the coercive population transfer of millions of Germans from Poland, Czechoslovakia, and Hungary.[88]

Conclusion

What conclusions can be drawn from the NTN trials? In sharp contrast to numerous show trials that were adjudicated by different standards, the NTN conducted its proceedings according to international and Polish domestic judicial norms as much as was possible in Poland's postwar political and emotional atmosphere. The NTN adopted several safeguards from the prewar Polish legal tradition such as a defendant's right to counsel and the imperative that conviction be predicated upon proof of guilt. Each determination of guilt or innocence was elaborated in the verdict in a section titled "justification" (*uzasadnienie*), in which the tribunal judged each defendant's crimes on the basis of existing legal norms. The variety of sentences indicated that the tribunal tried to base its decisions on the circumstances of each case. It is not surprising, therefore, that the NTN trials were quite different from the proceedings in local courts. Whereas NTN trials were administered by experienced and qualified Polish jurists, local courts were often administered by individuals of lower professional quality, who found themselves under pressure from party committees and a population that craved the severe punishment of war criminals.

Since, with the exception of Höss, all of the defendants who stood trial before the NTN vehemently denied their guilt, it is safe to assume that they were not subjected to physical or psychological pressure – a common practice in Soviet war crimes trials, in which most of the defendants admitted or even exaggerated their guilt. Moreover, to blunt potential accusations of unfairness, the Polish authorities made sure that German defendants in prison were treated equitably. For example, in a letter to the procurator of the special penal court in Kraków, the NTN prosecutor Tadeusz Cyprian emphasized that since foreign observers attended the trials of major Nazi criminals, it was crucial that these defendants be in optimal physical and psychological shape. To this end, Cyprian requested that they be placed under constant medical surveillance, receive clean clothes and linen, have access to books in German, and be allowed to write memoirs or notes for their defence.[89]

Such treatment paid off: the NTN proceedings received praise from the most unlikely source, SS-Obergruppenführer Erich von dem Bach-Zelewski, who in February 1947 arrived in Poland to testify as a witness at Fischer's trial. After returning to Germany, Bach-Zelewski expressed his admiration for the proceedings in the NTN. "The truly democratic form in which the trial was conducted," Bach-Zelewski declared, "is exactly the opposite of what German press reports on the authoritarian political form of Poland led me to expect."[90] Although prosecutors and the tribunal tended to exaggerate the death rate at Auschwitz – the figure of four million victims was commonly used – most crimes enumerated in NTN trials have been studied and authenticated by prominent historians.[91] Hence, NTN records represent a valuable source for studies of the Second World War, the German occupation of Poland, and postwar retribution.

Although the NTN trials tended to integrate the Holocaust as an inseparable element of the Nazi war of extermination against Poles, it became a central issue in the trials of Rudolf Höss, Amon Göth, and the Auschwitz administration. Critically, the NTN's recognition of the genocide of Jews took place at the same time that a wave of antisemitic rhetoric and violence was sweeping through Poland. Popular accusations against Jews ran the gamut – Jews were accused of everything from committing "ritual murder" and engaging in black marketeering to ardent support for communist rule. Between the German withdrawal from Poland and the end of 1946, the wave of anti-Jewish attacks and pogroms claimed as many as 750 lives.[92] In August 1946 the Presidium of the KRN discussed issuing a decree specifically directed at combating antisemitism. Under this decree, any expressions of antisemitism in the form of verbal offence or physical insult were to be punishable by a prison term of three years to life; cases involving the death of a victim were to be punishable by death. Heavy prison terms also included the confiscation of property of the culprit. It appears, however, that the decree was never promulgated.[93]

The NTN trials should not be perceived, however, as a flawless administration of justice, especially as the consolidation of the communist-dominated government rendered critical discussion of the Soviet Union impossible. Hence, it was the Germans who became the predominant and officially approved symbols of danger and hatred in the immediate postwar era. Fascism, Germany, and Germans were thought of as a single category of evil that did not require analytical explanation.[94] The NTN rulings on the illegality of the German regime and the concepts of criminal association and ill-intent in effect rendered all German functionaries in occupied Poland war criminals *in potentia*. Moreover, the prosecution certainly had more time and resources at its disposal than the defence. For example, the defence had neither sufficient time nor the capability to summon all desired witnesses (some of whom lived in Germany) and to collect necessary evidence.[95] The forty Auschwitz defendants were represented by nine attorneys, each of whom assumed the daunting task of defending four or five clients. In contrast, the prosecution team had at its disposal several groups of experts, each of whom worked on a specific case for at least two months before the beginning of the trial.[96] Although witnesses at the trials of the top Nazi officials described the horrific conditions in prisons and camps, only a few actually saw the defendants at these sites. It is possible that the notoriety of the Security Police and the SD guided the tribunal's hand when it sentenced Meisinger for crimes that were actually committed by his successor Ludwig Hahn. (In 1975, a court in Hamburg sentenced Hahn to life imprisonment for the deportations of Jews.) Similarly, the horrific images of Auschwitz may have determined the fate of Liebehenschel, who was undoubtedly a less sinister personality than some of his co-defendants.

Some NTN rulings were vague or controversial. At Greiser's trial the tribunal ruled that since the German occupation of Poland was illegal, Germany effectively lost its right of a belligerent as stipulated by the Hague Convention. In its verdict the tribunal defined German occupation as an "illegal seizure of foreign territories through violence and coercion." Conversely, the population of the occupied territories was fully justified in resisting the aggressor by any means, including those not prescribed by the Hague Convention. Such a formulation, however, was contradictory, for if German occupation was illegal, then the German administration was *not* bound by any international conventions. Yet the violation of international conventions was at the core of the indictment and sentencing of the high-ranking Nazi officials.[97] On

11 October 1949, the Supreme Court of Poland amended this concept, stressing that the "Hague Convention is binding for each occupation, even for an 'illegal' [bezprawna] one such as the German one."[98]

Similarly, the military codes of many countries (including Poland) made unquestioning obedience in the execution of superiors' orders incumbent on military personnel. Nevertheless, the NTN ruled that international laws regulating warfare and the culprit's "awareness of the criminality of his action" must take precedence over military codes. In fairness, it should be mentioned that the IMT and later American judges in other war crimes trials used a similar formulation, emphasizing that "army regulations are not a competent source of international law when a fundamental rule of justice is concerned."[99]

The Polish government skilfully utilized the NTN trials – they were filmed, as well as publicized in the press and on the radio – as a powerful propaganda tool. The positive opinion of foreign journalists and representatives of the Allied nations, who praised the meticulousness and impartiality of the tribunal, certainly added to its credibility. Correspondingly, the NTN's reputation reflected well upon the government, burnishing its democratic credentials and validating its desire – genuine or not – to re-establish an orderly and fair society driven by a sense of justice.[100] The trials also catered to Polish popular opinion, which expected swift retribution for Nazi crimes. The government even contemplated beginning the trial of Fischer and his co-defendants on 1 August 1946, the second anniversary of the 1944 Warsaw Uprising, even while the communist-dominated media were slandering that event as the "gamble of the adventurous clique in London" (the seat of the Polish government-in-exile). Apparently due to the time-consuming task of collecting evidence, the opening of the trial was postponed.[101]

Right after the war, Poles were concerned mainly about the political turmoil and economic disintegration their country faced. Even so, there was strong public interest in the trials, as reflected in the large numbers of spectators in the courtrooms, which were expanded to accommodate them; even so, crowds constantly converged outside the courtrooms. Emotional factors undoubtedly played an important role in the courtroom, for the prosecution succeeded – and, in light of the available evidence, it did not have to try too hard – in depicting all of the defendants in the worst possible light. For example, in his closing statements, prosecutor Siewierski called Greiser a career-climber with a "limited intellectual background ... and suffering from an inferiority complex" and referred to Göth as a "hedonistic murderer" who enjoyed inflicting pain and suffering. The judges, the prosecutors, and the media were aware of the trials' value as propaganda and manipulated popular sentiments, portraying the defendants as sadists and murderers and stressing the influence of Nazi ideology on all Germans – an ideology that, so they contended, effectively released them from all moral constraints. Prosecutor Siewierski referred to Göth as an individual "for whom murdering people became more than a profession, but pleasure and licentiousness." At the trial of Höss, Siewierski stated that the defendant was an "obedient, disciplined, utterly reliable killing automaton without any need for moral evaluation." Hitlerism thus turned all Germans into Hösses, Forsters, and Greisers.[102] A former Auschwitz inmate and the future prime minister of Poland, Józef Cyrankiewicz, who testified at the trial, noted that it would be understandable and better if Höss were an "anomalous, degenerate murderer. However, [the inmates] clearly understood that if one ordinary henchman were compelled to give up his position, he would have been immediately succeeded by another one, similarly capable of carrying out the same murderous functions."[103] The newspapers called Höss "the murderer of four millions" who had created a "vortex of tortures, brutalities, and death."[104] Some newspapers went so far as to allege that Höss trained his children to become killers and enjoyed watching executions with his family in tow. Some reports stressed that the defendants looked and behaved like ordinary men, which made their brutal conduct even more horrific.[105] Not surprisingly, given the scale of destruction wrought on Poland by the Germans, the death sentences met with overwhelming popular approval.[106]

So it is possible – and the defence attorneys argued as much – that the tribunal's decisions were influenced by prosecutors' inflammatory rhetoric that portrayed the defendants as the very symbols of Nazi tyranny. Similarly, the language in the courts of the Western Allies often included phrasing driven more by emotions than by legal definitions. Thus, the British judge advocate at the trial of Bergen-Belsen concentration camp personnel characterized the camp's regimen as a "system of cruelty," and his American counterparts at the *Einsatzgruppen* trial stressed that the crimes committed by the defendants "paled in comparison to Dante's inferno."[107]

Furthermore, the Polish media kept repeating that only a united Polish society, led by the new government in alliance with the Soviet Union, could effectively thwart the "German menace." The implication was that the opponents of the regime were helping the "new Greisers."

In late 1946 the media also began insinuating that whereas the Polish government was fully committed to prosecuting war criminals, the Allies were gradually losing interest.[108]

In the late summer of 1948, the NTN was abolished just as it was preparing for the trials of other high-ranking German Nazis, although there was no official decree to this effect.[109] Having helped solidify the image of Poland's suffering, the NTN was deemed no longer useful, and its prerogatives were transferred to the jurisdiction of the district and provincial courts. Its termination corresponded with the communists' assumption of total control over the country. By 1947 the secret police were evoking the "bourgeois" credentials of Greiser's attorney, Chmurski, who was subjected to a vicious slander campaign; his apartment was confiscated and he was forced to terminate his law practice. The NTN prosecutor Siewierski was less fortunate. In April 1948, immediately after participating in Albert Forster's trial, he was arrested and charged under the August Decree for his participation on the side of the prosecution in the prewar trials of communists and for functioning as a civil servant in the context of the "fascist constitution" of 1935. He was sentenced to five-and-a half years in prison and, ironically, placed in the same prison ward as Albert Forster.[110]

In June 1945, Justice Robert H. Jackson wrote to President Truman that the task of the Nuremberg International Tribunal was "so immense that it can never be done completely or perfectly, but which we hope to do acceptably."[111] Most certainly, the NTN attempted to reach the same goal, which was to punish the most notorious war criminals but also to provide guidelines for Polish law and judicial practices in the prosecution of war crimes. Although imperfect, the NTN did not become a blind instrument of postwar retributive justice in a country in political turmoil. Its adjudication of Nazi crimes was a substantial historical and legal achievement, in that it determined the penal liability of the defendants largely in accordance with existing international norms and domestic legislation and in a way that was comparable to similar proceedings in Western courts.

Chapter Four

Himmler's Men on Trial, 1948–1953

A particularly dark chapter in postwar Polish history was the era of "High Stalinism" – the years from 1948 to 1953 when the Polish Communist Party (and its counterparts in other Soviet-dominated Eastern European satellite states) launched a massive wave of political purges. Although Polish communists were in full charge of the country's political system by 1948, momentous international developments, including the proclamation of the Truman Doctrine and Tito's "revolt" in Yugoslavia in defiance of Moscow, provided the Stalinist leadership in Poland (and elsewhere in Eastern Europe) with a pretext to purge the country's "deviants" and "renegades." The establishment of the Federal Republic of Germany and the outbreak of the Korean War further exacerbated the regime's suspicions of "internal enemies." This deeply politicized era witnessed resumption of calculated assaults on remnants of the AK and what remained of the liberal opposition, who were charged under the special "Decree for the Protection of the State."[1]

In this highly charged atmosphere, political trials far overshadowed trials for Nazi crimes, which lost their ideological significance and public appeal. Indeed, two to three years after the war, official reports acknowledged that most people did not want to think about German crimes or Polish martyrdom. As one author astutely observed, people just "wanted to get on with their lives and forget. They enthusiastically participated in postwar reconstruction, mightily drank vodka, had fun, made love, and marched to the altar. From newspapers, movies, and radio they expected entertainment, forgetfulness, and not the irritation of old wounds."[2]

In September 1948, pursuant to an agreement between the Socialist Unity Party of Germany (Sozialistische Einheitspartei Deutschlands,

SED)[3] and the Soviet administration in eastern Germany, the Polish government began releasing German POWs who were deemed politically reliable to the Soviet zone of Occupied Germany. By April 1950, the last transports of German POWs had left Poland for the newly created German Democratic Republic (GDR, East Germany) and Federal Republic of Germany (FRG, West Germany).[4] In 1950 all district branches of the GKBZN, except for Kraków's, were closed (partly as a gesture to the newly established GDR). The Polish Military Mission for the Investigation of German Crimes by the Allied Control Council was disbanded, and in 1951 the extradition of war criminals to Poland was terminated. As a result, the number of trials of German and Austrian Nazis in Poland dwindled. In 1948, Polish courts convicted 893 extradited Germans accused of war crimes; thereafter, such cases became progressively rarer – 153 in 1949, 78 in 1950, 19 in 1951, and 10 in 1952–3. Most German war criminals sentenced by Polish courts had been released by the late 1950s.[5]

Weakening official and public interest directly affected the publicity surrounding these trials – except for high-profile cases, they received little or no press coverage – but not the conduct of the courts, which continued to function more or less in conformity with rule-of-law principles. Although some trials were administered in the speedy fashion of the special penal courts, pretrial investigation was generally thorough, and judges generally evaluated the available evidence and the degree of guilt in trials of German Nazis in accordance with standard legal procedures.

In general, Polish courts placed more emphasis on establishing the action or conduct that comprised constitutive elements of Nazi crimes (*actus reus*), and less on the mental state (*mens rea*) of individual perpetrators. That said, judges and prosecutors, as well as former inmates of German prisons and concentration camps, often attempted to comprehend the Nazi personality. For example, Professor Stanisław Batawia, a criminologist, psychiatrist, and lawyer, examined Amon Göth, Rudolf Höss, Josef Bühler, and Kurt Burgsdorf, the governor of the Kraków District, in an effort to understand their motivations when they functioned as Nazi officials. He concluded that they displayed no psychological deviations, but rather were "fanatics for superior orders." In other words, totalitarian systems transformed ordinary people into criminals who acted in the name of a higher ideal.[6] AK officer Kazimierz Moczarski analysed the character of his cellmate SS-Gruppenführer Jürgen Stroop, revealing the mechanisms of the Nazi (and, under closer scrutiny, the Soviet) totalitarian system. Similarly, former AK member and Auschwitz inmate Władysław Bartoszewski, who shared a prison cell with SS-Hauptsturmführer (Captain) Erich Engels,[7] wondered "why the ordinary, polite, and sensitive man who loves Bach and sheds tears when he hears music coming from somewhere outside had become a murderer."[8]

Despite the rapidly dwindling numbers of war crimes trials, between 1948 and 1953 Polish courts tried a number of notorious culprits, revealing a multitude of perpetrator personalities, ranging from "desk-killers" to Nazi zealots. These trials exposed the bifurcated character of the Nazi terror system: the Nazis' top brass determined the regime's genocidal policies, but it was the forces on the ground that were responsible for carrying out the leadership's decisions. To this end, local forces were afforded wide operational latitude. In practice, men of various ranks, from low-ranking functionaries to senior SS officers, boasting various backgrounds, personal characteristics, and motivations for participating, were instrumental to and integrated with the machinery of mass murder and repression. On the surface, the Nazi terror system seemed to be strictly regulated by Hitler and his senior lieutenants, but in fact that system was never uniform. Although the different Nazi agencies cooperated with one another, they just as often competed with one another, prioritizing their own objectives. Hence, Nazi rule was driven largely by personal initiatives, ambitions, motives, and character traits at all levels, and this generated constant changes and variations.[9]

In the daily application of terror, seemingly rigid orders and regulations were often implemented by mid- and low-level executioners who enjoyed wide latitude when it came to interpreting them. These individuals were not docile automatons; rather, they reinforced the terror system by twisting or even ignoring their superiors' orders to satisfy their own ambitions or to maximize their personal benefit. Many culprits were rabid Jew-haters; but that aside, the commission of anti-Jewish crimes, for which they were immune from penal liability in the Nazi system, enabled them to expand their authority and to line their own pockets. The very nature of the Nazi state allowed their ambitions and basest human instincts to flourish, and in this way even the worst atrocities were legalized.[10]

Josef Grzimek and Friedrich Riemann: Ideological Soldiers or Opportunists?

When in April 1948 Polish newspapers published an appeal for witnesses who could testify against Josef Grzimek, the former commandant of Jewish labour camps and ghettos in East Galicia, more than thirty individuals responded, describing him as a "savage," a "brute," or a "fiend" – the most violent German functionary they had encountered during the war.[11] Given that most of these witnesses had survived several ghettos and concentration camps, where they encountered many SS officials and guards, such descriptions testified to Grzimek's particular propensity to violence. A survivor from the labour camp at Jaktorów (near Złoczów) recalled that the first commandant treated prisoners relatively leniently, but in February 1942 he was replaced by Grzimek. Life for inmates immediately became a living hell. In June, Grzimek organized and directly participated in the execution of 160 Jews who were no longer capable of work. Other witnesses testified that Grzimek had many prisoners flogged for the slightest transgressions and drastically reduced daily food rations. He ordered executions of hostages for escape attempts and in the summer 1942 took part in the liquidation of several Jewish ghettos in East Galicia.[12]

When in January 1949 Gzimek was put on trial in the district court in Warsaw,[13] one Jewish or Polish witness after another recounted a litany of horrors as they recalled their wartime encounters with the defendant. In February 1943 Grzimek was appointed the commandant of the Jewish ghetto in Lwów, which the Nazis euphemistically named "Julag" (short for *Judenlager*). Survivors described the widespread fear of Grzimek and how Jews ran for cover whenever they saw him at a distance. For his amusement, Grzimek organized a musical band, which played when the prisoners were taken to work or to executions. Preaching "cleanliness," he flogged and beat prisoners who looked "unkempt" and had the so-called illegals – those who did not have a permit to work for the Wehrmacht – deported to the Bełżec death camp.[14]

As a specialist in the "Jewish question," Grzimek was transferred to other camps and ghettos, where he continued his murderous activities. One witness saw Grzimek kill the remaining Jewish militiamen in Rawa Ruska. He forced them to climb into two horse carts and shot them in the nape of the neck, until the carts were filled with bloodied bodies writhing in agony.[15] In the summer of 1943 Grzimek was appointed *Lagerführer* (a functionary responsible for the prisoner section) in the labour camp of Szebnie in southeastern Poland, where he stood out among the most brutal SS men, tormenting and killing prisoners at will. To suppress the screaming of the victims, Grzimek again organized a musical band that played during executions. He personally shot fifteen Jews who in his opinion laboured at a slack pace. In another instance,

4.1 and 4.2 Friedrich Riemann (left) and Josef Grzimek in Allied custody.
USHMM, RG-15.156M, Acc. 2010.12, trial of Friedrich Riemann
and RG-15.156M.0019, trial of Josef Grzimek.

he ordered the Ukrainian guards to shoot twenty Jews in reprisal for a prisoner's escape. In the fall, he took an active part in the liquidation of the Jewish ghettos in the Tarnów District, and when a transport of Jews came from the Tarnów Ghetto, he selected 300 people and sent them to be shot.[16]

Friedrich Riemann, who during the war headed the "Jewish Bureau" (*Judenreferat*) at the Sipo office in Tarnopol, had a similarly notorious reputation. Extradited to Poland by the British in October 1947, Riemann faced charges for the persecution and murder of Jews in several localities in East Galicia. In response to an appeal published by the Polish authorities, several witnesses submitted affidavits, describing Riemann as the "right hand" of Herman Müller, the Sipo chief in Tarnopol. In this capacity, Riemann literally acted above and beyond the call of duty. He came to the Jewish ghetto every day and preyed upon its residents. He assaulted those who happened to cross his path, viciously beat them, and escorted them to the Sipo prison, whence they were taken to execution sites. In several instances, he shot people on the spot.[17] Some witnesses testified that Riemann was a member of *Einsatzkommando 5*, which carried out mass executions in Lwów. On 4 July 1941, the commando, supported by the Wehrmacht and the Ukrainian militia, staged a pogrom of Jews in Tarnopol, where 4,000 people were murdered.[18]

On 17 December 1948, Riemann stood trial in the Warsaw district court, where witnesses and survivors described him as one of the most brutal SS functionaries. Bronisław Münz told the court that on 6 September 1941 he saw Riemann during the so-called *Intelligenzaktion* in Zbaraż, where the Gestapo organized the execution of seventy-two Jewish intellectuals and professionals. Münz saw Riemann personally shoot a woman and her child.[19] Julius Galber witnessed Riemann stumble upon a small Jewish girl who was playing in the garden. He viciously kicked her until she fainted and then ordered Galber to clean his bloodied boots.[20] Karol Brożyński told the court that Riemann was "bereft of any human feelings." Some witnesses never saw him personally but heard of his reputation. When Riemann arrived in Kamionka Strumilowa, the ghetto residents expected the worst, and indeed, the Germans organized a massive round-up.[21]

Grzimek and Riemann each made only a minimal admission of guilt. Grzimek claimed either that there were no beatings or murders under his command or that he "was not there at the time" of executions. When a number of witnesses testified that he personally shot several Jews, he conceded two cases in Szebnie, but claimed he did so on the orders of the Gestapo. He insisted that executions in the ghettos and camps were carried out mostly by Ukrainian policemen on the orders of the Gestapo and SSPF. By his own account, he "tried to treat the inmates humanely" and even "sympathized" with the Polish underground. When confronted by undeniable evidence, Grzimek complained that his long detention in prison – he was extradited to Poland in October 1947 – made him too weak to answer questions.[22]

British investigators had noted that Riemann possessed "little intellect or education ... He may be a war criminal, but it is unlikely that he will admit to any deed amounting to a war crime unless confronted with evidence."[23] Indeed, in British custody Riemann had admitted his membership in the Gestapo and posting to the KdS Warsaw, and he did the same in the courtroom in Warsaw. But he fought tooth and nail to deny all other charges. He claimed that in Warsaw he was responsible solely for food supplies at the Pawiak prison,[24] that he never mistreated prisoners, and that he often objected to beatings and tortures.[25] He further insisted that he arrived in East Galicia in September 1941, after the murder of the Polish intelligentsia in Lwów and the anti-Jewish pogrom in Tarnopol. By his own account, he "never killed a single person" or took part in ghetto-clearing operations (*Aktionen*) and executions. To the contrary, he claimed that he tried to treat Jews humanely, insisting that after he was transferred to Sokal he was arrested by the Gestapo for helping some Jews cross the Hungarian border.[26]

On 29 January 1949, in accordance with Articles 1, 2, 3, and 4 of the August Decree, the court found Grzimek guilty on all charges and sentenced him to death, stressing that in carrying out his murderous activities he had displayed particularly "sadistic" qualities.[27] Riemann's trial lasted one day, and on 17 December 1948 the court sentenced him to death for "criminal activities against Polish citizens of Jewish nationality, against Poland, and against humanity." In justification of the verdict, the judges conceded that Riemann's participation in the massacre of the Polish intelligentsia in Lwów and in the pogrom in Tarnopol was not fully proven, but that all other evidence was sufficient to impose the ultimate penalty.[28]

Although the courts did not specifically aim at composing a sociopsychological analysis of Grzimek's and Riemann's personalities and motivations, in both cases it was duly noted that the defendants' wartime postings and activities were more than coincidental. Indeed, the trial records show that the two most important factors that informed their conduct were their level of Nazification and the environment in which they operated during the war. It seems that Grzimek and Riemann derived pleasure from inflicting pain, cruelty, and degradation on their victims. The survivors of Nazi terror, including the witnesses who testified against Grzimek and Riemann, were wont to describe their tormentors as "beasts," "monsters," or "sadists" who lacked elementary human traits. These men seemingly enjoyed their "work" – humiliating, beating, torturing, and murdering their victims under any pretext or none at all. They were constantly in the midst of *Aktionen* and round-ups, selecting for executions those who were sick and those who were unable to work. While their colleagues took it easy after massacring people all day, they lurked in the streets of ghettos or in the shadows of concentration camp barracks, hunting down potential victims. But was their conduct exceptional in the context of the German occupation?

The biographical data collected by the Allied investigators reveal that Grzimek and Riemann were typical of a broad stratum of the SS recruited from the lower middle class and that they possessed average intellectual abilities; many SS personnel had only a middle school diploma or a certificate from a trade school. Too young to participate in the First World War, they lived through the collapse of the German Empire in 1918 and the postwar socio-economic and political ordeal.

Riemann finished primary school, but due to a frail physique he did not join his father's horse-slaughtering business and became a cattle dealer instead. He was twenty-four when, in 1931, he joined the SA and NSDAP, becoming an early volunteer for the Nazi cause. After enlisting in the Nazi movement cost him his job, he survived on the dole, while carrying out various tasks for the Nazi Party, including spying on opponents of Nazism. In 1934 he joined the Gestapo and was made responsible for gauging the mood of industrial workers in his area. His reports to his superiors led to the deportation of some political offenders to concentration camps. Before the German invasion of Poland, Riemann was assigned to *Einsatzgruppe* IV; he arrived in Warsaw in October 1939. When KdS Warsaw was established, he was dispatched to the Pawiak prison, where (contrary to his court testimony) he functioned as a liaison officer between KdS headquarters and the prison administration.[29]

Grzimek, too, was a young man (born in 1905) when he joined the Nazi Party in 1930 and the SS in 1932. The fact that he was born in Silesia may have contributed to his radicalization, for many notorious SS men came from the territories that had been affected by the Treaty of Versailles.[30] Grzimek's SS superiors must have considered him a devoted Nazi, for they selected him for a particularly secret mission. In August 1939 he and other Polish-speaking Germans were sent to Berlin, where they were handed Polish uniforms and equipment and then dispatched to the German–Polish border. On 30 August they attacked the German customs post in Hohenlinden (near Bytom); German authorities immediately accused the Poles of mounting the attack. This and similar covert operations that were carried out along the German–Polish border were used by Hitler as the pretext to attack Poland. Upon completing this task, Grzimek received additional instruction in an SS training unit and was dispatched to the staff of the SSPF in Kraków; from there, in 1942, he was dispatched to East Galicia.[31]

Long before the outbreak of the war, Riemann and Grzimek had been indoctrinated into the Nazi racial and xenophobic *Weltanschauung*.[32] Neither was a creative thinker (nor were many other Nazis), and their low level of education mirrored their low status within the SS. They were particularly attracted to the rigid military structure of the Nazi hierarchy, which provided them with a certain amount of guidance and structure, and which placed a strong emphasis on toughness, extreme authoritarianism, obsession with power, and the racial ideology of National Socialism. In Germany proper, Riemann and Grzimek had been mere NCOs whose authority was sharply defined and limited.[33] A posting to Poland or Russia changed all of this – it opened a door to the "wild East," a land of undreamed-of opportunities where thousands of German functionaries could fulfil their most impossible dreams of power and personal enrichment under the cover of an ideological crusade.[34]

In the territories slated for Hitler's *Lebensraum*, SS men like Riemann and Grzimek acquired literally unlimited power over thousands of people and acted as local satraps. Their greed and base instincts no longer encountered limits. The Jewish ghettos were a crucial feature of the Nazi "Final Solution." The Germans transformed many ghettos into what for all intents and purposes were labour camps; the Nazis exploited the Jewish inhabitants, and when Jews were incapable of hard labour, they were murdered. Much like the camps, the ghettos became "world[s] without restraint" where German functionaries and guards could express their power through any imaginable act of cruelty and where they could satisfy with impunity their personal ambitions and greed.[35]

Riemann systematically extorted valuables from Jewish families after promising to save some of their members from deportation and certain death, all the while looting Jewish apartments left vacant after *Aktionen*. One witness who worked at the warehouse where confiscated Jewish goods were collected saw Riemann almost every day, when the latter helped himself to the valuables, furs, and rugs of those whom he had sent to their deaths.[36] A member of the Soviet Extraordinary State Commission for the Investigation of the German Fascist Crimes, the writer Vladimir Belyaev, who investigated Nazi crimes in western Ukraine, described Grzimek as an individual driven by hate, violence, and greed. In Lwów, where he was literally master over life and death, Grzimek called himself "king of the ghetto." He took over a spacious apartment, had it renovated by a detail of Jewish labourers, and purchased an estate near Lwów, which had a stable where Jewish prisoners laboured. In Szebnie, Grzimek made it a point to meet new transports of Jews, robbing them of their money and valuables and shooting those who tried to conceal their possessions.[37]

By Himmler's order, SS men "acting out of self-seeking, sadistic, or sexual motives should be punished by a court of law,"[38] and as a rule, the Nazi leaders were wary of sadists, who could fly out of control when carrying out their functions. They preferred to rely on those who carried out their gruesome tasks promptly and efficiently; in this context, cruelty was considered but a side effect. Survivors remembered thousands of perpetrators whose conduct matched that of Riemann and Grzimek, including Peter Leideritz in Kolomyja; Hans Krüger and Herman Müller, the Sipo commanders in Stanislawów (now Ivano-Frankivs'k) and Tarnopol, respectively; and the commandants of the Lwów Janowska camp, Fritz Gebauer and Gustaw Willhaus. All of them were known for their ferocious ingenuity when torturing and murdering their victims.[39]

An entire corps of such individuals passed through SS special "schooling" that made them willing and resourceful servants of the system. They honed their skills in Poland or Russia, where, as chiefs of Sipo branch offices, as "Jewish experts" (*Judenreferenten*), and as the commandants of ghettos and labour and concentration camps, they exercised unlimited power over thousands of defenceless people. They represented the fusion of two types of perpetrators – the ideological soldier, and the *Exzesstäter* (excessive perpetrator) who thrived on hatred and violence. They organized and carried out round-ups and selections, but they also robbed, brutalized, and personally killed scores of people. In the words of Dieter Pohl, "they constituted a core segment of the personnel in the 'Final Solution' and without their participation, it would have been impossible to implement the carnage in this manner."[40]

Waldemar Macholl: Career Policeman

During the occupation of Poland the Nazis murdered about three million of the country's Jews – almost 90 per cent of its prewar Jewish population. At the same time, more than two million Poles perished in Nazi concentration and labour camps, through collective executions in prisons and on city streets, and in the course of the "pacification" of entire villages and districts. Nazi terror policies in Poland were a part of a deliberately planned political project, predicated on Hitler's vision of *Lebensraum*, whereby the Slavic lands to the east of Germany were to be "emptied" and repopulated by ethnic Germans. On 22 August 1939, Hitler confided to a circle of German dignitaries that the war against Poland would be radically different from the war in the West and must be waged with no mercy. This speech became the ideological underpinning of the terror campaign, which was to accelerate German victory and the destruction of the Polish state. Until the invasion of the Soviet Union, Poland was the only country where the Nazis applied mass "preventive" terror and ambiguously termed "reprisals" (*Sühnenmassnahmen* and *Vergeltungsmassnahmen*). Both aimed at the liquidation of real and potential opponents of the regime and were carried out regardless of whether the local population had anything to do with the acts of resistance. Any sign of hostility or defiance was to be met with acts of overwhelming ferocity. The names of executed persons were published or broadcast, and corpses were often left for several days at the site where the killing had taken place.[41]

Although many members of the resistance fell victim to reprisals, the Nazi terror mostly affected the population at large, which lived in constant fear and anticipation of violence. Indeed, those who survived the German occupation remembered their wartime existence as "life as if" (*życie na niby*), in that death had become a daily possibility.[42] Jan Parandowski, a prominent Polish writer and translator, recalled:

> We experienced things that shook us every day, every night, every hour. They poisoned and threatened every moment of our existence. At every moment, violence snatched somebody – off the street, from a cafe, a house, out of a family, society, and humanity itself. What only yesterday used to be the epicenter of life, love, devotion, responsibility, hope, and help, was now tossed into nothingness, of which we knew that it was but some dump, filled with dirty rags and scraps of human flesh, left to rot and burn.[43]

Frequent public executions traumatized large segments of Polish society. A woman in Lublin could not forget how "innocent people, with their mouths covered, formed lines against the walls and were shot by a bullet in the back of the head. The next group of people had to make room for themselves, removing the corpses. The blood-curdling cry of a mother in the crowd pierced the air and did the rest."[44]

Spearheading this campaign of relentless terror was Himmler's SS and police apparatus. During the invasion of Poland, the special killing units – the *Einsatzgruppen* – murdered thousands of Polish intelligentsia and Jews. Later, these units were dissolved and transformed into KdS stationary offices, which the population dreaded because of the suffering and death they inflicted. Local residents remembered well the names of the KdS's commanders and its most abominable functionaries.

When the trial of Waldemar Macholl began on 8 March 1949 in Białystok, the courtroom could not accommodate the large number of people who wanted to attend, and the court had to issue special passes for select individuals and groups. Former members of the Polish resistance were particularly keen to hear the testimony of the defendant, who had headed the "anti-resistance" section of the Białystok Gestapo.[45] In this capacity SS-Hauptsturmführer (Captain) Macholl participated in the arrests and interrogations of captured resisters and civilians and supervised the executions of more than 1,850 hostages seized by the KdS. He also took part in the destruction of eighteen villages for their alleged links to the resistance and in the executions of about 3,000 residents. In July 1944, as a member of *Sonderkommando* 1005, Macholl supervised a Jewish labour detail that exhumed thousands of corpses at the sites of mass executions in the Białystok District; on the completion of this task, he ordered the execution of the Jewish labourers.[46]

At the beginning of Macholl's trial, the court heard the expert opinion of Szymon Datner, the head of the Białystok branch of the CKŻP. Datner testified that during the AB Action in the Suwałki region, where Macholl temporarily served as the *Grenzkommissar* (border commissar), the Gestapo and the police shot several members of the Polish intelligentsia. In the Białystok region, German terror claimed 350,000 victims; the KdS Białystok contributed heavily to this tally of deaths.[47] Former prisoners testified that Macholl was often present during brutal interrogations at KdS headquarters, although he did not personally torture prisoners. (Only one witness testified that Macholl beat him.) Having extracted necessary information from the captives, Macholl and his subordinates would begin another series of arrests and interrogations. He also often decided a prisoner's fate, which was usually either deportation to a concentration camp or execution. According to Datner, the machinery of destruction thus ground on without pause.[48]

Some witnesses saw Macholl participate in arrests and round-ups of hostages, who were later shot; some never saw him but knew that he had decided their fate by signing arrest warrants. Without exception, all witnesses described horrible conditions in the KdS prisons, which were overcrowded; in 1942–3, thousands of inmates died of mistreatment, malnutrition, and epidemics. Those who had survived brutal pacification operations told the court how the SS and police wiped out entire villages.[49] The prosecution summoned Macholl's former colleague Fritz Friedel, who had headed the Judenreferat at the KdS Białystok and was awaiting his own trial. Friedel confirmed that in accordance with German anti-guerrilla doctrine, no difference was made between "partisans" and "bandits," and that Macholl played the key role in combating the resistance. On his orders at least 250 people were shot, and although he himself did not shoot anyone, he was frequently present at executions.[50]

The main tool of the KdS in Białystok (and elsewhere in German-occupied Europe) was native informants, turncoats, and agents provocateurs, who informed their masters about all aspects of life in the region and infiltrated the ranks of the resistance. According to the official Polish version of recent history and common popular conviction, Poland was the only nation that produced no Nazi collaborators.[51] The fact that the Gestapo had on its payroll native informants was a highly sensitive topic, and perhaps for this reason the court did not ask too many questions about this aspect of Macholl's testimony.[52] Still, according to Macholl, many of his agents either were anti-communists (Ukrainians and Byelorussians as well as Poles) or were after financial rewards paid by the KdS, and they contributed heavily to German terror in occupied Poland. In one instance, an agent revealed to his Gestapo controllers the whereabouts of a Soviet partisan unit. The German police inflicted heavy losses on the partisans and in June 1943 "pacified" a village suspected of helping the resistance. The village was burned to the ground and thirty-six of its residents were shot.[53]

While Macholl's primary objective was combating the underground, his participation in the Holocaust indicates that, regardless of their specialization, most KdS functionaries participated in the genocide. They were regularly assigned to escort Jewish victims to execution sites, where some took part in the shooting or supervised the death squads, which were comprised of Ukrainian, Byelorussian, and Lithuanian policemen.[54] According to Datner, in November–December 1942 the KdS in Białystok played a leading role in the deportation of 130,000 Jews to Treblinka and Auschwitz. In August 1943 the KdS and the police carried out the last *Aktion* in Białystok, during which 30,000 Jews were sent to Treblinka or Auschwitz.[55]

In the fall of 1943, the head of *Sonderkommando* 1005, Paul Blobel, arrived in Białystok to begin the eradication of traces of Nazi crimes. By courtesy of the KdS in Białystok, Macholl joined Blobel's staff, for which he organized a unit of Jewish prisoners who were chained and ordered to exhume mass graves and burn thousands of corpses. In July 1944, when they had almost completed their task, Macholl ordered the execution of the entire unit. The prisoners attempted to escape, but only nine out of forty managed to get away.[56]

A survivor, Amiel Szymon, submitted an affidavit to the court in which he described in vivid detail how the Jewish exhumation detachment carried out its macabre work. The prisoners worked every day, digging up hundreds of corpses – men, women, and children; in some graves, mothers still clung to their babies. After the corpses were put in piles and set on fire, their bones were ground up and the ashes were filtered for valuables, which were taken by SS functionaries. Szymon asserted that in the course of eight weeks, the detachment exhumed and burned about 40,000 corpses in the districts of Grodno, Augustów, and Białystok. Macholl was present at the sites. He solemnly promised the prisoners that they would not be shot, but in the late summer of 1944 he ordered the liquidation of the entire unit.[57]

The prosecution had the court summon Chaim Wróbel, the unit's only surviving member living in Poland at the time of Macholl's trial. On 14 April 1948 he was brought to court for a confrontation with Macholl and instantly recognized him as the SS officer who headed the "incineration detachment." In the courtroom, Wróbel testified that after murdering most Jews, the Germans retained about a hundred Jewish specialists, who worked in garages and workshops. They were confined in the Białystok prison; there, Macholl selected about forty able-bodied men and had them taken to Augustów, where they were chained and deprived of shoes to prevent their escape. Under armed guard, they dug deep ditches, laid wooden planks over them, put corpses on top, and covered the corpses with fuel. Altogether the prisoners built between sixty to seventy such makeshift ovens. Another group of prisoners used long hooks to pull corpses by their skulls out of previously dug mass graves. Prisoners known as "gold searchers" (goldzukhers in Yiddish) searched the corpses for earrings, rings, and gold teeth. After the fire died down, the unit's members used special crushing devices to smash bones and sifted the ashes in search of any valuables. The unit was well fed and even received alcohol, which some prisoners understood as a sign that the Germans were not going to leave them alive.[58]

Despite overwhelming incriminating evidence, Macholl pled not guilty. He argued that at the KdS in Białystok he merely carried out his professional police duties, and he insisted that, although he took part in pacification operations, he personally neither killed nor tortured anybody. He contended that all arrests in the district were carried out on the orders of the KdS commanders (Wilhelm Altenloh and his successor, Herbert Zimmermann), and that when Altenloh, Zimmermann, or the SSPF ordered the executions of hostages, he faced a choice: either take part in the killings or face court martial. Macholl vehemently denied that he had supervised the incineration detachment and claimed that he was merely responsible for supplying it with food. Furthermore, he asserted in the courtroom that he was "deeply shaken" when he found out that the incineration detachment had been liquidated.[59]

In his closing statement, Macholl justified his actions by reference to his superiors' orders and complained that four years of imprisonment and separation from his family had already "punished him enough, whereas those who had given orders were walking free in Germany."[60] On 25 March 1949, on the basis of Articles 1, 2, and 7 of the August Decree (in line with its December 1946 amendment), the court sentenced Macholl to death. President Bolesław Bierut turned down Macholl's appeal, and on 26 October he was executed.[61]

At first glance, Macholl's defence that he merely carried out his professional duties in a mechanical fashion appears plausible. In the hierarchy of the Sipo and the SD there was a distinction between career police officials and ideologically motivated members of the SS proper. The former were supposed to be somewhat more moderate, whereas the latter represented the most radical group within Himmler's apparatus. The fact that Macholl joined the Weimar police in 1920 and became a NSDAP member only in 1940 could be interpreted as indicating that he was much less an ideological warrior than an opportunist who continued his career under the new regime. At his trial, most witnesses testified that during interrogations at the KdS Macholl looked totally emotionless; whereas other Sipo functionaries screamed at their victims, he asked questions in a flat, colourless voice. Sometimes, when prisoners were subjected to a particularly gruesome treatment such as burning with electric current, Macholl seemed disgusted and looked away.[62]

Yet under closer scrutiny, the investigation and trial records in Macholl's case reveal details that go beyond mere professional habit and point to a personality that combined careerism with at least partial embrace of Nazi ideals. To begin with, Macholl belonged to a generation from which the Nazi regime recruited many of its members. Born in 1900, he was raised in a typical German lower-middle-class family; his mother was deeply religious and his father was a policeman who worshipped the Kaiser. Macholl fought briefly on the Western Front in the First World War, earning the Iron Cross, and upon his return to Germany found himself with neither work nor prospects. He shared his father's bitterness about Germany's defeat. In 1920 he joined the police force in East Prussia, rising to NCO and then receiving training as a police detective. In 1930 he was transferred to the criminal police (Kripo); then in 1933 he joined the political police, in which role he combated "anti-state activities" – at the time, a euphemism for suppressing leftist and liberal organizations. After the Nazi takeover, the political police force in East Prussia was renamed the Gestapo. Macholl worked in its counter-intelligence section and was promoted to *Kriminalrat* (criminal commissar).[63]

Macholl thus passed through a special socialization process long before he joined the Nazis. The Weimar police were subjected to an ideological indoctrination that was profoundly anti-democratic as well as anti-communist; also, rigorous physical training, along with participation in the dispersals of strikes and demonstrations and in brutal interrogations of prisoners, conditioned many policemen for later service in the Nazis' repressive apparatus.[64] In 1929, even before the Nazi takeover, Hitler named Himmler the Reichsführer-SS, and when Himmler was appointed chief of the German police in 1936, all police and security services were effectively unified under the SS. A crucial aspect of this was the ideological training conducted by all police branches. In his capacity as a member of the Kripo and the Gestapo, Macholl must have undergone intense ideological indoctrination that incorporated the xenophobic and racial doctrines of National Socialism. At the same time, the police were purged of unreliable elements, and the fact that Macholl remained in its service indicates that he had proved his fealty and trustworthiness.[65]

Macholl was not, strictly speaking, an SS official. After the SD, the Gestapo, and the Kripo were unified in the Reich Main Security Office (Reichssicherheitshauptamt, RSHA), he became an SS "uniform bearer" (*Uniformträger*). Neither his low-level status in the SS nor the fact that he joined the NSDAP relatively late should be regarded as indicating a lack of ideological enthusiasm on his part, for a number of notorious Nazi perpetrators entered the party between 1937 and 1940.[66] Crucially, Macholl's socialization through the "regulated" violence in the Weimar police and then the Gestapo came in handy when he was dispatched in August 1939 to *Einsatzgruppe* V; upon the German invasion of Poland that unit committed atrocities against Jews and Poles in the Masovian region in northeastern Poland. It also carried out deportations and expulsions of Jews from the Suwałki region to Lithuania and Białystok. (Under the German–Soviet agreement, the Białystok region was assigned to the Soviet zone of occupation.)[67]

Macholl's experience and performance must have satisfied his superiors, for in November 1939 he was appointed border police commissar (*Grenzpolizeikommissar*) in Suwałki, which was integrated into East Prussia. In this capacity, he supervised all police forces in the district. In the spring of 1940 the Gestapo in Suwałki carried out an *Intelligenzaktion*, arresting 1,000 Polish intellectuals, doctors, lawyers, and political activists, many of whom were executed or perished later in concentration camps. In August 1940 Macholl changed his Polish-sounding name Macpolowski to his wife's name of Macholl; a year later he assumed the position of the chief of the Gestapo IV-A3 section (resistance) at the Białystok KdS.[68]

Whether Macholl fully embraced National Socialist ideology remains unknown, but there is no doubt that the Nazi regime offered him many opportunities for career advancement. In return, Macholl and his like placed their police experience and professional skills at the disposal of the regime. Inured to "regulated" violence under the Weimar Republic, they embraced it as an indispensable tool of their trade during the war, and alongside members of the SS proper, they became pillars of Himmler's terror apparatus.[69]

Jürgen Stroop: "The Right Man for the Job"

In July 1951, Jürgen Stroop became one of the top SS senior officers tried in Poland for Nazi-era crimes, in particular for his role in the liquidation of the Warsaw Ghetto and the suppression of the Warsaw Ghetto Uprising in April and May 1943.[70]

Born in 1895 into a family that strictly upheld Catholic and Prussian militarist traditions, at the outbreak of the First World War the young Stroop immediately volunteered for the German army, seeing action in France, Poland, and the Balkans. He was wounded three times, received medals for his service, and was promoted. After the end of the war, like many demobilized soldiers, Stroop was disillusioned by what struck many as Germany's precipitous surrender. The frustrated Stroop gravitated towards gatherings of war veterans who missed the comradeship of the battlefield and who bemoaned Germany's disgraceful defeat and the humiliating terms of the Treaty of Versailles, all the while feeling betrayed by the country's leaders. He joined the Nazi Party in June 1932, and by July he had been recruited to establish an SS unit in Detmold. He showed his mettle with alacrity, galvanizing local support for the Nazis, largely through intimidation and the demonization of Social Democrats, communists, and Jews, who were harassed by his SS minions, whom he had organized into an auxiliary police battalion under his command. From modest origins, Stroop suddenly became a man of the moment, and he rose quickly through the ranks of the SS. In

January 1938 he attended a course for SS officers near Dachau, where he immersed himself in the Nazi world view, in which antisemitism figured prominently, and further internalized the SS values of blind obedience, unswerving discipline, and unconditional willingness to sacrifice one's life for the fatherland. Himmler took note of Stroop early. He chose Stroop to join him in leading the SS men marching past Hitler in the 1938 Nazi Party rally at Nuremberg. By the time the Second World War broke out in September 1939, Stroop had attained the rank of SS-Oberführer (Brigadier General).[71]

On Himmler's order, in October 1939 Stroop was sent to Poznań (Posen) in Nazi-annexed western Poland (the Warthegau) to take command of the "self-defence" (*Selbstschutz*) formation of local ethnic Germans. This unit killed around 2,000 Polish civilians under Stroop's command; most of the victims were political figures. In March 1940 Stroop was appointed commander of the SS unit in Gniezno (Gnesen). In October 1942 he received a medal for his accomplishments in Poland – the persecution and mass murder of Poles. After the German invasion of the Soviet Union, Himmler consented to Stroop's request that he be transferred to the Eastern Front. From July to September 1941 he served along the Eastern Front with the infantry regiment of the 3rd SS Totenkopf Division. After he recovered from a shrapnel wound, he filled various temporary posts in Ukraine. He oversaw the construction of the so-called Durchgangsstraße IV, built by Soviet POWs, Jews, and Ukrainian labourers, designed to bring coal, industrial goods, and agricultural products into Germany from Ukraine. Stroop rapidly climbed the rungs of the promotion ladder, attaining the rank of SS-Brigadeführer (Major General) in September 1942. In October 1942 he was assigned to Himmler's personal staff and for several months attended a training course in Berlin for high-ranking officers in the SS and police. The course was held at the RSHA, which was the epicentre for the coordination and commission of Nazi anti-Jewish and other genocidal crimes. In February 1943 he was named SSPF for Lemberg (the German name for Lwów or L'viv), where he assisted in the extermination of thousands of Jews in hiding and in labour camps and in the formation of the Ukrainian SS-Division "Galizien."[72] His success at pacifying enemies of the Reich in Poland and the Soviet Union earned him a favourable reputation among Nazi leaders, from Himmler on down.

In February 1943, Himmler ordered the liquidation of the Warsaw Ghetto and the deportation of its remaining Jewish inhabitants to Treblinka or to forced labour camps. However, when German forces under the command of Ferdinand Sammern-Frankenegg entered the ghetto on 19 April, some 750 young Jewish men and women mounted what was then the largest urban revolt in any Nazi-occupied country since the outbreak of the Second World War – the Warsaw Ghetto Uprising. Spearheaded by the leaders of their Zionist and Bundist[73] youth groups, the Jewish resisters temporarily disrupted the Germans' plans for further deportations. (Units of the Jewish Military Union [Żydowski Związek Wojskowy, ŻZW], followers of the Zionist Revisionist movement, took part in the uprising under their own command structure.) Outraged, Himmler ordered Stroop to Warsaw to take command of the SS and police. In the words of historian Yosef (or Joseph) Kermish (Józef Kermisz in Polish), "Stroop was just the right man for the job. His previous activities in Poland, his mass murders and persecution of the population bore witness to his talent for carrying out the task assigned to him – to exterminate and destroy the Warsaw Ghetto, the most powerful stronghold of Jewish resistance throughout the occupied countries."[74]

After two days of heavy fighting, Stroop shifted tactics. Unable to defeat the insurgents using conventional means, he decided to set fire to the ghetto, forcing its inhabitants, overcome by fire, heat, and smoke, out of burning buildings and underground hideouts, while his forces chased Jewish combatants emerging from the conflagration. He further ordered his soldiers to unearth and attack the hundreds of bunkers built and used by both civilians and fighters. Stroop's strategy of setting the ghetto on fire proved decisive in crushing the uprising. A small group of Jewish fighters escaped from the ghetto through the sewers; most of the remaining Jewish militants were killed in combat. During the uprising the Germans apprehended or killed more than 56,000 Jews. The Germans deported the surviving Jews to Treblinka, Majdanek, and the forced labour camps at Trawniki and Poniatowa. Stroop celebrated the final liquidation of the Warsaw Ghetto by ordering the dynamiting of Warsaw's Great Synagogue.[75]

Although the Warsaw Ghetto Uprising had been defeated, it immediately became a symbol of heroic Jewish resistance, one that inspired Jews in other ghettos and in partisan units throughout Nazi-occupied Europe and that made a lasting impression no less on leaders of the Polish underground.[76] After the war the uprising became the focal point of Jewish commemorations of the Holocaust in Poland and throughout the Jewish world. The Warsaw Ghetto Monument, the world's most famous monument to the Holocaust, which features ghetto resistance fighters cast in high relief, was unveiled on 19 April 1948 in Warsaw

4.3 Jürgen Stroop (second from left) gathers information from a civilian on the
second day of the suppression of the Warsaw Ghetto Uprising, 20 April 1943.
Accompanying Stroop are officers of his command staff, including Franz
Konrad (left) and Karl Brandt (second from right), a member of the Sipo
in Warsaw, responsible for the supervision of the ghetto.
United States Holocaust Memorial Museum, courtesy of Louis Gonda.

on the fifth anniversary of the uprising. In attendance were surviving Jewish fighters, Jewish communal leaders, and Polish dignitaries.
Although the authorities, abetted by communists of Jewish extraction,
exploited subsequent commemorations of the uprising, which were
held in front of the monument, to extol the virtues of communism – a
staple of the Polish communist version of the war years was the exag-
geration of the assistance rendered by the communist underground to
ghetto fighters – the image of the uprising remained fixed in the minds
of Jews and Poles alike in the immediate postwar era.[77]

In June 1943, Stroop was officially named SSPF in the Warsaw District
(SS- und Polizeiführer im Distrikt Warschau). In recognition of his

successful suppression of the uprising, Himmler awarded Stroop the coveted Iron Cross 1st Class. Later, he served as HSSPF in Greece, where he was promoted to SS-Gruppenführer (Lieutenant General), and then as HSSPF in Reich-Westmark, with its headquarters in Wiesbaden. At the end of the war, Stroop organized an abortive guerrilla organization, "Werewolf," composed mostly of teenagers, to oppose invading Allied forces behind enemy lines.[78]

Stroop surrendered to American troops in Germany a few days after the cessation of hostilities in May 1945 under the assumed name of an army captain. He revealed his true identity only in July 1945 after the Americans had recovered incriminating documents, including his copy of his report on the liquidation of the Warsaw Ghetto and the suppression of the Warsaw Ghetto Uprising. The Polish government's delegation to the Nuremberg Trial requested and received the report after the trial.[79]

On 21 March 1947 a US military tribunal established in the former concentration camp at Dachau found Stroop guilty of having ordered the summary execution of nine downed American airmen between October 1944 and March 1945 and sentenced him to death. The Americans had surrendered to Stroop's troops after making a forced landing in the military district under his control. (Twelve other Germans who were under his command were convicted of murdering the pilots and received the death penalty; other German defendants received prison sentences; one defendant was acquitted.) Despite the death sentence, the Americans, in response to entreaties by the Polish Military Mission in Berlin, extradited Stroop to Poland in May 1947 to stand trial there for his role in the liquidation of the Warsaw Ghetto, the suppression of the Warsaw Ghetto Uprising, and the murder of ethnic Polish civilians.[80]

Stroop sat in prison for four years while authorities in the Polish Ministry of Justice prepared his trial. He was questioned repeatedly by representatives of the ministry and the GKBZH.[81] Although Stroop's pending trial generated strong interest in Poland, especially among Polish Jews, it was delayed. One reason for the delay was that the prosecutors' preparations were interrupted midstream when Yosef Kermish, deputy director of the ŻIH in Warsaw, who was slated to testify for the prosecution as an expert witness, emigrated from Poland to Israel in 1950 and had to be replaced.[82]

While awaiting trial at Mokotów prison in Warsaw, Stroop shared his cell for 255 days, from 2 March to 11 November 1949, with Kazimierz Moczarski (1907–1975), an ex-AK officer during the war. A brave leader in the underground, as well as a trained lawyer and journalist, Moczarski was a member of the small Democratic Party (Stronnictwo Democratyczne, SD). The AK had assigned him the task of identifying Polish collaborators, and during the Warsaw Uprising in August and September 1944 he edited the AK's underground newspaper. In prison since August 1945, Moczarski, who was falsely accused by the communist regime of collaborating with the Nazis, was tried twice. In January 1946 he was sentenced to ten years' imprisonment (later reduced to five years), and in November 1952 he was sentenced to death (later commuted to life imprisonment). In November 1956, in the wake of political liberalization in Poland, the Warsaw district court declared Moczarski innocent of all charges and he was fully rehabilitated. Although he was initially stupefied when prison authorities placed him in a prison cell with Stroop and other Nazis, Moczarski resolved to use his proximity to Stroop, a "mass murderer" (*ludobójca*) in his eyes, "to extract as much of the truth about Stroop and his life as possible." After his release from prison, Moczarski, who became an investigative journalist for a Warsaw daily, made voluminous notes of his conversations with Stroop and examined wartime documents to verify Stroop's assertions. The result, *Rozmowy z katem* (Conversations with an Executioner), was published in the monthly periodical *Odra* between 1972 and 1974. It was then published in book form in 1977, after Moczarski's death in 1975, and became a bestseller in Poland. Although the absolute accuracy of Moczarski's renditions of his conversations with Stroop, recorded several years after they took place, is open to debate, Moczarski's book is nevertheless an invaluable exploration, based on first-hand impressions, of the Nazi mind, for which Stroop was Moczarski's case study.[83]

Moczarski's book cast a glaring light on Stroop's character traits. By Moczarski's account, Stroop was self-absorbed, vainglorious, arrogant, chauvinistic, militant, and racist. He also held most of the human race in contempt, yet he was hypersensitive when the probity of his wartime behaviour was questioned. He was slavishly loyal and subservient to authority. He was wont to excuse his actions through resort to slogans like "Befehl ist Befehl" (An order is an order.) He harboured a perverse sense of legality and was oblivious to common morality. He may have been unscrupulous in the line of duty, but he was not a misfit. That said, there was a steely edge to Stroop's personality. When Moczarski castigated him after one of his particularly perverted descriptions of Jews who were apprehended in battle, Stroop turned crimson. "He had lead in his eyes," writes Moczarski. "I imagine that he had looked at Jews fighting in the ghetto with a glare like that made of lead."[84] Although Stroop's formal education was minimal, he was a wily and calculating man. He was unrepentant, but he was not oblivious to the incriminating evidence of his wartime conduct that the authorities by then possessed. Therefore, although he was boastful, he held his tongue when conversation in their cell turned to crimes for which, he thought, Polish authorities lacked sufficient evidence to convict him. In his view, Hitler and Himmler were two of the greatest men of the twentieth century, and he subscribed unwaveringly even after the war to Nazism's vision and objectives, which included a world without Jews. Although he expressed grudging admiration to Moczarski for the tenacity of the Jewish fighters in the Warsaw Ghetto, he was and remained an out-and-out antisemite. In addition to Jews, he counted Social Democrats, communists, Freemasons, and many others among Germany's enemies, even after the war. The portrait of Stroop that develops in Moczarski's book is of a dyed-in-the-wool Nazi who committed mass murder without qualms or hesitation. In Stroop's case, there was no push, only pull.[85]

On 18 July 1951, Stroop and Franz Konrad were escorted under armed guard into the courtroom of the Warsaw district court. The case was heard by three judges. The presiding judge was A. Pyszkowski, who was the vice-president of the district court. Leon Penner and Jan Rusek represented the prosecution; Penner was responsible for conducting the proceedings against Stroop, Rusek against Konrad. Each defendant had his own defence attorney: J. Nowakowski defended Stroop; J. Palatyński defended Konrad. As historian Katarzyna Person notes, "in accordance with the demands of Jewish organizations, Stroop's trial was perceived, from the beginning, as a comprehensive reckoning for crimes committed in the Warsaw Ghetto."[86] Although both Stroop and Konrad stood in the dock, the trial's focus was on Stroop. Konrad's inclusion was more or less an afterthought.[87]

Stroop faced charges on four counts. The first count accused him of belonging to the SS, a criminal organization. The second count addressed his role in the liquidation of the Warsaw Ghetto and the suppression of the Warsaw Ghetto Uprising. According to the second count, Stroop,

from 19 April to 16 May 1943, in Warsaw, in command of the operation [*akcja*] whose objective was the deportation from the Warsaw Ghetto of the rest of the Jews, numbering about 100,000, confined there to the Lublin District for the purpose of exterminating them in extermination camps as well as liquidating the ghetto, issued the order for the murder of at least

56,065 persons, the deaths of tens of thousands of others in burning underground canals and other hideouts, the destruction of building complexes
that constituted the ghetto, and the burning of the synagogue outside the
wall of the ghetto; moreover, he ordered the plunder of property belonging to the murdered.

The third count charged Stroop, as SSPF in the Warsaw District, with
ordering the execution of 100 Poles on 16 July 1943 in retaliation for
an attack with a hand grenade by an anonymous person on a marching column of SA men that resulted in the injury of some Germans. It
was further alleged in the fourth count that Stroop, as commander of
the Selbstschutz in Poznań from October 1939 to March 1940 and then
as commander of the SS unit in Gniezno from March 1940 to October
1941, took part in the persecution and murder of the Polish civilian
population.[88]

The indictment charged Konrad with taking part in "Operation
Reinhard" – the euphemism for the mass murder of Jews in the General
Government. Under the command of SSPF-Lublin Odilo Globocnik,
Konrad was responsible for the so-called *Werterfassung* – the requisition
and registration of property left behind by murdered or deported Jews
– and for looting their property for the Third Reich. While engaged in
these activities, Konrad pocketed some valuables and money for his
own benefit.[89]

The prosecution's key piece of evidence was Stroop's own report,
which he had compiled for Himmler. Bearing the self-congratulatory
and smug inscription "The Jewish quarter of Warsaw is no more!" (*Es
gibt keinen jüdischen Wohnbezirk – in Warschau mehr!*) across its cover, it is
one of the few contemporary chronicles of the Warsaw Ghetto Uprising
and constitutes the only evidence of several otherwise undocument-
ed skirmishes between Stroop's forces and Jewish fighters. Robert H.
Jackson, the chief prosecutor for the United States, mentioned Stroop's
report in his opening address at the Nuremberg Trial, and in December
1945 Jackson's assistant, American prosecutor William F. Walsh, introduced it into evidence, reading excerpts from it into the court record.[90]
But the report's significance is magnified by what Andrzej Wirth, cultural editor of the Warsaw weekly *Polityka* in the 1950s, labels "the language of fascism," which appears in it "practically unfiltered through
any kind of ideological screen."[91] This fascist form of language oscil-
lates between euphemisms and bureaucratic speech, both used in am-
ple quantities to describe – or to be more precise, obfuscate – the act of

mass murder. Thus in the report's first section, the ghetto, the site of forced Jewish segregation, is called "the Jewish quarter" (*der jüdischer Wohnbezirk*) or "quarantine district" (*Seuchensperrgebiet*), which the Germans established "in the interest of preserving the health of German troops and also the civilian population." The German liquidation of the ghetto receives the name "grand operation" (*Großaktion*). According to the report, 310,322 Jews were not deported to their deaths in Treblinka but rather "resettled" (*ausgesiedelt*) between 22 July and 3 October 1942. The report blames Jews for their own destruction because they "no longer considered voluntary resettlement [*freiwillige Umsiedlung*] but were determined to resist with all weapons and means at their disposal." The report is obsessed with the numbers of German and Jewish casualties; yet the figures for German fatalities and wounded in it are probably underreported, and the numbers of Jewish dead among the fighters and of the apprehended among the ghetto's inhabitants are likely inflated. The report mentions Jewish fighters and criminal elements in the same breath – thus the ubiquitous coupling of "Jews and bandits" or "Jews and Polish bandits." Yet the report cannot help but resort frequently to what Wirth calls "the object-language of mass murder."[92] In this sense the report celebrates "apprehended or destroyed Jews" (*erfassten bzw.* [*beziehungsweise*] *vernichteten Juden*). And on 8 May the report, signed by Stroop, reads: "The undersigned is determined not to terminate the grand operation until the last Jew has been destroyed" (*bis auch der letzte Jude vernichtet ist*).

The report also contains fifty-three photographs, many taken by Stroop's co-defendant Konrad. Captions under most of the photographs praise the Nazi triumph over the Jews of Warsaw. The photographs show German forces, led by Stroop, in action, as well as their round-up of Jews and the liquidation of the ghetto. One of the report's photographs is particularly well-known. It shows a bedraggled and anxious group of Jewish men, women, and children, their hands in the air, being led out of a building by armed German soldiers. The photograph attained iconic status after the war owing to the figure of a boy, standing just off-centre ahead of the rest of the group, who appears to be between eight and ten years of age. An SS soldier stands a few feet behind him, his gaze and the muzzle of his firearm directed at the boy. Unlike the woman standing beside the boy, who seems to steal a glance at this soldier, the boy, hands raised, stares straight ahead into the unknown, gripped by fear, which is evident by his facial expression. The caption below the photograph reads "Taken out of bunkers with force."

4.4 Jews captured by SS and SD troops during the suppression of the Warsaw Ghetto Uprising are forced to leave their shelter and march to the Umschlag-platz for deportation. United States Holocaust Memorial Museum, courtesy of National Archives and Records Administration, College Park

In all likelihood the Jews under arrest, including the boy, were killed.[93] Later, when the Polish prosecutor showed Stroop the photograph during cross-examination at his trial in Warsaw, Stroop asserted that the boy and the other Jews could not have been shot. What he failed to add was that they were probably transported to their deaths in Treblinka.[94]

The indictment paid tribute to Jewish fighters, while praising Poles, especially communists, for rendering assistance in the uprising. The indictment, which focused on Jewish victimhood and rebellion, was adapted largely from the two expert opinions submitted by researchers for the ŻIH, Artur Eisenbach and Bernard (Ber) Mark, the institute's director. The last part of the indictment described the killing of Polish civilians by the Selbstschutz unit under Stroop's command in 1939–40 and the execution of about 100 Poles in Warsaw on Stroop's orders on 16 July 1943.[95]

The first witness was Franz Konrad. His testimony was marked by self-serving contortions of the facts and by his efforts to distance himself both from Nazi ideology – in which he claimed to have no interest – and from Nazi anti-Jewish operations in the Warsaw Ghetto. To be sure, he had been head of the *Werterfassung*, but he now made every effort to minimize his own importance and the scope of its requisitions of Jewish property. He claimed to have no knowledge of the *Werterfassung*'s connection to Operation Reinhard. By his own account, his German colleagues had given him the nickname "king of the ghetto" because there were two Germans named Konrad. He denied that he had pocketed valuables that the *Werterfassung* requisitioned. He denied further that he had Jewish labourers in his labour battalion shot; indeed, he blamed Stroop for the shooting. On the contrary, by his own account he enjoyed the trust of Jews in the Warsaw Ghetto and did his best to protect them during German operations to liquidate it. He even claimed that he secretly transported the son of a Jewish family out of the ghetto. But his defence strategy mainly involved efforts to have his case overshadowed by Stroop's; this included deflecting blame for the suffering of Jews in the Warsaw Ghetto away from himself and placing it squarely on Stroop's shoulders. He recounted several instances in which Stroop personally ordered the execution of hundreds of Jews by firing squad during the liquidation of the ghetto, including 2,000 Jews in the courtyard of the Jewish Council (*Judenrat* in German). He testified further that Stroop was present at the execution of 500 Polish political prisoners from the Pawiak prison in the courtyard of the Jewish Council. When the prosecutor, Penner, asked him whether he took part in the murder of Jews during the liquidation of the ghetto, he shot back, "I was not active, I took photos."[96] Indeed, he cast himself in the role of a uniquely placed eyewitness to Stroop's crimes, as someone who was always by his side during the brutal suppression of the uprising. To a question from Stroop's defence counsel, Nowakowski, he replied: "I was like a neutral observer of all these things that took place there ... I knew that somehow I had to remember them, and, therefore, I even took photographs and made notes in my notebook." Those photographs and notes, he told Nowakowski, were intended to serve as proof "against Stroop" regarding "the liquidation of the Warsaw Ghetto and the liquidation of people."[97] But when Nowakowski asked Konrad whether he had heard of Treblinka, he answered that he heard of it only after the liquidation of the ghetto and that even then he thought it was a labour camp. As historian Katarzyna Person observes, "it is difficult today, at least, to determine what parts of his testimony were an account of actual events and which parts resulted from a line of defense based on a contrast between Konrad as a casual observer and Stroop, the brutal initiator of the pacification of the uprising."[98]

Stroop took the stand on the second day of the trial, 19 July 1951. He categorically denied the charges levelled against him in the indictment. His defence strategy was to shift blame onto others, deny that he was an antisemite, make excuses for treating the fighting in the Warsaw Ghetto as a frontline battle against an opposing army, paint the Jewish fighters as a formidable military opponent that was no different from an opposing army, and tell bald-faced lies in an effort to save his neck.

Stroop gave short shrift to Konrad's accusations against him. Indeed, he asserted, his adjutant had warned him to keep an eye on Konrad because of his duplicity and greed. Konrad, Stroop explained, had it in for him because he (Konrad) had been Sammern's right-hand man and accrued significant personal wealth due to Sammern's patronage – both were tied to Ostindustrie GmbH (Osti).[99] On arriving in Warsaw, Stroop had weakened Konrad's control in the ghetto, including his capacity to exploit the ghetto's inhabitants.

Stroop acknowledged that he had headed the Selbstschutz, but he denied that the ethnic German unit was responsible for the murder of any Poles.

By Stroop's own account, when he took over from Sammern his assessment of the situation, influenced by the heavy casualties on both sides, was that a battle was under way, and he responded as one would expect a soldier to respond. He denied responsibility for the tactical decision to set the ghetto on fire. He attributed the first recourse to fire during the uprising to the rebels' attempt to destroy a workshop in the ghetto. He asserted that he offered protection to inhabitants of the ghetto who voluntarily reported for resettlement, and he claimed that eventually thousands went voluntarily to the *Umschlagplatz*, a plaza on the edge of the ghetto to which Jews were led by force and where they were made to board trains bound for Treblinka. He denied any responsibility for deportations from the *Umschlagplatz*. Rather, to his chagrin, the rebels refused to go there voluntarily and took up arms instead. He presented the Jewish underground as a well-armed opposition force. He tried to convey the impression that the underground was equivalent to a conventionally equipped and trained military.

4.5 Defendant Jürgen Stroop in the witness box during his trial,
18–23 July 1951. United States Holocaust Memorial Museum, courtesy of
Leopold Page Photographic Collection.

On his own, Stroop invoked the Hague Convention to justify the kill-ing of the underground fighters, equating them to "francs-tireurs" or "partisans" – that is to say, unlawful combatants who upon capture were not entitled to prisoner-of-war status and could be subject to the death penalty. Stroop called them "bandits."[100] A judge then asked him whether it had occurred to him that Himmler's order to destroy the ghetto's Jewish civilian population and parts of the city that were un-armed was in violation of the Hague Convention. Stroop refused to budge from his position. "In that moment," he replied, "when sud-denly Himmler's order arrived, I was unable not to be aware of the fact that I was fighting, that Germany found itself in a state of war, I had an order for the cleansing of the ghetto, I was in combat, I had to wage combat."[101] When pressed by the judge whether after almost a month of liquidating the ghetto he had become aware that he was not waging conventional warfare, he replied that he had become aware that he was fighting "a battle, resistance that must be broken." He found justifica-tion for his treatment of *francs-tireurs* under the Hague Convention, to which, he claimed, Himmler had referred in his order to kill captured ghetto fighters. He claimed further that Himmler ordered him to de-stroy the ghetto's synagogue on the grounds that the rebels were stor-ing arms and congregating there. He asserted that he never killed any children or elderly.

But immediately after Stroop proffered his version of the events during the uprising, the judges and prosecutors confronted him with his report, which belied his testimony. For example, when Judge Hańczakowski asked him where apprehended Jews were transported to and to what end, Stroop claimed that Sammern had informed him that they and the machines from workshops located in the ghetto (in which goods for the German military were manufactured) would be transferred to Lublin or another camp, where Jews from Warsaw would continue with their previous tasks. But the judge pointed out that in his report from 25 April 1943 Stroop had written that darkness made the immediate liquidation of 1,690 captured Jews impracticable and that if he could not procure a train to T-II – that is, the extermination camp at Treblinka – they would be executed the following day. Stroop, who seemed discomfited by the question, replied that "T-II was a purely administrative matter." When the judge pressed him to explain why he used the term "liquidation" in the report if the ghetto's inhabitants were being sent for labour, he turned testy: "This is an editorial error … I didn't care about these reports, but that the order to cleanse the ghetto and that it would disappear, as Himmler had clearly and distinctly commanded, would be carried out by Sammern."[102] When the prosecutor asked him during cross-examination whether he knew the goal of deportations to T-II, he denied authorship of the reference in the introduction to his report to the deportation of 310,000 people for extermination between 22 July and 3 October 1942, and he attributed responsibility for the report's introductory narrative to Krüger and to Ludwig Fischer, governor of the Warsaw District. During his questioning of Stroop, Judge Hańczakowski further pointed to the report from 24 April that noted that the Jews and the "bandits" preferred to return to the flames rather than submit to Stroop's forces. He then pointedly asked Stroop whether he [Stroop] could treat as serious his testimony that he counted on the ghetto inhabitants whom he summoned to surrender voluntarily. "Yes," replied Stroop.[103] Stroop must have realized by now that the report was his undoing.[104]

The prosecution subjected Stroop to a withering cross-examination. An excerpt from it is illustrative of the prosecution's line of questioning and Stroop's evasive tactics. It also illustrates his ingrained Nazi mindset.

PROSECUTOR PENNER: Allow me to ask the defendant whether he admits that he carried out Himmler's orders to liquidate the ghetto in a resolute and determined manner, with complete meticulousness, and with complete precision.

DEFENDANT: Yes and no. There was no discussion of liquidation in my order. The order that I received from Sammern-Frankenegg and that he received personally from Himmler, read: "Cleanse the ghetto, move all people, machines, and stock elsewhere, in Lublin." Transportation lay in Globocnik's hands, and only then [was I to] demolish the ghetto as quickly as possible to make it disappear from the surface, so that in its place, where the ghetto had been, a green flat area, which would be suitable, with small cottages in a country style, would be built.

PROSECUTOR: If I understand the answer correctly, the burning of people, the melting, the murder of people, was the result of the resistance they mounted.

DEFENDANT: It was connected with the resistance, but it also resulted from the order that read that the ghetto should be destroyed and made to disappear from the surface.

PROSECUTOR: And from what resulted the order for the burning of children, women, and the elderly who mounted no resistance?

DEFENDANT: It was like this that buildings were emptied and we continually summoned these people to leave their homes.

PROSECUTOR: Yesterday an incident was presented to the defendant that when children appeared on ledges [of buildings], the defendant then gave the order to shoot the children.

DEFENDANT: I didn't see children on rooftops.

. . . .

PROSECUTOR: Does the defendant know that the resolutions of the Hague and Geneva Conventions do not apply to cases of aggressive war, in concrete cases the aggressor, who invades a country, may not use these clauses. What does the defendant think, did Germany commit aggression against Poland and other countries?

DEFENDANT: I am not a politician.

PROSECUTOR: The defendant calls himself a general, in addition he is a war criminal.

DEFENDANT: No, I am a general.

. . . .

PROSECUTOR: Does [the defendant] consider a crime such as the murder of children in accordance with his conscience?

DEFENDANT: As far as I know, children were not murdered. I am not charged with that. I have tried during my life always to act in a chivalrous manner.

. . . .

PROSECUTOR: Does the defendant today, in light of all that he has heard, in light of the material that has been revealed during the investigation, regard himself as a soldier or not?

DEFENDANT: I have always acted in my life as a soldier. I have always been a soldier and it seems to me that I'm not able to shed my skin.

PROSECUTOR: I believe that it is not befitting the position of a soldier and does not belong to the duties of a soldier to shoot children and the elderly as well as demolish buildings.

DEFENDANT: I didn't shoot at the elderly and children, but I was suppressing an uprising and resistance. It happens during war that buildings have to be demolished.

PROSECUTOR: In war – against whom? Against civilians?

DEFENDANT: In this case it doesn't matter. According to my understanding, if a country finds itself at war and wages a hard struggle for [its] existence, if an uprising, resistance broke out, it's appropriate to suppress it. If a state didn't do this, then in this case it would be committing suicide.[105]

The prosecutor further asked Stroop to clarify his view of Jews: "And what would be the defendant's position on the Jewish question?" Stroop approached this line of questioning gingerly, but he did himself no favours. His tortuous answers to the prosecutor's question and his convoluted digressions – all in an effort to distance himself from Nazi antisemitism – proved hard to swallow. For example: "When I arrived in Warsaw and there was resistance here, it didn't matter to me who mounted resistance, whether they were Jews or others. Such is my outlook." And: "I knew that the party has antisemitism as a goal. However, this is not proof that I had to be an active antisemite [just] because I was a [Nazi] Party member." The prosecutor asked: "When he burned down the ghetto, was the defendant aware of its [the operation's] antisemitic aim?" To which Stroop replied: "I think it has nothing in common with antisemitism."[106] Stroop's awkward and self-serving denials that he was antisemitic only reinforced the impression that he was indeed a stalwart antisemite.

The prosecution produced more than a dozen witnesses. They included, *inter alia*, ethnic Polish activists in the PPR who took part in its underground cell during the Nazi occupation, and Marek Edelman, Ryszard Walewski, and Bernard Borg, all three of them ghetto fighters. Edelman was the Bund's representative in the command structure of the Jewish Fighting Organization (Żydowska Organizacja Bojowa, ŻOB), its last commander who remained in Poland, since all the others had emigrated in the immediate postwar years. Walewski was a member of the PPR who had fought in the uprising in the ranks of the ŻZW. Borg, who had fought in the ŻOB, was also a PPR member and an activist in the Union of Former Political Prisoners (Związek Byłych Więźniów Politycznych). In the immediate postwar years he had served as a judge on the Polish Jewish honour court, which adjudicated cases of alleged Jewish collaborators with the Nazis.[107]

Person notes that "by 1952 there was no need to exploit the trial as an element of political struggle, while there remained a distinct aspiration to place Stroop's crimes in a historiographical narrative of Polish Stalinism."[108] The testimony of several witnesses supported this narrative, led by the first prosecution witness, Franciszek Łęczycki, a political activist whose testimony – or, to be more precise, speech – amounted to an ideological paean to the PPR-led communist underground, in which he had participated, embroidered with inflated details about how it had assisted Jewish fighters in the Warsaw Ghetto. Łęczycki made a point of underscoring the brotherhood of Poles and Jews and of refuting contemporary attempts – which evidently rankled him and other Poles – to blame Poles for the genocide of the Jews. Łęczycki, however, did not address the suffering of Poles in Warsaw and restricted himself in his testimony to the Jewish tragedy.[109]

Perhaps the most dramatic testimony of the trial was Edelman's. He stressed the wanton violence and disregard for human life that Stroop's SS units exhibited while suppressing the Warsaw Ghetto Uprising. He placed particular emphasis on the tactic Stroop devised to defeat the uprising: he set fire to the entire ghetto. Tens of thousands of Jews were killed in the flames, while Stroop's forces rounded up those who emerged from their bunkers and transported them to camps. Edelman contrasted the Germans' actions with the response of Jewish fighters: the latter acted in accordance with the rules of warfare, whereas Stroop's SS units were driven, in Edelman's words, "to commit murder and destruction."[110] Edelman laid the blame for the Germans' brutal destruction of the Warsaw Ghetto and its inhabitants squarely on Stroop's shoulders. "All the people burned in the ghetto and the blood of the murdered – this is Stroop."[111]

Walewski was another Jewish fighter who testified. His articulate and emotional testimony painted a vivid picture of a ferocious battle between Stroop's forces and the Jewish militants in the Warsaw Ghetto. Deeply imprinted on his memory were a ghetto ablaze as a result of the fires set by the Germans and their mass executions of apprehended Jews. He described Jewish fighters' attempts, fraught with danger, towards the end of the uprising to escape to the Polish or so-called Aryan side of the city through underground tunnels in the hope of joining partisan formations and fighting another day. He made much of the appearance of Soviet airplanes over Warsaw on the evening of 13 May, which prompted German forces to disperse. The flyover of Soviet military aircraft was an important psychological moment, but, he conceded – perhaps in an ideological slip-of-the-tongue – it did not render actual assistance to Jewish fighters on the ground.[112] In a nod to the political spirit of the times, Walewski punctuated his testimony with a rousing expression of faith that "nowhere and never again would there be a ghetto" in "a new era of progress, an era of humanism, and era of justice, that an era was approaching in which all of humanity, all corners of the world will become socialists. And this will be our greatest victory, this will be our greatest [article of] faith, that the nightmarish days of the occupation have vanished forever and a new happy life will come into existence."[113]

Although Stroop was the focal point of the trial, Konrad was not forgotten. The prosecution produced several witnesses who testified against him. For example, Karolina Markowa, a Jewish woman who worked in the office of the *Werterfassung*, testified that he remained indifferent as thousands of Jews who laboured under his command were deported; that he took part in the selection of 6,000 Jews who worked in a workshop taken over by the German industrial concern Toebbens, who were then led to the *Umschlagplatz* for deportation; that he ordered seven to nine Jewish workers shot; and that he led the *Werterfassung*'s personnel to the *Umschlagplatz* during the German operation to liquidate the ghetto in January 1943.[114]

The last prosecution eyewitness to testify was Marek Bitter, a leading figure in the Jewish community in postwar Poland. Like several witnesses who preceded him, Bitter described in vivid terms the suffering of the ghetto's Jewish inhabitants during the assault by Stroop's units. Their flame-engulfed bunker – in which Bitter and his family had hidden with other Jews – was discovered by the SS, who with wanton cruelty herded them to the *Umschlagplatz* for deportation. There, Bitter testified, he saw Stroop, while supervising the operation, shoot and kill a young Jew from his bunker and an additional twenty to thirty Jews with his own hands. Bitter concluded his testimony on an emotional note: "I would like to add one thing, I bid the court. Today I am seeing this bandit for the second time. It makes no difference whether he was present at a particular act of murder or not, Stroop is answerable for everything. Everyone who perished at that time in the ghetto perished at his hands."[115] On cross-examination Bitter conceded that he learned from an acquaintance that Stroop had killed the young man with his own hands. In other words, in this regard his testimony was hearsay. Bitter's testimony provoked a vehement reaction from Stroop, who requested permission to speak in rebuttal. "Never in my life," Stroop sought to assure the court, "have my hands ever shot anyone, never in my life have they killed anyone, nor grabbed, nor hit. How is it possible that I, in my position, as a general, went and started shooting. Such a thing never happened and never would."[116] Incensed by what he perceived as Stroop's impertinence, the prosecutor tried to wring an admission out of him that he had issued orders to shoot Jews or to burn buildings that they inhabited, but Stroop would not budge.

The prosecution solicited several expert opinions. Stanisław Kubiak, an employee at Polish Radio in Poznań who had researched German crimes in the Warthegau, described for the court the Nazis' policy to Germanize the region by importing ethnic Germans living in other parts of Poland while expelling ethnic Poles eastward. In addition, leading Polish civilians were targeted for execution, which was entrusted to various regional units of the Selbstschutz, whose manpower was supplied by ethnic Germans. Stroop led the Selbstschutz in Poznań in 1939 and then in Gniezno 1940 and was responsible for the execution of hundreds of innocent Poles.[117]

Bernard Mark, the director of the ŻIH, read his expert report into the record. Mark's testimony largely toed the Communist Party line. In his report he bent over backwards to accentuate Polish support for Jews in the Warsaw Ghetto, especially from the PPR. Leading the resistance in the ghetto was the ŻOB, which, Mark claimed, was inspired to act by the Soviet victory over the Nazi military machine at Stalingrad – a victory that had undermined the myth of the Nazis' invincibility. Mark made it a point to link the Jewish and Polish resistance. He quoted one of Stroop's answers to the questionnaire he received from the ŻIH while he was sitting in jail awaiting his trial that his superiors had stressed that "'the uprising in the ghetto can become the beginning of a general uprising in Warsaw.'" Mark further emphasized that the liquidation of the Warsaw Ghetto presented the Germans with a challenge that the liquidation of other ghettos did not present: doing battle not only with Jewish fighters in the ghetto but also with Polish fighters outside the ghetto. The incompetent and ineffectual Sammern-Frankenegg was not suited to the task. "It was necessary," according to Mark, "for the implementation of Himmler's order [to liquidate the ghetto] to make use of a strong person (in the sense of Hitlerite ideology) and [a person] without scruples, a person from the first ranks of Himmler's school, a Hitlerite 'knight,' without fault and unblemished, a person ready [to commit] the most atrocious crimes. Such a person was Jürgen Stroop."[118] Mark added: "This is a fascist robot, the product of a fascist machine."[119] A large part of Mark's expert opinion was devoted to the heroism of Jewish fighters. Furthermore, his report directly addressed Stroop's actions. As he correctly observed, although Himmler ordered the "cleansing" of the ghetto, it was Stroop who decided on his own initiative to set the entire ghetto ablaze, street by street, apartment block by apartment block. In this part of his expert opinion Mark used Stroop's report to great effect, deftly demonstrating with Stroop's own words that setting fire to the ghetto became his main tactic in his overall effort to defeat the uprising, liquidate the ghetto, and eliminate thousands of Jews, thus relieving some pressure on the operation to deport them. According to Mark's detailed estimate, Stroop's report actually *under*counted the number of his victims – the true number was closer to 70,000. The final section of Mark's report amounts to a eulogy for Jews from all walks of life, in particular members of the Jewish community's intelligentsia, who fell victim to Stroop's forces. "Jürgen Stroop," concludes Mark's expert opinion, "is answerable for the organized murder of the last part of the Jewish people of Warsaw."[120] Also testifying for the prosecution in the name of the ŻIH was Artur Eisenbach.[121]

Additional reports in support of the prosecution's case by experts who did not testify in court were introduced into evidence. For example, in their report Ludwik Hirszfeld, a professor of medicine at the university in Wrocław and a world-famous microbiologist who himself had escaped with his family from the Warsaw Ghetto, and Jan Czekanowski, a professor of anthropology at the universities in Poznań and Lublin, debunked the scientific pretensions of the Nazis' racial relegation of Jews and Slavs to an inferior human status and their claim, which they used to justify ghettoization, that the Jews were natural carriers of diseases and the reason for the spread of epidemics.[122]

The two prosecutors – Penner, who conducted the prosecution against Stroop, and Rusek, who prosecuted Konrad – and the two defence attorneys – Nowakowski for Stroop and Palatyński for Konrad – made closing arguments. In an obligatory preamble, Penner paid obeisance to the Soviet Union, "the bastion," in his words, "of democracy and socialism," compared the fires in the North Korean capital of Pyongyang during the Korean War to the fires set in the Warsaw Ghetto, and castigated West German imperialism. That aside, Penner's preamble contained an analysis of the Third Reich's imperialistic ambitions and the pivotal role played by the Nazis' racial world view in their drive for *Lebensraum* in Eastern Europe, which encompassed the invasion of Poland and, above all, the destruction of the Soviet Union. "German fascism," he continued in this vein, "realized political discrimination of its making by directing it in the first instance against the population of Semitic extraction. The destruction of Jews was to be the first step in the realization of political Hitlerism; the second, which was to follow directly after the extermination of the Jews, was to be the subjugation and the systematic destruction of the Slavic peoples."[123] His preamble concluded, Penner got down to business. Setting aside three days' worth of testimony by the defendants and eyewitnesses and several expert opinions, Penner asserted Stroop's guilt solely on the basis of his notorious report, which Penner wielded like a rhetorical bludgeon, evoking the defendant's perfidy, Jewish suffering, the heroism of Jewish fighters led by the ŻOB, and, of course, the assistance rendered to the armed Jewish underground by the PPR. "Because of the fact that he destroyed people, burned people, wanted an earth without people," Penner said in his final appeal to the court, "sentence him to the only sentence that he deserves – the death sentence."[124] Rusek followed suit. After his own lengthy preamble in which he linked German capitalism to the confiscation of Jewish property and the destruction of the Jews, Rusek, invoking Eisenbach's expert testimony, situated Konrad in the context of the Nazis' exploitation of Jewish labour and looting of Jewish property. "Konrad," he averred, "was an active member of staff, very well oriented in the plans of the Hitlerite regime, and trusted officer among the commanders of the SS and police in the Lublin District, to whom Himmler entrusted ... the liquidation of the Jews on the territory of occupied Poland."[125] Moreover, Konrad not only played an integral role in Operation Reinhard and its offshoot, Osti, but also took advantage of the exploitation and despoliation of Warsaw's Jews to line his own pockets while turning a blind eye to their suffering, including that of those who laboured under him for the *Werterfassung*. His perfidy was cast into sharp relief when he personally led 3,000 of them to the *Umschlagplatz*, misleading them about the Germans' intentions; he had assured them that they and their families were being transferred to a labour camp, though he well knew they were being deported to Treblinka. Rusek asked that Konrad be sentenced to death.

Stroop's defence counsel, Nowakowski, turned the tables on the prosecution's accommodation to communist dogma to cast Stroop in the role of a hapless stooge of "capitalist patrons." "Stroop," Nowakowski argued, "was a condottiere of imperialistic capital," that is, a leader of a group of mercenaries in thrall to the interests of Nazi German capitalism.[126] Stroop, moreover, could not help but be affected by the cascade effect of Nazi racist and antisemitic propaganda, so that the actions associated with the crime of which he was accused "are not Stroop's acts, that there is no actual individualism in it, but that they are the acts of Hitlerism and the results of the ethnical and legal nihilism that were characteristic of Hitlerism."[127] Palatyński resorted to a similar line of argument in his representation of Konrad. "Konrad," in his words, "was

not the originator of these [Hitlerite criminal] forces but their product
– the product of capitalism, fascism, and imperialism."[128] Moreover,
Palatyński disputed the prosecution's version of the facts. Testimony by
several eyewitness demonstrated that Konrad was involved in the requisition of abandoned Jewish property but not in the physical destruction of the Jews – so asserted Palatyński. In the final analysis, the court
did not put much stock in the arguments of either defence counsel.

Stroop and Konrad were each given an opportunity to have the final
word before the court retired to consider a verdict. Stroop, by his own
reckoning, essentially followed the orders issued by his superiors. "As
a soldier, I carried out orders, believing that they were ultimately for
the fatherland," he said. To a question by the presiding judge, Stroop
expressed his faith that the verdict would be just. Konrad denied any
part in the annihilation of the Jews, insisting that his role was limited to the requisitioning of property left behind by deported Jews. He
claimed further that he tried to help Jews and that he informed Jews
who worked under him for the *Werterfassung* of impending deportations. He asked the court for a "just verdict." Neither defendant expressed remorse, neither pled for forgiveness, neither demonstrated a
scintilla of regret for the tens of thousands of lives lost.[129]

The judges then retired to their chambers. They returned to the courtroom the same day to announce the court's decision. It returned guilty
verdicts on all counts listed in the indictment. It found Stroop guilty of
membership in the SS, of the persecution and mass murder of Polish civilians while he was commander of the Selbstschutz in Poznań in 1939
and 1940, of ordering the execution of Poles in retaliation for an attack
by an anonymous perpetrator on a column of SA troops in July 1943
while he was SS and police leader in the Warsaw District, and, primarily, "from 19 April to 16 May 1943 in Warsaw," of

> leading an operation [*akcja*] whose objective was the evacuation [*wysiedle-
> nie*] from the Warsaw Ghetto of the remainder of the some 100,000 Jews
> shut there to the Lublin district for their extermination in extermination
> camps as well as the liquidation of the ghetto, with his orders he caused
> the apprehension and murder of 56,065 people as well as the death of ad-
> ditional tens of thousands of people in burning hideouts and underground
> canals, and moreover the demolition of building complexes in the ghetto,
> of synagogues located in the area outside the ghetto, as well as the plunder
> of the possessions of those apprehended and murdered.[130]

Konrad, for his part, was convicted of membership in the SS, of plundering Jewish property, and of taking part in the mass murder of the Jewish population in the Warsaw Ghetto in April and May 1943. For these crimes both Stroop and Konrad received the death penalty.

The court's justification for its judgment showed deference to communist dogma – but only to a small degree – while taking into account the victimhood of Poles and Soviet citizens. However, in the main, it stressed the pernicious and lethal role played by antisemitism in Nazi aggression. After announcing its guilty verdicts, the court commenced its delineation of the grounds for its ruling in the following words:

> Among the immeasurable crimes committed against conquered nations by the Hitlerite clique, which thanks to German and international big capital seized the government in 1933, the persecution of the Jews constitutes the most shameful and shocking chapter. The history of humanity does not know an example organized with such meticulousness and executed with such inhumanely bestial cruelty. Antisemitism was embraced in the program of the Hitlerite party and propagated by Nazi doctrine. After the Hitlerites' seizure of power, it was expressed in a series of regulations that gave the start to the systematic persecution of the Jews in the territory of the German Reich. After the beginning of war aggressions and the achievement of conquests, the Hitlerites extended their policy of extermination vis-à-vis the Jewish people in occupied territories and worked out a plan for the final annihilation of the Jews, the so-called Endziel, making preparations for the preparation of similar methods with reference to the Slavic peoples. Millions of innocent people, through horrible suffering, fell victim to his policy.
>
> This crime of genocide [ludobójstwo], unprecedented in its scope, was for the German Reich at the same time an undertaking fetching enormous profits. Through Operation Reinhard and the Ostindustrie the Hitlerites seized properties confiscated from Jews, exploited the workforce of Jewish slaves, then after killing their victims stole the personal belongings of the murdered. The lion's share of these profits fell to the large German industrialists and financiers, whose businesses were closely associated with American and English corporations and cartels.[131]

In workmanlike fashion the court addressed Stroop's accountability for the killings of Polish civilians by the Selbstschutz in Poznań and Gniezno when he was its local commander in 1939 and 1940 and for the reprisal killings of Polish hostages in Warsaw in July 1943. On the grounds that all shootings by the Selbstschutz had to be confirmed by the local commander and that the reprisal killings had been ordered by Stroop, the court found Stroop liable for the killings of the Polish civilians by the Selbstschutz when it was under his command, in line with the Nazis' repression of Polish national feelings in the annexed parts of Poland, and for the execution of the Polish hostages in Warsaw. When it came to Konrad, the court gave credence to the evidence that showed that he was Globocnik's deputy for the requisition of property left by deported Jews and that he helped Stroop with the final liquidation of the Warsaw Ghetto, in part by participating in the selection of Jews who worked for Osti; he sent some directly to their deaths and others to labour camps with deceitful promises to save them from annihilation. In other words, Konrad was responsible not only for the plunder of Jewish property, from which he profited handsomely, but also for participating in mass murder. The court categorically rejected his attempt to portray himself at trial as a defender of Jews, when he was in fact their persecutor.

But the focal point of the verdict was Stroop's role in the liquidation of the Warsaw Ghetto. The court meticulously described the Nazi genocide of the Jews in Poland. "The final objective of the Hitlerites in relation to the Jewish people," wrote the court, "was their complete destruction."[132] The court outlined the erection of ghettos in occupied Poland and then the deportation of their Jewish populations to death camps under the aegis of Operation Reinhard. After the second evacuation operation in the Warsaw Ghetto in January 1943 was suspended in the face of resistance by the ŻOB, Himmler issued an order in February to destroy the ghetto, but when SS and police leader Sammern-Frankenegg proved unsuited for the task, Stroop assumed command of the operation:

> The period encompassing the following twenty-eight days was a chain of the most brutal crimes committed systematically against the civilian population of the ghetto by units of the "Waffen-SS," Gestapo, police, and Wehrmacht. The human imagination fails at the attempt to reconstruct the course of events that led to the apprehension or annihilation of tens of thousands of inhabitants of the ghetto and the razing to the ground of this part of the city of Warsaw.[133] The key piece of evidence, to which the court resorted repeatedly, was Stroop's report. To be sure, its evidentiary value was complemented by eyewitness and expert testimony, but by assembling the report, Stroop had quite unwittingly – and literally – put his head in a noose.

The court categorically rejected Stroop's superior orders defence. It ruled:

> The whole operation of the liquidation of the ghetto, all the acts of murder and all the destruction, was Stroop's handiwork. The defendant's defense that he had only performed his duty as a soldier and followed the orders of his superiors, judging that they were in conformity with international law, are disputed by the facts ... The organization and the extent of the brutal acts of murder and executions prove that they were not spontaneous acts of immediate murderers but that the method of action was imposed by the commander of the operation ... by the person specially chosen for this operation, the defendant Stroop, who was fully conscious of his part in conducting the Hitlerite's anti-Jewish policy and embraced the countless murders of the inhabitants of the ghetto as expressive of his own will and intentions.[134]

The court roundly dismissed Stroop's reliance on the Hague Convention for justification of his troops' executions of the militants on account of his own dirty hands; Nazis, who had committed criminal acts in Poland, could not now seek refuge in the principles of the Hague Convention. Moreover, the judges were clearly irked by the cynicism inherent in this ploy. "Enlisting the Hague Convention in justification of these acts, which do not apply to the perpetrators of treacherous attacks like those committed by the Hitlerites in Poland in 1939, and the attempt to desecrate the participants in the heroic resistance with the stigma of 'bandits' create an impression of cynical derision."[135]

The court grappled with the actual number of those who fell victim to the operations of forces under Stroop's command and found itself unable to establish an exact figure. The number 56,065 was reported by Stroop in his report. Taking into account people who perished in the ruins of apartment buildings, bunkers, and canals, the court considered 56,065 the low end of the estimate of Stroop's victims. Based on the eyewitness testimony of Edelman and Walewksi and Mark's expert opinion, the court assumed that apart from these 56,065 people, thousands of additional people were seized and murdered by Stroop's units, while only a minimal number managed to survive.

Given the spirit of the times, it is not surprising that the verdict lauded the cooperation of the PPR and the Gwardia Ludowa (GL) – the underground fighting force formed by the PPR and supported by the Soviet Union – with the ŻOB in defending the ghetto, to which Jewish as well as Polish witnesses had testified. In the words of the court, the cooperation of the Jewish and Polish communist militants was "evidence of unbroken heroism and faith in the principles of Marxist-Leninist ideology." The verdict recounts attacks by the PPR and the GL on German forces outside the walls of the ghetto and efforts to save and hide Jewish fighters who escaped through the underground canals. The court concluded its praise of the cooperation between Jewish and Polish militants by quoting the Polish witness Łęczycki, a PPR activist: "'The ghetto did not wage a struggle between life and death, but only for a worthy death that would leave behind a deep, warm memory of fraternal struggle, of superhuman effort, among all honest people. The power of endurance of this small handful of the Jewish nation that remained fills us with a deep faith that the casualties, their blood overflowing, were not in vain, that truth and justice shall triumph.'"[136] Obligatory paeans to the assistance – however modest in reality – rendered by the communist underground to the Jewish armed resistance notwithstanding, the court's last word in this regard was in praise of the courage of the Jewish rebels.

According to the court, the August Decree, the law under which Stroop was indicted, prescribed the "severest punishment" for Stroop's crimes and indeed demanded an "obligatory death penalty." Moreover, it could find no mitigating circumstances in Stroop's case. The court's ultimate condemnation of Stroop was categorical and unequivocal:

> The character and extent of the crimes committed by Stroop, his arrogant attitude and evasive explanations, demonstrating not only a lack of remorse but also, on the contrary, that he still sticks to a Hitlerite worldview, did not permit the Court to discern any extenuating circumstances in Stroop's conduct. His actions attest to the fact that he is a type of person devoid of all human feelings, a fascist hangman [kat], tormenting his victims with cold brutality, whose utter elimination from human society is necessary.[137]

Public interest in the trial was high. *Folks-shtime*, a Yiddish-language newspaper supportive of the communist regime, reported that the courtroom was full for Stroop's and Konrad's trial and that the majority of those who attended "bore the pain and suffering during the period of the Hitlerite occupation in the Warsaw Ghetto."[138] The *Folksshtime* dubbed Stroop "the Hitlerite hangman."[139] Several mainstream periodicals, including *Życie Warszawy* and *Trybuna Ludu*, also sent correspondents to the trial. In general, the Polish press, while noting Stroop's assaults on Poland's overall population, stressed his anti-Jewish crimes – without, however, neglecting to toe the party line regarding the help rendered to Jewish ghetto fighters by the Polish leftist camp, particularly the PPR. After the verdict was returned, Polish radio reported that Stroop and Konrad were sentenced to death "for exterminating the Jewish population in the Warsaw ghetto during the German occupation."[140]

The convictions of Stroop and Konrad, and the sentences handed down to them, were upheld on appeal by Poland's Supreme Court on 7 December 1951. Their lawyers faulted the district court for reaching erroneous conclusions based on indirect and incomplete evidence of their level of participation in the crimes of which they were convicted. The high court, however, discovered no errors in the district court's establishment of the facts.[141] Stroop and Konrad and their attorneys then submitted petitions for clemency to the Polish president, Bolesław Bierut. Also, both men's wives wrote Bierut to plead for their husband's lives. Stroop had not changed his tune since the trial, and his own petition reflected this. He wrote that he had been raised as a soldier to follow orders and that he had always been indifferent to politics and political policies that implicated groups of people (bevölkerungspolitische Dinge). "My entire life was devoted to my fatherland and my family," he asserted. "Never in my life had I done or undertaken anything with the awareness that I could be punished for it."[142] Konrad's petition for clemency, written in Polish and probably translated from German, mirrored his testimony at trial. By his own reckoning, he had done his best to save a number of Jews from deportation and had "nothing in common" with Stroop's liquidation of the ghetto. "I tried to fulfill my duties in the spirit of a true soldier, avoiding all expressions of severity," he wrote. "I did not cover my hands in blood."[143] Because he considered Stroop a war criminal, he had felt it incumbent upon himself to testify against him before American military authorities as well as in Warsaw. Konrad went so far as to claim that since his imprisonment in Warsaw he had made a positive contribution to Poland's postwar reconstruction by working diligently in the prison's print shop. Both men's petitions for clemency, which were utterly devoid of introspection or remorse, were rejected in February 1952.[144]

Stroop and Konrad were hanged at the Mokotów prison on 6 March 1952.

One might ask whether this was a fair trial. Political elements infiltrated the proceedings in the form of an occasional nod to communist
dogma or expressions of praise for the Soviet Union from the judges,
lawyers, and witnesses associated with the PPR. But it would be incorrect to deem the trial politicized, since in 1951, when the trial was conducted, the communist regime had no compelling reason to pressure
legal officials to make it political in character. The prosecution's emphasis on the anti-Jewish dimension of Stroop's and Konrad's crimes,
which resonated with the court, further militates against an interpretation of the trial as politicized. To be sure, Stroop's request that a German
lawyer represent him was rejected by Polish legal officials, and no witnesses were summoned to testify on either Stroop's behalf or Konrad's.
That said, they were allowed to defend themselves robustly on the witness stand, and reasonable defences were mounted by their respective
attorneys. Both cases, however, were open-and-shut, Stroop's in particular; the evidence in support of their individual culpability was incontrovertible, and their convictions were, for all intents and purposes,
never in doubt. It is fair to say that in the trial of Stroop and Konrad,
justice – albeit imperfectly – was done.

Conclusion

In examining the Nazi terror system and the implementation of the
"Final Solution," a modern researcher faces several crucial and difficult questions: What motivated the German perpetrators to cast their
scruples to the wind? Were many German Nazis indeed oblivious to
the moral ramifications of their evil deeds, and did they act without
any hatred in their hearts for their victims, as Hannah Arendt argued in
her controversial 1963 book *Eichmann in Jerusalem*? Did the brutalizing
and corrosive effects of war impel the perpetrators to genocidal actions,
as emphasized by Christopher Browning? Were a large number of perpetrators diehard Nazis who hated Jews and Slavs and others whom
Nazism deemed racially inferior to the degree that they were willing to
resort to any means, including unfathomable violence, to eliminate or
enslave them? Or must the researcher assume that, as Mark Roseman
argues, "there was never just one kind of perpetrator"?[145]
    Having observed the trial of Adolf Eichmann, Hannah Arendt con-
cluded that the key to his personality was the "banality" of his character, the implication being that many Nazis were morally opaque,

indifferent to their victims and bearing them no malice. In other words, most Nazis were not bloodthirsty creatures but "ordinary" men who were just following orders or going through the motions, doing what was expected of them, precisely as they argued in their trial defences. To be sure, some German war criminals fit Arendt's conclusions, but many others were driven by ideological conviction or self-serving motives.

While Polish courts in general exposed the *modus operandi* and sheer brutality of the Nazi terror system, the trials of Himmler's men demonstrated that the perpetrators were a highly heterogeneous group, hailing from different age groups and social backgrounds and exhibiting different personalities. The men who perpetrated the destruction varied not only in background but also in their psychological attributes. Some were so-called *Exzesstäter* or gratuitously brutal murderers who enjoyed humiliating, torturing, and killing their victims out of greed, ideological conviction, and other base motives. The top Nazi leadership did not promote excessive brutality – indeed, high-ranking Nazis preferred fast, orderly, and "clean" killing. That said, serial murderers like Riemann and Grzimek played a decisive role in the killing process in the Jewish ghettos and the concentration camps. Many had served in the Weimar police and after the Nazi rise to power (*Machtergreifung*) applied their skills, diligence, and energy to carrying out the ensuing terror and genocide. Still others were *Weltanschauungstäter* (ideologically motivated perpetrators, perpetrators who were true believers) who perceived the Nazi struggle through the prism of Social Darwinism, which explained all problems in racial and biological terms. Accordingly, they carried out mass murder as part of a "crusading mission" against Jews, followed by Slavs, communists, liberals, and "social undesirables." Naturally, all of these personality types often overlapped; sheer zeal folded together a number of categories.

Still, upon joining the SS one did not instantly become a "willing executioner." One prominent psychologist has argued convincingly that many who joined did not "become mass murderers as soon as their environment allowed it."[146] In his study of SS personality types, George Browder concluded that their behaviour was rooted not in "defective personalities, but in the processes they experienced that legitimized participation in mass inhumanity."[147] Many defendants, besides having been thoroughly indoctrinated by various Nazi organizations, acquired substantial "field experience." Thus, as a career policeman Macholl fought the political opposition during the Weimar Republic; then in 1939 he was assigned to an *Einsatzgruppe* V. Similarly, Riemann was a member of *Einsatzgruppe* IV and then joined the Pawiak prison crew, while Grzimek served with the SSPF office in Kraków before his departure for East Galicia. Stroop developed a reputation for liquidating civilians in Poland and Ukraine before leading the erasure of the Warsaw Ghetto and suppression of the Warsaw Ghetto Uprising. Thus, Riemann, Grzimek, Macholl, Stroop, and their ilk shared a crucial commonality – ideological training and professional development prepared them to execute the regime's infernal program. They had been socialized to do evil.

Yet when they came face to face with judicial retribution, the defendants' tough personae vanished into thin air and none of them stood by their beliefs and convictions. To the contrary – when confronted with overwhelmingly incriminating evidence, they resorted to calculated self-justifications and outright lies to save their skins, claiming to have acted out of duty, under orders, or for the "good of Jews." Not one of them admitted to having harboured "bad feelings" towards his victims, and all appealed their sentences as "unfair." Riemann willingly betrayed his Gestapo colleagues to the Allied authorities and expressed his eagerness to help combat the Nazi underground movement. In his appeal of his death sentence, he accused all the witnesses of being Gestapo confidants who wanted to get rid of him as an "undesirable" witness.[148]

Interviewed in his cell by Aleksander Omiljanowicz, a functionary of the Polish security service and amateur author, Macholl conceded that he knew full well about the massacres of civilians and the gassing of Jews and the mentally ill.[149] In the courtroom, however, he claimed that only "some" of the arrestees were shot and that he never heard of extermination by gas. When, in the prosecutor's office, Macholl encountered Chaim Wróbel, who would offer important testimony against him, he begged him not to testify against him in court, justifying his actions by his duty to obey superior orders. In the courtroom, he blatantly denied knowing anything about the gruesome tasks of *Sonderkommando* 1005.[150] Likewise, Stroop denied all responsibility for his actions. By his reckoning, he had done what he had been trained to do ever since he had become a soldier: obey the orders of his superiors.

Some of the key defendants in the Polish trials of Nazis held between 1948 and 1953 had conducted themselves as exemplars of an extraordinarily violent culture, one that Himmler's SS and the Nazi police state had brought into being and carefully fostered. Indoctrination into a cruel and xenophobic ideology had been essential for transforming them into willing and reliable tools of the regime. SS training effectively promoted a double-morality. That training rationalized their actions as being in Germany's best interests; at the same time, it unleashed their basest drives while offering total immunity for the crimes they committed while giving in to those drives. After the outbreak of the war, they specialized in different forms of violence, according to what specific circumstances required. Setting aside their varying degrees of acquiescence to evil, the different types of perpetrators complemented and reinforced one another. This greatly strengthened the Nazi terror system as it strove to establish Hitler's "utopian" society.[151]

Chapter Five

Jews, Poles, and Justice

Polish antisemitism bedevilled relations between ethnic Poles and Polish Jews not only during the Nazi occupation of Poland but also in the post-war era, even "after Auschwitz." Moreover, Stalinization in Poland, which manifested itself in the communist regime's suppression of independent Jewish organizational life in the late 1940s and early 1950s and in the intimidation of certain prominent Jews in 1952–3, alienated the ever diminishing number of Jews who remained in Poland. Thousands who had clung to the dream of rebuilding Jewish life in Poland even after several antisemitic pogroms, culminating in the massacre of forty-two Jews in Kielce in July 1946, left the country by the end of the decade, while those 70,000 who stayed after 1950 – by 1961 barely 37,000 remained – were constantly looking over their shoulders. Yet from the end of the war through the 1950s there was a meeting of the minds between Poles and Jews regarding punishment for Nazi criminals, and both were eager to see German Nazis stand trial in a Polish dock. In harmony with the sentiments of ordinary Poles and Jews, the authorities in the postwar communist state and the reconstituted Jewish leadership in Poland after the Holocaust shared a strong mutual interest in prosecuting Nazi criminals in Polish courts. But Polish Jews had no intention of being relegated to the sidelines while the government pursued Nazis; they were determined to take part in the effort to bring German perpetrators to justice. Polish legal officials and institutions mostly welcomed their assistance in this effort.

But Jewish participation in Polish trials of Nazis did not come without a cost. As Natalia Aleksiun points out, "Jewish preparations for future trials required support of the Polish authorities."[1] In the volatile political climate that prevailed in Poland immediately after the war, Jews had to be careful not to provoke official disapproval by arguing too aggressively that Polish Jews had suffered uniquely under the Nazis. Jews were acutely aware of their dependence on the regime and that they would have to adjust if they wanted to contribute to Poland's legal pursuit of Nazis. So in this chapter we explore Jews' stake in bringing Nazi criminals to justice, the part they played, and the constraints under which Jews, especially Jewish historians, were forced to operate if they hoped to play a role in the trials.

History in the Service of Justice

During the Holocaust, many Polish Jews painstakingly recorded the Jewish plight under the Nazis in personal diaries and ghetto chronicles and contributed to underground ghetto archives like *Oyneg Shabes*, the clandestine archival endeavour in Warsaw spearheaded by Emanuel Ringelblum. Inspired by their example, many survivors dedicated themselves after the war to documenting the Holocaust and commemorating the victims. The first contingent of Jewish survivors to arrive in liberated Lublin organized an *ad hoc* historical commission in August 1944. Although this embryonic effort stalled, it was followed by the formal creation in Łódź in December 1944 of the CŻKH (Tsentrale Yidishe Historishe Komisye in Yiddish) under the leadership of Philip (Filip in Polish) Friedman (1901–1960). Local branches of the CŻKH existed in several Polish cities; the most active were in Warsaw and Kraków. In 1947 the central office of the CŻKH moved to Warsaw and was reorganized into the ŻIH. Nachman Blumental (1905–1983), director of the CŻKH after Friedman, then became the ŻIH's first director, followed by Bernard (Ber) Mark (1908–1966), who took over in 1949. The CŻKH's founders and the personnel of the CŻKH and the ŻIH were university-trained historians and journalists, writers, and other members of the Jewish intelligentsia.

The CŻKH and then the ŻIH operated under the aegis of the Central Committee of Jews in Poland (Centralny Komitet Żydów w Polsce, CKŻP) until the communists dismantled the latter in 1950. The CKŻP was the principal representative body of Polish Jewry until its dissolution, and until the late 1940s it helped promote a sense of ethnic solidarity among Jewish survivors, both those who remained in Poland during the war and those who returned there afterwards. But its financial support of the CŻKH and then the ŻIH was unreliable, and the more the CKŻP came under the influence of Jewish communists, the more pressure it exerted on Jewish historical institutions to toe the Communist Party line.

The Social and Cultural Association of Jews in Poland (Towarzystwo Społeczno-Kulturalne Żydów, TŻSK), the CKŻP's successor, was unable to finance the ŻIH; it came under the control of the Ministry of Education and Science and was supervised by a public board of trustees, but the TŻSK's leadership, which was dominated by communists, still kept it on a tight leash. In the 1950s – especially in the first half of the decade, when Poland was in the grip of Stalinism – the ŻIH faced enormous political pressure to help legitimize communist rule in Poland. Jewish leaders who were close to the centre of power in Warsaw expected the ŻIH to represent the Holocaust through a Marxist and universalizing lens. This entailed de-emphasizing Jewish suffering and overstating the role of communists in Jewish resistance to Nazism, while assigning blame for the rise of Nazism to capitalist countries, in particular the United States, which even now, according to communist propaganda, was in league with a revanchist West Germany and other fascist holdovers to overturn the social progress initiated by the Soviet Union and its allies, not least of which was Poland.[2] If the personnel of the CŻKH and then the ŻIH hoped to do justice to the Jewish victims of Nazi atrocities while remaining mindful of communist dictates, they would have to undertake a delicate balancing act.

Diarists and ghetto chroniclers had made a point of establishing a record of German anti-Jewish crimes. Both Jewish historical commissions set out to document the fate of Polish Jewry during the German occupation; as part of this mandate, and in an effort to bring Nazi criminals to justice, they gathered evidence of Nazi anti-Jewish crimes.[3] Indeed, the commissions' founders and personnel considered recovering wartime evidence of Nazi crimes – especially documents generated by Jews – essential to their mission. To that end, the CŻKH's staff not only retrieved Jewish and German documents but also collected the testimonies of some 7,000 survivors. Yosef Kermish, one of the CŻKH's founders, pushed for the collection of survivor testimony. In an instructional manual for interviewers of survivors, he emphasized the "sacred duty" of survivors to give testimony, a "first-class ... source," in his view, "for compiling an indictment against the entire German people and every German ... who took part in a specific crime."[4] "The main thought of all surviving Jews," he later wrote in a 1947 report on the CŻKH's activities, "was to collect the entire documented record of incriminating materials in order to mete out punishment to all criminals [and] in order to show the world what fascism is capable of."[5] Blumental referred to the collection of documentary evidence for use in trials of Nazis as "practical history."[6] Personnel at the CŻKH and later the ŻIH maintained two extensive card files on some 10,000 suspected Nazi war criminals, one organized alphabetically, the other according to the places where they committed their alleged crimes, whether it be cities and towns or labour, concentration, and extermination camps. They also prepared documents for use not only at trials but also in extradition requests.

The CŻKH's and then the ŻIH's personnel worked closely with Polish judicial authorities and institutions from the end of the war through the 1950s. They assisted high-ranking officials at the Ministry of Justice and the state-sponsored GKBZN, as well as officials at the NTN, Polish representatives at the UNWWC, prosecutors at Polish provincial courts, and even the Ministry of State Security (Ministerstwo Bezpieczeństwa Publicznego, MBP), which was notorious for its persecution of noncommunist elements), in the endeavour to investigate Nazi war crimes and prosecute them in Polish courts. Along the way, the CŻKH and ŻIH exchanged information about Nazi criminals with Jewish organizations in other countries that were working with their own local authorities to haul German Nazis into their national courts.[7]

The involvement of individual Jews and Jewish institutions took various forms. In 1945, representatives of the CŻKH and the GKBZN conducted joint investigations of various concentration and death camps. In 1946 the CŻKH prepared a report and sent documents to the Polish delegation at the IMT through the GKBZN. Jewish historians and activists questioned Jürgen Stroop before his trial. The CŻKH and later the ŻIH compiled documents for prosecutors pertaining to Nazis who had been active in Poland, and representatives of both Jewish institutions appeared as expert witnesses for the prosecution at several high-profile trials. Jewish eyewitnesses also testified. Meanwhile, not only Nazi trials held in Poland but also the Nuremberg Trial (and even the Eichmann Trial in Jerusalem in 1961) received extensive coverage in the resuscitated postwar Jewish press in both Yiddish and Polish; along the way, Jewish newspapers proudly reprinted the expert opinions of Jewish historians in Polish courts.[8] In other words, Jews, driven by what they considered their sacred duty, were deeply involved in trials of Nazis in Poland.[9]

Philip Friedman and the Nuremberg Trial

Polish Jews were eager to have a say in the prosecution of the major war criminals standing trial before the IMT. The CŻKH envisaged for itself a key role in the proceedings. It was keen to assist in the preparation of the indictment and the production of evidentiary materials for the tribunal. In this vein, it passed documents and survivors' testimonies in its possession pertaining to the death camps of Treblinka, Sobibór, and Bełżec to the GKBZN, which in turn transmitted them to the Polish delegation at Nuremberg. Moreover, in the fall of 1945 the CŻKH appealed to the leadership of the CKŻP to create a public forum for Polish Jews to react to the Nuremberg Trial, and the historical commission convened a public meeting of representatives of Jewish political parties and social organizations to discuss the trial and to mobilize support for sending a Jewish delegation to Nuremberg.[10]

Philip Friedman in particular was behind the effort to promote the involvement of Polish Jews and the CŻKH in the Nuremberg proceedings. Friedman emerged from his hiding place on the "Aryan" side of Lwów when it was liberated by the Soviets in 1944, but he had lost his entire family. A highly respected historian of Polish Jewry even before the war, in November of the same year he went to Lublin, where the survivors gathered there placed him in charge of the newly formed CŻKH, which, relocated to Łódź, burgeoned swiftly under his direction into a serious research institute devoted to the documentation, study, and commemoration of the Holocaust in Poland. Friedman himself developed into a prolific scholar of the Holocaust, publishing several important studies in the first several years after liberation. He forged close ties with the GKBZN, serving on the board of its Łódź branch, taking part in the delegation sponsored by the Polish and Jewish commissions to Auschwitz and Chełmno, and consulting with the GKBZN and Polish prosecutors while they were collecting materials pertaining to Nazi anti-Jewish crimes for impending war crimes trials. During a trip to Nuremberg in the summer of 1946 to observe the IMT in action, Friedman decided not to return to Poland and resigned from the CŻKH. He visited the tribunal in the summer of 1946.[11] Like many other Jews, he initially planned to stay in Poland and rebuild Jewish life there after the war; however, he was induced to leave by Polish antisemitism and his apprehension about the independence of historical scholarship, which was coming under increasing pressure from both Jewish communists and the regime to serve as a vehicle for propaganda. Arriving in New York in 1948, he remained a prolific scholar of the Holocaust until his death.[12]

In the preface to his 1945 book on the destruction of the Jews of Lwów, Friedman stressed the urgency of preparing material for the IMT. In the introduction, dated December 1945, he wrote: "It is necessary at this very moment to give a systematic overview of the Lwów events ... It is a necessity now, when before the free nations of the world, the criminals sit on the bench in order to receive their just punishment."[13] Thanks to Friedman's close ties with the GKBN, the Jewish historical commission forwarded materials to the Polish delegation to Nuremberg, and he received an invitation from Stefan Kurowski, the delegations' head, to submit a report to it on the destruction of Polish Jewry at the hands of the Nazis.[14] The two-part report was written in German, which Friedman knew well, given that his doctorate was from the University of Vienna. The title of the longer first part was "Deutsche Verbrechen gegen die jüdische Bevölkerung in Polen" (German Crimes against the Jewish Population in Poland), the title of the second "Die Motive des Verbrechens" (Motives for the Crime). What did Friedman highlight in the report?

Friedman required no time to come to the point. In the report's very first sentence he wrote: "The absolute annihilation of the Jewish population in Europe was one of the goals that the German regime wanted to achieve in its provocation of a second world war."[15] The report proceeded thoroughly and systematically to depict the Nazi genocide of Polish Jewry in both annexed western Poland and the General Government from the moment of the German invasion to the end of the war. It listed the multitude of anti-Jewish decrees that set the stage for the commission of German crimes against Jews. Highlighted and described in detail were the establishment of ghettos and the deterioration of living conditions in them from bad to worse, with an emphasis on the ghettos in Warsaw and Łódź; the conscription of Jews for forced labour; the liquidation of ghettos; and the deportation of Jews to concentration and death camps and their annihilation there, with an emphasis on Auschwitz and Treblinka. Also discussed in the report were the creation of Jewish councils, the confiscation of Jewish property, and the organized hunt for Jews who tried to evade the Nazi dragnet by going into hiding. The report painstakingly counted up the Jewish population in Poland on the eve of the war, the number of Jews in German-annexed western Poland, in German-occupied central Poland, and in Soviet-occupied eastern Poland, and the number of Jewish fatalities, which it put at around 3,000,000. The report assigned responsibility for German anti-Jewish crimes from Hitler on down through the top brass in the military to the SS and the civil administration in the General Government, particularly Hans Frank. But, the report concluded, it was the German people, who in their enthusiastic support for the Nazi regime had morphed into a "criminal nation" (*Verbrechervolk*), who bore ultimate responsibility for the crimes.[16] In short, the report was an exhaustive history of the Holocaust in Poland, remarkable especially when one takes into account that it was written within one year after the end of the war and under fluid conditions for scholarship, during a period of gathering documentation and testimony.

Since Friedman's report was undated, it is unclear when he started or completed it and when it reached the hands of the lawyers in the Polish delegation to Nuremberg. Since the language in the Polish indictment's description of the anti-Jewish crimes in Poland and of the fate of Polish Jewry under Nazi occupation did not appear to be influenced by Friedman's report, it probably arrived in Nuremberg after the Soviets had presented the Polish indictment, dated 22 January 1946, to the IMT. Support for this conjecture comes from a document dated 11 January 1946 in which Friedman listed and corrected errors in the December 1945 penultimate draft of the Polish indictment pertaining to the Nazis' anti-Jewish crimes, followed by one-and-a-half handwritten pages of a few suggested supplements to the indictment's enumeration of the Nazi persecution of Polish Jews. Friedman indicated that to the Polish indictment's catalogue of anti-Jewish crimes he would have added the denial of Jews' civil rights, the economic exploitation of Jews, the Nazi campaign of terror and pogroms in which thousands of Jews perished, and round-ups and executions. He also would have stressed the destruction of Jews in hundreds of labour camps. It stands to reason that he would not have had sufficient time between 11 and 22 January to write a lengthy report and then have it reach the Polish delegation in time to have what he wrote incorporated in the Polish indictment before its submission to the tribunal. If Friedman sent a comprehensive report to the Polish delegation after the presentation of the Polish indictment to the IMT, it might have been intended largely for the edification of the delegation's members and to provide them with more thorough knowledge of the Nazi genocide of the Jews when the Polish lawyers discussed the trial with representatives of the various prosecution teams.[17]

In the Fields of Treblinka

A high level of cooperation characterized relations between the two Jewish historical institutions and the state-sponsored GKBZN. As mentioned already, the appointed task of the GKBZN, established in March

1945 by the presidium of the KRN, and vested in November of the same year with statutory authority, was, in cooperation with the Polish justice and foreign affairs ministries in their pursuit of Nazi war criminals, to document details of German crimes committed on Polish soil. Established in Lublin, it moved to Warsaw, and like the CŻKH it had branch offices in various Polish cities. Its remit and the briefs of the two Jewish historical bodies were in total agreement, and the GKBZN welcomed their assistance. In this spirit, Friedman was appointed to the GKBZN's Łódź branch; and, with the participation of a representative of the Jewish historical commission, the Warsaw branch created a special section for the investigation of Nazi crimes against Jews.[18]

In May 1945 the CŻKH and the GKBZN dispatched to Chełmno (Kulmhof) the first of several joint delegations to investigate the sites of former death camps. Subsequent joint expeditions travelled to Auschwitz, Majdanek, and Treblinka.[19] The first volume of the GKBZN's annual journal, *Biuletyn Głównej Komisji Badania Zbrodni Niemieckich w Polsce*, published in 1946, included articles on Chełmno and Treblinka that were written as a result of the official visits to those former camps. An English-language translation of the first volume was given to prosecutors at Nuremberg.

The visit to Treblinka on 5–7 November 1945 exemplified these joint investigations. The leader of the delegation to Treblinka was Zdzisław Łukaszkiewicz, a judge from the provincial court in Siedlce, a town southeast of the camp. Other participants in the delegation from the Polish state commission included J. Maciejewski, a district attorney in Siedlce, and M. Tratsald, a licensed surveyor. The judge and the district attorney had been conducting their investigation since August of the same year, inspecting the former grounds of the camp and interviewing witnesses. Representing the CŻKH were Rachel Auerbach and Yosef Kermish. Accompanying them were five Treblinka survivors, including Samuel Rajzman (the same Samuel Rajzman who testified at Nuremberg), several local officials, and a press photographer. When it arrived, the delegation toured the site of the former death camp and interviewed local residents. After the site visit, the delegation wrote a report for the judicial authorities.

The official report was signed by Łukaszkiewicz and Maciejewski and dated 22 November 1945. It was a professional and compact overview of the origins, physical layout, and operations of Treblinka based on the inspection of its former grounds and interviews with twelve of its survivors and twenty-three local residents, including railway employees who had a hand in transporting Jews to the camp. The Germans had made efforts to conceal their crimes by ploughing over the camp before leaving the area. The report, however, was able to make note of the large number of bones and other human remains on or just below the surface, in addition to personal valuables and an unusual amount of ashes covering the pits in which the corpses of the victims had been burnt. The report described in detail the transporting of Jews from Poland and throughout Europe in freight trains to the gates of Treblinka, their selection on arrival, their murder in the gas chambers, the burial of their bodies in mass graves, and later their disinterment and burning, followed by the disposal of the ashes. It also described the composition of Treblinka's personnel, consisting of German staff supported by subordinate Ukrainian guards. It further depicted the grisly labour assigned to the small number of ill-starred Jews who were selected to take part in the *Sonderkommando*. The report estimated that, based on an assessment of the number of transports to Treblinka and their capacity, the death toll at Treblinka was between 1,300,000 and 1,500,000. (Contemporary scholars put the number of victims at 875,000 to 925,000.) According to the report, apart from Jews, a significant number of Roma (Gypsies) and a small number of Poles were among the camp's victims. But, the report concluded, the Nazis' primary aim in constructing Treblinka was unequivocal. "The annihilation camp at Treblinka ... was meant without any doubt to be for the annihilation of the Jews." Although the report was written largely in a matter-of-fact style, emotionally charged words and phrases were scattered throughout it. Thus when prisoners alighted on the platform after their train had arrived at the camp, the guards treated them "in a brutal way." The report added that "the treatment [of prisoners selected to work] ... was marked by brutality and cruelty."[20]

In the wake of the delegation's visit to Treblinka, Łukaszkiewicz wrote a slim book intended for an ethnic Polish audience. *Obóz straceń w Treblince* (Extermination Camp in Treblinka), published in 1946, was a polished piece of expository prose in which the author, now freed from the constraints entailed in writing an official report, was able to vent his emotions. Early in the book he drew the readers' attention to the mounds of ashes from burnt corpses and the presence of bones visible on the surface. Drawing heavily from the testimonies of Treblinka survivors, Łukaszkiewicz described the camp's establishment and *modus operandi* in great detail. He listed the camp's SS authorities, viewing them, along with the Ukrainians under their command, with obvious contempt. "Normal people," he wrote, "will never be able to understand how those individuals, living and executing their hellish functions among the constant wailing of the victims, in the fetid air caused by the corpses, in the stench of burning bodies, did not lose the external trait of what it is to be human. It is certain only that the human sprit did not remain in them."[21]

By contrast, he portrayed their Jewish victims in sympathetic terms, and Jews who were selected to labour inside the camp with admiration. Despite the horrific conditions that prevailed in the camp, "there were, however, among the workers people who did not crack spiritually."[22] Lest his readers presume that Jews were passive victims, he devoted several pages to the prisoner uprising in August 1943. In describing what transpired at the camp, Łukaszkiewicz took pains to situate it in context. "It is necessary to remember," he wrote, "that Treblinka is the type of annihilation camp on a scale [previously] unencountered."[23] As becomes evident from his different estimates of the number of victims in his initial report, in the article in the first volume of *Biuletyn Głównej Komisji Badania Zbrodni Niemieckich w Polsce*, and in his book, Łukaszkiewicz was continually grappling with and adjusting his figures. In his book he estimated that Treblinka claimed around 800,000 victims, taking pains to calculate as accurately as possible on the basis of the testimony of Jewish prisoners and Polish railway employees the number of transports and the number of Jews in each transport. But, in his view, the precise number of victims of an atrocity of this scale was beside the point. "Treblinka is such an exceptional place in the history of atrocious crimes that an inflation of the number of victims is not necessary for imparting its great terribleness. Is a number of about 800,000 people killed still too small?"[24] Nevertheless, Łukaszkiewicz felt compelled to complete this exercise in response to people who, fortunate enough not to have lived in Poland under Nazi occupation, doubted his estimates. He wrote: "To these people I pose a simple question: What became of millions of European Jews?"[25] He concluded that the evidence "left no doubt that Treblinka was intended for the destruction of individual members of the Jewish people."[26]

Like Łukaszkiewicz, Rachel Auerbach (Rokhl Oyerbakh in Yiddish) (1903–1976) was inspired to write a book about the delegation's visit to Treblinka. But her book, *Oyf di felder fun treblinke* (In the Fields of Treblinka), published in 1947, was written not in Polish but in Yiddish and was intended for a Jewish readership. She made her intention clear early in the foreword: "Let all Jews know [what was done to

Jews]: It is their national duty *to know the truth.*"[27] Auerbach herself was a survivor. A journalist before the war, she was a key participant in Emanuel Ringelblum's clandestine archive in the Warsaw Ghetto. After the war she played a leading role in the CŻKH until her emigration to Israel in 1950.[28]

Auerbach's book was very different from Łukaszkiewicz's in style. It was a poignant and impressionistic collage inspired by the delegation's tour of Treblinka: a description of how Jews were killed, culled largely from the accounts of the survivors who were her travelling companions as well as from testimonies in the CŻKH's possession; a description of the German SS and Ukrainians who manned the camp; a portrait of several Treblinka victims and survivors; a snapshot of the landscape in which the camp was situated; and the reactions of the survivors in the delegation when they set foot there – all interspersed with philosophical digressions. Although Auerbach was able to flee and hide outside the ghetto, thereby evading deportation to Treblinka, she was no stranger to the camp. While still residing in the ghetto, she recorded the testimony of Abraham Krzepicki, one of the first escapees from Treblinka, for the underground archive.[29]

Like Łukaszkiewicz, Auerbach viewed Treblinka's Jewish prisoners with admiration. Although a few of them may have beaten other Jews or informed on them out of fear of the Germans or succumbed to the Germans' dehumanization of them, many "remain human beings as before. No, they develop even further." Evidence of their successful effort to preserve a flicker of humanity was the revolt. For Auerbach the revolt was positive because the prisoners' "plan placed emphasis not so much on saving the lives of participants as much as on *executing tasks*: destroying the camp, killing the SS, and even freeing Jewish workers at the neighboring penal camp, Treblinka I."[30]

Auerbach developed a special affinity for the Treblinka survivors who took part in the delegation's visit to the camp. Especially poignant was Auerbach's depiction of their reactions to Treblinka's landscape.[31] Walking the length and breadth of the grounds of the camp in the company of the survivors, she spied a plethora of human bones and even flesh and of Jewish religious objects strewn over, jutting from, or buried just beneath the surface of the ground. Then the surreal happened:

We found ourselves in the area where the gas chambers had been, the colossal mass graves, and the burning pits. In some places the smell of death mingles with the odor of fire. Indeed, here and there we see heaps of white ashes and petrified bones, mounds of soot ... In one place a huge crater had been ripped open by several bombs once laid in the ground. In the depth of the crater one sees dimly, through the fog, contours.

'These aren't just bones,' says the district attorney, 'Pieces of half-rotted bodies, bundles of intestines are still lying there, plastered in sand.'

...

The Treblinka [survivors] are running back and forth. They know [things], they point [to things], they argue with one another. They make mistakes and they recognize places again. They would like to do something, make extraordinary gestures that would at least reflect their feelings, so intertwined with this place. They just had to gather bones. They jump into the ditches, reach with bare hands into the rotted remains of corpses, they want to show that they are not repelled.

...

'Look, there at the edge of that hole," says the judge, "there is a skeletal remain of childlike foot.'

But the one who held it after taking it, wraps it in a newspaper with a gesture reminiscent of a pious Jew wrapping an *etrog* [a citron used in observance of the Jewish holiday of Sukkot that must remain unblemished]. He covers it in the lining of his coat, then places it in his breast pocket, clasping it to his heart.

'Maybe it's the foot of my little boy, whom I brought here,' he answers. And the uncanny aspect of it is that although everyone among us wants to utter something flowery, irrespective of whether flowery language is in order or utterly superfluous, it might just be the truth, the simple, matter-of-fact truth.

...

We climb into the car and drive back to Siedlce.
My head starts to pound.
A heavy weariness overtakes all of us.
Night falls over the field of Treblinka.[32]

Though inspired by the same investigation at Treblinka, the reports and book by Łukaszkiewicz and the book by Auerbach were different. He was a Polish judge, she a Jewish journalist who was a survivor and dedicated to preserving the memory of the Holocaust; the intended readership of his reports was Polish legal officials and of his book a wider ethnic Polish audience, the intended readership of her book was fellow Jews; his writings, especially his reports, belonged primarily to the sphere of empirical observations as distinct from impressions and ruminations, with which her book, along with facts, was suffused. It is noteworthy, however, that in her book she viewed Łukaszkiewicz and district attorney Maciejewski as sympathetic professionals and partners in the quest to uncover evidence of German crimes perpetrated against Jews at Treblinka. "The district attorney and the judge," she wrote, "already know every nook and cranny here. They have already been conducting the investigation for some time. They've interviewed both Jewish and non-Jewish witnesses, taken measurements and carried out small excavations."[33] Łukaszkiewicz, for his part, demonstrated not only steady determination to gather evidence to prove German anti-Jewish crimes but also appreciable empathy for the Jewish tragedy.[34]

The joint investigations of Treblinka and the other former camps helped lay the groundwork for a close working relationship between the GKBZN and the Jewish historical institutions in their common pursuit of Nazi criminals with the cooperation of the Polish legal system. This relationship endured through the second half of the 1940s and into the 1950s. Without it, the prosecution of Nazis in Polish courts might have evolved quite differently, with less emphasis on the Jewish dimension of the crimes perpetrated by the Nazi regime. The active participation of the Jewish historical commissions ensured that the fate of Jews in Nazi-occupied Poland was aired in open court.

Putting Questions to Stroop

Yosef Kermish (1907–2005) was a core member of the CŻKH who played a significant role in the trial of Jürgen Stroop. Kermish received a PhD in history in the 1930s and belonged to a circle of young Jewish historians headed by Emanuel Ringelblum. He survived the Nazi occupation in hiding in eastern Poland, and after the Soviet liberation of the area in 1944 he joined the Polish army that had been organized in the Soviet Union under the command of General Zygmunt Berling, rising through the ranks and teaching history at the army's historical institute. At the same time he started collecting testimonies from Jewish survivors. He joined the CŻKH in 1944 immediately after its creation, serving as a member of its directorate and head of the archives. He composed an instructional booklet for those gathering documents and taking testimony from survivors, and in 1946 he published a study of the Warsaw Ghetto Uprising. When the CŻKH was converted into the ŻIH in 1947, he became its director general. He immigrated to Israel in 1950 and became affiliated with Yad Vashem, founding its archive in 1953.[35]

After Stroop's extradition in 1947 to stand trial in Poland, Kermish was assigned to write the expert opinion in the name of the ŻIH for the prosecution. To that end, he received permission from Stefan Kurowski, who after participating in the Polish delegation at Nuremberg was appointed chief prosecutor of cases tried before the NTN, to interview Stroop in his jail cell at Mokotów prison in March 1948 and then present him with a questionnaire of forty-two items, which Stroop answered in writing. Kermish wished to question Stroop because existing documents, practically all of non-Jewish origin, and testimony were insufficient to paint a full picture of the Warsaw Ghetto Uprising and the battles between the Jewish fighters and the SS forces under Stroop's command; also, given Stroop's leading role in suppressing the uprising, no one was in a better position to shed light on what happened. Kermish avoided asking questions whose answers would implicate Stroop in the crime so as not to raise any suspicion in Stroop's mind that those answers could be used against him in court. Thus, Kermish restricted himself to questions that would help researchers gain a fuller understanding of the Warsaw Ghetto Uprising. Kermish asked Stroop, for example, what he knew about the preparations made by Jewish forces on the eve of the liquidation of the Warsaw Ghetto and how he judged them from an organizational and military standpoint. He also asked him about Polish assistance to the Jewish insurgents and the role of various German officials in the suppression of the uprising. Stroop answered most of the questions put to him. In response to a request from Kermish, Stroop added supplemental information.[36] Stroop seemed genuinely impressed by the Jews' preparations for the Germans' incursion into the ghetto and by the Jewish fighters' initiative, leadership, and fighting spirit. In his description of the initial confrontation between his German forces and Jewish fighters, Stroop wrote: "They [the Jewish fighters] were prepared for everything and were not even afraid of tanks."[37] Stroop was less impressed by what in his view was the apathetic attitude of the Polish population and the anemic assistance rendered by the Polish underground to the Jewish rebels during the uprising.[38] Stroop offered Kermish bits of information, but he claimed that he could not recall many details. Ultimately, Kermish did not prepare an expert opinion or testify for the prosecution because he left Poland for Israel before Stroop's trial commenced.

With the help of Tadeusz Cyprian, who after the Nuremberg Trial prosecuted cases brought before the Supreme National Tribunal, Kermish also arranged for Marek Edelman and Shalom Grajek, two former Jewish

fighters in the Warsaw Ghetto Uprising, and Rachel Auerbach, separately to question Stroop in his jail cell. They all pressed Stroop for a
full accounting of his individual responsibility for German actions during the uprising and for his assessment of the strength of the Jewish
insurgents, whose tenacity had made a lasting impression on him. As
he told Edelman, "Naturally, no one assumed that the individual insurgent cells would stand their ground so long."[39] Still, Stroop must have
largely disappointed his Jewish questioners, for many of his answers
were patently untrue. For example, he denied responsibility for the order to set the ghetto ablaze with flamethrowers, blaming the fires and
the use of flamethrowers on the Jewish fighters, and he denied that he
had a close relationship with Himmler. Edelman would later testify at
Stroop's trial.

It was not beyond Stroop to throw his Jewish questioners a bone and
concede the tenacity of the Jewish fighters during the Warsaw Ghetto
Uprising. All told, the information Stroop provided them that could be
said to be new was, however, limited and occasionally even of dubi-
ous veracity. But the fact that representatives of the ŻIH – Kermish and
Auerbach – and former ghetto fighters – Edelman and Grajek – were
permitted to pose questions to Stroop, even in his jail cell, was significant. It indicates that there existed a deep level of mutual trust between
representatives of the postwar Jewish community and Polish legal officials who were in charge of putting war criminals on trial.[40]

Mietek Pemper: Star Witness

In the first issue of *Dos naje lebn*, the Yiddish-language organ of the
CKŻP, Friedman counselled returning survivors to "take revenge" by
demanding the trials of the murderers and urged them to discharge
their "historical duty" in part by providing testimony for possible use in
judicial proceedings.[41] The CŻKH and then the ŻIH helped find Jewish
witnesses for trials of Nazi criminals in Poland. Jewish survivors were
eager to testify, for they agreed with Friedman that it was their duty.

The 1946 trial of Amon Göth in the NTN is a prominent example of
Jewish survivors' impulse to testify at Nazi trials. Prosecutors called
seventy-six eyewitnesses to the stand; sixty-four of them were Jews,
twelve were ethnic Poles.[42] In addition, the witness statements of
nineteen Jews who were residing in the American zone of Occupied
Germany in 1946 were read into the court record. Most of the Jewish witnesses were survivors of the Płaszów forced-labour and concentration

camp on the outskirts of Kraków. But a significant number came from the ghettos of Kraków, Tarnów, and Szebnie and Jewish communities in Mielec, Rzeszów, and Bochnia – all located in southeast Poland – whose liquidations were directed by Göth. Mieczysław (Mietek) Pemper, a survivor of the camp, related that when Göth saw the witness list, he reportedly exclaimed: "'What? So many Jews? And they always told us not a single one of the pricks would be left.'" "I've never forgotten that response," Pemper wrote, "for it suggests how vulgar Göth was, and why his brutality and that of the others was so unrestrained. They acted in the conviction that they would never be brought to justice because no witnesses would survive."[43] Of course, a few did indeed survive, and those who remained in Poland after the war were anxious to see those who had caused them such great torment punished. One of those Jews was Mietek Pemper (1920–2011), who was the prosecution's star witness at Göth's trial.

Pemper was born in Kraków. He studied law at the Jagiellonian University and business administration and accounting at the Academy of Economics. At Jagiellonian he and his fellow Jewish students were disciplined when they protested the university president's order in 1938 that they sit only on segregated "Jewish benches" in the lecture halls. In March 1941 the Nazis confined in a ghetto, along with their families, 15,000 of Kraków's Jews, most of whom were skilled factory workers producing goods for the war effort. The thousands of Jews who were not permitted to resettle in the ghetto were expelled from the city. Pemper received permission to move to the ghetto. Fluent in German and a competent typist – in 1940 he secretly transcribed BBC broadcasts for an underground newspaper – he was hired by the ghetto's Jewish Council (Judenrat) as an administrative clerk. Privy to correspondence between the council and German authorities, he was able to follow and came to grasp the administration of the German occupation from a distinctive vantage point. He was eventually able to bring his parents and brother, who were living illegally in the city, into the ghetto. The first two German transports of Jews from the ghetto to the extermination camp of Bełżec took place in June 1942. By the time of the third transport in October 1942, Pemper, working in the office of the Jewish Council, had learned how to predict when such transports were imminent. More important, he came to realize that the ghetto was only temporary and that only a few Jews who were well trained would be spared and employed in jobs the SS considered useful.

Pemper caught his first glimpse of Göth in the Jewish Council's offices in February 1943. But he became familiar with him only after the
fourth and final bloody liquidation of the ghetto in March 1943, which
Göth directed. Under Göth's command, the surviving 8,000 Jews were
herded into the Płaszów camp. The vicious and ruthless Göth personally murdered hundreds of innocent camp inmates and subjected count-
less others to harsh punishment to make an example of them, even for
the slightest offences and often for no reason at all. Since Pemper was
a skilled typist and spoke Polish and German, Göth commandeered
him to be his personal secretary, an assignment fraught with danger. "I
knew that Göth mistreated even the people who worked in his immediate environment," wrote Pemper in his memoir, *The Road to Rescue.*
"Some were cruelly tortured, others shot. Now, day in and day out, I
had to work for a mass murderer. There was no possibility of escape
from the job I was forced to do. My chances of survival were slim."[44]

In March 1943 Pemper was ordered to type his first letter to the German industrialist Oskar Schindler. The letter, signed by Göth, informed
Schindler that Jewish workers could no longer walk from the camp to
his enamelware factory because Schindler had regularly flouted SS security regulations. Schindler socialized with Nazis and lavished them
with liquor and cigarettes, but he did not share their hatred of Jews. He
pretended to be Göth's loyal friend and fellow Nazi, and he charmed
Göth into granting him permission to build barracks for his workers on
factory grounds, where they would be largely insulated from Göth's
attacks and those of his subordinates.

Pemper's imprisoned friend Izak Stern, who worked as an ac-
countant at Płaszów, persuaded Pemper to trust Schindler. Schindler
and Pemper would meet secretly in the main camp of Płaszów and
Schindler would inquire after the fate of its Jews. Schindler's concern
for the Jewish inmates rallied Pemper. "In the summer of 1943," Pemper
wrote, "I saw in Schindler the road to rescue I had been searching for
since the beginning of the war. With his help, I thought, we would
have to try to organize our survival. No one except Schindler evinced
any interest in our fate. His courage restored my faith in humanity."[45]
From his precarious perch in Göth's office, Pemper summoned sufficient guile and guts to gain access to classified information. He learned
that most Jewish work camps would be dismantled and only those that
produced arms and materiel essential to the German military would
remain open. The closing of smaller labour camps meant certain death

for their Jewish inmates. Since uniforms and boots were manufactured at Płaszów, Pemper was convinced that it was in line to be closed unless some kind of arms production was added to its manufacturing program. Pemper shared what he knew with Schindler and urged him, for the sake of his workers, to add the manufacture of arms to his production of enamelware. Schindler expanded his factory's capacity and began manufacturing grenade parts. Göth eagerly accepted Schindler's offer to place the operation in Płaszów because it would keep the camp open. To prove the operation's viability to the satisfaction of Göth and his superiors, Pemper produced reams of documentation brimming with inflated production tables. The smokescreen produced its intended effect, and the decision was made in late 1943 to keep Płaszów open; this prolonged the lives of its inmates, whose numbers had reached a maximum of about 25,000 by the summer of 1944. In all, under Goth's command, 8,000 Jews were murdered in the Płaszów camp.

As the Eastern Front approached, deportations and the liquidation of labour camps accelerated and important factories were transferred to Germany. After large deportations of inmates from Płaszów to Auschwitz, Mauthausen, and Stutthof in mid-1944, there were only about 7,000 inmates left in the camp, and it was clear that Płaszów was about to be dismantled. In September and early October 1944, Schindler pulled out all the stops to rescue the Jews in his factory, persuading the Nazi authorities – Göth had been arrested in mid-September 1944 and was under investigation by the SS for embezzlement – to allow him to take 1,000 Jewish workers from his factory to Brünnlitz in the Sudetenland. He contended that they were essential to the production of the grenade parts. It was Pemper and several other inmates who typed their names, and having noted that there were still openings on the list because the number of inmates authorized by the SS was larger than the actual number of workers left in Schindler's factory by the end of September 1944, they used subterfuge to add the names of other inmates to the now famous "Schindler's List." Schindler had Pemper, his parents, and his brother inserted on the list, saving them. But in his farewell speech to his Jewish workers before he departed Brünnlitz on the night of 8–9 May 1945, Schindler declined their thanks. Instead, he urged them to thank the "'fearless Stern and Pemper'" for their help in the rescue operation and others who made sacrifices, "'staring death in the eye every moment as they thought of the good of all and looked out for all of you.'"[46]

The then twenty-six-year-old Pemper testified on the first day of Göth's trial on 27 August 1946. He described the liquidation of the

Kraków Ghetto, which Göth directed. He explained Płaszów's topography, organizational structure, and chain of command, with which he was thoroughly familiar from his work in the former camp's headquarters. Since he was Göth's personal stenographer and typist, he had thorough knowledge of Göth's personnel file, and through stealth he had gained access to classified and secret correspondence between Göth and other Nazi officials. From his perch in Płaszów's headquarters Pemper continuously observed Göth and was utterly familiar with his actions and methods. For even minor infractions Göth favoured the death sentence, which required his approval before his subordinates could implement it, but which he often carried out himself, fatally shooting hapless inmates. Those who were fortunate enough to evade death were sentenced to solitary confinement in a cramped isolation cell or cruelly whipped. Göth embezzled Jewish property with the assistance of the senior Jewish inmate Wilek (Wilhelm) Chilowicz, but Göth eventually had Chilowicz killed, along with his family, because he knew too much and could incriminate the camp's commandant. In Pemper's own words, written sixty years after the trial, by virtue of his perch in Göth's office, he was "the only witness who could give a complete and exact overview."[47]

The centrepiece of Pemper's testimony was his description of the "health roll call" that was conducted at Płaszów in early May 1944. Pemper secretly monitored Göth's classified correspondence, and in this way he learned that in response to a request from SS headquarters in Berlin to accommodate several thousand new Jewish arrivals from Hungary, Goth had received permission in return to send current inmates no longer capable of full-time work to Auschwitz for "special treatment" (*Sonderbehandlung*). The "health roll call" was in effect a selection, and those whom the camp's German physician, Dr Max Blancke, deemed unfit – especially older and ill inmates – were sent to Auschwitz. Pemper learned from a telegram Göth sent to Auschwitz that the transport on 14 May 1944 contained 1,400 people, including 286 children. As Pemper testified, "for those of us acquainted with the practices of the SS, there was no doubt that these people were going to their death. I stress that the concept of '*Sonderbehandlung*' was synonymous with gassing; it was a concept well known to the SS. Goth's plan went in this direction, in order to cleanse the camp of unproductive elements, wanting to relieve the camp of them." In a subsequent telegram Göth sent to Auschwitz he requested the return of the striped prisoners' uniforms worn by the inmates on the transport. He must have made this request because prisoners' uniforms were in short supply.[48] The inference was that Göth was aware that he was sending the inmates who failed to pass muster at the "health roll call" to their deaths. As Pemper reflected on his testimony sixty years later in his memoir, Göth had testified in his own defence that he had no idea that the inmates who were transported to Auschwitz would be gassed. As Pemper observed, "this telegram is clear evidence that contrary to his testimony, Goth knew very well what the concept of *Sonderbehandlung* meant ... As an administrative matter, [Berlin's] initial inquiry about how many Hungarian Jews Goth could accommodate on a temporary basis had no criminal intent. However, Goth's suggestion in response was clearly criminal."[49] As was evident in the court's verdict, this was, indeed, the inference that it drew from Pemper's testimony.[50]

Pemper was recalled to the witness stand on the second day of the trial for cross-examination by the defendant. Göth, who subjected Pemper to intense interrogation, was dumbfounded by Pemper's encyclopedic knowledge of what transpired in the camp and of presumably confidential information. "How does the witness know?" was a constant refrain during Goth's cross-examination of Pemper. Göth strained to puncture Pemper's credibility, but in vain; Pemper stood his ground, impressing the court with both his phenomenal memory and his composure under fire. Meanwhile, Göth's questioning of Pemper did his own credibility no great service. When Göth asked Pemper how he knew that the inmates who were transported to Auschwitz on 14 May were going to their deaths, the presiding judge, Alfred Eimer, interrupted the cross-examination, reminding the defendant that he had already admitted during his own testimony that Auschwitz was an extermination camp. "This was known to all SS men," the judge added for emphasis.[51] Sixty years later, Pemper recalled Göth's cross-examination of him:

> While testifying I avoided eye contact with Göth, so I can only imagine his stunned look ... He had instituted such a reign of terror in the camp that it never would have occurred to him that anyone – much less a Jewish inmate! – would dare to read classified camp correspondence, telegrams, and official memoranda.
>
> But now, three years later, he suddenly became aware that Mietek Pemper, his most dutiful slave, had been systematically gathering information and using it to help fellow prisoners. It was surely not the first time he must have regretted not shooting this Pemper fellow, for my testimony was clear and incontrovertible. As an intelligent man, Göth must have now begun to realize what he was in for.

From then on, although he challenged certain details and made a comment here and there, he was no longer able to deny the truth of what I was saying. In fact, I had the impression that he wasn't even trying to do so anymore. He was probably coming around to the reality of his situation: His time was up. The game was lost.[52]

The sixty-odd Jewish witnesses who testified after Pemper followed suit, describing Goth's volatile temperament, cruelty, ruthlessness, and indiscriminate acts of torture and murder. But although Göth was securely in the hands of prison authorities, Jewish witnesses were still afraid of him and, like Pemper, avoided eye contact with him when they testified in open court. For their part, Jews from Płaszów whose own behaviour in the camp had been questionable advised Pemper in 1946 not to testify against Göth. But since his own behaviour had been beyond reproach, Pemper did not fear that Göth would be able to say anything in court that would discredit or compromise him. Pemper was resolute in his decision to testify and was not to be diverted from his cause. In his memoir he wrote:

> Again and again during the trial, I couldn't help reflecting that Göth had two defense attorneys, an interpreter, and medics waiting outside the courtroom in case he needed them, all the services that he never would have provided for his victims. And so, in view of what he did to so many innocent human beings, I regard his trial as an act of justice. For no other reason than that we were members of a Jewish "race" (which doesn't even exist), we were systematically humiliated, persecuted, tortured, and finally murdered – children, and adults, the old and the young. As a survivor, I regarded it as my duty to testify at Göth's trial.[53]

Notwithstanding their disquiet in the courtroom, it's fair to assume that the other Jewish witnesses who testified against Göth felt the same way.

Jewish Expert Witnesses

Personnel from the CŻKH filed reports and testified for the prosecution in the trials conducted before the NTN of Ludwig Fischer, Amon Göth, Josef Bühler, Rudolf Höss, and forty former SS officials and guards from Auschwitz. Also, staff from both the Central Jewish Historical Commission and the Jewish Historical Institute were expert witnesses in several trials held in Polish district courts, including the trials of Hans Biebow and of Jürgen Stroop and Franz Konrad. Over the course of a decade, Nachman Blumental, Yosef Kermish, Michał Borowicz, Artur Eisenbach, Bernard Mark, and Abram Rozenberg-Rutkowski testified for the prosecution in war crimes trials in the name of the CŻKH and the ŻIH.[54]

Two men who were called to testify as expert witnesses more than once were Natan Blumental and Artur Eisenbach, the former in the trials of Bühler, Höss, and the Auschwitz staff, the latter in the trials of Biebow and of Stroop and Konrad. Blumental (1905–1983), holder of a master's degree in literature from Warsaw University, survived the war in hiding in Poland. He joined the CŻKH shortly after its creation in Lublin and served as the first director of the ŻIH in 1947–48. In 1950 he immigrated to Israel, where he was affiliated with Yad Vashem.[55] Eisenbach (1906–1992) studied Jewish history at Warsaw University. In Warsaw he participated in a circle of young historians led by Emanuel Ringelblum and Raphael Mahler. He survived the Holocaust in the Soviet Union, but his wife, Ringelblum's sister, and child were killed in Poland. When he returned to Poland in 1946, he joined the CŻKH in Łódź and then in Warsaw. After the ŻIH was established, he became its head archivist and then a researcher. In the immediate postwar years he dedicated his life to research on the Nazi genocide of Jews: it was the topic of his doctoral dissertation in 1953 and his habilitation in 1955. He was appointed director of the ŻIH in 1966 but was forced under intense pressure to resign in 1968 in the wake of the regime's infamous anti-Jewish campaign. Even so, he was able to protect its archival collection from an attempt by the Communist Party's "anti-Zionist" faction to requisition it. Eisenbach immigrated to Israel in 1991, one year before his death.[56]

For the prosecution in Höss's trial in March 1947 Blumental wrote and then read into the court record a lengthy expert opinion, in which, using broad, sweeping strokes, he painted a picture of Nazi political objectives, which, he argued, were undergirded by antisemitic policies and perfidy and culminated in the death camps. In Blumental's view, the key to Nazi political ambitions was *Lebensraum* or "living space" for Germany's population, whose growth, it was claimed, had been constricted when the country was forced to forfeit territory after the First World War. But Germany's territorial expansion would have dire consequences for people living in countries overrun by the Germans. Blumental wrote: "'*Lebensraum*' for Germans – this is actually

'*Todesraum*' [dying space] for people in conquered countries ... It turned out that *Lebensraum* is actually ... a code name [*Deckname*], meaning death to conquered peoples."[57] Blumental saw a link between the acquisition of *Lebensraum* and the Nazi regime's antisemitic policies, and this link was the lynchpin of his argument. "On the road to the implementation of this final goal Hitlerism was served – as an intermediate phase – by the complete annihilation of Jews in countries under its control."[58] Antisemitism functioned to the benefit of the Nazis in multifarious ways both in Germany's domestic politics and in its foreign affairs. But, most important, the regime's antisemitic policies primed every German to believe that "the only enemy of Germany is the Jew."[59]

The sweep of Blumental's expert opinion was impressive. It described in detail Nazi propaganda; the accommodation of German science to Nazi ambitions; the step-by-step marginalization of Jews in Germany, especially though legal measures; the oppression of Polish Jews after the German invasion of Poland, including the denial of legal protections; the liquidation of ghettos; the construction of concentration and death camps; and the Nazis' ruthlessness.

One brief section of the expert opinion was devoted to Auschwitz. From Blumental's perspective, the Germans' initial intention in establishing Auschwitz was to create a forced-labour camp for "criminals" from Poland and other European countries. At first, the majority of inmates were political prisoners. But the character of Auschwitz changed with the German invasion of the Soviet Union. The labour shortage created by the pressing need for front-line troops delayed the liquidation of productive ghettos like the one in Łódź. In turn, German losses in the east and the gradual shift of the front line westward hindered the deportation of Jews from Western and Central Europe to the Operation Reinhard extermination camps located in eastern Poland, whose operations were further disrupted by revolts of Jewish prisoners at Treblinka and Sobibór. Auschwitz was expanded and developed into a killing facility, therefore, to relieve pressure on death camps farther east and to divert transports of Jews to a death camp situated closer to their countries of origin. Blumental wrote: "The place of Treblinka, Sobibór, and Bełżec, and then shortly Majdanek is taken by Auschwitz, to which transports from abroad also begin to flow, from the west and south, after unsuccessful attempts to liquidate these Jews in situ."[60]

Blumental then turned his attention to Jewish losses. By his estimates, three million Polish Jews and one million Jews from other countries perished on Polish soil. Three million were killed in death camps located in Poland. Auschwitz alone claimed the lives of one million Jews from outside Poland, and when the number of Polish Jewish victims of the camp was added, the total number of Jews killed there was between 1,300,000 and 1,500,000.[61] After this statistical excursus, he entreated the tribunal to see beyond the numbers and take full measure of the victims' humanity. "I have spoken objectively by all means – as if it were a matter not of people but of mathematical equations. We often forget that behind each number hides a human life."[62]

Contrary to what one might have expected, Blumental hardly mentioned Höss in his expert opinion. He left the description of the defendant's crimes largely to other witnesses. He did employ heavy irony once, drawing a comparison between the "humanitarian" Höss, who strove to make the asphyxiation of Jews in the gas chambers of Auschwitz as efficient as possible, and the rebellious spirit of Jewish women destined for death who, in the summer of 1943, attacked their guards on their way to the gas chamber and were killed. "Here is our hero – a specialist in his profession – worthy of his great nation."[63] These women, however, like other women who attacked a guard in a satellite camp of Auschwitz in the summer of 1942 and the members of the Jewish *Sonderkommando* who, in August 1944, damaged a crematorium with explosives and killed and wounded SS – they were the true heroes. Clearly, in Blumental's eyes, Höss was a pompous and contemptible man, but he was also an insignificant cog in the wheel. Blumental maintained that "in this system the individual could accomplish a lot," and that given his high rank, "Höss could have accomplished many things if he had been [a person] of good will – but he was not."[64] There were documented times when he could have prolonged the lives of Jews but instead allowed them to be led to the gas chambers.

Höss had not acted alone. From the SS to the manufacturers of the poison gas used at Auschwitz to the publisher Karl Baedeker, whose travel guides offered readers an airbrushed version of a Poland without Jews – in Blumental's words, "tens of thousands, even hundreds of thousands of Germans took part in these 'actions.'"[65]

Although Nazi anti-Jewish policy was paramount in Blumental's written expert opinion and testimony, he stressed repeatedly that the genocide of the Jews was a rehearsal for the mass murder of other ethnic groups, including at Auschwitz. He made this point early in his expert opinion. "That, however, the final goal of Hitlerism," he wrote, "was not only the extermination of the Jews is proven irrefutably by a number of facts. The death camp at Majdanek expands at the moment that there were nearly no Jews. A new crematorium is being built ... The same is true of the expansion of the death camp at Auschwitz." The intended victims of the enlarged killing facilities were – so intended high-ranking Nazi officials – "thirty million Slavs," whose annihilation would have embodied "the true meaning of *Lebensraum*."[66] Blumental wrote that there "was no doubt that the idea about the extermination of the Jews and not only Jews" occupied the minds of Nazi leaders after the German invasion of Poland in September 1939.[67] He contended that since the number of Jews Eichmann planned to deport to Auschwitz from Rumania and Bulgaria exceeded the Jewish populations of those countries, his intent must have been to send non-Jewish Romanians and Bulgarians to be killed at the camp. Blumental wrote: "Hitler had already accustomed the world to the killing of Jews .... So it was possible to liquidate other peoples along with Jews. The expansion of Auschwitz and Eichmann's plans served this goal."[68] Nevertheless, between the presentation of the written version of his expert opinion, dated 25 March 1947, to the tribunal and his oral testimony in open court the following day, Blumental, perhaps in consideration of the contemporary political climate in Poland, must have resolved to revise the expert opinion and explicitly point to the Poles and Russians by name. On the witness stand he said: "Auschwitz is the final phase of Polish Jewry. Here were dying survivors who miraculously evaded Treblinka, Sobibór, or Majdanek. Auschwitz is the nail in the coffin of Polish Jewry. If we remember beyond this that in reality Auschwitz was not a Jewish camp, that hundreds of thousands of citizens of other countries died here, above all Poles, Czechs, and Russians, then we will understand what Auschwitz was and what it was meant to be. For this reason, in Auschwitz there flourished a great industry of death."[69] In other words, after the Jews the Poles and other Slavs were next in line for extermination. This courtroom utterance did not appear in the written version of Blumental's expert opinion.

Blumental's testimony for the prosecution in the trial of the forty SS men who served at Auschwitz partly followed his expert opinion for Höss's trial, even borrowing passages from it. But if the centrepiece of Blumental's argument in his previous expert opinion was the German drive for *Lebensraum*, in this iteration it was the Nazi fixation with the Jew, personified by ideologue Alfred Rosenberg and percolating down to SS units and the public consciousness. Blumental situated the Nazis' anti-Jewish animus in their overall embrace of political biology, which dictated the annihilation of not only Jews but also thirty million Slavs and Roma (Gypsies), all of whom were deemed enemies of the Nazi state. Blumental ventured, moreover, to explain the psychological basis of Nazi criminality. Convinced that the world was divided between friends and enemies of the Reich and confident in the Führer's approbation of their actions, which afforded them legal protection, SS men had no scruples about killing. For this reason they could never bring themselves to admit guilt. In Blumental's view, the defendants personified the Nazi mind.[70]

Eisenbach testified at the trials of Hans Biebow in April 1947 and of Stroop and Konrad in July 1951. In his expert opinion for the prosecution in the Biebow trial, Eisenbach immediately articulated his argument, which mirrored and encapsulated Blumental's in the latter's expert opinion for the Höss trial: "The plan for the total extermination of the Jewish people in Europe was considered by the leadership of the Nazi party for a long time before the Second World War. In the NSDAP's political program it occupies one of the top places. The eradication of the Jews was to be the preface to the annihilation of tens of millions of Slavs for the conquest of new colonized territories, new *Lebensraum*."[71] Like Blumental, Eisenbach linked the fates of Poles and Jews, describing the expulsion of 200,000 Poles and 100,000 Jews in November 1939 from the annexed western part of Poland, the Warthegau, to the General Government and the execution of 4,000 Poles and the same number of Jews in Poznań and its environs in 1940.

As Biebow was under indictment for his administration of the Łódź Ghetto, Eisenbach focused on the Germans' use of terror and administrative measures to oppress the city's Jewish population from late 1939 onward. The forced resettlement of the city's Jews in a ghetto began in January 1940 and lasted until April 1940. What distinguished Eisenbach's expert opinion from Blumental's was the former's economic analysis of the Nazis' motives in Łódź. By 1941, Eisenbach observed, the ghetto functioned like a labour camp and the goal of the German authorities was "exploitation of its productive capacity in service to the German war economy."[72] But the exploitation of Jewish labour took precedence over the ghetto's liquidation only temporarily. When Germany invaded the Soviet Union and German forces embarked on the mass murder of Jews on Soviet territory, for all of its productive usefulness to the German war effort, the fate of the ghetto was sealed, even if it lasted until August 1944, when it was the last ghetto to be liquidated. In Eisenbach's words,

[t]he economic plans were ... not a goal in and of themselves, they were only means to the realization of the party's political plans. Likewise the exploitation of the Jews was only one phase [in attainment of] the goal. In the transitional period it was also possible to extract substantial benefits from them for the war economy. But even consideration of these benefits cannot stand in the way of the realization of the main political goal – the annihilation of the Jewish people.[73]

In 1941 Biebow, as head of the ghetto administration (*Ghettoverwaltung*), not only directed the requisition of Jewish property; he "was ... well informed of what was transpiring already during preparations for the annihilation of the Jews."[74] In other words, he promoted the exploitation of the ghetto's Jews, knowing full well what their end would be.[75] Eisenbach concluded his testimony with a long list of Biebow's individual crimes, ranging from his active role in deportations to his embezzlement of the deportees' property.[76] In this light, Eisenbach's expert opinion both indicted Biebow personally and cast him in the role of representative of the overall criminality of the Nazi regime.

The focus of Eisenbach's expert opinion for the prosecution in the 1951 trial of Stroop and Konrad was Konrad's activities. Eisenbach described the economic function of utilization of Jewish property and the exploitation of Jewish labour in Operation Reinhard, which was directed by Odilo Globocnik. Liquidation of the ghettos in Poland was the impetus for the establishment of the so-called Ostindustrie GmbH (Osti) in the Lublin District under Globocnik. Osti had recourse to Jewish forced labour and textile machinery transferred from evacuated ghettos, including the Warsaw Ghetto, to concentration camps under Globocnik's command. Osti also profited from the property left behind by deported Jews. Globocnik's representative in Warsaw was Konrad. It was Konrad who, as the person in charge of the *Werterfassung*, acquired control over abandoned Jewish property, and he formed a battalion of some 4,000 Jewish forced labourers in the Warsaw Ghetto to requisition and store it in several large warehouses. When their turn came to be deported with their families, Konrad turned a blind eye to their plight. "The activity of the defendant Konrad in both Warsaw and other cities in occupied Poland," concluded Eisenbach, "was closely connected with the general plan of the Hitlerite authorities for the mass murder of the Jewish people."[77] Eisenbach was subjected to a vigorous cross-examination by Konrad's lawyer, who attempted to distance his client from the deportation and especially the murder of Jews during Stroop's suppression of the Warsaw Ghetto Uprising. In response, Eisenbach stressed that the requisition of Jewish property was a key aspect of the liquidation of the ghetto.[78]

Noteworthy are the passionate reactions of their colleagues in the CŻKH in March 1947 to Eisenbach's and Blumental's expert opinions in the Biebow and Höss trials, respectively, in anticipation of the experts' testimony in court. Regarding Eisenbach's expert opinion, the commission's scholars debated Eisenbach's argument that German policy in Poland was driven by the exploitation of Jewish labour "as long as the technical possibility of mass murder did not exist."[79] Isaiah Trunk went further, pointing out that the Łódź Ghetto, whose Jewish leadership aggressively promoted the productive capacity of its inhabitants to Biebow, was the last in line for liquidation. Other colleagues disagreed. Journalist Wolf Jasny maintained that the Germans never harboured plans to preserve a Jewish labour force and that their exclusive goal had been extermination. After all, they had murdered the Jews in the Łódź Ghetto when their productive capacity was at its peak.[80] Another bone of contention was whether or not Eisenbach's expert opinion should focus on Biebow's individual crimes or make him stand for the criminality of the entire Nazi system. Backed by Kermish, Eisenbach favoured "a trial against the entire German policy and all levels of authority."[81] Representing the view that Biebow ought to be at the centre of Eisenbach's expert opinion, Leon Szeftel expressed misgivings at the prospect that a focus on the Nazi system rather than on Biebow's own actions would excuse him from personal responsibility on the grounds that he had no choice but to heed high-ranking Nazi authorities.[82] In the event, Eisenbach devoted the lion's share of his expert opinion to German anti-Jewish policy in general, while indicting Biebow for his part in its implementation.

Blumental's expert opinion for Höss's trial likewise ignited a vigorous debate within the CŻKH on the eve of his testimony in court. At the meeting, Blumental announced that he and prosecutor Tadeusz Cyprian had agreed that the theme of his expert opinion should be "Hitler's political extermination of the Jews" and that, for this reason, it had "to be a trial not only of Höss but also of the entire system, all of fascism." It was necessary to represent Höss in such a way that he was "incidental" and "would stand here for others." For his part, Blumental would have to discuss "the general background, Hitlerite ideology." He explained to his colleagues that the trial possessed "tremendous political significance," for it was to coincide with the meeting of the Council of Foreign Ministers of the Four Powers in Moscow, at which a peace settlement in Germany was the main item on the agenda. According to Blumental, "it [the trial] can have influence on the course of the conference."[83]

Blumental told his colleagues he was planning to argue that the Nazis' ultimate political goal was *Lebensraum* or living space, which entailed the destruction of territories and peoples through warfare. "One phase in the attainment of this goal," he continued, "was the extermination of the Jews." According to Blumental, the Nazis exploited antisemitism for larger objectives. It allowed them to divert the attention of the German people from important domestic and international issues. It allowed them to plan a war that the German people did not want. It allowed them to exert influence and create fifth columns in foreign countries. It partly had an economic objective – the enrichment of individual Germans and of the state's treasury. Furthermore, it afforded them freedom of action because they had no reason to fear intervention from foreign governments as they might have in the case of groups other than Jews. "The destruction of the Jews was," therefore, "preparation for the destruction of other peoples."[84] But not only Nazis took part in the annihilation of Jews. Blumental planned to indict the entire German people. "All devices serving the liquidation of the Jews, for example, railway cars, automobiles, crematoria were built by great engineers."[85] The "whole people" (*cały naród*), he added, referring to the Germans, "were involved in anti-Jewish actions."[86] As Höss was commandant of Auschwitz, Blumental thought it important to explain the camp's chronology. "At the beginning Auschwitz [Oświęcim] was not a camp only for Jews," he stressed to his colleagues. In 1941 most of its inmates were Poles, and only in 1942 did the extermination of Jews there commence.[87] Although Blumental clearly measured which way the political wind was blowing, he was still the quintessential scholar. Thus, for him, it was also important to establish the number of Polish Jewish victims, and in this regard he was dissatisfied with the estimates of other scholars, including Philip Friedman. In a detailed exposition of his methodology, he explained and defended his own estimate of three million Polish Jews dead, one million foreign Jews killed on Polish soil, and six million Jewish victims across Europe. Auschwitz, he concluded, had claimed one and a half million Jewish lives (in contrast to contemporary figures of two and a half million or even four million, the latter mentioned by Cyprian in his meeting with Blumental). Only 300,000 Polish Jews survived, the majority of them in the Soviet Union.[88]

After Blumental finished his presentation, several of his colleagues took issue with his approach. Emotions ran high. In particular, they thought he had failed to draw sharp distinctions between the Germans' victimization of Jews and that of other nationalities. A colleague named Mosiężnik admonished him: "The expert witness must remember that he is appearing as accuser in the name of all Jews who perished. The tribunal at Nuremberg distinguished crimes against humanity; it is necessary to underline that what took place here [in the case of Jews] was genocide. It will be necessary to distinguish the situation of Jews in camps from the situation of other peoples."[89] Another colleague, Michał Rajak, followed suit: "A lot of work, a lot of knowledge, has been incorporated in this expert opinion, but [our] colleague Blumental must remember that he is appearing as accuser in the name of six million Jews who were killed. The expert opinion has two goals: 1) to make clear the entire ugliness of Hitlerism before the world; 2) to become part of the history of the Jews."[90] In addition, there appears to have been general discontent with Blumental's downward estimate that one and a half million Jews were killed at Auschwitz. But Michał Mirski, a journalist and communist who was secretary of the CKŻP and an influential figure in the postwar Jewish leadership, registered an objection of a different kind. To his mind, Blumental's expert opinion was not sensitive enough to the political spirit of the times:

> I think that the expert opinion is too scholarly. Accuracy is necessary for scholarly purposes. In this trial political goals shine through. This trial has to be a demonstration before the Council of [Foreign Ministers of the] Four [Powers] debating in Moscow. It's not important whether one and a half, two, or three million Jews died at Auschwitz. It's important to treat Auschwitz as [part of] a system, as a symbol of fascist power. Stepping forward against Auschwitz, we step forward against all camps, against the Hitlerite system. It's necessary to jump over this arithmetic accuracy. Auschwitz is equally responsible for one million of those who died in the ghetto. Justified is the assertion that Jews were only the first victim; it [the murder of Jews] was only a preparatory laboratory ... What matters are actions and practices.[91]

Other colleagues came to Blumental's defence. Leon Szeftel was in favour of accurate calculations of Jewish victims, while Aleksander Rozenberg was wary of the appearance of political bias in Blumental's testimony because "political coloration in an expert opinion loses intensity," that is to say, compromises its integrity. That said, Rozenberg's dismissal of political considerations in the expert opinion was not unqualified. He did want that opinion to demonstrate the current resurgence of the Nazi system – presumably, in line with contemporary political orthodoxy, in the West and in the Western zones of Occupied Germany.[92]

Blumental stood his ground. In his own mind he was appearing not in the role of "accuser" in the name of Jewish victims but "as an expert witness who has to speak objectively about the topic he is given." Moreover, it was the prosecutor's task to address legal questions such as genocide, and the prosecutor had accepted his estimate that Auschwitz had claimed one and a half million Jewish victims. Of all the reservations that were expressed about his expert opinion, he felt most compelled to address the demand that he highlight the distinctive character of the Jewish fate under Nazi rule in Poland. "I think that it's not necessary in this expert opinion to underline the difference between the status of a Polish and a Jewish inmate. It's not necessary at this moment to advance this [opinion], but rather we should settle accounts with our common enemy."[93] Blumental took pains in court to do just that.

These heated internal debates were precipitated in large measure by the Jewish scholars' fears of provoking renewed antisemitism in Polish society after the eruption of antisemitic violence of the previous year, 1946, had largely subsided. During discussion of Eisenbach's expert opinion, Kermish expressed his apprehension that Poles might accuse Jews of collaboration with the Nazis if it drew attention to the fact that Jews in the Łódź Ghetto had produced uniforms for the German army.[94] Moreover, although the attention Eisenbach and others paid to the Nazis' economic exploitation of the Jews reflected current political orthodoxy, it was also indicative of two honestly held conflicting tendencies among commission members – some put great stock in a Marxist, economic explanation for the Nazis' persecution of Jews, whereas for others, the Nazis' economic exploitation of Jews was always subordinate in principle to outright extermination of the Jews. Indeed, in his testimony on the witness stand Eisenbach argued that however important the exploitation of Jewish labour was to certain Nazi officials in Poland, when push came to shove and the full-scale killing of Jews commenced, the annihilation of the Jews assumed paramount significance in Nazi anti-Jewish policy. Finally, Blumental's resolve to make note of Polish suffering in his expert opinion seems to have been motivated in large part by a pragmatic assessment of the constraints under which Jewish historians had to operate if they wished to remain relevant to the prosecution of war criminals in Poland. Indeed, his expert testimony for the prosecution in Höss's trial received positive reviews in the Polish press because of his analysis of the role of *Lebensraum*, which he equated with *Todesraum* or "death space" for all people living under Nazi occupation, thereby linking the fates of Jews and Poles in the minds of Polish commentators.[95] But by the time of the trial of the Auschwitz staff only half a year later, the CŻKH had to seek the justice minister's intervention, arguing that the participation of Jewish expert witnesses in Nazi trials had become a "Polish national tradition," before it received an invitation to prepare expert testimony for the prosecution.[96] To be sure, Blumental, Eisenbach, and other Jewish historians were under intense pressure from the communist authorities and the party's Jewish adherents to "universalize" the Jewish fate – that is, to place Jewish and Polish suffering (and resistance) on the same footing and thereby help legitimate the regime's claim to rule in that it represented a unified body politic.[97] In fact, in the first few years after the defeat of Nazism and even to a certain (albeit diminishing) extent from the end of the 1940s through the 1950s, there were Jewish scholars in postwar Poland, who, if they were not pro-regime, were not anti-regime, either, and who "subscribed" – as Laura Jockusch aptly puts it – "to the new government's promise to right the wrongs of fascism by building a better society in which social equality, political reaction, and anti-Semitism had no place."[98] Although Jockusch is describing the sentiments of the CŻKH's historians in the second half of the 1940s, these were still the lingering sentiments of the diehards who remained at the ŻIH in the 1950s.

It is important to point out, moreover, that Blumental and Eisenbach were not alone in seeing the fate of Polish Jews as linked to that of ethnic Poles. When they asserted on the witness stand that the Nazis had plans to annihilate the Poles after they had obliterated the Jews – "First the Jews, then the Poles" – they were not just throwing a bone to apparatchiks. Many Jews had harboured the same thought during the Holocaust. Abraham Lewin was a Jewish educator and a Zionist. In the Warsaw Ghetto he had helped Ringelblum with the underground archive. His wife was deported to Treblinka in 1942. He either died in the ghetto or was transported, along with his teenage daughter, to Treblinka in January 1943. Lewin kept a diary in the ghetto. On 7 June 1942 he wrote: "Let us not forget: the Poles are in second place in the table of tragic losses among the nations, just behind the Jews."[99] On 7 January 1943, he made a similar observation: "They have almost completely wiped out the Jews, now it looks as if it is the turn of the Poles."[100] In 1947, in an expanded version of the essay he authored on the Nazis' extermination of Polish Jews for the GKBZN's first volume of its yearbook in 1946, Philip Friedman, now in the American zone of Occupied Germany – and thus out of Poland and no longer vulnerable to communist political pressure – wrote: "As the fate of Soviet prisoners-of-war and of hundreds of thousands of Russian and Polish civilians murdered by the German authorities shows, the Poles and the Russians, as ethnic elements posing a threat to German expansion in the east, were the next candidates for mass extinction."[101] Without discounting the palpable pressure that communist officials and Jewish communists imposed on Jewish scholars after the war to universalize their representation of the Jewish fate under Nazi occupation, Blumental's invocation of a "common enemy" in the charged atmosphere of the March 1947 meeting of the CŻKH, therefore, expressed a belief – shared by many of his Jewish contemporaries – in the interconnectedness of Jews' and Poles' wartime fate and in the existence of shared interests even in the present day between Poles and Jews, despite the ruptures that existed between them.

Conclusion

In her incisive examination of the roles that Jewish individuals and organizations played at the Nuremberg Trial, Laura Jockusch notes that "it is a striking fact that so far historians of Allied postwar justice have mainly focused on Jews as the Nazis' *murdered victims* ... Questions as to what Jewish observers in the immediate postwar years had to say about the representation of the Jewish catastrophe in Allied war-crime trials and what roles Jews played in and around these tribunals," she continues, "have hardly been raised."[102] As she argues, investigation of the roles that Jews played in war crimes trials has the potential to amplify our understanding of not only Jewish responses to the Holocaust and the rebuilding of Jewish communities in its aftermath but also the intricacies of postwar justice.

Jockusch focuses on Jewish individuals and organizations located in the West and aligned primarily with the United States. But her line of inquiry can be extended to Jews and their institutions in postwar Poland. Jews who participated in trials of Nazi criminals desired to vindicate their own claim to a stake in Poland's future as well as to exact retribution for the deaths of three million souls from the Jewish community. Vindication in this sense entailed not only Jews' joining forces with Poles in condemnation of their common enemy but also their concerted effort to neutralize the marginalization of Jewish memory of the Holocaust in Poland. But Polish Jews had to tread a fine line if they wanted to take part in war crimes trials: they needed to draw attention to the Jewish fate under Nazism without appearing too aggressive; at the same time, they had to acknowledge the suffering of Poles. This was a daunting challenge, but they found it worthwhile to try to meet Poles halfway, even if it meant having to stomach occasional exaggerations, half-truths, and even distortions for the sake of legal recognition of the Jewish tragedy and the pursuit of retributive justice through Poland's courts. And some Jews who pressed for the participation of Jewish victims in trials of Nazi criminals might even have seen in Jewish and Polish cooperation in bringing Nazis to justice in Poland the potential to build bridges between Jews and Poles – the potential for convergence rather than conflict, for a reconciliation of sorts.

Of course, not only Jews in Poland but also Jews in other countries, through their own historical commissions and documentation centres, helped their local judicial authorities investigate and prosecute Nazi criminals. The most famous example is the Jewish Documentation Center in Vienna under Simon Wiesenthal.[103] But the close working relationship between the CŻKH and the ŻIH, each in its own time, and judicial authorities in Poland was, while it lasted, distinctive and not replicated anywhere else.

Chapter Six

History and Politics in the Last Trials, 1954–1959

In May 1954 the Warsaw provincial court tried the former SSPF in Warsaw, Paul Otto Geibel, and in March 1959 the same court sentenced to death Erich Koch, the former chief of the Białystok District administration and the Reich commissar (*Reichskommissar*) for Ukraine. Both defendants played a prominent role in Nazi Germany's brutal occupation of Poland, but by the mid-1950s, when Geibel faced trial, the drive to prosecute Nazi offenders had lost momentum in Poland and elsewhere in Europe. For all intents and purposes, Koch would be the "last Nazi" tried on Polish soil.[1]

It is in the nature of things that war crimes trials are political trials, in that they inherently disseminate, be it more or less purposefully, the prevailing official ideology. The trials of Geibel and Koch were no exception. Those trials were shaped by the interplay of politics and the official communist interpretation of the history of the Second World War. Since the end of the war, the communist government had consistently and systematically revised the story of Polish resistance, accrediting its heroism and sacrifices exclusively to partisans in the communist People's Guard (Gwardia Ludowa, GL), later the People's Army (Armia Ludowa, AL). Conversely, the non-communist AK was branded "the wretched dwarf of the reaction" (*zapluty karzeł reakcji*) – in other words, an inveterate enemy of the new Poland. In particular, state propaganda vilified the AK for launching the 1944 Warsaw Uprising, inspired by the "criminal adventurism" of the Polish government-in-exile in London, which was in command of the AK. Although the worst excesses of High Stalinism were over by 1954, a public trial of Geibel, a key German commander during the Warsaw Uprising, had the potential to undermine the official ideology. Accordingly, his trial was administered in a restrained and inconspicuous manner, attended by only a few party and state officials.[2]

In contrast, Koch's trial became a huge media event attuned to the East–West ideological rivalry. In May 1955, in response to West Germany's joining NATO, the Soviet government announced the creation of the Warsaw Pact, a defence alliance among the Eastern European states. The integration of some former Nazis into the West German civil service and armed forces helped fuel anti-Western propaganda in the Eastern Bloc.[3] In this context, Koch's trial was meant to highlight the fairness of communist justice as well as to assail the judicial system in West Germany, where the courts routinely acquitted defendants on trial for Nazi crimes or handed out light sentences to convicted Nazi war criminals.

Given the politicization of the two trials, how was the history of war and occupation treated in the courtroom? Robert Kempner, a member of the American prosecution staff at the IMT, called the Nuremberg Trial the "greatest history seminar ever held." Deliberately or not, all war crimes trials have a didactic dimension, in that they reconstruct history and shape memory through the traditional tools of justice – the law of the land, evidence in the form of documents and testimony from witnesses and the accused, and the utterances of judges and attorneys – as part of their efforts to determine the defendant's criminal liability.[4] Indeed, on close examination, it is clear that the trials of Geibel and Koch made a valuable contribution to a reconstruction of the history of the war and the occupation in Poland. But they also refracted what was still a fresh and vivid memory in the minds of adult Poles through a political prism. In this regard, the last Nazi war crimes trials conducted in Poland are significant not only in their own right but also because they shed light on the role played by Poland's criminal justice system in the construction of official memory of the war years after the end of High Stalinism but still very much in the shadow of Cold War politics.

Death of the City: The Trial of Paul Otto Geibel

In October 1947 the Czech government extradited Paul Otto Geibel to Poland. Until the last year of the war, Geibel had a rather unexceptional career: a gendarmerie officer, in 1939–1941 he served in the Protectorate Bohemia–Moravia (the German-occupied Czech lands); this was followed by a short spell with the HSSPF "South" in Russia, after which he was employed by the Main Department of the Order Police in

Berlin. In March 1944 Himmler promoted him to colonel and appointed him SSPF for the Warsaw District in place of Franz Kutschera, who had been assassinated by the Polish underground. Geibel apparently owed his promotion less to talent than to his unconditional obedience to his superiors. When the uprising in Warsaw under the leadership of the AK erupted in August 1944, Geibel played an active role in its suppression and in the total destruction of the city. In February 1945 he was sent back to Prague and placed in command of the Order Police. After the war, US authorities arrested him and handed him over to the Czechs, and in May 1947 a court in Prague sentenced him to five years' imprisonment. Five months later he was extradited to Poland.[5] The Allies repeatedly turned down Polish requests for the extradition of Geibel's superior, the supreme German commander in Warsaw and SS-Obergruppenführer (General) Erich von dem Bach-Zelewski, although they had "loaned" him to testify at Fischer's trial. The British explained their refusal to extradite SS-Gruppenführer (Lieutenant General) Heinz Reinefarth, whose units in Warsaw gained particular notoriety for atrocities, with reference to "matters of security," triggering a sarcastic inquiry by the Polish Foreign Ministry as to whether the "security of the British [occupation] zone depended on Reinefarth's expertise in the destruction of cities and deportations of civilians."[6] Thus Geibel was to be the only senior officer to stand trial for Warsaw's destruction, which as it turned out was the culmination of Nazi terror policies in Poland. As early as December 1939, Himmler stressed that Warsaw must be destroyed as the embodiment of the Polish national spirit. Hans Frank, head of the General Government, wrote in his diary that Warsaw "has been and will ever be the source of all trouble, sending the ripples of turmoil through the entire country."[7] In 1943 the General Government was declared an "area [overrun] by [criminal] gangs," a Nazi euphemism for an area infiltrated by partisans, and it thereby formally came within the jurisdiction of Heinrich Himmler and his SS and police apparatus. Orders to suppress resistance by any means that ensued from this declaration effectively sanctioned atrocities and removed any moral constraints.[8]

The Warsaw Uprising literally cut the lives of many Poles of the wartime generation into two distinct halves – "before and after the uprising" (przed powstaniem i po powstaniu). Their lives having been marked indelibly by the war and the occupation, the majority of Poles considered the AK the spearhead of the anti-German resistance. AK sympathizers placed flowers and wreaths by the graves of resisters and on sites of German executions, and soon after the war Polish workers attempted to erect a marker to commemorate the uprising.[9] Despite the reconstruction of Warsaw since the end of the war, traces of the uprising were still quite visible in the 1950s. The ruins reminded the city's inhabitants of the AK's valiant effort to oust the Germans.[10]

The communist government attempted to "correct" the history of the resistance. To this end, in September 1944, a PKWN radio broadcast from Lublin branded the AK commander General Tadeusz Bór-Komorowski as a "rabid fascist and Hitler's hireling" and threatened to put him on trial for collaboration with the Germans. That said, until the communists consolidated their power, they felt constrained to yield to popular sentiments. The Warsaw administration placed official plaques throughout the city that commemorated the martyrdom of the Polish people, while diminishing or passing in silence over the AK's role in the uprising. On 31 July 1945, government representatives placed wreaths at a symbolic sarcophagus in the military cemetery in Powązki and praised the heroism of the AL and the AK rank-and-file, but condemned the London exile government for "provoking" the uprising.[11] After the death of Stalin, the persecution of the AK lost momentum, but its members were still subjected to chicanery and discrimination. Often, under the slightest pretext, they were fired from their jobs as "class-aliens."[12] The media continued to vilify the AK's leadership and the Polish émigré community in the West. For example, on the tenth anniversary of the Battle of Monte Cassino, *Życie Warszawy* attacked the "London Poles" for "trying to turn Poland into a colony of the US and West Germany.[13]

This deep chasm between popular and official memories of the occupation and the uprising formed the backdrop to the Polish authorities' dilemma regarding how to try Geibel. An open trial could serve as a venue for highlighting Poland's supreme sacrifice during the war, as well as the West's soft treatment of Nazi war criminals. But it would certainly also draw considerable public attention, and the testimonies of the defendant and witnesses had the potential to challenge the official history of Polish resistance and martyrdom. From all appearances the latter consideration prevailed, and in lieu of an open trial, which might have exposed such a sensitive topic to public scrutiny, the government decided to hold closed-door proceedings.

Indeed, the text of the indictment, which Geibel received in December 1953, clearly reflected the official communist version of the Warsaw Uprising. It began with the declaration that the KRN and PKWN had been the only legal representatives of the "people's power" in Poland, arrayed against the forces of the Polish "reaction" – the "London clique." The latter, financed by American and British intelligence, had aimed first and foremost at seizing power before the Red Army was ready to strike across the Vistula. The "Polish bourgeoisie" had deliberately exploited popular patriotism and provoked the Warsaw population into a "hopeless struggle," one that resulted in the loss of 200,000 lives and the displacement of a million people.[14] Having thus paid lip service to the prescribed ideological dictates, the indictment then enumerated specific charges against Geibel: the mass executions of civilians in Warsaw between his appointment in March and the outbreak of the uprising in August 1944; massacres and the deportation of Polish civilians, carried out by the SS and by police forces under Geibel's command; participation in a collective criminal act – the systematic destruction of the city and plunder of property; and membership in the criminal organization of the SS – all charges in accordance with Articles 1, 2, and 4 of the August Decree.[15]

Crucially, the court had access to a full array of evidence, including eighty affidavits, announcements of executions signed by the SSPF in Warsaw (though without Geibel's signature on them), the testimonies of Bach-Zelewski at the IMT and at the trial of Ludwig Fischer, forensic reports that had been collected in the first years after the war, and the statements that Geibel had given Polish interrogators while in prison. Nine witnesses were summoned to appear in court.[16] In other words, Geibel's trial did not differ in essence from standard war crimes trials that were conducted in the West (except that it was conducted behind closed doors), and while the official communist interpretation of history discouraged any memorialization of the war that contradicted it, the evidence presented in court could not but facilitate a trustworthy rendering of the past.

Seven years after his extradition, on 25 May 1954, Geibel stood trial in a closed proceeding before the Warsaw provincial court, whose function was to pass judgment on the most important cases.[17] After Michał Kulczycki, the chief judge of the Warsaw provincial court, read the indictment, Geibel took the stand. He adopted the defence tactics all too familiar in war crimes trials. In Prague he had steadfastly denied all charges regardless of the evidence or had tried to minimize his role as a top Nazi functionary. Now, in court in Warsaw, he claimed that his SS rank was merely nominal or "honorary" and that the executions of 991 people between March and May 1944, which were publicly announced, were actually ordered by the KdS Ludwig Hahn in the name of the SSPF.[18] During his pretrial interrogation in Warsaw, Geibel maintained further that, upon the outbreak of the uprising, he had lost contact with his troops and was, therefore, not responsible for their actions.[19] In this vein, he maintained that in early August 1944 the insurgents besieged the so-called Polizeigebiet – the headquarters of the SS, security, and police forces – where he and his subordinates remained under constant attack for several days. Hence, he had no control over SSPF units in the densely populated Mokotów district, where they shot thousands of civilians or locked them in houses and burned them alive. Geibel insisted further that his main duty was command of the anti-air defence of the Polizeigebiet (despite the fact that the insurgents had no aircraft!).[20] Geibel surpassed himself when he told the court that he had "heard" of German crimes for the first time only during the investigation. Yet without blinking an eye, he then declared that he had tried to mitigate the "excesses" of the KdS, the SS, and the Order Police.[21]

Skipping over his role in massacres and executions, Geibel was more than willing to implicate his former colleagues and superiors. In December 1950, Bach-Zelewski's former chief of staff, Ernst Rode, wrote to Bach-Zelewski that he was concerned that in Warsaw Geibel would "spill all kinds of unpleasant things … He had already spoiled much in Prague."[22] Indeed, Geibel "spoiled" much in Warsaw, too, divulging numerous details so long as they did not incriminate him. Combined with the evidence collected by the GKBZH and Polish legal authorities, Geibel's testimony exposed the magnitude of German crimes in Warsaw.

Hitler's "*Vernichtungsbefehl*" became a key issue in Geibel's defence. On 1 August 1944, upon learning of the uprising in Warsaw, Himmler hurried to Hitler's headquarters. Concerned that his reputation was badly damaged – since his SS and police forces were responsible for maintaining order in Poland – Himmler told Hitler that the uprising provided a unique opportunity to destroy the Polish capital, the political and spiritual hub of the nation "that for seven centuries has impeded [German] expansion to the East." Hitler indeed was infuriated and ordered that Warsaw be razed and its entire population erased as a grim warning to the rest of Europe.[23]

After the war, all senior German officers who were implicated in the brutal suppression of the Warsaw Uprising justified their actions on the basis of Hitler's order "to kill everyone," and their testimonies differed only insofar as the form of the order and the time that they received it were concerned. At Ludwig Fischer's trial, Bach-Zelewski stated that upon dispatching him to Warsaw, Himmler told him in unequivocal terms that "every city resident, including women and children, must be killed and no prisoners should be taken."[24] Questioned by the Polish Military Mission in Berlin, Heinz Reinefarth claimed that he had "heard" of Hitler's order from Bach-Zelewski in Warsaw.[25] But some of Reinefarth's subordinates testified that since all civilians were rebels (the Germans did not recognize the insurgents as enemy combatants), Reinefarth ordered that everyone standing in the path of the troops was to be shot on the spot.[26] When questioned by Polish officials in Berlin, Bach-Zalewski's chief of staff, Rode, testified that he had seen Hitler's pencil-written order to destroy Warsaw and its inhabitants.[27]

The German army's chief of staff, Generaloberst (General) Heinz Guderian, told Polish prosecutor Jerzy Sawicki in Nuremberg that he had only "heard" of the order, but never received it. He, therefore, had nothing to do with atrocities, since the destruction of Warsaw was the prerogative of the SS, whose leaders "were never [his] colleagues."[28] Guderian thus clung to the "clean Wehrmacht" myth, which became popular in West Germany after the war and resulted in many German officers being exonerated of criminal responsibility. In fact, Guderian was well informed of the situation in Warsaw, since the insurgents had severed the crucial east–west communication lines that ran through Warsaw, with the result that German troops heading to the Eastern Front had been compelled to take a long detour. The suppression of the uprising, therefore, became a top priority for the Wehrmacht. On 3 August, Hans Frank recorded in his diary that Guderian personally assured him that the army would use the most radical means at its disposal to make Warsaw "suffer harsh and well-deserved retribution."[29] Already on 2 August, Wehrmacht units entered the monastery on Makowiecka Street, herded the nuns, monks, and refugees into the cellar, and tossed in hand grenades, murdering everybody on the spot.[30] The former garrison commandant in Warsaw, General Reiner Stahel, was more candid. Interrogated by Soviet authorities, he admitted that after Bach-Zelewski told him about Hitler's order, he allowed his soldiers to loot and kill with impunity since "it was impossible to keep them under control."[31]

Not surprisingly, Geibel tried to dissociate himself from the order and changed his version of events several times. During the pretrial interrogation, he insisted that he had "heard" of the order only in early August from Ludwig Hahn.[32] He was lying, however – as the SSPF in

Warsaw, he would have been among the first recipients of the order alongside Reinefarth, Hahn, and Dirlewanger.[33] Still later he admitted that Himmler had conveyed to him on 1 August that "[Hitler's] unconditional wish is that the city be completely erased from the face of the earth." In either case, Geibel maintained that he did not pass the order on to his subordinates.[34]

Such divergent versions of the *Vernichtungsbefehl* emanated not only from a desperate attempt to avoid responsibility. Hitler often expressed his wishes to subordinates, who were then left to their own devices in implementing them in accordance with their individual dispositions and their assessments of facts on the ground. At one point, Hitler was so infuriated at the lack of success in Warsaw that he considered recalling all German troops and unleashing a massive air bombardment that would incinerate the city and its inhabitants. By this time, however, German forces were heavily engaged in combat inside the city, and he had to abandon the idea.[35]

By all appearances, in the matters of mass murder and total destruction Geibel was less "accomplished" than Himmler's preferred commanders, whose experience at committing genocide and imperviousness to human suffering made them particularly suitable for the task. The KdS forces in Warsaw under the command of Ludwig Hahn had vast experience in murdering Poles and Jews *en masse*. In the spring of 1943, under the command of Jürgen Stroop, Hahn's subordinates had played an active part in the liquidation of the Warsaw Ghetto.[36]

In early August 1944, several special formations, which had received Hitler's order to crush the uprising by any and all means, arrived in Warsaw. Headed by Reinefarth, SS and police units from Poznań included staff from the Chełmno extermination camp. As HSSPF in the Warthegau, Reinefarth organized mass reprisals against the civilian population.[37] A penal unit of ex-convicts of various nationalities, the special regiment "Dirlewanger," named after its commander, the reputed psychopath Oskar Dirlewanger, epitomized German anti-guerrilla warfare. As part of Bach-Zelewski's anti-partisan formations in Russia, Dirlewanger's men had committed numerous atrocities against civilians; they were the ideal genocidal killers who neither gave nor expected quarter.[38] The so-called Russian Liberation National Army (RONA) had a similarly sinister reputation. Comprised of Russian collaborators, this unit gained notoriety for loose discipline, drunkenness, and extreme brutality, which at times shocked even hardened SS veterans. Its commander, Bronislav Kaminski, was a heavy drinker and was feared by his subordinates.[39]

Formed into a combat group subordinated to Reinefarth, the German troops and their auxiliaries launched attacks eastward from the western suburbs of Wola and Ochota towards the city centre – the historic Old Town. Reinefarth's troops immediately committed mass atrocities against civilians. They shot all residents regardless of age or sex, looted apartments and houses, and gang-raped women, leaving behind streets and housing blocks littered with corpses. Hauptmann (Captain) Wilm Hosenfeld learned of Himmler's order to murder all Polish males from a police officer. He observed that men, women, and children were being ruthlessly murdered and wrote to his family that one "has to shut off his eyes and heart as the population was mercilessly annihilated."[40] According to Polish sources, by 10 August 1944 between 38,000 and 50,000 people had perished in Warsaw's western suburbs.[41]

In the courtroom, Geibel insisted that since Reinefarth's, Dirlewanger's, and Kaminski's units were not subordinated to him, he bore no responsibility for their actions; nor could he have known of atrocities they had committed.[42] While such an argument was certainly valid, Geibel refused to acknowledge that as the SSPF he should have been aware of and thus responsible for the actions of the SS and police forces in Warsaw. In fact, the first mass executions began on 1 August under the watch of the KdS office (located in the Polizeigebiet) and its commander, Ludwig Hahn. By 4 August, Hahn's subordinates had murdered about 2,000 people and forced Polish captives to set the corpses on fire. The odour of burning flesh rose over Warsaw. After liberation the GKBZH found more than five tons of human ashes at the KdS headquarters (though it is possible that many corpses were burned before the uprising).[43] The prosecution summoned several witnesses who had never met or seen Geibel personally but recalled the days of horror in early August 1944. Zofia Jackowska, who was detained in the KdS prison on Szucha Street, and Edward Kryszkiewicz, who was employed by the KdS as a hairdresser, witnessed how KdS functionaries machine-gunned about 2,000 people in one day in the ruins across the street and then burned the corpses. Both also saw gendarmerie details carry out executions of civilians in the area near KdS headquarters.[44]

Geibel insisted that Hahn was directly answerable to the RSHA. However, earlier Polish trials had established that, in accordance with the chain of command in Himmler's security apparatus, the Sipo and the SD offices received direct instructions from the RSHA but were answerable to the SSPFs in general security matters. Hahn, therefore, had to coordinate his actions with Geibel.[45]

Other witnesses told the court about massacres in the densely populated Mokotów district, where SS and police forces carried out mass executions. Tadeusz Gonałkowski and Antoni Pożegowski told the court how SS troops dragged men and women out of houses and shot them.[46] During his defence, Geibel made but a minimal admission, stating that he knew of "the events at the Sipo only in a general sense" and never heard about the burning of corpses. Regarding Mokotów, he flatly denied any connection to the massacres.[47]

Atrocities committed in early August served as a prelude to the main action. On 2 August, Himmler appointed Bach-Zelewski supreme commander of all German forces in Warsaw. After the invasion of the Soviet Union, Bach-Zelewski, a veteran of the Nazi movement, served as the HSSPF of central Russia. In June 1943 he was appointed commander of the anti-partisan formations, which acquired notoriety for extreme brutality, and Hitler praised him as a "man who could wade in a sea of blood."[48] Upon Bach-Zelewski's appointment, Geibel functioned as a key senior officer, both as SSPF and temporarily as Bach's chief of staff (he was replaced by Ernst Rode around 9 or 10 August 1944), and thus he bore responsibility for the atrocities committed by the SS and police forces during this period.

Bach-Zelewski arrived in Warsaw on 5 August (after the war he insisted that he arrived on 8 or 10 August) and immediately realized that the troops' immersion in plunder and wanton destruction was slowing their advance. He had no qualms about the murder of civilians, but unregulated atrocities took time and undermined Himmler's ultimate objective, which was to crush the uprising as soon as possible before the Soviet army resumed its offensive. Hence, Bach-Zelewski turned his attention to the logistics of killing. His staff officers, including Geibel, set out to redeploy German forces, which were ordered to abandon costly frontal attacks and concentrate on single city blocks or streets. These were first subjected to ferocious airstrikes and artillery barrage; platoon and company-size units then worked their way forward, supported by tanks or armoured vehicles. Using women and children as human shields, the troops moved from house to house, tossing grenades into cellars or incinerating everybody inside with flamethrowers. Sapper details then blew up buildings with explosives. German planes dropped bombs and incendiary devices on hospitals clearly marked by large red crosses. Such tactics followed a clearly defined purpose: to make entire areas unusable for the insurgents and unlivable for the population. Thousands of civilians escaped to the areas still controlled by the insurgents, aggravating sanitary conditions and exacerbating the shortage of supplies.[49]

Although Geibel temporarily served as Bach-Zelewski's chief of staff, when questioned in court he obstinately maintained that he "did not take part in any conferences, neither gave nor signed any orders, and was involved only in logistics."[50] The court, however, had evidence that Geibel had ordered that women be taken as human shields on German tanks. In fact, this episode became well-known in Warsaw among both Germans and Poles. For example, when interrogated by the Soviets, German Hauptmann Wilm Hosenfeld mentioned that Geibel used Polish women as "bulletproof vests" on German tanks.[51]

The court heard witness Wanda Odolska, who testified that in early August SS troops in the Polizeigebiet forced a group of women onto German tanks, which then attacked the insurgent positions. In the course of fighting, two tanks were destroyed and all the women on them burned to death.[52] Geibel now conceded that on 4 or 5 August he had indeed ordered civilians onto tanks, but in his version of events he wanted to "spare" Polish women as well as wounded German personnel. To this end, he ordered a group of Polish women to carry the wounded; other women were to walk ahead of the German column with white bandanas, signalling that it was a peaceful procession. For "protection," he ordered four tanks to move ahead as cover, but he "did not know" that the crews forced women to sit on the tanks. Later, when he found out about it, he "felt ashamed."[53]

After Rode took over as Bach-Zelewski's chief of staff, Geibel carried on in his capacity as SSPF.[54] Meanwhile, massacres of civilians and captured insurgents continued unabated as German troops moved forward. Since early August, Corporal Will Fiedler had been stationed at a tannery, where he witnessed how drunken SS men forced men, women, and children to undress and lie down on a pile of wood; mothers still clung to small babies. A shooting detail came forward and commenced firing at point-blank range, while their comrades divided the victims' cloths and valuables. After the next group of civilians was ordered to lie down on the corpses, the shooting resumed. "Accustomed to the shooting of Jews," Fiedler was shocked when he found out that all the victims were Poles. He calculated that at the tannery the SS shot about 200 people a day; by late August about 5,000 people had been shot.[55]

Pressed for time, Bach-Zelewski opted for a more constructive approach. Hauptmann Hosenfeld noticed that later only Polish males were shot, although he did not know whether it was due to Bach-Zelewski's intervention.[56] Then Bach-Zelewski proposed to Himmler that the insurgents be treated as POWs so long as they did not wear German uniforms; civilians who did not participate in fighting would be transferred to labour camps in Germany.[57] Concerned about the impending Soviet offensive, Himmler acceded to the proposal. On 2 October the AK command realized that the situation was hopeless and agreed to lay down arms. Under the terms of surrender, more than 17,000 resistance fighters, except communists, were sent to POW camps, while about 300,000 Polish civilians were collected in detention centres and then sent to Germany as a forced labour contingent.[58]

For two months Geibel acted in the shadows of his more prominent superiors such as Bach-Zelewski and Reinefarth, but in early October he came forward to play the key role in the destruction of Warsaw's infrastructure. Such plans had already been contemplated in the spring of 1944, when Hans Frank ordered the "immobilization operation" (*Lähmungaktion*), which involved the dismantling of Polish industries and the demolition of immovable infrastructure.[59] In accordance with Hitler's order, Himmler on 12 October appointed Geibel to oversee the operation and told him that Hitler "expressly wished that the city be wiped off the face of the earth and no stone left unturned."[60] Geibel thus enjoyed full executive powers to expel the population and to obliterate the Polish capital. Contrary to the postwar testimonies of German generals, the Wehrmacht fully endorsed the destruction of Warsaw in order to deprive the Red Army of the city's material and human resources and to turn it into a heap of ruins that would slow down the Soviet offensive.[61]

Under Geibel's supervision, sapper units of the 9th Army began their lethal work; they demolished not only power stations, water pumps, and tramway rails, but also museums, libraries, and theatres, which were marked as strategic points. One Wehrmacht commander in Warsaw complained to Himmler that Geibel's subordinates were blowing up buildings that from a military standpoint were useless.[62] Simultaneously, the city was thoroughly looted. The special "clearing unit" (*Räumungsstab*) collected paintings, carvings, frescos, altars, and weapon collections. The order to destroy had erased the thin line between military expediency and destructive lust, and the troops raped,

murdered, and plundered; some units that left the city resembled merce-
nary soldiers or *Landsknechte* of a bygone era, loaded down with goods.[63]

Amid almost apocalyptic images of the dying city, the SS formed
several "incinerating" brigades of Polish prisoners, who were forced to
collect and burn the corpses that littered the streets. A survivor of one
such brigade recalled that the prisoners poured fuel on piles of corpses
and watched in horror "as the fire engulfed human bodies, which began shrinking and twitching as if stretching their hands to the sky."[64]

In line with his total denial of culpability, Geibel told the court that
he tried to intervene with Himmler against the destruction, but when
he was shown photographs of the city ruins, he justified his actions by
invoking "military necessities."[65] As a last resort, he claimed to have a
certificate, signed by an ephemeral Polish underground organization
(the so-called Corps of State Security) that vouched for him, supporting his assertion that he did not participate in the terror campaign in
the city.[66]

Himmler called the fight in Warsaw the "hardest battle" since the beginning of the war, comparable only to the street fighting in Stalingrad.
Accordingly, Hitler rewarded all German units in the city with a special "Warsaw Shield" badge. On 30 September he bestowed upon
Bach-Zelewski and Oskar Dirlewanger the highest German order, the
Knight Cross. Reinefarth received the Oak Leaves to the Knight Cross,
and Hahn was awarded the Iron Cross 1st Class.[67] As for Geibel, on
22 September 1944, HSSPF "East" Wilhelm Koppe supported his promotion, praising him for "energetically and prudently carrying out
necessary actions against the resistance" and adding that "the police
forces under his command achieved outstanding results."[68] Geibel received the Iron Cross 1st Class and was promoted on 26 October to
SS-Brigadeführer (Major General) and Generalmajor (Major General)
of the Police.[69]

On 31 May 1954 the court pronounced sentence: life imprisonment,
which was quite rare for Polish war crimes trials.[70] The court acknowledged that it could not prove that Geibel acted on his own initiative and
therefore assumed that he acted under orders. Such a rationale seems
inexplicable, given that Polish courts routinely rejected the plea of superior orders. To be sure, the court ruled that as SSPF in Warsaw, Geibel
was part of a common criminal plan (the charge of common criminal
design was applied to a number of defendants in 1946–7), even if he
was not present at the sites of murder and destruction.[71] Most likely,

it was the long passage of time since the war that saved Geibel from the gallows. Indeed, the court acknowledged that it took into consideration Geibel's "partial remorse" (potentially affected by imprisonment in "socialist" Poland) and noted that ten years had elapsed since he committed his crimes. Also, in the context of the official interpretation of the Warsaw Uprising and given that Geibel's trial was a low-key affair, the sentence appears less striking. Upon Geibel's appeal, on 22 September 1954 the Supreme Court upheld the verdict and made his sentence retroactive to his imprisonment in May 1946.[72]

On 27 April 1956 the Polish government declared a general amnesty. This was hailed by the press as the "reflection of critical [positive] changes in Polish society, the success of socialist reconstruction, and the fact that most enemies were either defeated or acknowledged their errors." Accordingly, within a few years most German war criminals who were serving prison terms were released. Significantly, Article 7 of the amnesty specified that it did not apply to crimes committed under Article 1(a) of the August Decree (in the December 1946 reading) – that is, partaking in the murder of civilians and POWs.[73] Nevertheless, the Opole district court (Geibel served his term in Opole) decided to release Geibel "on grounds of good conduct." However, the justice minister authorized reconsideration of the decision after a protest by a group of participants in the Warsaw Uprising.[74] On 19 December 1959 the Supreme Court overturned the Opole court's decision, pointing out that it had been made "without taking into consideration the gravity of the crimes committed by the prisoner." Geibel, therefore, would have to serve his term in full.[75] On 12 October 1966 he committed suicide in his cell.[76]

The destruction of Warsaw and the massacre of its population was a uniquely horrifying event in wartime Europe, equal in magnitude and ferocity only to the notorious Nanjing Massacre.[77] Half of Warsaw was turned to rubble and between 150,000 and 200,000 people (out of a population of 720,000) lost their lives.[78] Yet except for General Reiner Stahel, the former commandant of Warsaw, Geibel was the only German senior officer tried for the largest single massacre of the Second World War.[79] When justice finally caught up with Bach-Zelewski in 1962, a West German court sentenced him to life imprisonment for murder perpetrated during the "Night of the Long Knives."[80] No charges, however, were filed against him for his role in the suppression of the Warsaw Uprising.[81]

The postwar career of Heinz Reinefarth is indicative of West German policies to immunize Nazi criminals from prosecution. After being questioned by the US War Crimes Investigation Committee (OCCWC), Reinefarth was cleared of any wrongdoing and released as an individual of "great potential military value" whose extradition to the east would be to the "detriment of the United States."[82] When questioned by the West German authorities, Reinefarth claimed to have come to Warsaw a week after the onset of massacres and denied that Kaminski and Dirlewanger were his subordinates.[83] In 1949 the de-Nazification commission exonerated Reinefarth from wrongdoing, declaring him a mere "follower" (*Mitläufer*) of Hitler and the Nazi Party.[84] Freed to enter West German politics, he eventually became mayor on the island of Sylt in Schleswig-Holstein.[85]

In response to protests mounted by West German liberal circles and requests submitted by the Polish authorities, the prosecutor's office in Flensburg launched an investigation of Reinefarth that lasted almost a decade. In the end, the investigation "found nothing that supported allegations of Reinefarth's criminal activities." A spokesman for the Ministry of Justice of Schleswig-Holstein went so far as to state that the population of Warsaw had violated the rules of warfare, whereas Reinefarth's troops "treated the civil population humanely."[86] In 1966 the investigation of Reinefarth was closed due to "lack of evidence" and he lived on peacefully until his death in 1979.[87]

In the 1960s Ludwig Hahn was arrested and released several times. Only in June 1973 was he sentenced to twelve years in prison for his activities as the KdS in Warsaw, but he was acquitted of any crimes perpetrated during the Warsaw Uprising. In July 1975 a court in Hamburg sentenced him to life imprisonment for the deportations of Jews to Treblinka. In 1983 he was released due to poor health; he died in 1986.[88]

The Trial of Erich Koch: Hitler's "Brown Tsar"

On 12 October 1958 the newspaper *Trybuna Ludu* announced that Erich Koch, the former Nazi president of East Prussia and governor of the Białystok District, would soon stand trial for the murder of thousands of Poles, Jews, and Soviet POWs. Furthermore, as *Reichskommissar* of Ukraine, Koch was held responsible for the killing and starvation of four million people and the deportations of two million more to labour camps. The newspaper stressed that if Koch had not eluded justice earlier, he would have sat in the dock among other leading Nazi officials at the IMT in Nuremberg.[89]

Koch's career in the Third Reich represented the spectacular rise of a "plebeian" – an individual born into the lower stratum of society who rose to positions of great power during the Nazi "revolution." Born in 1896 to a working-class family and raised in the Lutheran tradition, Koch graduated from a trade school and worked in a printing business and as a railway employee. He fought in the First World War, entered the Freikorps after the war, and in 1922 joined the Nazi Party, becoming a member of the Nazi elite – the so-called old fighters (*alte Kämpfer*). Koch initially belonged to the left wing of the NSDAP, led by Gregor Strasser, who advocated an "anti-capitalist" revolution and eventually came into conflict with Adolf Hitler's faction.[90]

In 1928 Hitler dispatched Koch to East Prussia to become the province's Gauleiter In September 1933, Koch was appointed president (*Oberpräsident*) of East Prussia, and under his watch the Nazis launched the persecution of Jews and a vehement anti-Polish campaign.[91] Notwithstanding his promotion, his past association with Strasser had tarnished his reputation in the Nazi Party, and until the end of the Third Reich he attempted to prove his loyalty to Hitler by acting as one of the most brutal Nazi officials in the East. Koch's jurisdiction expanded after the conquest of Poland, when the districts of Suwałki, Augustów, and Ciechanów were integrated into East Prussia. When Germany invaded the Soviet Union, the Białystok District was also placed under his civilian administration. The Nazi leadership intended to integrate that district into East Prussia; however, it remained under a special status throughout the war, and Koch governed it as Chief of Civil Administration (Chef der Zivilverwaltung für den Bezirk Bialystok), directly answerable to Hitler. In November 1941 the district was expanded by incorporating the city of Grodno and its environs.[92]

What would become Poland's longest war crimes trial had a twisted prelude. After Germany's defeat in 1945, Koch lived under an assumed name in the British zone of occupation. In May 1949 he was recognized by a refugee from East Prussia and arrested by the British police. The former *Reichscommissar* of Ukraine dreaded extradition to the Soviet Union, but by the late 1940s Moscow had seemingly lost interest in prosecuting German war criminals. Some notorious offenders such as SS Gruppenführer (Lieutenant-General) Bruno Streckenbach, who organized the *Einsatzgruppen* for the Russian campaign, received a "standard" twenty-five-year prison sentence and were treated as POWs.

After the creation of the German Democratic Republic, the Soviets began releasing German nationals from Soviet prison camps.[93]

Although the Soviet government did not request Koch's extradition, in the summer of 1949 Warsaw expressed interest in putting him on trial. The case was reviewed by the British Extradition Tribunal in Hamburg. His attorney argued in vain that, after Soviet Marshal Konstantin Rokossovski became Poland's defence minister, Koch's extradition to Poland was for all intents and purposes an extradition to the Soviet Union and that he would face a Soviet-style show trial. Nevertheless, in January 1950 the British extradited Koch to Warsaw on the condition that he be tried solely for his wartime activities in Poland.[94]

In preparation for the trial, Polish authorities launched a comprehensive search for evidence about his activities on Polish soil. They collected Koch's correspondence with Nazi officials, wartime German decrees and newspapers, medical reports on exhumations of mass graves, and several hundred affidavits of witnesses and survivors.[95] Although Koch's activities in Ukraine would not be the focus of his trial, they were included in the state's evidence for the sake of "highlighting the defendant's political profile." For example, Alexander Dallin's book *German Rule in Russia*, which addressed Koch's rule in Ukraine, was included in the collection of documents. The Soviet government also sent documentary evidence about Nazi crimes in Ukraine to Warsaw, while the East German authorities sent the Poles affidavits of German nationals about Nazi terror against the political opposition in East Prussia.[96]

Koch was indicted in February 1955. The indictment cited his complicity in preparing and waging an aggressive war against Poland; his membership in Nazi criminal organizations, that is to say, the SA and the upper echelons of the NSDAP; his organizing of the deaths of political activists and the Polish intelligentsia; his persecution and murder of Poles, Jews, and Soviet POWs on national, racial, and political grounds; the looting of Polish national resources; and the destruction of Polish culture and religion. Koch thus faced charges of crimes against peace, war crimes, and crimes against humanity; the last two charges fell under Articles 1 and 2 of the August Decree.[97] In other words, much like Greiser, Forster, and Fischer, Koch would be tried for the criminal leadership he had exercised over the area under his control.

Still, it was eight years after his extradition before Koch finally appeared in court. The trial was repeatedly postponed due to Koch's complaints about poor health; apparently, at one point he was mishandled by his fellow prison inmates. Concerned about Koch's health, the

Warsaw provincial court (where he would be tried) ordered that he be placed under constant medical surveillance.[98]

On 20 October 1958 the "trial that Poland awaited for many years had begun" – so wrote a Soviet journalist regarding the special significance of Koch's trial.[99] A few days later, *Folks-shtime* stressed that "even though a long time has passed since the Hitlerite murderer began his murderous work in occupied Poland and Ukraine, still fresh in one's memory are the horrifying crimes, for which he will now have to answer in front of a court of the Polish Republic."[100] Like previous trials, this one was intended to demonstrate Poland's resolve to punish Nazi war criminals regardless of time limitations. The publicity surrounding Koch's trial indicated that the Polish government considered it of particular symbolic value. In fact, Koch's trial began shortly after the trial of ten *Einsatzkommando* members in Ulm in July–August 1958, which revealed that many perpetrators had smoothly insinuated themselves into West German society and were living normal lives. Despite overwhelming evidence, most defendants in Ulm received light sentences. Later in the same year, the West German justice ministry established the Central Office for Investigations of Nazi crimes in Ludwigsburg. Koch's trial, therefore, was to serve as a podium from which to condemn West German policies of absolving former Nazis of their crimes. Special admission cards were necessary to enter the courtroom, and most of these were distributed among Polish dignitaries, representatives of professional associations, and members of the local state and PZPR branches. Thirty foreign and fifty Polish journalists would report on the trial.[101]

All eyes turned to the courtroom door through which Koch was escorted into the dock. The sickly and broken old man who entered hardly resembled an omnipotent Nazi dignitary. Presiding Justices Edward Binkiewicz and Ignacy Frydecki, both members of the Supreme Court, read the indictment aloud. As Gauleiter of East Prussia, Koch was held responsible for preparing an aggressive war against Poland. He was accused of overseeing the murder of about 100,000 Poles and 80,000 Jews while acting on his "own initiative" as governor of the Ciechanów District. In his subsequent role as Chief of Civil Administration in the Białystok District, he was held personally responsible for the murder of 72,000 Poles and the deportation of about 200,000 Jews to labour and death camps. German "pacifications" of villages in the Białystok District, which Koch was alleged to have overseen, involved burning or

6.1 Erich Koch on trial. Public domain:
http://euromaidanpress.com/2015/03/28/why-did-stalin-save-the-life-
of-hitlers-gauleiter-in-ukraine-who-sent-to-graves-4-million-people

destroying houses, executing village inhabitants, and deporting local populations to labour camps or prisons.[102]

Koch pleaded not guilty to all charges. Throughout the trial he would maintain that he was merely the civil administrator of the occupied provinces, carrying out the orders of Hitler and Himmler, that all crimes were committed by the SS and police forces subordinated to Himmler, and that he learned about "many horrible things" only from the indictment. As far as public announcements he made during the war were concerned, he claimed that they had been prepared by his subordinates and that he signed them without reading them. When facing particularly damning evidence, he would complain of poor health or the wretched conditions in his prison cell.[103]

The prosecution's case rested on extensive documentation, which included Koch's published anti-Polish speeches and administrative orders, discriminatory regulations for Białystok and Ciechanów issued by Koch and other Nazi authorities, and witness testimonies. The prosecution also referred to Alexander Dallin's book *German Rule in Russia*, in which the author discussed Koch's rule in Ukraine. To prove that Koch participated in preparing an aggressive war against Poland, the prosecutors presented his speech published on 2 November 1939 in the *Königsberger Allgemeine Zeitung*, in which he slandered Poland

and praised Germanizing efforts in Polish schools in East Prussia. On 31 December 1939 the same paper published an article by Koch in which he expressed satisfaction with the destruction of Poland, "which ravaged the old, cultural, German land."[104] The prosecution also had at its disposal the testimony of the former chief of the Judenreferat at the KdS Białystok, SS-Obersturmführer (First Lieutenant) Fritz Gustav Friedel, who told the interrogators that Koch was a rabid National Socialist.[105]

Apparently for the first time in Polish legal history, the court listened to recorded speeches, in this case two speeches made by Koch, one from June 1938 and the other from June 1939, in which he promoted aggressive German policies towards Poland.[106] To counter Koch's argument that he merely carried out Hitler's orders, the prosecution produced an affidavit by Albert Forster, who functioned in a similar capacity in Danzig. Forster unequivocally stated that as Gauleiter and president Koch controlled all state and party affairs in East Prussia.[107]

Charged with organizing and implementing Nazi terror policies in the area he administered, Koch had to answer for the notorious Działdowo (Soldau in German) camp. Erected in the winter of 1939 in the Ciechanów District, the camp became part of Aktion T4 (a program of forced euthanasia in wartime Nazi Germany), whereby 1,500 mental patients from East Prussia and 250 to 300 from the district were murdered by gas.[108] In the summer of 1941, Działdowo was reorganized into a labour education camp (Arbeitserziehungslager). Out of 30,000 inmates who passed through the camp, 13,000 were murdered or died of illness, mistreatment, and hunger.[109] Koch insisted that he had only "heard" about the camp and never issued orders to deport people there. However, the prosecution presented the court with the testimony of the former SSPF in Lublin, Jakob Sporrenberg, who told Polish investigators that in early 1941 he and Koch talked about the conditions in the Działdowo camp and that as a top Nazi official Koch knew about all concentration and labour camps in his area.[110]

Two other German functionaries also testified that all terror policies and anti-Jewish measures in the Białystok District were carried out with Koch's approval or acknowledgment. Friedel told interrogators that in February 1943 Koch ordered the resettlement of Poles and Byelorussians from the city quarters marked for the ghettoization of Jews. Koch also issued ordinances that forbade contact between Jews and non-Jews and ordered the "fur operation" (Pelz-Aktion), whereby Jews had to give up all warm clothes for the German army and later all gold and valuables.

Waldemar Macholl, the former chief of the "anti-resistance" section of the Białystok Gestapo, had earlier testified that Koch was known as an extremely harsh functionary and a fanatical follower of Hitler and that all decrees, regulations, and actions against Poles and Jews could not have been executed without his knowledge or approval. In August 1941 Macholl was present at a conference of Nazi officials in Białystok at which Koch urged them to govern the region with an "iron fist." On several occasions, Koch directed his subordinates to apply the strictest measures possible against the civilian population.[111]

The prosecution summoned more than fifty witnesses, including several from the GDR.[112] As the spouse of an NSDAP member, Magdalena Kolek met Koch at several social gatherings. She testified that Koch approved mass reprisals against Poles for the murder of a single German.[113] Witness Kazimiera Rybicka-Zawadzka, who worked for the German administration in Białystok, recalled Koch's speech to the city administration in August 1941 in which he stressed the "German" character of the land and promised to liquidate the Jewish ghetto.[114] A former telephone operator in East Prussia, Paul Bredlov, told the court about Koch's conversations with other German officials in which they planned the deportations of Poles to Ukraine. Bredlov alleged that Koch personally took part in the executions of twenty Poles during the evacuation of the German population from East Prussia.[115] Recently released from prison, where he had spent several years as an "enemy of socialist reconstruction," Kazimierz Moczarski testified that the AK command knew full well of Koch's sinister role in Białystok and Ciechanów.[116]

The prosecution summoned Professor Marian Pospieszalski, an expert witness from the ŻIH, who outlined the Nazi plans to exterminate the Jews; this was to be a prelude to a similar extermination of Slavic people.[117] Pospieszalski told the court that relations between the NSDAP, the civil administration, and the HSSPF in reality depended on personal connections between the top leaders of these organizations. Hence, although he was directly responsible to Himmler, the HSSPF had to coordinate its activities with the civil administration and its leadership. As such, Koch must have known about Hitler's genocidal plans to annihilate the Jews as well as the so-called Generalplan Ost, which stipulated the resettlement of millions of Slavs to Siberia.[118]

Another expert, Professor Mieczysław Siewierski, who was a prosecutor at the trial of Amon Göth, stressed that the trial of Koch was similar to those of Greiser and Forster in that all three were supreme rulers in their respective domains, supervising NSDAP cells, the civil administration, and the SS and police apparatus. Since Koch was charged with crimes against peace – which involved a conspiracy to wage aggressive war – Siwierski explained to the court that a "conspirator" need not necessarily directly participate in crime but could coordinate it from afar. Therefore, the IMT's formulation of the commission of criminal conspiracy (the planning, preparation, initiation, and waging of wars of aggression) and the definition of genocide in the UN Convention on the Prevention and the Punishment of the Crime of Genocide of 9 December 1948 fit Koch's crimes exactly. For this reason, he was not eligible for the amnesty of 1956.[119]

Naturally, Koch's own rendition of his activities differed sharply from that in the indictment. In fact, all sense of proportion had vanished entirely from Koch's statements since his arrest by the British.[120] Interrogated by the Polish authorities for the first time in April 1950, Koch denied all charges, and he would consistently do so till the bitter end. In a letter to President Bierut, Koch called himself an "honest socialist" who was concerned about the situation in West Germany and referred to Konrad Adenauer as a "dangerous personality." He went so far as to propose the creation of a new political party in West Germany that he would lead down a path towards socialism.[121]

He continued this line of defence in the courtroom, vigorously refuting all allegations or claiming that he had no prior knowledge of any incriminating evidence.[122] The high point in his denials was his insistence that the civil administration had nothing to do with the "Jewish question," that he found out about Nazi crimes only during his extradition trial in Hamburg or from the indictment, and that he tried to treat Poles and Jews humanely and intervened on their behalf before the SS. Thus, when he "accidentally" found out that the SS deported Jews from Białystok to Warsaw, he rushed to the station, ordering more transports so that they would not be cramped inside their freight cars.[123]

Straining to dissociate himself from Hitler, Himmler, and the SS, Koch maintained that he was a National Socialist in the "social-revolutionary" mould of a Strasser – that is, the total opposite of Hitler and his racial ideology. Constantly in conflict with the SS, he could not have known of mass executions, the concentration camps, or the persecution of Jews and Poles. Furthermore, he claimed that after antisemitic legislation was set in motion, he helped Jews leave East Prussia. Not surprisingly, such remarks generated derisive laughter among the onlookers in the courtroom. For their part, the judges found such excuses repellent, and on several occasions they reprimanded Koch for rambling.[124]

Koch's conduct may have been indicative of his cynicism and lack of remorse. After all, when an attorney at the IMT in Nuremberg asked Ernst Kaltenbrunner why he refused to accept any responsibility for the actions of the SS, the latter mockingly replied that "a trial is a game and everybody plays to win."[125] But Koch quite possibly also saw which way the wind was blowing in Europe: the drive to prosecute Nazi criminals had subsided, and that wind seemed to be blowing in his favour. Most Nazi war criminals in West Germany were given mild sentences or were let go. More than once Koch complained in court that "all guilt lay with those who at this time are free." Moreover, the April 1956 amnesty for convicted accomplices in Nazi war crimes had emptied Polish prisons of most German culprits. By the time of Koch's trial, they had left Poland for Germany.[126]

In all likelihood, Koch had also heard about the harsh sentences meted out by Polish courts to war criminals. He must have realized that his life was at stake and have been determined to fight for it to the bitter end. In prison, he had plenty of time to familiarize himself with the main arguments made by defendants in Nuremberg and at other war crimes trials. On several occasions he complained about the court's "violation of human rights," pointing to the fact that his wartime activities were not considered criminal by German law at the time they were committed. To prove this point, he requested the opinion of experts from the International Court in The Hague.[127]

Koch looked relatively confident during the first few days of the trial, but as it went on he became perceptibly more nervous. The testimonies of witnesses and the hostile reactions of the gallery visibly unsettled him, and increasingly he found the psychological strain too hard to endure. Consequently, although the press repeatedly reported that the sentence would be pronounced soon, the trial was postponed several times due to the defendant's deteriorating health. For example, by 25 November, after the court had heard fifty-one witnesses and six affidavits had been read into the record, the press reported that the sentence would be announced on 20 December. Then it was reported that the trial was to resume in late January or early February 1959 "unless unexpected difficulties intervene."[128]

The prosecution asked for the death penalty. In late February Koch's lawyers delivered their summation. They pointed out that Koch was an old, sick, and broken man who condemned Hitlerism and was being tried fourteen years after the war – the implicit suggestion was that he was being tried as a symbol of the German occupation. They further argued that Koch was not responsible for the actions of the SS and the police. They insisted that since he was being tried for crimes committed against Poland, his activities in East Prussia and Ukraine should be removed from the text of indictment.[129] Crucially, the defence stressed that Article 1.1 of the August Decree stipulated the death penalty only for direct participation in murder, which the prosecution was unable to prove since its case rested entirely on circumstantial evidence. In this context, argued defence counsel Professor Jerzy Śliwowski, Koch's case fell under the jurisdiction of Article 8.1 of the April amnesty (according to which all cases except those under Article 1.1 were to be terminated). Underscoring the ideological slant of the trial, the defence appealed to the court to consider Koch's partial "re-education" by Polish justice, evidenced in his display of anti-Nazi inclinations.[130]

On 9 March 1959 the court assembled for the last time to pronounce judgment. The courtroom was packed with onlookers, including newspaper and television reporters; the overflow filled the hallway.[131] In the view of the judges, Koch had been a key and willing participant in Nazi crimes who now deserved the ultimate punishment. As Gauleiter of East Prussia, he had been among the Nazi elite who enjoyed Hitler's complete trust, and he was fully responsible for implementing the Nazis' terror policies in the Białystok and Ciechanów districts.[132] As a senior Nazi official, Koch "must have been aware" of Hitler's intentions, was in ideological harmony with Hitler's genocidal policies, and helped implement these policies in East Prussia and in Poland. Such practices, which were entirely consistent with the NSDAP's world view, had been formulated in the 1920s and applied after the Nazi takeover in the 1930s, and had reached their zenith during the war. Under Koch's supervision, 200,000 innocent Poles and Ukrainians had been executed with bullets or exterminated in concentration and death camps.[133]

Koch was found guilty of persecuting and murdering entire groups on the basis of their politics, nationality, or race and of depriving Jews of freedom and imposing forced labour on them in ghettos and concentration camps. The verdict emphasized that the Holocaust was a crucial component of a comprehensive Nazi effort to exterminate the Polish nation. For crimes against humanity, war crimes, and crimes against peace, and in accordance with Article 1 of the August Decree, the court sentenced Koch to death.[134]

On hearing the verdict, the courtroom erupted in applause. *Folksshtime* called the death sentence not revenge, but a just punishment imposed on "the basis of the [defendant's] guilt. For this reason it was met with satisfaction by all in Polish and Jewish society and it will also certainly be met with satisfaction by the entire world, among them thousands of people of good will in West Germany."[135]

Given Koch's position in the Nazi hierarchy, his guilt was never seriously in doubt, nor is it to this day. According to the evidence collected by Polish investigators and subsequently by contemporary researchers, Koch took part in a number of conferences during which terror and murder were discussed in unequivocal terms. For example, on 2 October 1940, Koch, Hans Frank, Baldur Schirach, and Martin Bormann met with Hitler, who declared that the General Government should become a sort of Polish "reservation," a huge labour complex, where the native elite would be immediately eliminated and the rest of the population would serve as a cheap labour force. To degrade the Polish people and keep them at the lowest intellectual level, the education system would be dismantled.[136]

Similarly, during the trials of Greiser, Forster, and Fischer it was proven that they had been aware of the crimes committed by the SS and police and often coordinated their activities. For example, in accordance with the instruction issued by the German Ministry of the Interior on 20 September 1936, the inspectors of the security police in Germany were subordinated directly to the presidents of provinces, facilitating closer cooperation between the two structures.[137] On 7 November 1939, Himmler's directive specified that regional police departments were to be subordinated to the civil administration, although they would answer directly to him.[138] To that effect, in June 1939 Koch appointed Wilhelm Rediess, the HSSPF for East Prussia, as his deputy in all police matters in the event of war. (The letter of appointment was included in the court evidence.)[139] Along the same lines, Sporrenberg testified that the SS and police in East Prussia were subordinated to the HSSPF, who in turn was answerable to Koch in all police-related matters. Koch, therefore, must have been well informed about SS terror and the conditions in the concentration camps.[140]

In October 1939, Hitler appointed Koch as regional commissar for the Reichskommissariat for the Strengthening of German Nationhood (Reichskommissariat für die Festigung deutschen Volkstums, RKFDV), which was subordinated to Himmler. The RKFDV's remit was to plan, implement, and control Germanization in occupied Poland and later in Occupied Russia; this encompassed population transfer projects.[141]

Furthermore, in accordance with the decree of the German Ministerial Cabinet of 4 December 1941, Koch ordered the establishment of a drumhead court martial for Poles and Jews in East Prussia.[142]

Since Koch's standard practice was to delegate multiple tasks to his subordinates, from the legal point of view it was difficult to establish his direct involvement in the genocide of Jews. For example, the court found that Koch displayed "conscious initiative" in promoting Hitler's racial and genocidal policies, but it also recognized that the implementation of the "Final Solution" rested in the hands of the SS. Still, Koch's involvement was far from marginal. He signed public announcements that restricted the movement and activities of Jews, and he called upon Poles and Byelorussians to help apprehend Jews.[143] On one occasion he participated in the discussion of deportations of Jews from East Prussia to the General Government or "elsewhere."[144] When on 9 October 1942 the NSDAP chancellery sent a memo to every Gauleiter that indicated that the final stage of the "Final Solution" had been set in motion, Koch certainly knew what the term meant. In October and November 1942 most ghettos in the Białystok District were liquidated (except in the city of Białystok itself)[145] and most Jews were deported to the death camps. In January 1943 Koch ordered that any remaining Jewish labourers be gradually replaced by Byelorussians.[146]

At the same time, Koch tried to spare "useful" Jews – those employed in German industries and enterprises. Possibly, this initiative reflected his pragmatism as well as an ongoing rivalry between him and the SS.[147] In June 1943 the Białystok District was declared a zone for anti-partisan operations (*Bandenkampfgebiet*), which were taken over by Koch's rival, Bach-Zelewski. Under the latter's command, the SS and the police "pacified" 147 villages; over the course of two months, 3,644 houses and farms were burned and almost 2,000 people were shot.[148] Koch tried to sabotage Bach-Zelewski's actions, but there is no doubt that his civil administration provided "technical" support for the SS, arranging transport and securing the loot.[149]

Moreover, on 25 February 1943, in a letter to Himmler, Koch wrote that he was dissatisfied with the activities of the police, who in his opinion were not doing enough to combat the partisans. As an ultimate measure, he suggested a total evacuation of the population and the creation of a security zone of 50 to 100 kilometres on both sides of the highway leading from Gomel to Brest.[150]

Cold War politics played a visible role in the conduct of Koch's trial. The Polish communist political establishment clearly intended to turn it into a symbolic trial of Germany and a podium from which to wage ideological warfare against the West. Accordingly, the press labelled Koch an "offspring of an ideology whose essence was murder and violence, an ideology alien to humanism and justice, the total opposite of social-ist ideology."[151] Koch's indictment emphasized that the "aspirations of American and German imperialisms were identical – both were poised to destroy socialism." To this end, the former deliberately provoked the latter to invade the Soviet Union.[152] The Polish press also alluded to the alleged guilt of the German Social Democratic Party in suppressing the post–First World War revolutionary process: the "social-democratic opportunists impeded the further revolutionary instincts of the [German] working class and allowed the bourgeoisie to establish the Weimar Republic."[153] Polish newspapers in particular highlighted the failure of de-Nazification in West Germany, where since 1951 thousands of former Nazi officials had been allowed to take jobs in the civil service. About 600 former Nazi judges were employed in the West German justice system, and the West German military (Bundeswehr) employed at least 200 former senior Wehrmacht officers. Many other former Nazis had assumed important positions in West Germany's economy and industries.[154]

While such accusations reflected the East–West ideological divide, they were not far-fetched. For example, in 1953 Konrad Adenauer's admin-istration appointed Hans Globke as Director of the Federal Chancellery. In Nazi Germany, Globke had played a key role in drafting anti-Jewish legislation and later served as chief legal adviser to the Office for Jewish Affairs in the Ministry of the Interior.[155] The West German courts rou-tinely treated Nazi atrocities as individual cases of "anomalous" con-duct and meted out mild sentences to the perpetrators or even acquitted them. For example, when in 1951 Bach-Zelewski faced trial for political murder during the "Night of the Long Knives," he was not charged with mass murder in Byelorussia and Poland.[156]

Polish and Soviet propaganda favourably compared Koch's trial with that of Adolf Eichmann in Jerusalem in 1961. In the same year, a book published in Moscow averred that Koch's trial was a "knock-out blow to the sinister forces of fascism, which dragged the German people again into an aggressive war and was [now] revived in West Germany." In contrast, the trial in Jerusalem allegedly entailed a tacit agreement between Tel Aviv and Bonn, whereby in exchange for profit-able trade contracts, the Israeli government agreed not to publicize the names of many of Eichmann's associates, who had become respectable businessmen and politicians in West Germany.[157]

After he was sentenced to death, Koch's defence sent several appeals to the State Council, which in December 1959 and in February 1960 turned them down. However, on 25 March 1960, *Trybuna Ludu* announced that the execution had been temporarily postponed due to Koch's ill health.[158] Having grasped that poor health might help him avoid the noose, Koch set out to worsen his health by refusing scheduled walks in the prison yard and through self-induced vomiting.[159] In 1963, 1964, and 1965 the Warsaw district procurator's office repeatedly queried the district court as to whether the carrying out of Koch's death sentence was still postponed, and each time it received an affirmative answer.[160] Thus, the execution was postponed indefinitely. In 1960, 1965, 1970, and 1973, Koch was examined by several medical commissions, all of which found him ill, although his condition was not life-threatening.[161]

Several factors seem to have played a role in determining Koch's fate. First of all, it seems that the Polish government was unsure whether it would make political sense to execute Koch. After all, sparing Koch's life served an ideological purpose. As the prison warden put it, "the case reflected the humanity of the [communist] system, which refused to carry out the death sentence against a sick individual."[162] Especially after the Treaty of Warsaw in December 1970, which improved Polish–West German relations, the execution of Koch would have been untimely. Indeed, after Willy Brandt's visit to Warsaw Koch hoped he would be extradited to West Germany. His cousin, however, informed Koch that the Federal Republic's ambassador to Poland showed no interest in his fate.[163]

Moreover, the Polish and Soviet governments were interested in the whereabouts of the famous Amber Room, which had been presented to Peter the Great by the King of Prussia in 1716. Installed in the Catherine Palace outside Saint Petersburg, it was a chamber decorated in amber panels and backed by gold leaf and mirrors. During the Second World War it was disassembled by the Nazis, who supposedly transported it to Königsberg in East Prussia, Koch's former domain. It disappeared, and its whereabouts remained a mystery.[164] The KGB and the attorney general of the Soviet Union were continuously asking their Polish counterparts for assistance in locating it, and in June 1964 Koch dispatched a letter to the Soviet ambassador, offering help in this matter in exchange for a visit by a relative. During a meeting with a Soviet representative, however, Koch did not offer anything new on the subject; rather, he suggested that he be transported to Kaliningrad, formerly Königsberg, where the Amber

Room was supposedly hidden.[165] Moreover, the Polish security service used Koch as a source of information; an agent planted in his cell received information from him about German politicians with a Nazi past and even received recommendations from Koch to his friends and acquaintances in West Germany![166] Koch also promised Polish authorities that he would divulge the criminal activities of some German politicians. In this vein, Koch requested that he be extradited to West Germany, where he would testify against Theodor Oberländer and Reinhard Gehlen.[167] In 1962, when Aleksander Omiljanowicz visited Koch in his prison cell in Warsaw, Koch recounted for him an alleged meeting in February 1940 between Himmler and Lavrentiy Beria, chief of the Soviet secret police apparatus (NKVD) under Stalin, in East Prussia, where they agreed to coordinate the efforts of their respective security services.[168]

In prison, Koch wrote his memoirs, which amounted to a self-absolving collection of lies and distortions. For example, he claimed that Hitler never advocated the total extermination of Jews, but rather tried to use the persecution of Jews as a bargaining chip in the conflict between Germany and the British and Americans.[169] Koch wrote to his relatives urging them to contact leading West German politicians such as Chancellor Helmut Schmidt and Foreign Minister Hans-Dietrich Genscher on his behalf.[170]

Koch spent the rest of his life in prison. In June 1983 the chairman of the GKBZH, Professor Czesław Pilichowski, wrote to the Foreign Ministry that the release of Koch was out of question since the prisoner possessed information "vital to the Polish state such as hidden Nazi loot in Poland." Such an assertion from an expert certainly sounded odd, given that Koch did not reveal any "vital" information for almost a quarter of a century after the verdict.[171] On 12 November 1986 Koch died of natural causes at the age of ninety in an Olsztyn hospital.[172]

Conclusion

The trials of Geibel and Koch represented a complex relationship between law, memory, history, and politics. The narrative of these trials was carefully drawn in accordance with the interests and agendas of the government.[173] Political agendas obviously affected the ways in which the trials of the "last Nazis" were conducted. Official Polish communist memory discouraged critical memorialization of the war, and the collision between official and popular memories became particularly acute in the case of the Warsaw Uprising. For the government, people's memories of the uprising represented a dangerous relic of the past; for Poles, that event was a cherished symbol of past trauma and heroism. Only after the partial rehabilitation of the AK began in April 1956 did official commemoration of the uprising become more open and were markers that carried the names of AK soldiers installed in many places in Warsaw and other cities:[174]

The trial of Geibel presented the official interpretation of the uprising, pointing to the AK's actions as the key factor in the destruction of the city and in fuelling German atrocities. Even so, history and popular memory insinuated themselves into the trial through Geibel's and witnesses' testimonies. Although he vehemently contested the charges, Geibel revealed a substantial amount of information, which in combination with other sources collected by the Polish authorities provided a fuller and more accurate history of German crimes in Warsaw.

Undeniably, the conduct of the German troops in Warsaw fit squarely within the wider context of the Nazis' ideological principles and anti-guerrilla warfare. Long before the Warsaw Uprising, the SS and Wehrmacht leadership had come to view the category of "bystanders" as meaningless. Hence, they treated the civilian population as potential guerrillas, as guerrillas' helpers, or at most as collateral damage. Although Geibel's role in the destruction of Warsaw paled in comparison with that of Bach-Zelewski, Reinefarth, Hahn, and Dirlewanger, his guilt for the crimes of which he was accused was incontrovertible.

Geibel's had been a "command responsibility trial"; in contrast, Koch's was one of "leadership responsibility." Koch did not directly participate in mass murder, but he occupied a much higher position in the Third Reich than Geibel and, consequently, his trial revealed a wealth of information about German rule in Poland. Because of his connections to Strasser, Koch initially appeared less radical than some of Hitler's cronies. But in order to remain near the top of the Nazi hierarchy, he adjusted his conduct to become an ardent and unscrupulous executor of Hitler's policies in Poland and Ukraine.[175]

The prosecution proved that as the chief civil servant in Białystok and Ciechanów, Koch controlled the party and state administration and enjoyed unlimited powers. On several occasions Koch declared that he intended to "cleanse" his domain of Poles and Jews, who stood in the way of his building process. In April 1940 he initiated the arrests of the Polish intelligentsia in Ciechanów and Suwałki, precipitating the infamous AB Action in the General Government. The captives were sent to the camp in Działdowo. In more general terms, Koch's trial demonstrated that terror was a method of Nazi rule – indeed, its very essence. As the court stated, "the realization of the criminal plans of the NSDAP and the establishment of the 'New Order' in Europe were impossible without a large-scale application of violence and murder ... which aimed at the removal of people who were considered dangerous for such plans. On Polish soil, it entailed the mass murder of Polish civilians and the total extermination of the Jewish population."[176]

Koch's trial, which lasted almost seven months – the longest trial of a Nazi official conducted in postwar Poland – brought a sense of finality to Polish prosecutions of German Nazi criminals, which had lasted more than a decade.

Epilogue

It's instructive to compare the legal pursuit of Nazis in Poland with the prosecution of Nazi culprits in other countries behind the Iron Curtain. Take, for example, East Germany, the German Democratic Republic or GDR, established under Soviet patronage in 1949. Between 1950, when they inherited the prosecution of Nazis from the Soviet authorities, and 1959, the East Germans convicted 4,717 defendants of Nazi-era crimes. (This figure includes the convictions of 3,324 alleged Nazis just released from Soviet detention in ten particularly arbitrary proceedings conducted in the town of Waldheim in 1950.) East Germany further prosecuted a handful of Nazi criminals in the early 1960s; the last major trial ended in 1966. But in reality, observes historian Christian Dirks, "at no time was there a systematic pursuit of Nazi criminals in the GDR."[1] Indeed, the East Germans followed in the footsteps of the Soviets. The East German trials of Nazis were essentially show trials, utilized by the authorities to suppress political opposition. The security services stage-managed prosecutions behind the scenes, heavy-handedly overseeing all aspects of the proceedings from selecting defendants and dictating indictments to prosecutors to vetting prosecution witnesses and prescribing verdicts even prior to the commencement of trial. As Dirks puts it, "SS murderers in the GDR could not expect a fair trial."[2] Because the East German trials were on the whole overtly political, the Jewish dimension was generally absent. In contrast, overall the Poles, unlike their East German counterparts, took the prosecution of Nazi criminals seriously.[3]

It's more instructive, in fact, to draw a comparison between Poland and a Western European country, since there is an assumption that trials of Nazi criminals in Western democracies were "better" than in countries that lay behind the Iron Curtain such as Poland. Of course, comparing the pursuit of war criminals in Poland and a Western European country is a lot like comparing apples and oranges because not only their immediate postwar political systems but also their experiences under German occupation were radically different. That said, given our argument that Polish trials for Nazi crimes were substantially similar to those held in the West, a brief comparison may be insightful. The Netherlands is a case in point.

Nazi rule in Poland was brutal, violent, and devastating. The death toll from the German occupation of Poland's Jews was around three million, of ethnic Poles about two million. In other words, the Germans and their accomplices were responsible for the deaths of 90 per cent of Polish Jewry and 10 per cent of the ethnic Polish population. (The victims from other ethnic groups in Poland numbered in the tens of thousands.)[4] In line with its racial program, Nazi Germany pursued the systematic and utter destruction of Poland's Jewish population on the one hand, and the harsh colonization of Poland and the terrorizing and enslavement of ethnic Poles on the other. Along these lines, the Nazis targeted Polish Jewry for isolation, persecution, slave labour, and ultimately physical annihilation, while subjecting ethnic Poles to a staggering and indiscriminate loss of life, despoliation of property, incarceration, forced labour, and forced resettlement. Since the Nazis intended not only to defeat the Polish state but also to destroy the Polish nation and turn the Poles into serfs, they had no interest in converting Poles to the Nazi cause.

Nazi rule in the Netherlands started from different premises. The Nazis desired to win the Dutch over for their occupation of the Netherlands and their larger ambition to dominate Europe. After their successful invasion in May 1940 the Nazis installed a civil administration, but it competed with the SS for primacy in the country. Although the occupation regime was bolstered by the collaboration of the Dutch civil service, police force, and industrial sector, not to mention an enthusiastic indigenous Dutch Nazi party, civic strife in the form of strikes and a Dutch underground hardened Nazi occupation policy over time. As Gerhard Hirschfeld writes: "With military collapse threatening [in early 1945], the last restraints fell away. In essence, policy was scarcely different now from Nazi tyranny in the occupied countries of Eastern Europe."[5]

The civilian death toll in German-occupied Holland was around 206,000. The Netherlands had the highest per capita death rate, 2.36 per cent, of all Nazi-occupied countries in Western Europe. More than half, 107,000, of the victims were Jews. Among them were thousands of German Jews who had fled Germany in the 1930s. The step-by-step destruction of Dutch Jewry was marked by the compulsory registration of Jews, their segregation from the non-Jewish population in Amsterdam and other cities, the incarceration of foreign and stateless Jews, followed by the concentration of native Dutch Jews at the transit camps of Westerbork and Vught, and finally the deportation of all Jews in the Netherlands, beginning in the summer of 1942 and lasting until September 1944, mostly to Auschwitz and Sobibór. Only 5,500 survived the camps; of the estimated 18,000 to 25,000 Jews who went into hiding, two-thirds survived. The Jewish death toll of 75 per cent was the highest in Western Europe. The collaboration of the Dutch civil service and police was instrumental in the identification and round-ups of Jews. The Dutch researcher Marnix Croes suggests, however, that an aggressive hunt conducted by the Sipo for Jews hidden in the provinces was key to the low survival rate of Jews in the Netherlands.[6]

The judicial authorities in both postwar Poland and the Netherlands, therefore, had every reason to want to bring German criminals to justice in their respective national courts. It goes without saying that the German apparatus of occupation was much more extensive in Poland than in the Netherlands, but there was no shortage of potential German (and Austrian) defendants who, if the Dutch authorities could lay their hands on them, could be put on trial. As we have shown, Polish judicial officials vigorously pursued the prosecution of Nazi criminals, and Polish courts put more German nationals on trial between 1945 and 1959 than the courts in any other Soviet satellite. The fact that Poland was a communist country operating in the long shadow cast by the Soviet Union naturally makes one question the legitimacy and seriousness of its war crimes trials. We have argued, however, that trials of Nazis in Poland were different from trials of collaborators, both real and imagined, which were by and large show trials. But were the procedures and outcomes in Polish war crimes trials similar to those in a Western country like the Netherlands? Although the German occupation regimes in Poland and the Netherlands were not the same by any stretch of the imagination, it cannot be denied that the occupation in the Netherlands was oppressive and even severe at times. Furthermore, the high rate of destruction of Dutch Jewry was only about 15 per cent lower than the rate of destruction of Polish Jewry. This raises a question: Was the pursuit of justice for German Nazi criminals in Poland comparable to that in the Netherlands?

Shortly after liberation, the Dutch authorities arrested 150,000 people accused of collaboration. In the summer of 1945 the Ministry of Justice assumed responsibility for collaborators, and special courts, part of a special legal campaign (Bijzondere Rechtspleging), were established to try them. Yet of the 150 defendants who were sentenced to death, only 40 were executed. In the course of the late 1940s and 1950s Dutch attitudes softened, and the government adopted a policy of dispensing conditional release for those whose offences were deemed "minor cases," as well as pardons and, with the support of the churches, clemency. Most convicted collaborators were rehabilitated within five to ten years. They included men who had been found guilty of persecuting Jews or of betraying them to the Germans. The effort by the Dutch authorities to sweep the issue of collaboration under the rug was later challenged in the 1960s and 1970s by discontented elements in Dutch society, led by former members of the Dutch resistance.

The prosecution of German officials who had been active during the occupation lagged behind the punishment of indigenous collaborators. The parliament passed a law that granted jurisdiction over German nationals to Dutch courts only in July 1947. Dilatory Dutch judicial officials struggled to identify the legal authority to judge German nationals in Dutch courts, but their procrastination was abetted by the government's preoccupation with collaborators. Dutch special courts eventually tried 232 Germans, convicting 205. Eighteen of those were sentenced to death, but in the end only five were executed. The vast majority of the defendants were sentenced to fixed prison terms. The most prominent Nazi who was executed was SS-Brigadeführer (Major General) Hans Albin Rauter, an Austrian who was Higher Police and SS Leader and Generalkommissar for Security Matters in the Netherlands. A Dutch special court sentenced him to death in 1948. (Arthur Seyss-Inquart, the *Reichskommissar* in the Netherlands, was sentenced to death at Nuremberg and executed.) Rauter's deputy, Wilhelm Harster, commander of the Sipo and SD in the Netherlands, who was in charge of police measures against the Jews and organized their deportation, was more fortunate. He was sentenced to only twelve years in prison and released early in 1955. (In 1967 he was retried with other defendants in Germany and sentenced to fifteen years in prison.) The death sentences of Willy Lages, Ferdinand Hugo Aus der Fünten, and Franz

Fischer, underlings who were all convicted of anti-Jewish crimes, were commuted to life in prison. Lages, who was Harster's deputy SD chief in Amsterdam and head of the Central Office for Jewish Emigration (Zentralstelle für jüdische Auswanderung), directed the arrest and deportation of the city's Jews and even led raids himself. He was released in 1966. His deputy, Aus der Fünten, who was responsible for the day-to-day administration of the Zentralstelle, and Fischer, who organized the deportation of 13,000 Jews from The Hague, were released in 1989. By 1949–50 the Dutch government had lost its appetite for the prosecutions of Germans, partly in response to pressure from the newly established Federal Republic of Germany to draw a line under the trials in Dutch courts.[7]

What does a comparison between the pursuit of justice against Nazi criminals in Polish and Dutch courts teach us? It's clear that settling accounts with domestic collaborators (and, in Poland's case, with political opponents of the nascent communist regime) was a top priority for both Polish and Dutch officials and that in both countries the prosecution of collaborators took precedence over trials of Germans. The difference was that Dutch society backed its government's ardent campaign against collaborators, whereas Polish society was suspicious of its government's crackdown on alleged collaborators – with good reason. It demonstrates further, however, that, even though the Poles operated behind the Iron Curtain and the Dutch in the democratic West, the Polish effort to bring Nazi criminals to justice did not look all that different from that of the Dutch. They both exerted themselves to put perpetrators on trial – witness their mutual resort, albeit temporary in the case of the Poles, to specially convened courts – and they both tended to achieve convictions, including in cases in which the defendants were accused of crimes against Jews. Moreover, the prosecution of Nazi war criminals both in the Netherlands and in Poland eventually ran out of steam, in the former by 1950, in the latter by 1960. Public discussion in the Netherlands over whether to release Lages, Aus der Fünten, and Fischer from prison was heated, but it did not signal revived interest in Dutch society in bringing more cases to court. Likewise, the fate of Erich Koch in Poland, whose death sentence in 1959 was deferred repeatedly until it was finally commuted to life in prison, was a topic of debate within and outside the government, but his case marked the definitive end of an era of war crimes trials in the country. We think, therefore, that it's fair to say that the legal undertaking to put Nazi criminals on trial in communist Poland was substantially the same as, if not even more robust than, in the Netherlands, a Western European country. What are the implications of this similarity? There are at least two.

Even in Western democracies there has historically existed a tension between political discourse and political practice in the realm of law. Western democracies have both extended and violated rights enshrined in law and the promise of rights guaranteed by law. Without a doubt, postwar communist regimes promised the moon when it came to legal rights, but for the most part these regimes actually violated them. But at least in Polish trials of German Nazis, courts managed to limit the usual practice of flouting the law. One reason for this was that in contrast to the politicized environments in which the legal system was implicated in the regime's heavy-handed efforts to achieve a desirable outcome, such as in collaborator trials, in trials for Nazi crimes the regime was more or less content to leave the conduct of the trials in the hands of lawyers and judges whose basic instincts had been shaped by a prewar rule-of-law legal culture. Another reason was that the regime's promise of law could translate into the fulfilment of that promise in trials of German nationals precisely *because* they were not Polish citizens, who, unlike the Germans, in principle should have been able to claim the enjoyment of rights that had been promised to them, even if only on paper. In other words, process and substance in the Polish trials of Nazis remained framed by law because the new Polish government could afford to do so and because the trials satisfied the postwar popular demand for retribution against Germans.[8]

Moreover, the fact that the trials were shaped by holdover rule-of-law instincts allowed Jewish survivors to reassert their dignity, reclaim agency of which the Nazis had deprived them, and give voice to their traumatic ordeals both in their close working relationship with Polish judicial officials and on the witness stand. By giving voice to the traumatic private and collective injuries inflicted by the Nazi genocide, the testimony by both eyewitnesses and expert witnesses at many of the trials – imperfect though these trials may have been and however subject they were to communist biases – helped restore closure and normative coherence to the survivors' world, as Mietek Pemper's testimony at Göth's trial in 1946 showed. (Testimonies of ethnic Poles at many of the trials could not help but perform a similar function for them.)[9] In the process Jews' private traumatic memory became public memory. The fact that the trials were legitimate rather than sham helped Jewish memory of the Holocaust in Poland emerge, through the legal process, from its contemporary invisibility.

In general, Polish–Jewish relations in communist Poland were strained.[10] There were several reasons for friction between Poles and Jews, and one was that the regime and Polish society appropriated Jewish collective memory of the Nazi occupation.[11] The trials, however, created an institutional space in which Jewish memory could unfold largely uncompromised and without being shoehorned into and submerged and distorted by Polish communist collective memory. Indeed, these trials may have been the only such institutional space that existed in immediate postwar Poland.

This particular institutional platform was especially significant because, as Lawrence Douglas argues, the transformation of testimony into legal evidence is a judicially potent act that is constitutive of memory, reifies it, and imparts to it an imprimatur of authenticity.[12] It is often argued that, as opposed to the Nuremberg Trial, the first (and perhaps only) bona fide "Holocaust trial" – that is, the trial that paid satisfactory attention to Jewish suffering (and heroism) and in which the Jewish fate under Nazi rule was thoroughly aired in open court – was the 1961 Eichmann trial in Jerusalem. Douglas calls the Eichmann trial the "Great Holocaust Trial" in large measure because, thanks to the attention it enjoyed worldwide, it "served to *create* the Holocaust: it helped remove an episode of unprecedented atrocity from the silences of shame, unexamined horror, and purposeful avoidance and transform it into an episode of world historical significance and collective meaning."[13] Polish trials clearly paled by comparison on the global stage. But if the Eichmann trial was, as Douglas puts it, "the legal proceeding in which the tasks of doing justice to unprecedented crimes, clarifying a tortured history, and defining the terms of collective memory conjoined and collided in the most provocative fashion,"[14] certain trials held in Poland such as the 1946 trial of Göth and the 1951 trial of Stroop performed similar functions. Even if the Eichmann trial was the "Great Holocaust Trial," the trials of Göth, Stroop, and others Nazis can be seen as prefiguring it.

The title of our book is *Justice behind the Iron Curtain*. Was justice practised in Poland in the first decade and a half after the Second World War? Generally speaking, the answer is no, as the trials of thousands of putative collaborators who were opponents or imaginary opponents of the communist regime demonstrated. The judicial juggernaut of Kazimierz Moczarski is a case in point. But the trial of Moczarski's longtime cellmate, Jürgen Stroop, was conducted with a palpable degree of legal integrity. So were the trials of other German nationals tried in Polish courts for crimes they committed against ethnic Poles and Polish Jews during the Nazi occupation of Poland. Poles like Moczarski found the fact that German Nazis were afforded legal safeguards denied purported Polish collaborators hard to stomach, and with good reason. At the very least, though, in the cases of German Nazis a certain justice was done.

Notes

Introduction

1 Grabowski, "Raport," 16; Berendt, "Straty osobowe polskich Żydów," 62, 73.
2 Founded in 1918, the Polish Communist Party was dissolved in 1938 by the Communist International (Comintern) during the Stalinist purges. It was re-created in 1942 under the name PPR so that it would appear to be a diverse political group and in order to conceal its subordination to Moscow.
3 Quoted in Huener, *Auschwitz*, 46.
4 Borodziej, "'Hitleristische Verbrechen'" 431–2; also Borodziej, "Ściganie zbrodniarzy," 116. According to the data collected by the London-based United Nations War Crimes Commission (UNWCC), which was established in October 1943, by the spring of 1948 the Poles had charged 7,805 Germans with war crimes and convicted 5,445 of them. Plesch, *Human Rights after Hitler*, 91.
5 Paczkowski, "Poland, the 'Enemy Nation,'" 382.
6 Selerowicz and Garscha, "Die strafrechtliche Ahndung in Polen," 88; Kobierska-Motas, "Ściganie sprawców zbrodni hitlerowskich," 31.
7 The first Polish resistance movement – Service for Poland's Victory (Służba Zwycięstwu Polski, SZP) – was formed in late September 1939. In November of the same year it was renamed the Home Army (Armia Krajowa, AK). In February 1942 the ZWZ was renamed Armia Krajowa (AK), and under that name it eventually absorbed most of the non-communist underground groups and became one of the largest resistance forces in German-occupied Europe.
8 Moczarski, *Rozmowy z katem*; Selerowicz and Garscha, "Die strafrechtliche Ahndung in Polen," 88.

9 Pilichowski, "Udział Polski,"69; Kulesza, "Der Beitrag der polnischen Nachkriegsjustiz," 115. The vast majority of these investigations were conducted until 1970, when West Germany and Poland signed the Treaty of Warsaw, accepting the existing Oder–Neisse border line, imposed by the Allies at the Potsdam Conference in 1945. According to Dr Łukasz Kamiński, former director of the IPN, now on the faculty of the Institute of History at the University of Wrocław, over the past decade the IPN has re-opened a large number of cases, especially of Austrians accused of Nazi-era crimes in Poland, of whom only a small number were extradited to Poland in the 1940s and 1950s. In Kamiński's view, the resumption of investigations indicates a willingness in contemporary Poland to complete this process. Personal communication with Dr. Łukasz Kamiński, 12 June 2017.

10 For example, due to the conflict with Tito over Trieste, the Allies largely blocked Yugoslavia's extradition requests. The Yugoslav government had placed 17,500 war criminals on its wanted list (including 7,567 Germans, 395 Austrians, and 3,789 Italians), but the UN Commission in London reduced these numbers to 2,104, and by 1948 the Allies had handed over to Yugoslavia only 947 war criminals and "traitors." After the Tito–Stalin split in 1948 the Yugoslav government lost interest in prosecuting German and Austrian culprits. Jandrić, "Prijepori saveznika," 467–8n44.

11 In addition to war criminals extradited to Poland by the Allies, approximately 3,700 German and Austrian nationals had been captured by the Polish and Soviet authorities. According to Czesław Madajczyk, the Western Allies extradited 1,817 individuals to Poland. Madajczyk, *Polityka III Rzeszy*, 2: 364. Łukasz Jasiński's figures vary slightly. He writes that 1,776 individuals were extradited, 1,683 in 1946–47 and an additional 93 by the end of 1949. Jasiński, "Zarys działalności Głównej Komisji," 44.

12 In English, see, for example, Finder and Prusin, "Jewish Collaborators"; Prusin, "Poland's Nuremberg"; Gawron, "Amon Göth's Trial"; *Model Nazi*, ch. 9; Drumbl, "'Germans are the Lords"; Bazyler and Tuerkheimer, *Forgotten Trials*, 101–27. For Polish studies of the topic, see Cyprian and Sawicki, *Siedem wyroków Najwyższego Trybunału Narodowego*; Pilichowski, *Badanie i ściganie*; Musial, "NS-Kriegsverbrecher"; Borodziej, "'Hitlerische Verbrechen'"; Borodziej, "Ściganie zbrodniarzy"; Selerowicz and Garscha, "Die strafrechtliche Ahndung in Polen."

13 See Koźmińska-Frejlak and Finder, "Apart."

14 For example, see Deák, "A Fatal Compromise?" 64–7.

15 Finder, "Introduction," 12–19.

16 Rothberg, *Multidirectional Memory*, chap. 1.

17 Jewish Historical Institute (Żydowski Instytut Historyczny; hereafter ŻIH), Warsaw, Centralna Żydowska Komisja Historyczna (hereafter CŻKH), 330/XX/14, p. 20. See also Jockusch, *Collect and Record!* 114–16.

18 In 1939–41 the Białystok province was occupied by the Soviets and incorporated into the Byelorussian SSR.

19 Pendas, "Seeking Justice," 349n8.

1 A Restive Society Demands Swift Justice

1 Cooper, *Raphael Lemkin*; Sands, *East West Street*, pt IV; Konrat, "Rafał Lemkin's Formative Years," 66, 68–9.

2 Cooper, *Raphael Lemkin*, 17; Konrat, "Rafał Lemkin's Formative Years," 70; Schabas, *Genocide*, 25.

3 Lang, *Act and Idea*, 5. See also Sands, *East West Street*, pt VIII; Cooper, *Raphael Lemkin*, 57, 60; Korey, "Lemkin's Passion," 83.

4 Kochavi, *Prelude to Nuremberg*, esp. chs. 1–2.

5 Jankiewicz, "Przygotowania Rządu RP," 45n1.

6 Kobierska-Motas, *Ekstradycja*, 1: 13.

7 Cyprian and Sawicki, *Procesy*, 2; quote in Marrus, *The Nuremberg Trial*, 19.

8 Plesch, *Human Rights*, 46.

9 Kochavi, *Prelude to Nuremberg*, chaps. 2–3; Kobierska-Motas, *Ekstradycja*, 1: 14; Selerowicz and Garscha, "Die strafrechtliche Ahndung," 75.

10 Szyprowski, *Sąd kapturowy*, 56–62, 72.

11 Machnikowska, *Wymiar sprawiedliwości*, 256–7; Gondek, *Polska karząca*, 37–8, 112–24.

12 Jankiewicz, "Przygotowania Rządu RP," 47–8.

13 "Dekret Prezydenta Rzeczypospolitej z dnia 30 marca 1943 r. o odpowiedzialności karnej za zbrodnie wojenne," *Dziennik Ustaw Rzeczypospolitej Polskiej* (cited as *Dziennik Ustaw*), no. 3, pp. 13–14.

14 It was followed by the Soviet decree of 19 April 1943 and by the decree of the Free French Forces on 28 August 1944. Kubicki, *Zbrodnie wojenne*, 38, 69.

15 Kochavi, *Prelude to Nuremberg*, 57, 72–3; for the text of the Moscow Declaration, see Marrus, *The Nuremberg Trial*, 20–1.

16 Kobierska-Motas, *Ekstradycja*, 1: 29.

17 Musial, "NS-Kriegsverbrecher," 26; Borodziej, "'Hitlerische Verbrechen,'" 409; Jakubowski, *Sądownictwo powszechne*, 23; Pilichowski, *Badanie i ściganie*, 156.

18 Organized by the Polish communists in the Soviet Union, the union laboured to create the pro-communist armed forces made up of Polish

POWs and civilians, who were to fight side by side with the Soviet army. In April 1943, after the Soviet Union broke diplomatic relations with the Polish government in London, Stalin approved the formation of the first Polish infantry division, headed by General Zygmunt Berling.

19 Rojowska, "Wpływ dekretów radzieckich," 187.
20 Kersten, *Narodziny*, 38; Selerowicz and Garsha, "Die strafrechtliche Ahndung," 57.
21 In part, the Allied decision in Teheran implemented the secret protocol of the Nazi–Soviet Pact of 1939, which partitioned Poland and assigned its eastern provinces to the Soviet Union.
22 Text of the manifesto in *Konstytucja i podstawowe akty*, 9, 11–12. In contravention of the principles of the constitution of 1921, the April 1935 constitution limited the power of the Polish Sejm and enhanced the authority of the Polish president, Józef Piłsudski.
23 "Ustawa z dnia 15 sierpnia 1944 r. o tymczasowym trybie wydawania dekretów z mocą ustawy," *Dziennik Ustaw*, no. 1, 2.
24 "Dekret PKWN z dnia 31 sierpnia 1944 o wymiarze kary dla faszystowsko-hitlerowskich zbrodniarzy winnych zabójstw i znęcania się nad ludnością civilną i jeńcami oraz dla zdrajców Narodu Polskiego," *Dziennik Ustaw*, no. 4, 17–18.
25 Lityński, "Criminal Law," 356.
26 *Kodeks karny*, 58–9, 110–11, 114, 126–7.
27 Jakubowski, *Sądownictwo powszechne*, 45–6. For example, in January 1946, Kazimierz Moczarski, an officer in the AK, was charged under the 30 October 1944 decree "For the Protection of the State."
28 "Dekret z dnia 16 lutego 1945 o zmianie dekretu PKWN o wymiarze kary dla faszystowsko-hitlerowskich zbrodniarzy winnych zabójstw i znęcania się nad ludnością civilną i jeńcami oraz dla zdrajców Narodu Polskiego," *Dziennik Ustaw*, no. 23, 1–2; Sawicki, "O prawie sądów specjalnych," 57.
29 Biegański, "Kara śmierci," 179n20.
30 "Dekret z dnia 10 grudnia 1946 r. o zmianie dekretu z dnia 31 sierpnia 1944 o wymiarze kary dla faszystowsko-hitlerowskich zbrodniarzy winnych zabójstw i znęcania się nad ludnością civilną i jeńcami oraz dla zdrajców Narodu Polskiego," *Dziennik Ustaw*, nr. 69, 863–4; Sawicki, "O prawie sądów specjalnych," 57.
31 In 1945, after the PKWN was replaced by the Provisonal Government of the Republic of Poland (see below), the departments of various state branches were renamed ministries.
32 "Dekret z dnia 10 listopada 1945 r. o Głównej Komisji i Okręgowych Komisjach Badania Zbrodni Niemieckich w Polsce," *Dziennik Ustaw*,

no. 51, position 293. For a brief history of the GKBZN, see Jasiński, "Zarys działalności Głównej Komisji."

33 On 1 January 1945 the PKWN was replaced by the Provisional Government of the Republic of Poland (Rząd Tymczasowy Rzeczypospolitej Polskiej, RTRP), which proclaimed itself the legitimate government of Poland. In June 1945 the RTRP was transformed into the Provisional Government of National Unity (Tymczasowy Rząd Jedności Narodowej, TRJN), which, on the face of it, looked more like a coalition government than had its predecessors; in reality, however, this was a mere token gesture by Stalin to mollify the Western Allies.

34 Kobierska-Motas, *Ekstradycja*, 1: 28–9.

35 Lubecka, "Procesy," 50; Kobierska-Motas, *Ekstradycja*, 1: 30.

36 According to Plesch's research, over the course of the UNWCC's existence, the Polish government in London and then after 1945 in Warsaw brought in total 1,564 cases to the commission, of which 372 or 24 per cent involved anti-Jewish crimes. Plesch, *Human Rights*, 115, 123. It is unclear, however, from Plesch's book, how many cases were filed separately by the London and Warsaw governments. Ibid., 122–7, 222–40.

37 Kobierska-Motas, *Ekstradycja*, 1: 31–3.

38 Jasiński, "Zarys," 44.

39 Zaremba, *Wielka trwoga*, 561–73. The commission's name was changed in 1949 to the Main Commission for the Investigation of Hitlerite Crimes in Poland (Główna Komisja Badania Zbrodni Hitlerowskich w Polsce). The distinction between "Germans" and "Hitlerites" or Nazis was made to accommodate the sensitivities of the communist leadership of the German Democratic Republic, which took pains to differentiate East Germany from the Federal Republic of Germany or West Germany, a stronghold, according to East German propaganda, of former Nazis. After the fall of communism the commission was transformed in 1991 into the Main Commission for the Investigation of Crimes against the Polish Nation (Główna Komisja Badania Zbrodni przeciwko Narodowi Polskiemu), and its mandate was expanded to include crimes committed against Poles by the communist regime. In 1999 a parliamentary act establishing the Institute of National Remembrance – Commission for the Prosecution of Crimes against the Polish Nation (Instytut Pamięci Narodowej – Komisja Ścigania Zbrodni przeciwko Narodowi Polskiemu) effectively ended the Main Commission's independent status. Instead, the Main Commission for the Prosecution of Crimes against the Polish Nation became a department of the Institute of National Remembrance.

40 Sakson, "Niemcy," 409; Kalicki, *Ostatni jeniec*, 176.

41 Szarota, *Niemcy i Polacy*, 145.
42 Ibid., 170.
43 Kalicki, *Ostatni jeniec*, 177–8; Kiwerska, "W atmosferze wrogości," 47.
44 Kochanowski, *W polskiej niewoli*, 247, 252–4.
45 Szarota, *Niemcy i Polacy*, 168.
46 Borodziej, "Widma," 48.
47 Zaremba, *Wielka trwoga*, 396.
48 Browarek, "Próba periodyzacji," 235.
49 Borodziej, "Widma," 45–6; Kalicki, *Ostatni jeniec*, 185.
50 Machnikowska, *Wymiar sprawiedliwości*, 259; Lityński, "Criminal Law," 361.
51 "Dekret PKWN z dnia 31 sierpnia 1944," 18; Selerowicz and Garscha, "Die strafrechtliche Ahndung," 87; "Dekret Polskiego Komitetu Wyzwolenia Narodowego z dnia 12 września 1944 r. o specjalnych sądach karnych dla spraw zbrodniarzy faszystowsko-hitlerowskich," *Dziennik Ustaw*, no. 4, 25.
52 Rzepliński, *Sądownictwo*, 26; "Dekret z dnia 22 lutego 1946 r. o rejestracji i przymusowym zatrudnieniu we władzach wymiaru sprawiedliwości osób, mających kwalifikacje do objęcia stanowiska sędziowskiego," *Dziennik Ustaw*, no. 9, position 65–6.
53 Chajn, "Próba bilansu," 20–2; Fijalkowski, "Politics," 93; Rzepliński, *Sądownictwo*, 38.
54 Jakubowski, *Sądownictwo*, 37; Machnikowska, *Wymiar*, 265.
55 "Ustawa z dnia 11 września 1944 r. o organizacji i zakresie działania rad narodowych," *Dziennik Ustaw*, no. 5, 27–9.
56 "Dekret Polskiego Komitetu Wyzwolenia Narodowego z dnia 12 września 1944 r.," 25; Jakubowski, *Sądownictwo*, 84.
57 "Dekret Polskiego Komitetu Wyzwolenia Narodowego z dnia 12 września 1944 r.," 25–6; Kubicki, "Najwyższy Trybunał Narodowy," 10–11; Kobierska-Motas, "Ściganie," 25–6.
58 Sawicki, "O prawie sądów," 60–61; Biegański, "Kara śmierci," 183.
59 Rojowska, "Wpływ," 187; Biegański, "Kara śmierci," 189–90: Matusiak, "Zbrodniarze"; Zaremba, *Wielka trwoga*, 567.
60 On Majdanek, see Schwindt, *Das Konzentrations- und Vernichtungslager*; White, "Lublin."
61 Located near the town of Slavuta (Kmel'nyts'kyi *oblast*, Ukraine), the so-called *Grosslazarett* 301 was notorious for the ill-treatment and high mortality of Soviet POWs.
62 Werth, *Russia*, 890; Selerowicz and Garscha, "Die strafrechtliche Ahndung," 63.
63 Selerowicz and Garscha, "Die strafrechtliche Ahndung," 65.

64 Simonov, *Un Camp*, 3–4, 11. In April 1940, in the forest of Katyn (Smoleńsk oblast, Russia), the Soviet secret police secretly executed thousands of Polish officers captured in September 1939. Until its demise, the Soviet government blamed the Nazis for the murder. For more on Katyn, see chapter 2.

65 Putrament, *Pół wieku*, 2: 294–5.

66 Created in November 1942 by a decree of the Presidium of the Supreme Soviet, the Extraordinary State Commission for Ascertaining and Investigating Crimes Perpetrated by the German-Fascist Invaders and their Accomplices was delegated with the task of investigating crimes committed by the Axis powers and their accomplices against the Soviet Union and collecting documentation about Soviet material losses.

67 Formed under the umbrella of the PKWN, the bureau served as the political representation for Polish Jews. In October 1944 it changed its name to the Provisional Central Committee of Polish Jews, which on 12 November 1944 became the Central Committee of Jews in Poland (Centralny Komitet Żydów w Polsce, CKŻP).

68 Selerowicz and Garscha, "Die strafrechtliche Ahndung," 68–9.

69 Ibid., 71.

70 Kranz, "Die Erfassung," 235.

71 Selerowicz and Garscha, "Die strafrechtliche Ahndung," 69–70.

72 Putrament, *Pół wieku*, 2: 294–5; Zaremba, *Wielka trwoga*, 565–6.

73 Quoted in Kalicki, *Ostatni jeniec*, 179–80.

74 Wąsowicz, "Jerzy Sawicki."

75 *Majdanek. Rozprawa sądowa*, 13.

76 Zaborski, "Czy bronić 'zdrajców Narodu," 238; *Majdanek. Rozprawa sądowa*, 6–7.

77 *Majdanek. Rozprawa sądowa*, 8.

78 Ibid., 8–9.

79 Ibid., 9–10.

80 Ibid., 12.

81 Ibid., 14, 16–17, 23, 26–99.

82 Ibid., 48, 51–2.

83 Ibid., 62.

84 Ibid., 33, 35.

85 Ibid., 34.

86 Ibid., 26–9.

87 Ibid., 46.

88 Ibid., 58.

89 Ibid., 67–8, 74.

90 Cyprian, Sawicki, and Siewierski, *Głos ma prokurator*, 20–1.
91 Liebman, "Documenting the Liberation."
92 Dmitrów, *Niemcy*, 234.
93 *Majdanek. Rozprawa sądowa*, 85.
94 Ibid., 86–7.
95 Ibid., 88.
96 Rojowska, "Wpływ," 187; Selerowicz and Garscha, "Die strafrechtliche Ahndung," 96–7.
97 Quoted in Zaremba, *Wielka trwoga*, 566.
98 Załuski, *Czterdziesty czwarty*, 501.
99 Putrament, *Pół wieku* 2: 300.
100 Selerowicz and Garscha, "Die strafrechtliche Ahndung," 91.
101 Dmitrów, *Niemcy*, 89, 224, 231; *Głos Ludu*, no. 56, 7 March 1945, 1.
102 Rappaport, *Naród-zbrodniarz*, 7, 14–19, 21–9. Although German criminologists rejected Lombroso's theory of the born criminal, they shared many of his and his followers' basic assumptions about heredity, and genetic determinism played an instrumental role in Nazi racial policy. Wetzell, *Inventing the Criminal*, 300–2. Ironically, this glaring fact seems to have been lost on Rappaport, himself of Jewish origin.
103 Selerowicz and Garscha, "Die strafrechtliche Ahndung," 105; Dmitrów, *Niemcy*, 106.
104 *Głos Ludu*, no. 324 (1069), 24 November 1947, 4.
105 United States Holocaust Memorial Museum (USHMM), RG 15.156M, "Sąd Okręgowy w Warszawie = District Court in Warsaw, 1945–1960," (cited as District Court in Warsaw), "Akta w sprawie karnej Eustachego Prindyna [and others]," reel 4, frames 000004-007, 000024–025, 000131–132.
106 Ibid., frames 000132–134.
107 Ibid., frames 000093–097.
108 Ibid., frames 000101–103.
109 *Grenzpolizeikommisariat* included the Border Police, Sipo, and the SD.
110 USHMM, District Court in Warsaw, reel 1, "Akta w sprawie Petera Leideritza, Franza Schauera, Henryka Budera, Filipa Spanga i Pawła Simona," District Court in Warsaw, "Akta Simona," reel 1, frames 000127–128.
111 Ibid., frames 000129–135, 000461–463, 000635.
112 Ibid., frames 000139.
113 Ibid., frames 000877.
114 Ibid., frames 000132–000142, 000877–879.
115 Löw, *Juden*; Klein, *Die "Ghettoverwaltung"*; Crago, "Łódź."
116 On Biebow's role in Łódź, see Löw, *Juden*; Klein, *Die "Ghettoverwaltung."*

117 *Dziennik Łódzki*, no. 110, 23 April 1947, 1.

118 USHMM, RG-15.171M, "Proces Hansa Biebowa = Trial of Hans Biebow," (cited as trial of Hans Biebow), reel 1, file 3, indictment, 31 March 1947, 1–12. See also Lewiński, *Proces Hansa Biebowa*, 45–59.

119 USHMM, trial of Hans Biebow, reel 1, file 1, interrogation of Biebow, 19 August 1946, 65–6; see also reel 1, file 3, Biebow's letter to the court, 5 April 1947, 19.

120 Lewiński, *Proces Hansa Biebowa*, 60. For "genocide," Walewski interchangeably used two terms – *ludobójstwo* and *narodobójstwo*. We are using only the printed version of Biebow's trial in this instance because Walewski's references to *ludobójstwo* and *narodobójstwo* do not appear in the archival transcript of the trial. Indeed, the archival transcript appears to be an incomplete stenographic record of the proceedings, whereas the printed version seems to approximate more accurately a full record of the proceedings, leading us to believe that the printed version is based on a separate stenographic record of the trial. There are, however, strong correspondences between the printed version and the archival document in our possession. For this reason, we often cite both the archival and the printed transcript of Biebow's trial.

121 USHMM, trial of Hans Biebow, reel 1, file 3, testimony of Artur Eisenbach, 102–16 (pages 56–84 of trial transcript); testimony of Władysław Bednarz, 116–24 (pages 84–93 of trial transcript). See also Lewiński, *Proces Hansa Biebowa*, 186–217 (Eisenbach); 217–42 (Bednarz). For more on Eisenbach's testimony, see chapter 5.

122 Kulesza, "Der Beitrag," 122.

123 USHMM, trial of Hans Biebow, reel 1, file 3, testimony of Leon Szykier, 84–7 (pages 19–26 of trial transcript). See also Lewiński, *Proces Hansa Biebowa*, 107–23; *Dziennik Łódzki*, no. 25, 25 April 1947, 2.

124 USHMM, trial of Hans Biebow, reel 1, file 3, testimony of Donat Szmulewicz-Stanisz, 90 (pages 31–2 of trial transcript); testimony of Sasza Lewiatan, 95 (pages 41–2 of the trial transcript); testimony of Mendel Kaufmann, 99 (page 49 of trial transcript). See also Lewiński, *Proces Hansa Biebowa*, 133–7 (Szmulewicz-Stanisz), 154–8 (Lewiatan), 170–1 (Kaufman).

125 Lewiński, *Proces Hansa Biebowa*, 76–100.

126 USHMM, trial of Hans Biebow, reel 1, file 3, prosecutor's closing statement, 123 (page 98 of trial transcript). See also Lewiński, *Proces Hansa Biebowa*, 245–71; Kulesza, "Der Beitrag," 122.

127 USHMM, trial of Hans Biebow, reel 1, file 3, defence counsel's closing statement, 123 (page 98 of trial transcript). See also Lewiński, *Proces Hansa Biebowa*, 272–85; Kulesza, "Der Beitrag," 123–4.

128 *Dziennik Łódzki*, no. 113, 26 April 1947, 2.

129 USHMM, trial of Hans Biebow, reel 1, file 3, verdict, 30 April 1947, 126 (pages 1–2 of verdict). See also Lewiński, *Proces Hansa Biebowa*, 286–7; *Dziennik Łódzki*, no. 119, 2 May 1947, 2.

130 USHMM, trial of Hans Biebow, reel 1, file 3, verdict, 30 April 1947, 127–8 (pages 1–3 of justification for verdict). See also Lewiński, *Proces Hansa Biebowa*, 287–9. Max Stirner (1806–1856) was a German philosopher known as a prophet of nihilism and existentialism.

131 USHMM, trial of Hans Biebow, reel 1, file 3, verdict, 30 April 1947, 128 (page 3 of justification for the verdict). See also Lewiński, *Proces Hansa Biebowa*, 289–90.

132 USHMM, trial of Hans Biebow, reel 1, file 3, verdict, 30 April 1947, 128–30 (pages 4–7 of justification for verdict); See also Lewiński, *Proces Hansa Biebowa*, 291–7.

133 USHMM, trial of Hans Biebow, reel 1, file 3, verdict, 30 April 1947, 128 (page 3 of justification for verdict). See also Lewiński, *Proces Hansa Biebowa*, 289.

134 USHMM, trial of Hans Biebow, reel 1, file 3, verdict, 30 April 1947, 128, 131 (pages 4 and 10 of justification for verdict). See also Lewiński, *Proces Hansa Biebowa*, 290, 297–8.

135 *Dziennik Łódzki*, no. 161, 14 June 1947, 3; no. 171, 24 June 1947, 5.

136 Zaremba, *Wielka trwoga*, 108.

137 Ibid., 16, 46–7, 95–6.

138 Kalicki, *Ostatni jeniec*, 24–5.

139 Ibid., 180–1.

140 Zaremba, *Wielka trwoga*, 562–4.

141 Biegański, "Kara śmierci," 191; Wojciechowska, *Przestępcy*, 23, 49.

142 Pohl, *Nationalsozialistische Judenverfolgung*, 89, 148.

143 Pietrzak, "Hans Biebow," 186–7, 191.

2 The Poles at Nuremberg

1 Jockusch, "Justice at Nuremberg?," 107.

2 *Trial of the Major War Criminals*, 1: 8. See also Kochavi, *Prelude*, 224.

3 See Sands, *East West Street*, 112–16.

4 *Trial of the Major War Criminals*, 1: 11.

5 One defendant named in the indictment, Robert Ley, committed suicide in his cell in October 1945 and thus never stood trial. An excellent brief introduction to the Nuremberg Trial is Marrus, *The Nuremberg Trial*.

6 *Trial of the Major War Criminals*, 1: 13.

7 Jan Karski, for example, famously repeated his eyewitness account of Jewish suffering in the Warsaw Ghetto and at the death camp at Bełżec to the UNWCC in London and to British and American political leaders, including President Roosevelt. See Karski, *Story*, 384–8.

8 Tusa and Tusa, *The Nuremberg Trial*, 103–4.

9 Ginsburgs, *Moscow's Road*, 111. The Soviets, moreover, sought the agreement of the other Allied prosecution teams to prevent German defence counsel from raising Soviet–Polish relations during the war and other sensitive topics in open court, but to no avail. See Hirsch, "The Soviets at Nuremberg," here 719, 724–5; Cienciala, Lebedeva, and Materski, *Katyn*, 230–1.

10 *Zburzenie Warszawy*, 6; Sawicki, *Przed polskim prokuratorem*, 8. See also Motas, "Delegacja polska." 57–85.

11 Ginsburgs, *Moscow's Road*, 112.

12 Piotrowski, *Dziennik* (1957), ix.

13 Cyprian and Sawicki, *Materiały norymberskie*, 34; Motas, "Delegacja polska," 70–1.

14 Mushkat, "Yehudim betzeva'ot polin ha'amamit," 103.

15 "Sawicki, Jerzy," 10: 374; "Cyprian, Tadeusz," 2: 667; "Kurowski (Warszawski) Stefan," 6: 314.

16 Sawicki, at least among the lawyers in the Polish delegation, was deeply anti-German and believed that no punishment imposed on Germany and its people for Nazi-era crimes could be too severe. See Mushkat, "Yehudim betzeva'ot polin ha'amamit," 104.

17 Instytut Pamięci Narodowej (IPN), Główna Komisja Badania Zbrodni Hitlerowskich w Polsce (GKBZHwP) 1048, "Sprawozdanie delegacji Ministerstwa Sprawiedliwości z pobytu w Londynie w sprawie przestępstw wojennych i procesu w Norymberdze," 30 October 1945, quote on 2. Historian Anna Cichopek observes that written documents confirm that one Jewish survivor died and five additional survivors were wounded during the Kraków pogrom, but she notes, in addition, that an archival photograph of five coffins suggests that the pogrom claimed five fatalities and that a Polish press report mentioned two victims, which seems to be corroborated by a report in the 1946 American Jewish Yearbook. Cichopek, *Pogrom*, 86–7. The photograph is reproduced on page 259. Although Mushkat hints that Sawicki identified with his Jewish background, it does not appear that Sawicki acted as a Jew or as a representative of the Jews at the IMT. At this trial and at every war crime trial held in Poland in which he participated as a prosecutor, he offered no reason to doubt that he served the court first and foremost as a legal representative of the Polish state.

18 *Trial of the Major War Criminals*, 7: 196. The Polish indictment was revised
   before the Soviets submitted it to the IMT. Like most exhibits produced
   by Soviet prosecutors, the Polish indictment was not reproduced in *Trial
   of the Major War Criminals before the International Military Tribunal*, the
   official publication of the proceedings. (Its exhibit number was USSR-93;
   its official designation in the court record was "Official Polish Government
   Report.") For this chapter we use what appears to be the penultimate
   version of the Polish indictment, which is available in the archives of
   the IPN in Warsaw, listed under Międzynarodowy Trybunał Wojskowy
   w Norymberdze, I/Nor/1. Signed by Cyprian, it is dated 8 December
   1945, written in English, and titled "The Republic of Poland against 1.
   The German War Criminals [and] 2. Those Bodies and Organizations
   Indicted under Charge No. 1 before the International Military Tribunal."
   (We shall refer to it hereafter as the "Polish indictment.") The final version
   seems to have been produced in January 1946 and, according to Rudenko,
   was dated 22 January. A comparison of the December 1945 version with
   excerpts from the final version that were read into the court record by
   Soviet prosecutors shows strong similarities between the two. Indeed,
   they seem to have been largely identical. Compare, for example, *Trial of
   the Major War Criminals*, 8: 7–8, with IPN, Międzynarodowy Trybunał
   Wojskowy w Norymberdze, I/Nor/1, "Polish indictment," 22, 24 (pages
   20 and 22 of indictment); and *Trial of the Major War Criminals*, 8: 68–71, with
   IPN, Międzynarodowy Trybunał Wojskowy w Norymberdze, I/Nor/1,
   "Polish indictment," 17–19 (pages 15–17 of indictment), 25–6 (pages 23–4
   of indictment), 29 (page 27 of indictment), and 32 (page 30 of indictment).
   Minor apparent textual discrepancies between parallel sections in the
   December 1945 version and the January 1946 version may be attribut-
   able in part to the peculiarities of translation. When Soviet prosecutors
   read aloud excerpts from the January 1946 version into the court record,
   they spoke in Russian (reading from a Russian translation of the English
   original), while the simultaneous translation of their words into English
   is what we find in the official transcript of the proceedings. It would not
   be surprising, therefore, if certain words or phrases in the original English
   version of the Polish indictment were lost or garbled in the process of
   translation from English to Russian to English. That said, from *Trial of the
   Major War Criminals* it is clear that a few sections of the January 1946 version expanded on parallel sections in the December 1945 version, offering
   additional facts and summaries. This is true, for example, of the section
   on the deportation of the Polish civilian population for forced labour in
   Germany. Compare, for example, *Trial of the Major War Criminals*, 8: 134–6,

with IPN, Międzynarodowy Trybunał Wojskowy w Norymberdze, I/
Nor/1, "Polish indictment," 36 (page 34 of indictment). It also appears that
the January 1946 version that was ultimately presented to the IMT was
formatted differently from the archival version in our possession. See also
Motas, "Delegacja polska," 76–80.

19 Cyprian and Sawicki, *Materiały norymberskie*, 33; idem, *Ludzie i sprawy
   Norymbergi*, 166–7. Lachs, who had a post in the Polish exile government
   and who had served in the military during the Second World War,
   represented Poland on the UNWCC. He was of Jewish origin. He returned to Poland after the war and embarked on a distinguished career
   in diplomacy and law. He would become a member of Poland's delegation to the General Assembly of the United Nations, a legal adviser to
   Poland's Foreign Ministry, and ultimately a judge on the International
   Court of Justice in The Hague from 1967 to 1993. See Mushkat, "Yehudim
   betzeva'ot polin ha'amamit," 103; "Manfred Lachs." Bramson, who was
   in all likelihood of Jewish origin, would take part on behalf of Poland in
   the *travaux préparatoires* of the 1948 Genocide Convention. See Abtahi and
   Webb, *The Genocide Convention*.
20 Cyprian and Sawicki, *Materiały norymberskie*, 33; idem, *Sprawy polskie*, 709.
   See also Motas, "Delegacja polska," 75–6.
21 See Rojek, "The Government," 33; Zamojski, "The Social History," 204.
22 *Trial of the Major War Criminals*, 1: 39, 41.
23 Ibid., 1: 43–4.
24 Ibid., 1: 47.
25 See Kochanski, *The Eagle*, 101–2, 266–8; Łuczak, *Polityka*, 136–72.
26 See Cyprian and Sawicki, *Materiały norymberskie*, 33; idem, *Ludzie i sprawy*,
   164–9. On the first day of the trial, various Allied prosecutors from each
   of the Four Powers read the indictment aloud and adumbrated the facts
   on which the charges were based. Impressed by their summary of the
   anti-Polish and anti-Jewish crimes committed by the Nazis in Poland and
   of Hans Frank's role in them, Philippe Sands, an international lawyer and
   law professor, writes, "The events in Poland … were placed at the heart of
   the trial." Sands, *East West Street*, 272. Not all events, however. Hovering
   over the proceedings like a spectre was the massacre of Polish officers
   and police in the Katyn forest, near Smolensk. The Soviets insisted that
   the Allied indictment include a charge that the Nazi leaders on trial were
   responsible for killing the Polish officers in Katyn in September 1941. The
   number of victims specified in the original English text of the indictment,
   dated 6 October 1945, was 925; in the Russian text, dated three days later, it
   was 11,000, thanks apparently to Sawicki's intervention in the matter. IPN,

GKBZH 1048, "Sprawozdanie delegacji Ministerstwa Sprawiedliwości
z pobytu w Londynie w sprawie przestępstw wojennych i procesu w
Norymberdze," 30 October 1945, 2. (In the IMT's official publication of the
proceedings, it is 11,000. *Trial of the Major War Criminals*, 1:54.) Jackson and
British Attorney General Sir Hartley Shawcross, head of the British prosecution team, sought to dissuade the Russians from including the reference
to Katyn for fear that it would open up a can of worms because notwithstanding Soviet claims that the officers had been killed by the Germans,
the widespread view was that the Russians were guilty of the massacre.
German defence attorney Otto Stahmer, in an effort to relieve his client,
Herman Göring, who stood accused of all war crimes enumerated in the
indictment, of responsibility for the Katyn massacre, called witnesses, former German officers, for the defence. In turn, the Soviet prosecution called
three witnesses in rebuttal. Stahmer may have cleared the witnesses of
responsibility for the Katyn massacre, but Göring and almost all the other
Nazi leaders on trial were found guilty of war crimes on other charges.
Yet Katyn was not mentioned in the IMT's judgment. Nevertheless, the
issue, which the Russians had wanted to prevent the German defence from
raising, had been aired in open court, to the consternation of both Soviet
prosecutors and Soviet leaders in Moscow. See Cienciala, Lebedeva, and
Materski, *Katyn*, 229–32. See also Basak, *Historia*; Marrus, *The Nuremberg
Trial*, 57; Hirsch, "The Soviets," 725. "The London Poles," write Cienciala,
Lebedeva, and Materski, "made several attempts to present their information to the IMT but failed." Cienciala, Lebedeva, and Materski, *Katyn*, 232.
Although German guilt for the massacre was proclaimed by all Soviet and
other communist governments for almost half a century, the Polish indictment made no reference to it, probably because the lawyers in the Polish
delegation wished to avoid embarrassing the Soviet Union. The district
branch in Kraków of the GKBZN initiated a short-lived investigation of
the Katyn massacre in 1948 that aimed to pin the blame on the *Wehrmacht*
and the Gestapo rather than on the NKVD on the basis of speculation
rather than hard evidence. See Jasiński, "The Central Commission," 9–10.
We wish to thank Łukasz Jasiński for sharing his paper with us. Recent
research, spearheaded by Cienciala, Lebedeva, and Materski and collected
in their seminal volume, categorically affirms Soviet responsibility for the
massacre. They conclude that the NKVD shot some 14,500 Polish officers
and policemen who had been held in three special NKVD prisoner-of-war
camps in the spring of 1940 in the Katyn forest and likewise 7,300 Polish
prisoners who had been held in NKVD jails in the Ukrainian SSR and the
Belorussian SSR. Cienciala, Lebedeva, and Materski, *Katyn*, 121–48.

27 For Jackson's opening address, see *Trial of the Major War Criminals*, 2: 98–155, quote on 118.

28 For Shawcross's opening address, see ibid., 3: 91–145.

29 For Rudenko's opening address, see ibid., 7: 146–94, quotes on 153, 156.

30 IPN, Międzynarodowy Trybunał Wojskowy w Norymberdze, I/Nor/1, "Polish indictment," 8 December 1945, 3–4 (pages 1–2 of indictment).

31 Ibid., 13–21 (pages 11–19 of indictment), quote on 16 (page 14 of indictment); emphasis in original.

32 Ibid., 42 (page 40 of indictment).

33 Ibid., 43 (page 41 of indictment).

34 Ibid., 47–9 (pages 45–7 of indictment).

35 Ibid., 50–1 (pages 48–9 of indictment).

36 Ibid., 52 (page 50 of indictment).

37 *Trial of the Major War Criminals*, 1: 47.

38 Stroop's 1951 trial in Poland is described in chapter 4 below.

39 *Trial of the Major War Criminals*, 2: 106, 118–27, quotes on 127. Jockusch shows that Jacob Robinson of the World Jewish Congress (WJC) had a meeting with Jackson in June 1945 during which he argued that Jews as a people had suffered as victims of a Nazi conspiracy to commit systematic annihilation. For this reason, Robinson argued for a separate Jewish indictment and proposed that a Jewish delegation with the status of *amicus curiae* be permitted to take part at the IMT. Jackson rejected both suggestions, but it appears that Robinson's advocacy had an effect on Jackson, who accepted the idea that Nazi leaders had deliberately set out to destroy the Jews as a people. See Jockusch, "Justice at Nuremberg?," 111–16.

40 Rubenstein, "The War," 31.

41 Marrus, "The Holocaust at Nuremberg," 6.

42 See Bloxham, *Genocide*; and idem, "Jewish Witnesses," 539–53.

43 Douglas, *The Memory of Judgment*, 6.

44 IPN, Międzynarodowy Trybunał Wojskowy w Norymberdze, I/Nor/1, "Polish indictment, " 56 (page 54 of indictment; emphasis in original).

45 By all appearances, what the authors intended to write here was "10%."

46 IPN, Międzynarodowy Trybunał Wojskowy w Norymberdze, I/Nor/1, "Polish indictment," 54 (page 52 of indictment).

47 See Zimmerman, *The Polish Underground*, 204.

48 IPN, Międzynarodowy Trybunał Wojskowy w Norymberdze, I/Nor/1, "Polish indictment," 60 (page 58 of indictment).

49 Ibid., 24 (page 22 of indictment).

50 Ibid., 52 (page 50 of indictment).

51 Ibid., 55 (page 53 of indictment).
52 See *Trial of the Major War Criminals*, 7: 214–18 (Pokrovsky regarding aggressive war); 7: 428–9 (Pokrovsky regarding maltreatment of Polish POWs); 7: 476–8 (Smirnov regarding the German corruption of Polish law); 8: 7–8 (Sheinin regarding the plunder of Polish property); 8: 67–71 (Raginsky regarding the destruction of Polish culture); 8: 134–6 (Zorya regarding the deportation of slave laborers); and 12: 85, 98 (Smirnov's cross-examination of Bühler).
53 Ibid., 8: 239–40, quote on 240.
54 Marrus, *The Nuremberg Trial*, 201–2.
55 IPN, Międzynarodowy Trybunał Wojskowy w Norymberdze, I/Nor/1, "Polish indictment," 62 (page 60 of indictment).
56 *Trial of the Major War Criminals*, 18: 158.
57 IPN, Międzynarodowy Trybunał Wojskowy w Norymberdze, I/Nor/1, "Polish indictment," 62 (page 60 of indictment).
58 *Zburzenie Warszawy*, 147–73, quote on 169; see also Sawicki, *Przed polskim prokuratorem*, 107–24, quote on 121.
59 *Zburzenie Warszawy*, 97–146, quote on 137; see also Sawicki, *Przed polskim prokuratorem*, 72–106, quote on 99.
60 *Zburzenie Warszawy*, 174–276, quote on 276; see also Sawicki, *Przed polskim prokuratorem*, 125–97, quote on 197.
61 *Zburzenie Warszawy*, 17–77, quote on 48–9; see also Sawicki, *Przed polskim prokuratorem*, 17–59, quote on 33.
62 *Zburzenie Warszawy*, 77; see also Sawicki, *Przed polskim prokuratorem*, 59. Bach-Zelewski testified for the prosecution, summoned by US assistant prosecutor Telford Taylor and further questioned on direct examination by Soviet prosecutor Pokrovsky. But the exclusive focus of both the direct and the cross-examination of Bach-Zelewski was his command of SS anti-partisan units in Russia. His presence in Warsaw in 1944 was mentioned in cross-examination only once in passing. See *Trial of the Major War Criminals*, 4:, 475–96.
63 *Zburzenie Warszawy*, 145–6; see also Sawicki, *Przed polskim prokuratorem*, 105–6. We found the archival transcript of only one interrogation conducted by Sawicki; it is of his questioning of Guderian. The printed version is not an exact copy of the archival transcript. For the archival transcript, see AAN, 230/14. "Zeznania i relacje zbrodniarzy hitlerowskich dotyczące Powstania Warszawskiego."
64 We discuss Bühler's trial in chapter 3. A dispute between US and Polish officials over the postwar border between Germany and Poland brought

Guderian's pending extradition to Poland to a halt. See King, "Personal Reflections," 259. Negotiations between the Americans and the Poles over Bach-Zelewski's extradition to Poland were dissolved, overshadowed by the Cold War. See Conot, *Justice*, 283. However, Bach-Zelewski did appear in a Polish court in 1947, brought to Warsaw to testify for the prosecution in the trial of Ludwig Fischer, former governor of the Warsaw district.

65 *Zburzenie Warszawy*, 6–8; see also Sawicki, *Przed polskim prokuratorem*, 8–9. Although Sawicki is not the author of record of *Zburzenie Warszawy*, he was most likely the author of the preface in which this statement appears. In any event, it reflects his sentiments and those of other members of the Polish delegation and of the GKBZN who collected evidence of Nazi crimes in Poland.

66 *Zburzenie Warszawy*, 69–76; see also Sawicki, *Przed polskim prokuratorem*, 53–9.

67 *Zburzenie Warszawy*, 8; see also Sawicki, *Przed polskim prokuratorem*, 9.

68 Motas, "Delegacja polska," 81–2.

69 *Trial of the Major War Criminals*, 8: 317–22, quotes on 319, 320, and 322.

70 The other Jewish witnesses were Abraham Sutzkever and Izrael Eizenberg. Sutzkever, a Soviet prosecution witness, was a Yiddish poet who offered a horrific description of how the Nazis terrorized and massacred the 80,000-strong Jewish community of Wilno in Lithuania, the prewar centre of Yiddish culture. For Sutzkever's testimony, see *Trial of the Major War Criminals*, 8: 302–8. See also Jockusch, "Justice at Nuremberg?," 119–20. Eizenberg, summoned to testify by the British, was a Polish Jew who described the killing of Jews in the Lublin district in 1941–42. For his testimony, see *Trial of the Major War Criminals*, 20: 484–5. See also Jockusch, "Justice at Nuremberg?," 120. As Jockusch observes, the fact that mainly non-Jews testified about Nazi crimes against Jews and, in particular, that the Allied prosecution summoned two non-Jews (Szmaglewska and Marie-Claude Vaillant Couturier, a French resistance fighter) to the witness stand to testify about the mass murder of Jews at Auschwitz at the hands of Germans and their accomplices demonstrates that in line with the Allies' intentions, the IMT "focused not on victims and their narratives of persecution, suffering, and genocide but rather on the central figures of the Nazi regime … Individual victims from the periphery of the regime thus had limited value; indeed, prosecutors feared that their horrifying stories of human tragedy might be a distraction." Jockusch, "Justice at Nuremberg?," 122.

71 Menz was eventually convicted and sentenced to life imprisonment at the 1965 trial of Treblinka personnel that was held in Germany. See Sands, *East West Street*, 293.

72 *Trial of the Major War Criminals*, 8: 322–29, quotes on 322–3, 327, 328, and 329.

73 On the uprising at Treblinka, see Arad, *Belzec*, 282–305.

74 See Łuczak, *Polityka*, passim.

75 On Frank, see Fest, *The Face*, 209–19; Wulf, *Das Dritte Reich*, 340–73; Schenk, *Hans Frank*; and Sands, *East West Street*, pt VI.

76 *Trial of the Major War Criminals*, 1: 71.

77 Jasiński, "The Central Commission," 8.

78 IPN, GKBZHwP 1048, "Sprawozdanie delegacji Ministerstwa Sprawiedliwości z pobytu w Londynie w sprawie przestępstw wojennych i procesu w Norymberdze," 30 October 1945, 3–4.

79 Sands, *East West Street*, 235.

80 Präg and Jacobmeyer, *Das Diensttagebuch*, 30–1. Piotrowski published excerpts of Frank's diary both in the original German and in Polish translation in 1956 and 1957. See Piotrowski, *Dziennik* (1956); and idem, *Dziennik* (1957). Präg and Jacobmeyer's annotated version of the diary in the original German is more extensive than Piotrowski's versions.

81 *Trial of the Major War Criminals*, 3: 409. The excerpts (in the German original) from Frank's diary, IMT document 2233-PS, can be found in *Trial of the Major War Criminals*, 29: 356–581.

82 See, for example, ibid., 2: 12; 3: 409, 415; 5: 74, 78, 85; 12: 103, 106, 108, 113; 21: 468; 22: 223.

83 Sands, *East West Street*, 287.

84 The text of Piotrowski's brief, titled "Hans Frank – Der Mann und sein Werk: Der Generalgouverneur in seinen Tagebüchern," is available in Piotrowski, *Proces Hansa Franka*, 245–57. A Polish version of the brief can be found on 271–82.

85 Ibid., 248.

86 Ibid., 257.

87 *Trial of the Major War Criminals*, 2: 97.

88 Ibid., 2: 120.

89 Sands, *East West Street*, 279.

90 *Trial of the Major War Criminals*, 12: 7.

91 Ibid., 12: 8.

92 Ibid.

93 Höss, the former commandant of Auschwitz, appeared as a witness for defendant Ernst Kaltenbrunner, chief of the RSHA from January 1943 to

the end of the war, whose attorney tried to distance him from the killing process. But his attorney's strategy backfired because Höss, who offered a detailed and bone-chilling account of what transpired at Auschwitz, testified that he received orders signed by Kaltenbrunner. On cross-examination, Höss affirmed that his statement in an affidavit that he estimated that while he served as commandant of Auschwitz "at least 2,500,000 victims there were executed by gassing and burning, and another half million succumbed to starvation and disease making a total dead of about 3,000,000" was true. For Höss's testimony, see *Trial of the Major War Criminals*, 11: 396–422; quote on 415. Sands speculates that Frank, who testified after Höss and several particularly loathsome defendants, probably figured that he could help his own cause and avoid the gallows if, on the witness stand, he gave the judges the impression that he was less guilty than some of the other defendants and, instead of mounting a robust defence of his actions, he appeared introspective, pled ignorance to some of the atrocities that his fellow Nazis had committed in occupied Poland, and expressed a certain degree of responsibility. Sands, *East West Street*, 297. Höss was extradited and tried in Poland in 1947. We discuss Höss's trial in chapter 3.

94 *Trial of the Major War Criminals*, 12: 13.
95 Sands, *East West Street*, 299. Sands notes that several defendants expressed contempt for Frank because he had asserted in the courtroom that Germany would be disgraced for a thousand years. But the nephew of the French judge Henri Donnedieu de Vabre, who served as his legal secretary and was in court when Frank testified, told Sands that he and others who heard Frank testify were impressed that Frank seemed to accept a certain responsibility, however incomplete, and that fact distinguished him from the other defendants. Sands, *East West Street*, 299–301.
96 For Smirnov's cross-examination of Frank, see *Trial of the Major War Criminals*, 12: 26–39; cf. esp. 12: 28–31 and 12: 36–39 with Piotrowski, *Dziennik Hansa Franka*, 247, 249–50, and 253–4, respectively. For Dodd's cross-examination of Frank, see *Trial of the Major War* Criminals, 12: 40–3.
97 Sands, *East West Street*, 302.
98 For Seidl's closing argument on behalf of Frank, see *Trial of the Major War Criminals*, 18: 129–63, here 132.
99 Ibid., 146.
100 Ibid., 153.
101 Ibid., 154.
102 Ibid., 159.
103 Ibid., 150–1.

104 Ibid., 152–3.

105 Ibid., 160.

106 Sands, *East West Street*, 331.

107 For Jackson's closing argument, see *Trial of the Major War Criminals*, 19: 397–432 at 425.

108 Ibid., 416.

109 Ibid., 427.

110 For Shawcross's closing argument, see *Trial of the Major War Criminals*, 19: 433–529, here 491.

111 Ibid.

112 Erich Koch was party leader of the regional branch (Gauleiter) of the Nazi Party in East Prussia from 1928 to 1945, head of the civil administration of the Białystok district (Bezirk Bialystok) between 1941 and 1945, and Reich Commissar (*Reichskommisar*) of the Reich Commissariat Ukraine (*Reichskommisariat Ukraine*) from 1941 to 1943. He stood trial and was convicted of war crimes in Poland in 1959. We examine his trial in chapter 6.

113 Wilhelm Keitel, general field marshal and chief of the Armed Forces High Command (*Oberkommando der Wehrmacht*, OKW) from 1938 to 1945, was a defendant at Nuremberg. He was hanged.

114 *Trial of the Major War Criminals*, 19: 494.

115 Ibid., 497. For Shawcross's use of the term "genocide" in his closing argument, see Sands, *East West Street*, 335–6.

116 *Trial of the Major War Criminals*, 19: 501.

117 Ibid., 502.

118 Ibid., 517.

119 Ibid., 515.

120 For Rudenko's closing argument, *Trial of the Major War Criminals*, 19: 570–618 and 20: 1–14.

121 For Dubost's closing argument, *Trial of the Major War Criminals*, 19: 535–69, quote on 553.

122 Ibid., 605.

123 Ibid., 617.

124 Ibid., 606.

125 Ibid., 609.

126 Ibid.

127 *Trial of the Major War Criminals*, 19: 448 (Shawcross); 19: 568–9 (Dubost); 20: 14 (Rudenko).

128 Ibid., 19: 529.

129 Sands, *East West Street*, 256, 293, 302.

130 For Frank's closing statement, including all quotations, see *Trial of the Major War Criminals*, 19: 384–5.

131 Quoted in Sands, *East West Street*, 288.

132 For the judgment, see *Trial of the Major War Criminals*, 22: 411–523 (30 September 1946) and 22: 524–89 (1 October 1946), here 477.

133 Ibid., 478.

134 Ibid., 480.

135 Ibid., 481.

136 Ibid., 491.

137 Ibid., 494.

138 Ibid., 22: 491.

139 Ibid., 22: 541–4. Arthur Seyss-Inquart was Frank's deputy in the General Government from October 1939 until May 1940; he was then appointed Reich commissioner in the occupied Netherlands. He was convicted partly for supporting the exploitation of Polish agriculture, the AB Action, and the persecution of Polish Jews. See ibid., 22: 575. But the primary grounds for his conviction were his ruthless administration of the occupied Netherlands.

140 Ibid., 22: 588. French judge Donnedieu wanted to spare Frank's life and sentence him to life in prison, but he was overruled by the tribunal's seven other judges. Donnedieu's willingness to show leniency to Frank may have been motivated by their prewar acquaintance. See Sands, *East West Street*, 356–7.

141 Schenk, *Hans Frank*, 399–402.

142 See Piotrowski, *Proces Hansa Franka*, 211–16; Cyprian and Sawicki, *Materiały norymberskie*, 288–91.

143 For Walsh's presentation, see *Trial of the Major War Criminals*, 3: 553–8. See also Jockusch, "Justice at Nuremberg?," 115–16. We discuss Stroop's 1951 trial in Poland in chapter 4.

144 Marrus, "The Holocaust," 25. See also Marrus, *The Nuremberg Trial*, 201.

145 Cyprian and Sawicki attacked Western critics of the IMT; see Cyprian and Sawicki, *Sprawie polskie*, 782–9. On the Soviets' dissatisfaction with the trial, see Hirsch, "The Soviets at Nuremberg," 722–30.

146 Cyprian and Sawicki, *Sprawy polskie*, 710–11; see also Cyprian and Sawicki, *Materiały norymberskie*, 34–5. A Polish observer expressed similar satisfaction with the results achieved by the delegation, especially as seen in the judgment. See Małcużyński, *Oskarżeni*, 82.

147 In her valuable essay on the assistance rendered by the Central Jewish Historical Commission in Poland to the GKBZN and to the Polish

delegation, the reaction of Polish Jews to the IMT's verdict, and the delegation's representation of the plight of Polish Jewry in Nazi-occupied Poland, Natalia Aleksiun argues that "Polish authorities gave more emphasis to atrocities committed against Poles than to the even greater suffering of the Jews who were, in theory, equal citizens of Poland" and that for both Poles and Jews "the Nuremberg trial represented a disappointment and came to symbolize the lack of closure." Aleksiun, "Organizing for Justice," 191. As this chapter makes clear, we would qualify these statements. At least the Polish delegation at Nuremberg placed more or less equal emphasis on ethnic Polish and Polish Jewish suffering and viewed the proceedings and judgment as more positive than negative.

3 The Supreme National Tribunal

1 This chapter is partly based on Prusin, "Poland's Nuremberg"; and on Pendas, Jockusch, and Finder, "Auschwitz Trials."
2 Gumkowski and Kułakowski, *Zbrodniarze*, 173; Rojowska, "Wpływ dekretów," 188.
3 Dmitrów, *Niemcy*, 242–3.
4 *Głos Ludu*, no. 272, 3 October 1946, 1; no. 273, 4 October 1946, 2; no. 275, 6 October 1946, 2; Dmitrów, *Niemcy*, 244–9, 254.
5 "Dekret z dnia 22 stycznia 1946 r. o Najwyższym Trybunale Narodowym," *Dziennik Ustaw*, no. 5, 78–80.
6 "Dekret z dnia 22 stycznia 1946 r. o odpowiedzialności za klęskę wrześniową i faszyzację życia państwowego," *Dziennik Ustaw*, no. 5, 80–1.
7 In accordance with the decision of the KRN's Presidium, the issuance of the decree was "based on conviction that the cause of the September defeat was the *Sanacja* regime and unlawful activities of its former leaders, particularly their systematic violation of the basic laws such as the Constitution of 1921 and the introduction of fascist principles inconsistent with the Constitution." "Załącznik do protokołu z 4 posiedzenia," 280. The Sanacja "healing" was the name for the authoritarian political system that dominated Poland from 1926 to 1939.
8 For example, a US team led by Brigadier General Telford Taylor, assistant counsel to Robert Jackson at the IMT and then chief counsel of the twelve successor trials held before the US Nuremberg Military Tribunals, attended the trials of Rudolf Höss and Ludwig Fischer. *Życie Warszawy*, no. 72 (858), 14 March 1947, 2; Jakubowski, *Sądownictwo powszechne*, 37.

9 Jakubowski, *Sądownictwo powszechne*, 58.
10 Musial, "NS-Kriegsverbrecher," 54; "Cyprian, Tadeusz," 2: 667; "Sawicki, Jerzy," 10: 374. See also Cyprian, Sawicki, and Siewierski, *Głos ma prokurator*, 33, 83, 111, 169, 201, 213, 231; "Wacław Barcikowski," http://encyclopedia.interia.pl/; "Antoni Chmurski," http://pl.wikipedia.org; "Stanisław Hejmowski," http://wapedia.mobi/pl (accessed 23 May 2017).
11 In January 1947, after the national elections (falsified by the Polish and Soviet security services) to the Legislative Sejm (Sejm Ustawodawczy), the KRN, which held both legislative and executive powers, officially terminated its functions.
12 "Załącznik do protokołu z 4 posiedzenia," 291.
13 Borodziej, "'Hitlerische Verbrechen,'" 407–8; Jakubowski, *Sądownictwo powszechne*, 86; "Dekret z dnia 22 stycznia 1946 r. o Najwyższym Trybunale Narodowym," 79; *Głos Wielkopolski*, no. 168/473, 21 June 1946, 2; no. 168/472, 22 June 1946, 1.
14 USHMM, RG-15.169M,"Proces członków załogi Oświęcimia = Trial of the Staff of KL Auschwitz-Birkenau" (cited as trial of Auschwitz-Birkenau staff), reel 5, testimonies of witnesses, vol. 51, 9–25; Gumkowski and Kułakowski, *Zbrodniarze*, 98–9, 103, 169; Tadeusz Kułakowski, "Proces Józefa Bühlera," in Gumkowski and Kułakowski, *Zbrodniarze*, 178.
15 Pasek, *Przestępstwa*, 105–7; Kubicki, *Zbrodnie*, 147–9; Kobierska-Motas, "Ściganie," 33–4; Borodziej, "' Hitlerische Verbrechen,'" 413; Sawicki, *Przed polskim prokuratorem*, 251.
16 Kubicki, "Najwyższy Trybunał Narodowy," 11, 13–14; idem, *Zbrodnie*, 81; USHMM, RG-15.166M,"Proces Artura Greisera = Trial of Arthur Greiser" (cited as trial of Arthur Greiser), reel 2, indictment, vol. 21, 1–8; reel 14, testimony of Ehrlich, vol. 34, 2–5; ibid., vol. 35, 2–5; Sawicki, *Przed polskim prokuratorem*, 251, 255–7.
17 USHMM, RG-15.174M, "Proces Józefa Bühlera = Trial of Josef Bühler" (cited as trial of Josef Bühler), reel 12, testimony of Ehrlich, frames 35127–8, 35131, 35133.
18 Ibid., frames 35134–6.
19 Ibid., frames 35138–9.
20 *Głos Wielkopolski*, no. 167/471, 221 June 1946, 1; no. 171/475, 25 June 1946, 1; Basak, "Zagadnienie ludobójstwa," 284–5, 287f.
21 USHMM, RG-15.165M, "Proces Ludwiga Fischera, et al = Trial against Ludwig Fischer, 1946–1947" (cited as trial of Ludwig Fischer and others), reel 2, indictment, vol. 58, 1–6.
22 USHMM, trial of Arthur Greiser, reel 14, indictment, vol. 33, 1–8.

23 Ibid., reel 1, trial minutes, vol. 13, 17a-b, 75–6; vol. 14, 186, 194; reel 2, vol. 18, 1–4; reel 14, vol. 34, 15–27, 46–8; USHMM, trial of Ludwig Fischer and others, reel 2, indictment of Fischer, vol. 58, 17–18; vol. 60, 32; Basak, "Zagadnienie ludobójstwa," 286, 290, 298; Gumkowski and Kułakowski, *Zbrodniarze*, 9–10, 13–16, 22, 25–6, 29, 33, 45, 47, 51, 61–3, 70–1; Cyprian, Sawicki, and Siewierski, *Głos ma prokurator*, 218–19; Sawicki, *Przed polskim prokuratorem*, 266–9, 271.

24 USHMM, trial of Ludwig Fischer and others, reel 2, indictment of Fischer, vol. 58, pp. 9–10; vol. 60, pp. 41, 47–8, 50; reel 6, vol. 73, 431–3; reel 9, vol. 80, 75, 79–80; Gumkowski and Kułakowski, *Zbrodniarze*, 14, 18, 20, 22–3, 54–6, 66–70; Kułakowski, "Proces Józefa Bühlera," 183–6, 190, 217–18, 251, 258–9, 261–4; Cyprian, Sawicki, and Siewierski, *Głos ma prokurator*, 62; Płoski et al., *Okupacja i ruch oporu*, 1: 235; 2: 31, 48–50; Sawicki, *Przed polskim prokuratorem*, 269.

25 Bloxham, *Genocide*, 19–20; Cyprian and Sawicki, *Siedem wyroków*, 10–14; Kobierska-Motas, "Ściganie sprawców," 33; Sawicki, *Przed polskim prokuratorem*, 251.

26 USHMM, trial of Ludwig Fischer and others, reel 2, indictment of Meisinger and Daume, vol. 60, 6, 14–15; reel 6, vol. 73, 395, 438–9, 442–8, 457; vol. 71, 11; vol. 72, 199–201; reel 9, vol. 80, 66, 86–8, 90, 92–4, 104–6; Płoski et al., *Okupacja i ruch*, 1: 158–65, 235; 2: 31, 48–50; Sawicki, *Przed polskim prokuratorem*, 283–92.

27 USHMM, RG-15.170M, "Proces Amona Goetha = Trial against Amon Goeth, 1946," (cited as trial of Amon Göth), reel 3, indictment, vol. 42, 12–13, 14–16; vol. 45, 151; *Proces ludobójcy*, 11–13. For the Holocaust as a secondary issue in Allied courts, see Bloxham, *Genocide*, 74–5.

28 USHMM, trial of Amon Göth, reel 2, testimony of experts, vol. 43, 136–8.

29 Ibid., reel 1, vol. 42, testimonies of witnesses, 1, 22, 24–5, 32; reel 2, vol. 43, 42; reel 3, vol. 3, 12; vol. 45, 21, 26; Płoski et al., *Okupacja i ruch oporu*, 2: 442.

30 USHMM, trial of Amon Göth, trial minutes, reel 1, vol. 1, 74–5; vol. 41, 75–6, 78–9, 104–6; vol. 42, 22, 24–5, 32, 34, 42; reel 2, vol. 3, 112–13; vol. 43, 42; vol. 45, 21, 26–7; reel 3, vol. 3, 12; vol. 42, 12–13, 14–16, 29, 95; vol. 43, 29; vol. 45, 26, vol. 47, 15–17, 31, 33, 201.

31 USHMM, trial of Auschwitz-Birkenau staff, reel 12, indictment, vol. 77, 13–25; reel 15, vol. 84, 17–19, 22; Sosińska, "Powstanie i działalność," 44.

32 USHMM, trial of Auschwitz-Birkenau staff, minutes, reel 5, vol. 51, 41–5, reel 7, vol. 56, 107; *Wspomnienia Rudolfa Hoessa*, 94–9, 277, 299–301, 318–20; Gumkowski and Kułakowski, *Zbrodniarze*, 97–9, 102–3, 112–13, 117–18, 152.

33 USHMM, trial of Auschwitz-Birkenau staff, minutes, reel 6, vol. 55, 118–19; reel 12, vol. 80, 3.
34 Gumkowski and Kułakowski, *Zbrodniarze*, 99–100.
35 The trials before the NTN of Höss in March 1947 and of forty Germans from Auschwitz in November and December of the same year were but two of a large number of trials of Auschwitz staff conducted in postwar Poland. In all their Auschwitz trials, Poles tried and convicted almost 600 personnel from the camp. See Sydnor, "Auschwitz I," 207.
36 *Biuletyn Głównej Komisji Badania Zbrodni Niemieckich w Polsce*, vol. VII. Höss's autobiography was translated into many languages and appeared in several Western countries from 1958 onward with the publication that year in Germany of Höss, *Kommandant in Auschwitz*, which features an introduction and commentary by German historian Martin Broszat.
37 USHMM, RG 15.167M, 1998.A.0243, "Proces Rudofa Hessa = Trial of Rudolf Höss" (cited as trial of Rudolf Höss, reel 5, vol. 22, 2–4.
38 Ibid., 7.
39 Ibid., 18.
40 Ibid., 71.
41 Ibid., 84. This assertion is not unambiguous, since it could be read as attributing the mass murder of Jews by gassing to German efforts to relieve the camp's overcrowding, strained to the breaking point by an unexpectedly large influx of prisoners, as much as to German racial ideology.
42 Ibid., 61. The Polish word here for "extermination" is *zagłada*, the same term used earlier in the indictment to describe the mass murder of Jews.
43 In this vein, prosecutor Tadeusz Cyprian stated in his opening argument that Höss represented a criminal "system whose objective was the elimination no longer of individuals, groups, or strata of people but of entire nations [*narody*]" in service to the Nazi regime. USHMM, trial of Rudolf Höss, reel 6, vol. 23, 8. See also Gumkowski and Kułakowski, *Zbrodniarze*, 87.
44 USHMM, trial of Rudolf Höss, reel 6, vol. 23, 125–6.
45 Ibid., reel 6, vol. 24, 74–5.
46 Ibid., reel 7, vol. 31, 67–87 (Kowalski's report); ibid., reel 7, vol. 29, 182–205 (Kowalski's testimony).
47 For an interview more than five decades later with Dragan, now named Shlomo, and his brother, Abraham, who was also a member of the *Sonderkommando* at Auschwitz, see Greif, *We Wept without Tears*, ch. 3.

48 USHMM, trial of Rudolf Höss, reel 6, vol. 26, 149–66, quote on 150.

49 Ibid., 156 (Mandelbaum); reel 7, vol. 29, 40 (Tauber). For further attestation in secret diaries kept by members of the *Sonderkommando*, discovered after the war, that Poles were shot by Germans in the crematoria at Birkenau, see Piper, "Estimating the Number of Deportees," 84–5.

50 USHMM, trial of Rudolf Höss, reel 7, vol. 31, 1–66 (Blumental's report); ibid., reel 7, vol. 29, 119–81 (Blumental's testimony). For more extensive analysis of Blumental's expert opinion, see chapter 5.

51 The judgment has been published in Cyprian, *Siedem wyroków*, 92–136.

52 USHMM, trial of Rudolf Höss, reel 7, vol. 32, 5–6. Franciszek Piper, an acknowledged authority on Auschwitz, has revised this figure significantly downward. He estimates that 1,100,000 inmates were killed or died at Auschwitz; almost one million of these victims were Jews, 70,000–75,000 were Poles, and the remaining victims were nationals from various countries in Europe under Nazi occupation. Piper, "Estimating the Number of Deportees," 89–98; see also idem, "The Number of Victims," 61–76.

53 USHMM, trial of Rudolf Höss, reel 7, vol. 32, 29.

54 Ibid., 37.

55 Ibid., 33.

56 Ibid., 40.

57 Ibid., 44–6.

58 Ibid., 67.

59 Ibid.,. 32.

60 *Dziennik Ludowy*, no. 69 (544), 12 March 1947, 3.

61 *Głos Ludu*, no. 70 (815), 12 March 1947, 2.

62 *Dziennik Ludowy*, no. 69 (544), 12 March 1947, 3.

63 *Życie Warszawy*, no. 70 (856), 12 March 1947, 5.

64 *Życie Warszawy*, no. 85 (871), 27 March 1947, 2.

65 Epstein, *Model Nazi*, 320–1; Kulesza, "Der Beitrag," 126.

66 USHMM, trial of Arthur Greiser, Biebow's testimony, 26 June 1946, reel 13, vol. 28, 41; reel 15, vol. 38, 855–6.

67 Kulesza, "Der Beitrag," 128.

68 USHMM, trial of Ludwig Fischer and others, reel 6, Fischer's testimony, vol. 73, 313; reel 9, Meisinger's testimony, vol. 80, 63–5, 2500, 2502; Kułakowski, "Proces Józefa Bühlera," 179, 190–1, 265.

69 USHMM, trial of Amon Göth, reel 3, vol. 47, 9–14; trial of Auschwitz-Birkenau staff, reel 5, vol. 51, 65–6, 76–7; reel 7, vol. 56, 109–10 (defendants' testimonies); Gumkowski and Kułakowski, *Zbrodniarze*, 96–7, 99, 102, 104–5.

70 USHMM, trial of Arthur Greiser, defence arguments, 6 July 1946, reel 15, vol. 38, 727; reel 16, vol. 539, 1034–7, 1044–5; trial of Ludwig Fischer and

others, reel 9, testimonies of witnesses, vol. 80, 144–6, 155–7; vol. 81, 2793–801; Kułakowski, "Proces Józefa Bűhlera," 179, 201, 244, 254–6; *Dziennik Ludowy*, no. 347/466, 30 December 1946, 3. In the 1950s Hejmowski became known for his courageous defence of the members of the non-communist underground and, consequently, was placed on the security police's blacklist. We are grateful to Dr Łukasz Kamiński for this information.

71 *Proces ludobójcy*, 18, 19, 429–31, 433, 451; USHMM, trial of Auschwitz-Birkenau staff, reel 6, testimonies of witnesses, vol. 55, 119; reel 15, vol. 84, 27–9, 46; Gumkowski and Kułakowski, *Zbrodniarze*, 95, 111, 167, 170.

72 USHMM, trial of Auschwitz-Birkenau staff, reel 15, defence arguments, vol. 84, n.pag.

73 USHMM, trial of Arthur Greiser, reel 14, verdict, vol. 34, 70–1; trial of Ludwig Fischer and others, reel 2, verdict, vol. 58, 9–10; vol. 60, 41, 47–8, 50; reel 6, vol. 73, 431–3; reel 9, vol. 80, 75, 79–80; Gumkowski and Kułakowski, *Zbrodniarze*, 22–3, 54–6, 66–70; Kułakowski, "Proces Józefa Bühlera," 183–6, 190, 217–18, 251, 258–9, 261–4; Cyprian, Sawicki, and Siewierski, *Głos ma prokurator*, 62; Sawicki, *Przed polskim prokuratorem*, 269.

74 Kubicki, *Zbrodnie*, 99–100.

75 USHMM, trial of Ludwig Fischer and others, reel 2, verdict, vol. 58, 14; vol. 60, 9; reel 6, vol. 71, 105–8, 161–3; reel 9, vol. 80, 81–4, 104–6, 114–15.

76 USHMM, trial of Amon Göth, reel 3, vol. 45, 193, 204; trial of Auschwitz-Birkenau staff, reel 15, verdict, vol. 85, 35–54, 128–30. In their postwar recollections of Münch, former Auschwitz inmates described him mostly in a positive light. See Micheels, *Doctor #117641*, 85, 101, 107–8, 124–5, 127, 137, 141–5, 162, 197–8; Langbein, *People in Auschwitz*, 358–9. In aquitting him, the NTN's judges approvingly noted his declaration that he had never belonged to the NSDAP. However, according to his SS personnel file, which neither the prosecutors nor the judges saw, he had been a member of the Hitlerjugend and the NSDAP. See Lasik, "The Apprehension and Punishment of the Auschwitz Concentration Camp Staff," 109n12.

77 In 1944–47 some members of anti-communist armed formations were also executed publicly. Zaremba, *Wielka trwoga*, 389–90.

78 Ibid., 568.

79 Ibid.

80 "Załącznik do protokołu z 47 posiedzenia," 303–4.

81 *Głos Wielkopolski*, no. 187/491, 11 July 1946, 1; no. 198/502, 22 July 1946, 1; *Dziennik Ludowy*, no. 245/364, 8 September 1946, 1; Dmitrów, *Niemcy*, 236–40. During the execution of Höss, there were about one hundred spectators who possessed special passes. Zaremba, *Wielka trwoga*, 569.

82 Biegański, "Kara śmierci," 186n44.

83 Wittmann, *Beyond Justice*, 240.

84 Gumkowski and Kułakowski, *Zbrodniarze*, 170.

85 Dmitrów, *Niemcy*, 265–7.

86 Ibid., 266–7.

87 Ibid., 273.

88 Douglas, *Orderly and Humane*, 21–2, 160–1; Naimark, *Fires of Hatred*, 122–3.

89 Lubecka, "Procesy," 57–8. In contrast, German defendants in the provincial and district courts did not enjoy such amenities. Sometimes they were even compelled to clean execution sites and to witness the carrying out of death sentences, which certainly affected them psychologically. For example, Bühler's deputy Ernst Böpple was present at the execution of three AK members. Ibid. Böpple himself was sentenced to death and executed in December 1950.

90 Musial, "NS-Kriegsverbrecher," 52.

91 For example, Madajczyk, *Polityka III Rzeszy*; Łuczak, *Polityka ludnościowa*.

92 Zaremba, *Wielka trwoga*, 584.

93 "Załącznik do protokołu z 47 posiedzenia," 297–9.

94 Borodziej, "Widma przeszłości," 44–5.

95 For example, Greiser requested that 126 witnesses be summoned to testify on his behalf, but only a few appeared at trial. Epstein, *Model Nazi*, 320.

96 See the recollections of prosecutor Jan Brandys in Sosińska, *W czterdziesto-lecie powołania*, 52–3.

97 Kubicki, "Najwyższy Trybunał Narodowy," 14–15; Cyprian, *Siedem wyroków*, 361.

98 Machnikowska, *Wymiar sprawiedliwości*, 273.

99 Friedman, "Law and Politics," 87.

100 *Głos Wielkopolski*, no. 169/473, 21 June 1946, 1; no. 183/487, 7 July 1946, 2.

101 *Gazeta Morska*, no. 193 (312), 18 July 1946, 1.

102 Lubecka, "Procesy," 55; Dmitrów, *Niemcy*, 187.

103 Gumkowski and Kułakowski, *Zbrodniarze*, 159.

104 *Życie Warszawy*, no. 70 (856), 12 March 1947, 1–5; *Głos Ludu*, no. 70 (815), 12 March 1947, 2; *Głos Ludu*, no. 73 (818), 15 March 1947, 2.

105 *Tygodnik Powszechny*, no. 26, 27 June 1948, 2; *Przekrój*, no. 101, 16–22 March 1947, 5; *Chłopski Sztandar*, no. 13, 30 March 1947, 2.

106 Sosińska, "Powstanie i działalność," 47. See the recollections of Jan Brandys in idem, *W czterdziestolecie powołania*, 54. See also *Głos Wielkopolski*, no. 161/465, 15 June 1946, 1; no. 169/473, 21 June 1946, 1; no. 183/487, 7 July 1946, 2; no. 198/502, 22 July 1946, 1.

107 USHMM, trial of Auschwitz-Birkenau staff, reel 15, defence for Mandel, vol. 84, n.pag; Cyprian, Sawicki, and Siewierski, *Głos ma prokurator*, 44–5, 89; Basak, "Motywacje moralne," 256–8.

108 *Głos Wielkopolski*, no. 167/471, 21 June 1946, 1; no. 169/473, 23 June 1946, 5; no. 171/475, 25 June 1946, 1; *Dziennik Ludowy*, no. 344/463, 17 December 1946, 6; no. 346/465, 19 December 1946, 2.

109 Among potential NTN defendants were Erich von dem Bach-Zelewski, Jürgen Stroop, and Paul Otto Geibel, the last SSPF of the Warsaw district. Cyprian and Sawicki, *Oskarżamy*, 265. Stroop was eventually tried in Poland in 1951 and Geibel in 1954. Bach-Zelewski, on the other hand, never stood trial in Poland.

110 Borodziej, "Hitleristische 'Verbrechen,'" 414; Lubecka, "Procesy," 54.

111 Quoted in Baird, *From Nuremberg to My Lai*, viii.

4 Himmler's Men on Trial

1 "Dekret Polskiego Komitetu Wyzwolenia Narodowego z dnia 30 października 1944 r. o ochronie Państwa," *Dziennik Ustaw*, n. 10, position 50. For example, in November 1948 Kazimierz Moczarski, a member of the AK who had been in prison since August 1945, was again charged with crimes against the state. Machnikowska, *Wymiar sprawiedliwości*, 311.

2 Kalicki, *Ostatni jeniec*, 187.

3 The SED was created in April 1946 as a consequence of the merger of the Social Democratic Party of Germany and the Communist Party of Germany in the Soviet occupation zone. In October 1949, after the formation of the German Democratic Republic (GDR) that is, East Germany, the SED would become its governing party.

4 Ruchniewicz, *Warszawa–Berlin–Bonn*, 91, 93; Kochanowski, *W polskiej niewoli*, 95.

5 Selerowicz and Garscha, "Die strafrechtliche Ahndung," 106. Calculated on the basis of Kobierska-Motas, *Ekstradycja*, 2: 28–252. See also Borodziej, "'Hitleristische Verbrechen,'" 431–2.These numbers refer only to the trials of culprits extradited to Poland by the Allies.

6 Lubecka, "Procesy," 59; Szczepański, *Dzienniki*, 45.

7 Erich Engels played a key role in the genocide of Jews in East Galicia.

8 Kiwerska, "Władysław Bartoszewski." Non-communist activist, writer, and later politician Władysław Bartoszewski (1922–2015) twice served as a foreign minister in post-communist Poland.

9 Radziwończyk, "Rola i specyfika terroru," 239, 244.

10 Mallmann, "'Mensch," 126–8; Alexander, "War Crimes," 301.
11 *Dziennik Zachodni*, no. 91/1120, 1 April 1948, 6; *Słowo Polskie*, no. 90/501, 2 April 1948, 3.
12 USHMM, District Court in Warsaw, reel 18, "Akta w sprawie karnej Józefa Grzimka" (cited as trial of Josef Grzimek), letter of Jerzy Chyrowski to the Main Department of the Polish Union of the Former Political Prisoners, 27 December 1947, frame 000858; testimony of Henryk Altschüller to the Jewish Historical Commission in Kraków, n.d., frames 000772–773; testimonies of Stanisław Szafran, Chaim Winzelberg, and Adolf Wolfgang to the Jewish Historical Commission in Krakow, n.d., frames 000761–762.
13 Since the eastern region of Poland (Kresy Wschodnie) and East Galicia were incorporated into the Soviet Union after the Second World War, defendants who had committed crimes in these areas were tried in major cities such as Warsaw or Kraków.
14 USHMM, trial of Josef Grzimek, reel 19, testimony of Karol Ofenheim, 28 January 1949, frames 000250–251; testimony of Markus Winter, 28 January 1949, frame 000252; testimony of Rudolf Markel, 28 January 1949, frames 000255–257; testimony of Izydor Greiff, 28 January 1949, frames 000263–264.
15 Ibid., reel 19, written testimony of Imioła Wilhelm, 11 April 1948, frames 000402–403; courtroom testimonies of Leon Torczyner and Mordech Nass, 28 January 1949, frames 000258–259, 000261.
16 Ibid., reel 18, testimony of Abraham Landerer to the Jewish Historical Commission in Kraków, n.d., frames 000765–767; testimonies of Stanisław Szafran, Chaim Winzelberg, and Adolf Wolfgang to the Jewish Historical Commission in Kraków, n.d., frames 000761–762; testimony of Szewa Biederman to the Jewish Historical Commission, n.d., frame 000775; testimony of Edmund Schönberg, n.d., frame 000793; reel 19, the indictment, 4 September 1948, frames 000014–017; testimony of Wojciech Bednarz, 28 January 1949, frame 000262.
17 USHMM, District Court in Warsaw, "Akta w sprawie karnej Frederyka Wilhelma Riemanna, Fritza Weissa, Hugona Köhlera, Heinza Marwede" (cited as trial of Friedrich Riemann), reel 20, testimony of Romuald Papesisz, 17 December 1947, frame 000203; and 23 April 1948, frame 000053; testimony of Solomon Hirschberg, 17 December 1947, frames 000202–203; testimony of Solomon Hirschberg, 25 March 1948, frames 000049–050; testimony of David Frieman, 25 March 1948, frame 000051.
18 Ibid., reel 20, testimony of Solomon Hirschberg, 17 December 1947, frames 000202–203; testimony of Romuald Papesisz, 17 December 1947,

frame 000203; testimony of Solomon Hirschberg, 25 March 1948, frames 000049–050.

19 Ibid., reel 20, testimony of Bronisław Münz, 17 December 1948, frames 000191–192.

20 Ibid., reel 20, justification of sentence, frames 000275–276; testimony of Julius Galber, 17 December 1948, frame 000205.

21 Ibid., reel 20, testimony of Tadeusz Schaller, 17 December 1948, frame 000195; testimony of Karol Brożyński, 17 December 1948, frames 000200–201.

22 USHMM, trial of Josef Grzimek, reel 19, testimony of Josef Grzimek, 28 January 1949, frames 000222, 000225–231, 000251–252.

23 USHMM, trial of Friedrich Riemann, reel 20, the Allied interrogation report, 15 July 1945, frame 000452.

24 During the German occupation of Warsaw, Pawiak was the Sipo prison, notorious for the brutal treatment of inmates. Out of approximately 300,000 people who passed through Pawiak, about 37,000 were executed and 60,000 sent to the death and concentration camps. Domańska, *Pawiak*.

25 USHMM, trial of Friedrich Riemann, reel 20, court testimony of Friedrich Riemann, 17 December 1948, frame 000188–189.

26 Ibid.

27 USHMM, trial of Josef Grzimek, reel 19, verdict and justification of the sentence, 29 January 1949, frames 000295–297, 000326; *Trybuna Ludu*, no. 30 (44), 31 January 1949, 2.

28 USHMM, trial of Friedrich Riemann, reel 20, verdict, frame 000278.

29 Ibid., reel 20, appendix to the Allied interrogation report, 15 July 1945, frame 000457; note of the Polish Military Mission by UNWCC, 9 September 1946, frame 000447.

30 Roseman, "Beyond Conviction?," 95.

31 USHMM, trial of Josef Grzimek, reel 19, biographical data of Grzimek, frame 000548; indictment, 4 September 1948, frames 000012, 00000448, 000585–593; *Slowo Polskie*, no. 90 (501), 2 April 1948, 3.

32 On the ideological indoctrination of the SS, see Matthäus, "Die 'Judenfrage,'" 35–86.

33 Riemann's highest rank was SS-Oberscharführer (Staff Sergeant); Grzimek's was SS-Hauptscharführer (Sergeant 1st Class).

34 Mallmann, "'Mensch," 126. See also Lower, *Nazi Empire-Building*, 109.

35 Goldhagen, *Hitler's Willing Executioners*, 174.

36 USHMM, trial of Friedrich Riemann, reel 20, testimony of Solomon Hirschberg, 25 March 1948, frames 000049–050; testimony of Bronisław

Münz, 17 December 1948, frames 000191–192; testimony of Karol Broczyńsky, 17 December 1948, frames 000200–201; testimony of Abraham Ochs, 17 December 1948, frames 000196–199.

37 USHMM, trial of Josef Grzimek, reel 18, testimony of Abraham Landerer to the Jewish Historical Commission in Kraków, n.d., frames 000765–767; testimony of Szewa Biederman to the Jewish Historical Commission, n.d., frame 000775; testimony of Edmund Schónberg, n.d., frame 000793; reel 19, written testimony of David Sobol, 10 April 1948, frames 000411–412. Belyaev, *Razoblachenie*, 78–82, 114–17.

38 Büchler, "'Unworthy Behavior,'" 420.

39 Pohl, "Hans Krueger," 239–65; Tokarev, "V zamknutom kruge," 185–99.

40 Pohl, "Hans Krueger," 261.

41 Madajczyk, *Faszyzm* 2: 423, 425.

42 Załuski, *Czterdziesty czwarty*, 152.

43 Quoted in Madajczyk, *Polityka*, vol. 2, 238.

44 Cited in Zaremba, *Wielka trwoga*, 107.

45 USHMM, RG-15.164M, Sąd Okręgowy w Białymstoku = District Court in Białystok, 1945–69 (cited as District Court in Białystok), "Akta w sprawie karnej Waldemara Artura Augusta Macholla Macpolowskiego" (cited as trial of Waldemar Macholl), reel 6, letter of the Union of Political Prisoners in Białystok to the Białystok District Court, 22 March 1949, frame 000647.

46 Ibid., reel 6, indictment, 19 June 1948, frames 000442–000447, 000450; Omiljanowicz, *Zanikające echa*, 80, 106–7.

47 USHMM, trial of Waldemar Macholl, reel 6, expert opinion of Szymon Datner, 16 March 1949, frame 000690; ibid., 21 March 1949, frames 000660, 000684, 000686.

48 Ibid., reel 6, testimony of Roman Dybacki, 12 March 1949, frame 000741; testimony of Kazimierz Jurowiński, 8 March 1949, frame 000730; indictment, 19 June 1948, frames 000459–460; report of an investigator of the People's Militia, 15 January 1949, frame 000586; expert opinion of Szymon Datner, 16 March 1949, frames 000660–661.

49 Omiljanowicz, *Zanikajace echa*, 222–9.

50 USHMM, trial of Waldemar Macholl, reel 6, interrogation of Fritz Gustaw Friedel, 2 October 1948, frame 000659; testimony of Fritz Gustaw Friedel, 21 March 1949, frames 000774–776.

51 Unlike in most European countries they occupied, the Nazis did not attempt to establish any form of a native collaborationist administration in Poland. At the same time, thousands of Poles declared themselves to be ethnic Germans (*Volksdeutsche*), and the so-called Blue Police and low-ranking Polish bureaucrats were employed in the occupation

administration. In 1941 a number of Poles engaged in massacres of Jews in eastern Poland, while others benefited from blackmailing Jews or denouncing them to the police. Both the AK and the communist resistance suffered heavy losses due to the activities of agents, provocateurs, and informants working for the Gestapo or the German police.

52 The Polish security service, however, thoroughly interrogated Macholl and other individuals on this subject. For example, a security functionary and amateur writer, Aleksander Omiljanowicz, interviewed Macholl in his cell. Omiljanowicz, *Przed wyrokiem*, 15–21. See also USHMM, trial of Waldemar Macholl, reel 6, interrogation of Gestapo agent Jerzy Turowski, 4 December 1947, frames 000694–695.

53 USHMM, trial of Waldemar Macholl, reel 6, testimony of Adolf Bogucki, 8 March 1949, frames 000724–725; testimony of Antoni Klemensowicz, 10 March 1949, frames 000730–731; testimony of Stanisław Kondracki, 10 March 1949, frame 000732; testimony of Kazimierz Łytkiewicz, 10 March 1949, frame 000734; testimony of Maria Łycka, 10 March 1949, frame 000737.

54 Ibid., reel 6, trial testimony of Kazimierz Jurowiński, 8 March 1949, frame 000730.

55 Datner, "Niemiecki okupacyjny aparat bezpieczeństwa."

56 USHMM, trial of Waldemar Macholl, reel 6, indictment, 19 June 1948, frames 000461–464; Omiljanowicz, *Przed wyrokiem*, 90–2.

57 USHMM, trial of Waldemar Macholl, reel 6, affidavit of Amiel Szymon, n.d., frames 000567–568.

58 Ibid., reel 6, testimony of Chaim Wróbel, 15 March 1949, frames 000750–000752.

59 Ibid., reel 6, trial minutes, 8 March 1949, frames 000705–711, 000716, 000718–719; 12 March 1949, frame 000757.

60 Ibid., reel 6, Macholl's closing statement, 25 March 1949, frames 000817–818.

61 Ibid., reel 6, verdict, 25 March 1949, frames 000823–824.

62 Ibid., reel 6, testimony of Kazimierz Jurowiński, 8 March 1949, frame 000730; Omiljanowicz, *Przed wyrokiem*, 87–8.

63 USHMM, trial of Waldemar Macholl, reel 6, interrogation of Macholl in Allied captivity, 6 June 1947, 28 June 1948, frames 001035–1036; reel 7, autobiography of Macholl in Allied captivity, 28 June 1948, frames 000159, 000174–175.

64 Paul and Mallmann, "Sozialisation," 8–9; Hölzl, "Walter Nord," 166–7.

65 Breitman, "'Gegner Nummer eins'," 23–5; Westermann, *Hitler's Police Battalions*, 36–7.

66 Birn, "Heinrich Bergmann," 47.

67 Mallman and Bühler, *Einsatzgruppen in Polen*, 52; Wardzyńska, *Był rok 1939*, 123.

68 USHMM, trial of Waldemar Macholl, reel 7, record of Macholl's name change at the Gestapo in Suwałki, 26 October 1940, frame 000176; Omiljanowicz, *Przed wyrokiem*, 10–11, 14–15; see also Omiljanowicz, *Cienie powracają*, 12–13; Wardzyńska, *Był rok 1939*, 234–5.

69 Alexander, "War Crimes," 299; Wildt, *Generation*, 861–8.

70 Apart from Stroop, high-profile defendants included the SSPF in Kraków and East Galicia, Theobald Thier (tried in December 1948); the SSPF in Radom, Herbert Böttcher (tried in June 1949); the HSSPF in Danzig-West Prussia, Richard Hildebrandt (tried in November 1949); and the SSPF in Lublin, Jacob Sporrenberg (tried in September 1950).

71 Porat, *The Boy*, ch. 1; Kermish, *Mered geto varshah*, 95–6; see also idem, *The Warsaw Ghetto Revolt*, xli. The English edition is a condensed version of the Hebrew edition.

72 Kermish, *Mered geto varshah*, 96–7; also idem, *The Warsaw Ghetto Revolt*, xlii.

73 The Bund was the socialist General Jewish Workers Union in Poland.

74 Kermish, *The Warsaw Ghetto Revolt*, xlii–xliii, quote on xliii; see also idem, *Mered geto varshah*, 97–8.

75 On the Warsaw Ghetto Uprising and Stroop's tactics, see Gutman, *The Jews of Warsaw*, esp. chs. 7 and 10 to 14; idem, *Resistance* , esp. chs. 8 to 11; Patt, "Jewish Resistance."

76 See Zimmerman, *The Polish Underground*, 199–201.

77 See Kobylarz, *Walka o pamięć*; see also Young, *The Texture of Memory*, ch. 6.

78 Kermish, *Mered geto varshah*, 102–4; see also idem, *The Warsaw Ghetto Revolt*, xlv.

79 Kermish, *Mered geto varshah*, 108; Piotrowski, *Sprawozdanie*, 43.

80 Kermish, *Mered geto varshah*, 104–5; idem, *The Warsaw Ghetto Revolt*, xlv–xlvi; Person, "Mówi Jürgen Stroop," 382–3; English translation: "Jürgen Stroop Speaks." Appended to Person's article is Stroop's testimony at his trial in Warsaw in its entirety. Stroop's trial is mentioned in passing in the United Nations War Crimes Commission, "Trial of Ulrich Greifelt," 67.

81 Furthermore, Stroop faced questions in his cell from representatives of the ŻIH. On their encounter with him, see chapter 5.

82 Person, "Mówi Jürgen Stroop," 383.

83 Moczarski, *Rozmowy z katem*, quotes on 16. In English: Moczarski, *Conversations*. On Moczarski and the creation of his book, see, for example, Kunert, *Oskarżony*; Machcewicz, *Kazimierz Moczarski*.

84 Moczarski, *Rozmowy z katem*, 223. Pointing to this passage, Andzej Wirth writes that "Stroop's most striking characteristic may have been his coldness." Wirth, "Introduction," n.pag.

85 For an incisive analysis of Moczarski's portrayal of Stroop, see Tippner, "Moczarskis Gespräche mit dem Henker."

86 Person, "Mówi Jürgen Stroop," 384.

87 Person, "Filatelisty," 265; English translation: "The Adventures of a Stamp Collector."

88 IPN, GK 317/874, "Akta w sprawie Jürgena Stroopa, Franza Konrada i Hermana Höfla" (cited as trial of Jürgen Stroop and Franz Konrad), file 1, indictment, 5 July 1951, 1–2. (Citations from IPN, GK 317/874, files 1 and 2, are to folio pages in the file.)

89 IPN, trial of Jürgen Stroop and Franz Konrad, file 1, indictment, 2. The third person named in the indictment, defendant Hermann Höfle, was never tried in Poland. Höfle, chief of staff of Operation Reinhard, was charged with directing the deportation of Jews from the Warsaw Ghetto to Treblinka in the summer of 1942 and in January 1943. After Poland requested his extradition from Austria in 1948, he fled to Italy and remained there until 1951, when he returned to his native Austria, where he lived in the open until Austrian authorities arrested him in 1961. In 1962 he hanged himself in a Viennese jail before his trial could be conducted in Hamburg. See Person, "Mówi Jürgen Stroop," 384; Reich-Ranicki, *The Author*, 169.

90 For Jackson's reference to the report, see *Trial of the Major War Criminals*, 2: 126; for Walsh's introduction of it into evidence, see ibid., 3: 553–8.

91 Wirth, "Introduction," n.pag. See also the introduction ("Wstęp") by Żbikowski to a Polish translation of the report in Jürgen Stroop, *Żydowska dzielnica*, 10.

92 Wirth, "Introduction," n.pag.

93 Porat's book *The Boy* follows the separate but intersecting paths of various protagonists who played a role in this photograph, from Stroop, Konrad, and the German soldier holding the firearm, whose name was Josef Blösche – himself sentenced to death by an East German court in 1969 for his participation in the killing of Jews during the liquidation of the Warsaw Ghetto – to a survivor who claimed to be the child in the photo.

94 See IPN, trial of Jürgen Stroop and Franz Konrad, file 1, 19 July 1951, Stroop's testimony, 118.

95 Ibid., file 1, indictment, 3–18.

96 Ibid., file 1, 18 July 1951, Konrad's testimony, 62–90, here 79 (page 45 of trial transcript).

97 Ibid., file 1, 18 July 1951, 87 (page 61 of trial transcript).

98 Person, "Mówi Jürgen Stroop," 387.
99 Ostindustrie GmbH (OSTI) was the concern created by Odilo Globocnik in the Lublin District in March 1943. Linked to the SS Main Economic and Administrative Office (Wirtschafts- und Verwaltungshauptamt, WVHA), its main objective was to profit from Jewish property looted during Operation Reinhard and to create a network of labour camps and enterprises that would benefit from Jewish forced labour. See Person, "Mówi Jürgen Stroop," 400n63.
100 IPN, trial of Jürgen Stroop and Franz Konrad, file 1, Stroop's testimony, 19 July 1951, 90–133, here 104–5 (pages 28–9 of trial transcript).
101 Ibid., file 1, Stroop's testimony, 19 July 1951, 90–133, here 106 (page 31 of trial transcript).
102 Ibid., 106 (page 32 of trial transcript).
103 Ibid., 107 (page 33 of trial transcript).
104 It is not surprising that the prosecutors and judges refrained from drawing attention to the sensitive paragraph towards the end of the narrative section of Stroop's report that notes that the Polish population by and large welcomed the measures taken against the Jews. The paragraph describes the circulation in Warsaw of a poster, approved by Stroop, that justified the destruction of the ghetto in part by insinuating that the Jews were responsible for the deaths of Polish officers at Katyn, where mass graves had recently been discovered. Polish prosecutors sought a copy of the poster, probably to use in rebuttal as further proof of Stroop's deceitfulness – at this time Soviet and Polish communists publicly blamed the Germans for the executions of Polish officers at Katyn – should Stroop or his attorney refer to this passage in the report at trial in support of his defence, but apparently none was found. See IPN, GK 351/346, trial of Jürgen Stroop and Franz Konrad, internal memorandum written by Stefan Kurowski, chief prosecutor attached to the NTN, 2 October 1947, 56. Stroop's attorney understandably avoided mention of this paragraph because of its awkward and politically sensitive implications. It is unclear, however, why Stroop himself failed to mention it.
105 IPN, trial of Jürgen Stroop and Franz Konrad, file 1, Stroop's testimony, 19 July 1951, 108–10 (pages 36–9 of trial transcript).
106 Ibid., 110–11 (pages 40–1 of trial transcript).
107 On Borg and his service in the Jewish honour court, see Finder, "The Trial of Shepsl Rothoic."
108 Person, "Mówi Jürgen Stroop," 388.
109 IPN, trial of Jürgen Stroop and Franz Konrad, file 1, testimony of Franciszek Łęczycki, 19 July 1951, 133–6 (pages 85–91 of trial transcript).

110 Ibid., file 1, testimony of Marek Edelman, 19 July 1951, 146–9 (pages 111–18 of trial transcript), here 149 (page 117 of trial transcript).

111 Ibid., 149 (page 118 of trial transcript).

112 According to Bernard Mark, who testified after Walewski as an expert witness, the Soviet air attack was launched in response to an appeal from the leadership of the underground PPR in Warsaw to Soviet military authorities requesting help for ghetto fighters and retaliation for the Nazis' liquidation of the ghetto. Mark writes that Soviet planes dropped bombs on German military installations in Warsaw, inflicting numerous casualties on German forces and providing Jewish partisans with cover to attack distracted German guards and to attempt to escape from the ghetto to the Aryan side, while armed Poles facilitated their escape efforts. Mark, *Walka i zagłada*, 406–10; idem, *Der oyfshtand*, 132–3. The description of the Soviet air raid in the account by Mark, whose aim was to project the Soviet Union as a savior of the Jewish fighters in the ghetto, was a staple, appearing with slight variations, in the various editions of his studies of the Warsaw Ghetto Uprising. Soviet planes did in fact bomb Warsaw and drop leaflets over the city on 13 May 1943. But according to Israel Gutman, the eminent Israeli historian who was an authority on the Warsaw Ghetto Uprising and who fought in it, the Soviet planes did not come to help Jews and it is doubtful whether any Germans were killed in the bombing raid. Gutman, *Resistance*, 241. "Nor," adds prominent historian Lucy Dawidowicz, "was there any reliable evidence that the Polish Communists had ever requested Soviet aid on behalf of the Jews. As a matter of fact, by May 13, the uprising was nearly all extinguished and the Warsaw ghetto Jews were dead, dying, or deported to Treblinka." Dawidowicz, *The Holocaust*, 101–2. For his part, Yitzhak Zuckerman, legendary deputy commander of the uprising, called Mark's explanation of the Soviet air raid "nonsense." Zuckerman, *A Surplus of Memory*, 202.

113 IPN, trial of Jürgen Stroop and Franz Konrad, file 1, testimony of Ryszard Walewski, 20 July 1951, 153–67 (pages 8–35 of trial transcript), here 159 (page 19 of trial transcript).

114 Ibid., file 1, testimony of Karolina Markowa, 20 July 1951, 178–80 (pages 58–61 of trial transcript).

115 Ibid., file 1, testimony of Marek Bitter, 20 July 1951, 182–6 (pages 65–74 of trial transcript), here 185–6 (pages 72–3 of trial transcript).

116 Ibid., file 1, testimony of Jürgen Stroop, 20 July 1951, 186 (page 74 of trial transcript).

117 Ibid., file 1, testimony of Stanisław Kubiak, 20 July 1951, 187–91 (pages 76–84 of trial transcript).
118 Ibid., file 1, 20 July 1951, expert report (read into the court record) by Bernard Mark, dated 18 July 1951, 247 (page 15 of report).
119 Ibid., file 2, 20 July 1951, expert report (read into the court record) by Bernard Mark, dated 18 July 1951, 6 (page 22 of report).
120 Ibid., file 2, 20 July 1951, expert report (read into the court record) by Bernard Mark, dated 18 July 1951, 43 (page 59 of report).
121 For Eisenbach's expert testimony, see chapter 5.
122 IPN, trial of Jürgen Stroop and Franz Konrad, file 4, expert report (incorporated into the court record) by Jan Czekanowski and Ludwik Hirszfeld, dated 3 July 1948, 214–23.
123 Ibid., file 2, text of Penner's closing argument (incorporated into the court record), 23 July 1951, 49 (page 2 of Penner's closing argument).
124 Ibid., 61 (page 14 of Penner's closing argument).
125 Ibid., file 2, text of Rusek's closing argument (incorporated into the court record), 23 July 1951, 70 (page 9 of Rusek's closing argument).
126 Ibid., file 2, text of Nowakowski's closing argument (incorporated into the court record), 23 July 1951, 81 (page 5 of Nowakowski's closing argument).
127 Ibid., 86 (page 10 of Nowakowski's closing argument).
128 Ibid., file 2, text of Palatyński's closing argument (incorporated into the court record), 23 July 1951, 100 (page 1 of Palatyński's closing argument).
129 Ibid., file 2, testimony of Stroop and Konrad, 23 July 1951, 46 (page 5 of trial transcript).
130 Ibid., file 2, verdict, 23 July 1951, 112 (page 4 of verdict).
131 Ibid., 113 (pages 5–6 of verdict).
132 Ibid., 116 (page 12 of verdict).
133 Ibid., 117 (page 14 of verdict).
134 Ibid., 118 (page 16 of verdict).
135 Ibid., 118 (page 16 of verdict). It should be noted that in *The United States of America v. Wilhelm List et al.*, the seventh of the "Subsequent Nuremberg Trials" that was conducted between July 1947 and February 1948, which came to be known as "the Hostages Trial," the American judges held that under the current rules of war, as codified in the Hague Convention no. IV from 1907, anti-Nazi partisans in Greece, Albania, and Yugoslavia could not be considered lawful belligerents under article 1 of the Hague Convention and that, therefore, no criminal responsibility attached to Wilhelm List and his co-defendants, all German generals who had led German troops in southeastern Europe, for the execution of captured partisans. The tribunal

did find most of the twelve defendants guilty for the murder of hundreds of thousands of civilians by hostage-taking and reprisal killings by their troops in retaliation for guerilla attacks in excess of current rules under which the tribunal deemed hostage-taking and reprisal killings lawful. See United Nations War Crimes Commission, "Trial of Wilhelm List," 34–92, esp. 55–9.

136 IPN, trial of Jürgen Stroop and Franz Konrad, file 2, 119 (page 17 of verdict).

137 Ibid., 120 (page 20 of verdict).

138 "Der partsuf fun di yidn-merder (notitsn fun gerikhts-zal)," *Folks-shtime*, no. 118 (356), 25 July 1951, 4.

139 "Der hitlerisher talyen – jurgen stroop," *Folks-shtime*, no. 119 (357), 26 July 1951, 5.

140 "SS Men in Warsaw to Die," *New York Times*, 24 July 1951, 9.

141 IPN, trial of Jürgen Stroop and Franz Konrad, file 2, Supreme Court judgment, 7 December 1951, 201–9.

142 Ibid., file 2, Jürgen Stroop to president of the Republic of Poland, 12 December 1951, 196–7.

143 Ibid., file 2, Franz Konrad to president of the Republic of Poland, 19 December 1951, 219–20.

144 Ibid., file 2, B. Kowalewska, director of the Office of Pardons, to District Court for the city of Warsaw, 230.

145 Arendt, *Eichmann in Jerusalem*; Browning, *Ordinary Men*; Roseman, "Beyond Conviction?" 84.

146 Staub, *The Roots of Evil*, 134.

147 Browder, *Hitler's Enforcers*, 168.

148 USHMM, trial of Friedrich Riemann, reel 20, note of the Polish Military Mission by UNWCC, frame 000446, n.d.; Riemann's appeal, 8 March 1949, frame 000297.

149 USHMM, trial of Waldemar Macholl, reel 7, biography of Macholl in the Allied captivity, frame 000167; Omiljanowicz, *Przed wyrokiem*, 23–9.

150 USHMM, trial of Waldemar Macholl, reel 6, indictment, 19 June 1948, frame 000464.

151 Paul and Mallmann, "Sozialisation," 5; Paul, "Von Psychopathen," 61–2.

5 Jews, Poles, and Justice

1 Aleksiun, "Organizing for Justice," 184–94, quote on 186.

2 On the CŻKH see Aleksiun, "The Central Jewish Historical Commission," 74–97; Jockusch, *Collect and Record!*, ch. 3. On the ŻIH see Stach, "Geschichtsschreibung," 401–31.

3 See Stach, "'Praktische Geschichte,'" 245.
4 [Kermish], "Metodologishe bamerkungen," 2.
5 Kermish, "Dray yor tetikayt," 1. Kermish delivered this report in 1947 in Paris at the first conference of Jewish historical commissions and documentation centres held in postwar Europe. For a published synopsis of Kermish's report, see "Rapport du Dr Jozef Kermisz," 140–4.
6 Quoted in Cohen, "Holocaust Survivors," 295; see also Cohen, *Hadorot haba'im*, 133 and 133n13.
7 See Rozenberg-Rutkowski, "Działalność," 15–16; see also Kermish, "Dray yor tetikayt," 12–14. Michał Weichert, a Polish Jew who was acquitted in 1946 by a Polish court on charges of collaboration with the Germans, was recruited in a private capacity by Jerzy Sawicki and Tadeusz Cyprian to write reports for Polish prosecutors preparing for the trials of Fischer and Bühler on criminal measures initiated by Nazi civil authorities. See Weichert, *Zikhroynes*, 4: 183–7. We are unaware of other Jews unaffiliated with the Jewish historical commissions who prepared materials for Polish judicial authorities. The flow of information from Warsaw to Jewish documentation centres in Western Europe was steady in the first couple of years after the war, but it seems to have come to a virtual standstill after the rise of the Iron Curtain. There is evidence of cooperation between first the CŻKH, then briefly the ŻIH, and the Jewish Documentation Center in Vienna in 1947. See Stach, "'Praktische Geschichte,'" 259–61. But Simon Wiesenthal, legendary Nazi hunter and founder of the Jewish Documentation Center, testified in 1966 at a trial in Stuttgart of defendants accused of committing crimes in Lwów (Lviv) and at the Janowska labour camp on the outskirts of the city that his contact with Jewish documentation centres in Eastern Europe ended after 1948 on account of East–West tensions. Since then, he had not received archival documents from them about Nazis residing after the war in the West, and all he had received from the ŻIH in Warsaw since 1948 was its official periodical. Simon Wiesenthal Archive, Vienna, RG Lemberg 08, "Lemberg-Prozess," 20 December 1966, 2319–20 (page 17 of transcript from that day).
8 Among a large number of articles in the Jewish press, see, for example, on Biebow's trial, "Oskarżamy! Bibow – kat łódzkiego ghetta stanie wkrótce przed sądem. Rozmowa z prowadzącym dochodzenie w sprawie Bibowa wiceprokurat. Sądu Spec. ob. J. Lewińskim," *Nasze Słowo*, 29 July 1946, 10; on Göth's trial, Yosef Wulf, "Talyn fun krokever yidn farn gerikht," *Dos naje lebn*, 30 August 1945, 2; on the trial of Auschwitz personnel, Halina Nelken, "Na oświęcimskim procesie w Krakowie," *Nasze Słowo*, 31 December 1947, 9; on Stroop's trial, "Der partsuf fun di yidn-merder

(Notitsn fun gerikhts-zal)," *Folks-shtime*, 25 July 1951, 4; on the trial of Erich Koch, Sh. Tenenblat, "Di fardinte strof (oyfn rand funem urtayl iber erikh kokh," *Folks-shtime*, 12 March 1959, 2; on the Nuremberg Trial, "Der urtayl in nirnberger protses ruft aroys gefiln fun bafridikung un protest," *Dos naje lebn*, 4 October 1946, 1; and on the Eichmann Trial, "Aykhman shuldik in farbrechens kegn yidishn folk, kegn der mentshheyt," *Folks-shtime*, 13 December 1961, 1–2. For examples of reprinted expert opinions, see on Göth's trial, "Miliony oskarżaja (Z przemówienia M. Borwicza, biegłego w procesie Amona Goetha)," *Nasze Słowo*, 30 September 1946, 5; on Höss's trial, Nachman Blumental, "Żydowska ekspertyza w procesie Hoessa (Fragmenty wystąpienie przed Najwyższym Trybunałem Narodowym)," *Nasze Słowo*, 31 March 1947, 7–8; on Biebow's trial, Artur Eisenbach, "Likwidacja łódzkiego ghetta (fragment z ekspertyzy w procesie Hansa Biebowa)," *Nasze Słowo*, 17 May 1947, 7; and on Stroop's trial, B[ernard] Mark, "Der hitlerisher talyen–jurgen stroop," *Folks-shtime*, 26 July 1951, 5, 8.

9 Moreover, Jerzy Sawicki and Jerzy Lewiński, both of Jewish origin, were prosecutors in the trials of Nazis. Sawicki took part in several trials; Lewiński was the prosecutor in the trials of Hans Biebow, administrator of the Łódź Ghetto, and Walter Pelzhausen, commandant of the Radogoszcz prison. (Lewiński had been a policeman in the Warsaw Ghetto, but he was cleared of collaboration with the Nazis. See Finder, "The Politics of Retribution," 555–6.) Michał Mirski, secretary of the CKŻP, was an assessor, assisting the main judge, in the trial of Biebow. At least one judge on the NTN, Emil Rappaport, was of Jewish origin. Mietek Pemper, a witness at the trial of Amon Göth, served as an interpreter between Polish and German at many Nazi trials. He also helped draft the clemency plea of Johann Paul Kremer, a doctor who was a defendant at the 1947 Auschwitz trial. Kremer's court-appointed defence attorney, Berthold Rappaport, was Jewish. On Pemper's role as an interpreter and an aid to Rappaport, see Pemper, *The Road to Rescue*, 181–8. And a survivor of the liquidation of the Radom Ghetto and former prisoner in a labour camp constructed there after liquidation, Tuviah Friedman, who would, like Simon Wiesenthal, become a Nazi hunter (from his adopted home in Israel), joined a Polish militia unit for a short period after liberation and was assigned the task of interrogating suspected Nazis apprehended in Gdańsk (Danzig) and identifying members of the SS and Gestapo among them for Polish security forces. By his own account, Friedman, consumed by hatred for Germans, did not recoil from beating suspected Nazis during his interrogations of them. Friedman, *Sixty Years*, 127–39, 144. See also Nagorski, *The Nazi Hunters*, 27–30.

10 See Aleksiun, "The Central Jewish Historical Commission," 87; idem, "Organizing for Justice," 188–9.
11 Jockusch, "Justice at Nuremberg?," 118.
12 See Stauber, *Laying the Foundations*, 8–32.
13 Filip Friedman, *Zagłada Żydów lwowskich*, 4; quoted in Aleksiun, "The Central Jewish Historical Commission," 87n84.
14 See Grüss, *Rok pracy*, 21–2. The report did not include its author's name. But it bears a striking resemblance to the article "Zagłada Żydów polskich w latach 1939–1945" (Extermination of the Polish Jews in the Years 1939–1945), which appeared in the first volume of *Biuletyn Głównej Komisji Badania Zbrodni Niemieckich w Polsce* under Friedman's name. The author of the report and the article were, in light of their similarities, in all probability one and the same.
15 [Filip Friedman], "Deutsche Verbrechen gegen die jüdische Bevölkerung in Polen," ŻIH, CŻKH 303/XX/272, 4 (page 1 of document).
16 [Filip Friedman], "Die Motive des Verbrechens," ŻIH, CKŻP 303/XX/272, 119 (page 30 of document).
17 See IPN Nor/2, [Filip] Friedman, untitled document, 11 January 1946, 8–12 (1–5 of document); and IPN Nor/2, [Filip] Friedman, "Proponowane uzupełnienia," 11 January 1946, 12–13 (pages 6–7 of document). See also Aleksiun, "Organizing for Justice," 187. According to Natalia Aleksiun, "Friedman's efforts met with only partial success and he was disappointed with the nature of the indictment and the overall approach, which stressed Polish martyrdom." Aleksiun, "The Central Jewish Historical Commission," 86n81. We argued in chapter 2 that rather than emphasizing Polish martyrdom, the Polish indictment was relatively even-handed as far as Nazi crimes against ethnic Poles on the one hand and Polish Jews on the other were concerned. To be sure, disappointment in the Polish indictment on Friedman's part is entirely plausible, but what can be discerned with certainty in both his lists – one of corrections, the other of suggested additions – and his report is an impulse for exactitude and comprehensiveness in describing the Nazis' persecution and murder of Jews. Friedman himself was wont in 1945 to situate the fate of Jews in the broader context of suffering by Poles and other groups under Nazi rule. See Jockusch, *Collect and Record!*, 112. In any event, this universalizing trend was not evident in the Polish indictment. That said, without a doubt Friedman would have liked to see more of his arguments incorporated into the Polish delegation's case. As it turns out, he left Poland before the conclusion of the trial. As far as Polish Jews in general were concerned, Aleksiun notes that although the IMT's verdict "brought a partial sense

of moral satisfaction to both Jewish and non-Jewish victims of the war in Poland … both Polish and Jewish commentators complained that all those who had been indicted should have been found guilty and deserved death sentences." Aleksiun, "Organizing for Justice," 189.

18 Aleksiun, "The Central Jewish Historical Commission," 82–83; Jockusch, *Collect and Record!*, 112.

19 See Grüss, *Rok pracy*, 20–1; Kermish, "Dray yor tetikayt," 15; see also Aleksiun, "The Central Jewish Historical Commission," 83–4.

20 "Sprawozdanie z wyników dochodzenia w sprawie obozu unicestwienia w Treblince (obóz Nr. II), osiągniątych w okresie czasu od 24 września 1945 do 22 listopada 1945 r.," 22 November 1945, signed by Z. Łukaszkiewicz and J. Maciejewski, ŻIH 301/1095; available on microfilm at USHMM, RG–15.084M, 1095–1100, quotes on 3 and 4 (pages 1097 and 1098 of document). The chapter on Treblinka in the first issue of *Biuletyn Głównej Komisji Badania Zbrodni Niemieckich w Polsce*, published in 1946 by the GKBZN, an English translation of which was given by the Polish delegation to Allied prosecutors at Nuremberg, was an expanded version of the report, which Łukaszkiewicz reworked for publication. There were some differences between the report and the article. In the words of the article, "In the extermination camp at Treblinka mostly Jews, Polish citizens, were put to death," and the article estimated that the number of victims murdered at Treblinka was at least 731,600. But the language in the article obviously drew from that in the report, and the gist of the report was identical with that of the article. See [Łukaszkiewicz], "Obóz zagłady Treblinka," 133–44, quote on 142. In English: "The Treblinka Extermination Camp," 93–106. An undated report from the same visit to Treblinka was prepared for the CKŻP in Warsaw. Signed by Łukaszkiewicz, Maciejewski, Auerbach, Kermish, Rajzman, and another Treblinka survivor, it pointed out that the site had been disturbed by local inhabitants in search of valuables left behind by the victims. The report urged Jewish leaders to request that the government intervene because the digging was leading to the desecration of the victim's human remains and the destruction of criminal evidence. "Odpis sprawozdania Głównej Komisji dla Zbadania Zbrodni Hitlerowskiej w Polsce o Treblince," n.d., signed Łukaszkiewicz, Maciejewski, Kermisz, Auerbach, Mittelberg, and Rajzman, ŻIH, CKŻH 303/XX/209, 41.

21 Łukaszkiewicz, *Obóz straceń*, 18.

22 Ibid., 20.

23 Ibid., 26.

24 Ibid., 33.

25 Ibid., 40.

26 Ibid.

27 Auerbach, *Oyf di felder fun treblinke*, 9 (emphasis in original). An English translation of the book appears in an anthology: Auerbach, "In the Fields of Treblinka." The translation here is ours.

28 On Auerbach see Kassow, *Who Will Write Our History?* 198–208.

29 For an English translation of Krzepicki's testimony, see Krzepicki, "Eighteen Days in Treblinka."

30 Auerbach, *Oyf di felder fun treblinke*, 81 (emphasis in original). Treblinka I was a midsize labour camp within walking distance of the Treblinka death camp (occasionally referred to as Treblinka II), whose prisoners were mostly local ethnic Poles, but it also interned Jews.

31 Calculating from the number of transports and the number of deportees in each transport, Auerbach estimated that more than a million Jews were killed at Treblinka. She noted, moreover, that several thousand Roma and several hundred local Poles perished at Treblinka. She was critical of those who exaggerated the number of victims as a way of making the monstrous seem even more so. As she wrote, "Believe me that already one million people murdered over the course of one year in a tiny place is one million more than human brains can comprehend. And even half a million is also more than enough." Auerbach, *Oyf di felder fun treblinke*, 73.

32 Ibid., 106–7, 109.

33 Ibid., 106.

34 Łukaszkiewicz returned to Treblinka with a representative of the CŻKH and the Organization of Jewish Religious Communities, apparently in 1947, to continue his investigation of the camp's former grounds. They found scattered bones, hair, personal items, and household goods, the result of the local inhabitants' ongoing search for valuables left behind by the victims. Józef Kermisz, "W Treblince poraz drugi," n.d. [probably 1947], ŻIH, CŻKH 303/XX/280.

35 See the obituary by Krakowski, "Josef Kermisz," 161–3; see also Aleksiun, "The Central Jewish Historical Commission," 75–6n3.

36 For the questionnaire and Kermish's preface to it, see Kermish, "Stroops teshuves," 166–94. The preface and questionnaire and Stroop's supplemental comments can be found in Kermish, *Mered geto varshe*, 117–18 and 195–210; and in idem, *The Warsaw Ghetto Revolt*, li. The questionnaire and the supplement are in Wulf, *Das Dritte Reich*, 180–94.

37 Kermish, *Mered geto varshe*, 206; Wulf, *Das Dritte Reich*, 190.

38 Kermish included Stroop's view of Polish conduct during the uprising in *Bleter far geszichte*, which was published in Poland as Stalinism was

strengthening its grip on the country, but in a footnote he added a caveat that Stroop's comment was "an incorrect generalization." Kermish, "Stroops teshuves," 177n7. It's noteworthy that even after he had been out of Poland for a while and was safely ensconced in Israel, Kermish retained the same comment in a footnote in a Hebrew-language book that included a translation of the questionnaire. See Kermish, *Mered geto varshe*, 201n23.

39 Wulf, *Das Dritte Reich*, 204; see also Kermish, *Mered geto varshe*, 221.

40 Stroop was not the only German Nazi questioned in person by personnel of the Jewish Historical Institute. In July 1949, Szymon Datner conducted an interview with Waldermar Macholl in his prison cell in Białystok. As discussed above, Macholl was the chief of IV-A3 section (resistance) at the Białystok KdS. Datner's intention was to gather incriminating evidence about Erich Koch's war crimes. Between 1941 and 1945, Koch was chief of the civil administration in the Białystok District. He was also commissar of the Reichskommisariat Ukraine from 1941 to 1943. Datner used the interview with Macholl to establish Koch's authority and duties, his antisemitism and anti-Polish sentiments, and his role in anti-Jewish and anti-Polish initiatives. See the untitled report on the interview of Waldemar Macholl conducted on 27 July 1949, Szymon Datner, 31 October 1949, Spuścizna Bernarda Marka, ŻIH S/333/948. On Koch's trial, see chapter 6.

41 Philip Friedman, "Undzer historishe oyfgabe," *Dos naje lebn*, 10 April 1945, 6.

42 USHMM, trial of Amon Göth, reel 2, witness list, 17 August 1946, signed by presiding judge A[lfred] Eimer, 17 August 1946, vol. 46, 41–4.

43 Pemper, *The Road to Rescue*, 173.

44 Ibid., 41.

45 Ibid., 71.

46 Ibid., 166. In the 1993 film *Schindler's List*, which was adapted from Thomas Keneally's 1982 non-fiction novel *Schindler's Ark*, director Steven Spielberg created a composite character based on Pemper and Stern, naming him Mr Stern (portrayed by Ben Kingsley).

47 Ibid., 174.

48 USHMM, trial of Amon Göth, reel 2, trial transcript, 27 August 1946, vol. 47; also in *Proces ludobójcy*, 66–8, quote on 66. This published version of the transcript of Goth's trial is extensive but incomplete.

49 Pemper, *The Road to Rescue*, 97.

50 USHMM, trial of Amon Göth, reel 2, verdict, 5 September 1946, vol. 46, 209–10 (20–1 according to internal pagination of verdict); also in *Proces ludobójcy*, 485.

51 USHMM, trial of Amon Göth, reel 2, trial transcript, 28 August 1946, vol. 47; also in *Proces ludobójcy*, 85.

52 Pemper, *The Road to Rescue*, 180.

53 Ibid., 177–8. Pemper would later testify at the 1951 trial in Poland of Gerhard Maurer, who controlled the work assignments of the prisoners in all concentration camps in Germany and in German-occupied territories, including Płaszów. He also testified at Nazi trials held in Germany. See ibid., 91–3, 181, 183–4.

54 In addition, Marek Bitter, Salo Fiszgrund, and others testified in the name of the CKŻP in a few cases.

55 Jockusch, *Collect and Record!*, 209.

56 Ibid., 210. See also Polonsky, "Foreword," xiii–xxvii; Polonsky, "Artur Eisenbach," 423–6.

57 USHMM, trial of Rudolf Höss, reel 7, expert opinion (report), 25 March 1947, vol. 31, 1–66, here 2; for Blumental's testimony in court, see the trial transcript, 26 March 1947, reel 7, vol. 29, 119–81. An incomplete version of Blumental's report is reprinted in Pilichowski, ed., *Ekspertyzy i orzeczenia*, 8: 82–112.

58 USHMM, trial of Rudolf Höss, reel 7, expert opinion (report), 25 March 1947, vol. 31, 3.

59 Ibid., 4.

60 Ibid., 44.

61 Ibid., 46–50. Historian Franciszek Piper estimates that about 1 million of the 1.1 million Jews deported to Auschwitz were killed there. See Piper, "Estimating the Number of Deportees," 49–103; idem, "The Number of Victims," 61–76.

62 USHMM, trial of Rudolf Höss, expert opinion (report), 50.

63 Ibid., 52.

64 Ibid., 62.

65 Ibid., 64.

66 Ibid., 7.

67 Ibid., 33.

68 Ibid., 51–2.

69 USHMM, trial of Rudolf Höss, trial transcript, 26 March 1947, reel 7, vol. 29, 159. Franciszek Piper estimates that 70,000–75,000 Poles, out of around 140,000 Polish deportees, were killed at Auschwitz. Unlike the Jews who were killed at Auschwitz-Birkenau, the death camp, Polish victims were killed mainly at Auschwitz I and Monowitz. However, thousands of non-Jewish victims, including Poles, Soviet POWs, and Roma, perished at Birkenau as well. See Piper, "Estimating the Number of Deportees"; idem, "The Number of Victims." See also idem, "Auschwitz II-Birkenau Main Camp," 209.

70 See USHMM, trial of Auschwitz-Birkenau staff, RG-15.169M, reel 14, NTN 166, vol. 83, expert opinion of Nachman Blumental, 11 December 1947, 31–46. An incomplete version of Blumental's report is reprinted in Pilichowski, ed., *Ekspertyzy i orzeczenia*, 8: 113–20.

71 Lewiński, *Proces Hansa Biebowa*, 147. We are using the printed version of Eisenbach's testimony at Biebow's trial because, unlike the version of his testimony in the archival version of the trial transcript, it appears to be complete. In both the archival and printed versions of the proceedings in the Biebow trial, there is no record of Eisenbach's printed expert opinion; in both he is reading it into the court record.

72 Ibid., 158.

73 Ibid., 160–1.

74 Ibid., 161.

75 See ibid., 167.

76 Ibid., 170.

77 IPN, GK 317/874, trial of Jürgen Stroop and Franz Konrad, file 1, 20 July 1951, expert report (read into the court record) by Artur Eisenbach, dated 18 July 1951, 230 (page 32 of report).

78 Ibid., file 1, testimony of Artur Eisenbach, 20 July 1951, 192–4 (pages 85–9 of trial transcript). An incomplete version of Eisenbach's report is reprinted in Pilichowski, ed., *Ekspertyzy i orzeczenia*, 8: 231–54.

79 Minutes of meeting of CŻKH personnel, 17 March 1947, ŻIH, CŻKH 330/XX/14, 5.

80 See ibid., 2–3.

81 Ibid., 5.

82 Ibid., 2.

83 Minutes of meeting of CŻKH personnel, 21 March 1947, ŻIH, CŻKH 330/XX/14, 12 (page 1 of document).

84 Ibid., 13 (page 2 of document).

85 Ibid., 14 (page 3 of document).

86 Ibid., 17 (page 6 of document).

87 Ibid., 15 (page 4 of document).

88 Ibid., 16–17 (pages 6–7 of document).

89 Ibid., 18 (page 7 of document).

90 Ibid., 19 (page 6 of document).

91 Ibid., 18 (page 7 of document).

92 Ibid., 19 (page 8 of document).

93 Ibid., 20 (page 9 of document). For further discussion of the CŻKH's meetings on 17 March and 21 March 1947, see Jockusch, *Collect and Record!*, 113–16.

94 Minutes of meeting of CŻKH personnel, 17 March 1947, 2.
95 See Jockusch, *Collect and Record!*, 116; Stach, "'Praktische Geschichte," 250.
96 Stach, "Praktische Geschichte," 250.
97 See Jockusch, *Collect and Record!*, 110–12.
98 Ibid., 110.
99 Lewin, *A Cup of Tears*, 124.
100 Ibid., 235. See also his entry from 11 January 1943: "They began with us and finish with other peoples: Poles, Czechs, Serbs, and many others." Ibid., 239.
101 Friedman, "The Extermination," quote on 238. Contemporary Jewish commentators who did not come from Poland and who observed the unfolding of events there from a distance shared a similar view. In his epic 1942 study of Nazi rule, *Behemoth: The Structure and Practice of National Socialism*, which he wrote from exile in New York, Franz Neumann, a German Jewish lawyer and political scientist, discussed the structure of Nazi racial politics in occupied Poland: "The theory of German racial superiority and Jewish racial inferiority … establishes a hierarchy of races – giving no rights to the Jews, a few to the Poles, a few more to the Ukranians … and full rights to [ethnic] Germans … Next to these Germans are the Ukranians … and the White Russians … Next to them are the Poles and next to the Poles, at the bottom of the scale, are the Jews." Neumann, *Behemoth*, 126. Regarding Polish perceptions, historian Timothy Snyder writes that in 1943, as Operation Reinhard, the campaign to deport Jews to death camps in Poland, was drawing to a close, and as Generalplan Ost, the German campaign to deport 100,000 Poles from the Zamość region, many to Majdanek and Auschwitz, to make way for a racially German colony in the Lublin district of the General Government, was under way, "many Poles saw it [the deportation of Poles from Zamość] as the beginning of a Final Solution to the Polish problem. This was not quite correct, since Generalplan Ost envisioned the destruction of most but not all Poles; but it was a logical conclusion in the circumstances." Snyder, *Bloodlands*, 294.
102 Jockusch, "Justice at Nuremberg?," quote on 110 (emphasis in original).
103 See Jockusch, *Collect and Record!*, chs. 2 (France) and 5 (Austria); see also Stach, "'Praktische Gescichte,'" 251–9. On Wiesenthal in particular, see Segev, *Simon Wiesenthal*.

6 History and Politics in the Last Trials

1 Reitlinger, "Last of the War Criminals," 31.
2 Interview with the then director of IPN's archive, Dr Stanisław Biernacki, Warsaw, 21 July 1997.
3 Lediakh and Reshetnikov, "Kazhdyi natsistkii prestupnik," 25–7.
4 Douglas, "The Didactic Trial," 513–14.
5 IPN, GK 317/890, "Akta w sprawie Paula Ottona Geibla" (cited as trial of Paul Otto Geibel), the Prague court verdict, 2 May 1947, 73.
6 Borodziej, "Ściganie zbrodniarzy," 123n27.
7 Quoted in Płoski et al., *Okupacja i ruch oporu*, 1: 382–3.
8 Archiwum Akt Nowych (AAN), 230/14, "Zeznania i relacje zbrodniarzy hitlerowskich," 8–10; Blood, *Hitler's Bandit Hunters*, 214–15.
9 Orla-Bukowska, "New Threads," 178.
10 Ibid., 181.
11 Markiewicz, "Materielle Ausdrucksformen," 194–8.
12 Komorowski, "Polityka PRL," 195, 201.
13 *Życie Warszawy*, no. 124 (3296), 26 May 1954, 3; Komorowski, "Polityka PRL," 205. In January–May 1944 on the way to Rome, Allied forces, which included the Polish 2nd Corps, tried to break through the German defence line at Monte Cassino (80 miles southeast of Rome). The Polish 2nd Corps was a part of the Polish army that had been subordinated to the London government-in-exile; in a series of ferocious assaults on the Monte Cassino monastery, it suffered heavy casualties.
14 IPN, trial of Paul Otto Geibel, indictment, 28 December 1953, 6.
15 Ibid., 5–7.
16 Ibid., witness list, January 1954, 9–12; see also Geibel's testimony, 15, 16, 18, 21, 23, 25 October and 3 November 1948, in *Zbrodnie okupanta na ludności cywilnej*, 409-25.
17 It is unclear whether the trial was officially closed to the public or whether the empty courtroom resulted from the silence of the media. Interview with Dr Stanisław Biernacki, Warsaw, 21 July 1997.
18 IPN, trial of Paul Otto Geibel, trial transcript, 26 May 1954, 156–76.
19 Ibid., Geibel's letter to the Warsaw District Court, January 1954, 46, 24. See also Geibel's testimony, 15, 16, 18, 21, 23, 25 October and 3 November 1948, in *Zbrodnie okupanta na ludności cywilnej*, 416–18.
20 IPN, trial of Paul Otto Geibel, trial transcript, 26 May 1954, 165–6.
21 Ibid., trial transcript, 25 May 1954, 150–2; 26 May 1954, 156–7.
22 Barelkowski, "Vom 'Schlagetot' zum 'Kronzeugen,'" 160–1.

23 *Zbrodnie okupanta na ludności cywilnej*, 306.

24 IPN, 1100z/III, "Zbiór materiałów dotyczących zbrodni hitlerowskich w Polsce," 765; *Zburzenie Warszawy*, 33.

25 Interrogation of Heinz Reinefarth, 19 September 1946, in *Powstanie Warszawskie 1944*, 677, 679, 681, 685.

26 Marti, *Der Fall Reinefarth*, 58.

27 *Zburzenie Warszawy*, 33.

28 Bundesarchiv-Ludwigsburg (BAL), 211 AR 1507/61, "Ermittlungsverfahren gegen Ludwig Hahn," 3: 534; ibid., II211 AR 178/71, 1: 31–32; 2: 288; AAN, 230/14, "Zeznania i relacje zbrodniarzy hitlerowskich dotyczące Powstania Warszawskiego," 162.

29 Płoski et al., *Okupacja i ruch oporu*, 2: 538–9.

30 IPN, trial of Paul Otto Geibel, indictment, 28 December 1953, 7.

31 Interrogation of Reiner Stahel, 25 August 25 1945, in *Powstanie Warszawskie 1944*, 615.

32 Interrogation of Geibel, in *Zbrodnie okupanta na ludności cywilnej*, 419.

33 IPN, 1100z/II, "Zbiór materiałów dotyczących zbrodni hitlerowskich w Polsce," 448–9; *Zburzenie Warsawy*, 33; Marti, *Fall Reinefarth*, 309n294.

34 IPN, trial of Paul Otto Geibel, trial transcript, 26 May 1954, 156; IPN, 1100z/III, "Zbiór materiałów dotyczących zbrodni hitlerowskich w Polsce," 765; Geibel's statement, October 1954, in *Powstanie Warszawskie 1944*, 1025, 1027.

35 Sawicki, *Rozkaz*, 24–5.

36 BAL, II211 AR 178/71, "Ermittlungsverfahren gegen Ludwig Hahn," 2: 274–7; ibid., 211 AR (Z) 1/1966, "Pawiak Komplex und KdS Warschau," 3: 336–7.

37 IPN, 1100z/I, "Zbiór materiałów dotyczących zbrodni hitlerowskich w Polsce," 75; AAN, 230/14, "Zeznania i relacje zbrodniarzy hitlerowskich," 45; Leszczyński, *Heinz Reinefarth*, 19–23.

38 IPN, 1100z/I, "Zbiór materiałów dotyczących zbrodni hitlerowskich w Polsce," 189–91; "Relacja von dem Bacha," 308–9, 316; Michaelis, *Die SS-Sturmbrigade "Dirlewanger*," 11–12.

39 National Archives and Records Administration (NARA), situational reports of the Army Group "Center," T-501, roll 61, frame 000197; NARA, Berlin Documentation Center, A-3343, SSO-150A, file of Bronislav Kaminski, frames 752–755; "Dziennik Iwana Waszenko," 324–5, 327.

40 Vogel, "'Mann muss seine Augen,'" 237–8.

41 IPN, 1100z/III, "Zbiór materiałów dotyczących zbrodni hitlerowskich w Polsce," 611; AAN, 230/14, "Zeznania i relacje zbrodniarzy hitlerowskich," 79; ibid., 230/15, 1–4, 7–11.

42 Statement of Geibel, before October 1954, in *Powstanie Warszawskie 1944*, 1025, 1029. After the war, all key participants in the destruction of Warsaw defended themselves in a similar manner. For example, in his postwar testimonies, Bach-Zelewski blamed the RONA and Dirlewanger's unit for most of the atrocities. However, he conveniently forgot his report in the aftermath of the uprising, wherein he had stated that "in the first instance, our success depended on the personal service of SS-Oberführer Dirlewanger, who led his men by personal example." Barelkowski, "Vom 'Schlagetot' zum 'Kronzeugen,'" 154n99.

43 IPN, trial of Paul Otto Geibel, witness testimonies, 29 May 1954, 165–7; IPN, 1100z/II, "Zbiór materiałów dotyczących zbrodni hitlerowskich w Polsce," 401, 405, 406, 448, 496–8, 507; 1100z/III, 750, 756, 760; BAL, 211 AR (Z) 1/1966, "Pawiak Komplex und KdS Warschau," 3: 214–15, 218–21.

44 IPN, trial of Paul Otto Geibel, indictment, 28 December 1953, 6; trial transcript, 26 May 1954, 162.

45 Ibid., Geibel's letter to the Warsaw provincial court, January 1954, 41–4, 24; trial transcript, 25 May 1954, 141–9; GG ordinance of the chain of command of the SS and police forces, 8 July 1943, n.pag.

46 Ibid., trial transcript, 26 May 1954, 161.

47 IPN, 1100z/III, "Zbiór materiałów dotyczących zbrodni hitlerowskich w Polsce," 743–6; interrogation of Geibel, in *Zbrodnie okupanta na ludności cywilnej*, 415–16, 421, 425.

48 AAN, 230/14, "Zeznania i relacje zbrodniarzy hitlerowskich," 76–8.

49 Ibid., 79; AAN, 230/14, "Zeznanie i relacje zbrodniarzy hitlerowskich," 230/15, 1–4; IPN, 1100z/III, "Zbiór materiałów dotyczących zbrodni hitlerowskich w Polsce," 750, 756, 760; *Zburzenie Warszawy*, 29, 33.

50 IPN, 1100z/III, "Zbiór materiałów dotyczących zbrodni hitlerowskich w Polsce," 743–6; interrogation of Geibel, in *Zbrodnie okupanta na ludności cywilnej*, 415–16, 421, 425.

51 Vogel, "'Mann muss seine Augen,'" 238.

52 IPN, trial of Paul Otto Geibel, trial transcript, 26 May 1954, 160.

53 IPN, 1100z/II, "Zbiór materiałów dotyczących zbrodni hitlerowskich w Polsce," 289–91, 294; *Ludność cywilna w powstaniu warszawskim*, vol. 1, pt 1: 449–50; interrogation of Geibel, in *Zbrodnie okupanta na ludności cywilnej*, 420–1.

54 IPN, trial of Paul Otto Geibel, trial transcript, 26 May 1954, 158.

55 AAN, 230/15, "Zeznania i relacje zbrodniarzy hitlerowskich," 7–11.

56 Vogel, "'Mann muss seine Augen,'" 237–8.

57 IPN, 1100z/II, "Zbiór materiałów dotyczących zbrodni hitlerowskich w Polsce," 320–1, 333–4; BAL, II211 AR 178/71, "Ermittlungsverfahren gegen Ludwig Hahn," 3: 559.

58 NARA, RG-242, T-312, situational reports of the Army Group "Center," October 1944, roll 344, frames 7917750–7917763; IPN, 1100z/I, "Zbiór materiałów dotyczących zbrodni hitlerowskich w Polsce," 192; AAN, 230/14, "Zeznania i relacje zbrodniarzy hitlerowskich," 149–52.

59 Łuczak, *Polityka ludnościowa*, 632, 636.

60 *Dziennik Ludowy*, no. 32 (506), 2 February 1947, 3.

61 IPN, trial of Paul Otto Geibel, trial transcript, 25 May 1954, 141–2; AAN, 230/14, "Zeznania i relacje zbrodniarzy hitlerowskich," 103, 162–3; Płoski et al., *Okupacja i ruch oporu*, 2: 607–8.

62 IPN, 1100z/III, "Zbiór materiałów dotyczących zbrodni hitlerowskich w Polsce," 729, 765–6; Borodziej, "Ściganie zbrodniarzy," 125.

63 IPN, trial of Paul Otto Geibel, trial transcript, 29 May 1954, 166–7; IPN, 1100z/II, "Zbiór materiałów dotyczących zbrodni hitlerowskich w Polsce," 274; 1100z/III, 693, 714, 738–43; Łuczak, "'Aktion Warschau,'" 202–4, 206–7.

64 NARA, RG-242, T-312, roll 344, situational reports of the Army Group "Center," frame 7917902; AAN, 203/X-47, "Zbiór materiałów dotyczących zbrodni hitlerowskich w Polsce," 1; Franecki and Kisiel, "Raporty i meldunki," 78–9, 82–3, 88–90, 94–7; Klimaszewski, *Verbrennungskommando*, 29, 36, 52, 54–6, 82.

65 IPN, trial of Paul Otto Geibel, Geibel's letter to the Warsaw District Court, 24 January 1954, 38–42; trial transcript, 26 May 1954, 157; IPN, 1100z/II, "Zbiór materiałów dotyczących zbrodni hitlerowskich w Polsce," 289–91, 294, 296–7; Geibel's statement, in *Powstanie Warszawskie 1944*, 1031.

66 Statement of Geibel, n.d., in *Powstanie Warszawskie 1944*, 1053. The Corps of State Security was a small underground group that at times cooperated with the AK.

67 IPN, 1100z/III, "Zbiór materiałów dotyczących zbrodni hitlerowskich w Polsce," 768; AAN, 230/16, "Zeznania i relacje zbrodniarzy hitlerowskich," 5; NARA, Berlin Documentation Center, RG-242, A3343, SSO-053A, file of Ludwig Hahn, frame 144.

68 IPN, trial of Paul Otto Geibel, indictment, 28 December 1953, 6.

69 Interrogation of Geibel, in *Zbrodnie okupanta na ludności cywilnej*, 409–10.

70 In most cases, between 1945 and 1954 life sentences in Polish courts were the result of the commutation of the death penalty.

71 IPN, trial of Paul Otto Geibel, verdict, 31 May 1954, 172–6.

72 Ibid., decision of the Supreme Court in Warsaw, 22 September 1954, 184, 196–7; decision of the Supreme Court in Warsaw, 4 January 1958, 227.

73 "Ustawa z dnia 27 kwietnia 1956 r. o amnestii," *Dziennik Ustaw*, no. 11, 59–61; *Trybuna Ludu*, no. 117 (2630), 27 April 1956, 3; no. 119 (2632), 29

April 1956, 3. The last prisoners were released in the 1960s. For example, Karol Grams, who was serving a life term for being a wartime assistant to the executioner in Poznań, was released in January 1962. Kobierska-Motas, *Extradycja*, 2: 86.

74 Interview with Stanisław Biernacki, 21 July 1997. Article 1, pt 1, of the 29 May 1957 decree specified the conditions of the amnesty: "A person sentenced to imprisonment may be conditionally released if his or her lifestyle, character, personal circumstances, and behavior during imprisonment permit a presumption that, after release, he or she will comply with the principles of social coexistence and, in particular, will not commit a new offense." "Ustawa z dnia 29 maja 1957 r. o warunkowym zwolnieniu osób odbywających karę pozbawienia wolności," *Dziennik Ustaw RP*, no. 31, 395.

75 IPN, trial of Paul Otto Geibel, decision of the Supreme Court in Warsaw, 19 December 1959, 236–8.

76 Ibid., report of Geibel's suicide, 17 October 1966, 261.

77 During the Second Sino-Japanese War (1937–45), in December 1937 Japanese troops initiated a six-week massacre of Chinese civilians and POWs in Nanjing, then the capital of the Republic of China. About 200,000 Chinese were murdered and thousands of women were gang-raped. See Chang, *The Rape of Nanking*.

78 About 30 per cent of the city had been destroyed during the siege of 1939 and the liquidation of the Warsaw Ghetto in April–May 1943.

79 In 1951 a Soviet court sentenced Stahel to a long prison term for his participation in the war against the Soviet Union. His role in the suppression of the Warsaw Uprising was included in the indictment. Indictment against Stahel, 4 December 1951, in *Powstanie Warszawskie 1944*, 977–81.

80 In June–July 1934, the SS and the Gestapo carried out a purge against Hitler's potential opponents within the SA and the military. The purge consolidated Hitler's grip on power in Germany.

81 *Trybuna Ludu*, no. 360 (3577), 28 December 1958, 2. Bach-Zelewski's evasion of Polish justice rankled Poles, communists and non-communists alike, for many years. See Bartoszewski, *Prawda o von dem Bachu*. Bartoszewski, who was a steadfast opponent of the communist regime, supported a trial of Bach-Zelewski in Poland for atrocities perpetrated under his command during the Warsaw Uprising.

82 Marti, *Fall Reinefarth*, 81–2, 85–6.

83 Interrogation of Heinz Reinefarth, 19 September 1946, in *Powstanie Warszawskie 1944*, 677, 679, 681, 685; Marti, *Fall Reinefarth*, 57.

84 De-Nazification was an Allied program to rid German and Austrian society of any vestiges of the National Socialist regime and its ideology, including

the removal from politics and the civil service of Nazi Party members and individuals associated with Nazism. It was terminated in 1951.

85 In 1957 the East German DEFA film studio released a documentary that recounted the story of the "henchman of Warsaw" who successfully entered West German politics. Barelkowski and Klessmann, "Die Wahrnehmung des Warschauer Aufstands," 249–50.

86 *Trybuna Ludu*, no. 283 (3500), 10 October 1958, 2; no. 291 (3508), 18 October 1958, 2; no. 335 (3552), 1 December 1958, 2; no. 345 (3562), 11 December 1958, 2.

87 Leszczyński, *Heinz Reinefarth*, 102.

88 BAL, II211 AR 178/71, "Ermittlungsverfahren gegen Ludwig Hahn," 3: 477.

89 *Trybuna Ludu*, no. 285 (3502), 12 October 1958, 5.

90 IPN, "Akta w sprawie Ericha Kocha" (cited as trial of Erich Koch), GK 318/753, justification of verdict, 9 March 1959, 31–2. In 1934 Strasser was murdered during the "Night of the Long Knives."

91 IPN, trial of Erich Koch, GK 318/753, verdict, 9 March 1959, 31–7.

92 Ibid., 38, 48–9; Gnatowski, "Nationalsozialistische Okkupationspolitik," 161–2.

93 Parrish, *The Lesser Terror*, 127. In 1955, after the establishment of diplomatic relations with West Germany, Khrushchev ordered the release of remaining German prisoners.

94 IPN, trial of Erich Koch, GK 318/755, exchanges between Allied officials and the Polish Military Mission in Berlin, 2 July 1949, 70, 77; Fuhrer and Schön, *Erich Koch*, 197–8. In order to exercise tighter control of the Polish communist regime, in October 1949 Stalin dispatched several thousand Soviet officers to Poland, where they headed or supervised Polish military units. Of Polish stock, Rokossovski was one of the most distinguished Soviet wartime commanders and in Stalin's vision, most fitted to be appointed Polish Minister of National Defence, with the appropriate title of Marshal of Poland. In 1952 Rokossovski was elevated to Deputy Chairman of the Council of Ministers of the People's Republic of Poland.

95 IPN, trial of Erich Koch, GK 318/756, affidavits of eyewitnesses, 98–111; 318/742, lists of witnesses and documentary materials, 65–75.

96 Ibid., GK 318/743, bulletin about Dallin's book, 384–89; 318/759, protocol of Soviet evidence, 81–91; 318/760, testimonies of Elize Schütz and Paul Gier, 99–106.

97 IPN, trial of Erich Koch, GK 318/742, indictment against Koch, 5 February 1955, 14–15; Fuhrer and Schön, *Erich Koch*, 114.

98 IPN, trial of Erich Koch, GK 318/742, note of the Attorney General Office to the Warsaw District Court, 5 February 1955, 12; GK 318/742, doctors'

opinion of Koch's health, 12 August 1955, 128–9; IPN, Biuro Udostępniania i Archiwizacji Dokumentów (notes to Koch's trial, cited as BU), 01917/22, decision of the Warsaw District Court, 8 September 1958, 556.

99 Orlovskii and Ostrovich, *Erich Koch*, 80.

100 *Folks-shtime*, no. 166 (1856), 23 October 1948, 3.

101 *Trybuna Ludu*, no. 293 (3510), 20 October 1958, 1; Fuhrer and Schön, *Erich Koch*, 201.

102 IPN, trial of Erich Koch, GK 318/742, indictment, 5 February 1955, 14–15; *Trybuna Ludu*, no. 293 (3510), 20 October 1958, 1.

103 *Trybuna Ludu*, no. 294 (3511), 21 October 1958, 1–2.

104 IPN, trial of Erich Koch, GK 318/742, indictment, 5 February 1955, 29; GK 318/762, excerpts from Koch's speeches and announcements, n.pag.

105 Ibid., GK 318/760, interrogation of Friedel, 28 April 1952, 53–8.

106 *Trybuna Ludu*, no. 324 (3541), 20 November 1958, 1; no. 8 (3588), 8 January 1959, 1.

107 IPN, trial of Erich Koch, GK 318/760, testimony of Albert Forster, 25 April 1952, 27–31.

108 Browning, *The Origins*, 34, 189.

109 IPN, trial of Erich Koch, GK 318/742, indictment, 5 February 1955, 33–5; Gnatowski, Monkiewicz, and Kowalczyk, *Wieś białostocka oskarżą*, 21.

110 IPN, trial of Erich Koch, GK 318/760, testimony of Jakob Sporrenberg, 26 April 1952, 35–7.

111 Ibid., GK 318/747, interrogation of Macholl, 27 July 27 1949, 218; GK 318/753, verdict, 9 March 1959, 77; Omiljanowicz, *Przed wyrokiem*, 33.

112 IPN, trial of Erich Koch, GK 318/756, affidavits of eyewitnesses, 98–111; GK 318/742, lists of witnesses and documentary materials, 65–75.

113 IPN, trial of Erich Koch, GK 318/753, verdict, 9 March 1959, 76.

114 *Trybuna Ludu*, no. 325 (3542), 21 November 1958, 3.

115 Ibid., no. 338 (3555), 4 December 1958, 1; no. 340 (3557), 6 December 1958, 2.

116 Orlovskii and Ostrovich, *Erich Koch*, 170–1; *Trybuna Ludu*, no. 20 (3600), 20 January 1959, 3.

117 *Życie Warszawy*, no. 4 (4378), 5 January 1959, 2; *Trybuna Ludu*, no. 22 (3602), 22 January 1959, 3.

118 IPN, trial of Erich Koch, BU, 1917/22, testimony of Marian Pospieszalski, 8 February 1959, 502–4.

119 *Trybuna Ludu*, no. 322 (3539), 18 November 1958, 3.

120 IPN, trial of Erich Koch, GK 318/759, Koch's testimony, 9–11 November 1949, 97–113; Meindl, *Ostpreussens Gauleiter*, 481.

121 IPN, trial of Erich Koch, GK 318/759, interrogation of Koch, 24–7 April 1949, 145–72; GK 318/760, interrogation of Koch, 16 April 1952, 15–20; Orlovskii and Ostrovich, *Erich Koch*, 74–6.

122 *Trybuna Ludu*, no. 302 (3519), 29 October 1958, 2; no. 303 (3520), 30 October 1958, 1.

123 IPN, trial of Erich Koch, GK 318/760, interrogation of Koch, 16 April 1952, 18–20; *Trybuna Ludu*, no. 301 (3518), 28 October 1958, 6; *Życie Warszawy*, no. 264 (4685), 3 November 1958, 4.

124 IPN, trial of Erich Koch, GK 318/759, interrogation of Koch, 9–11 November 1949, 97–113; Meindl, *Ostpreussens Gauleiter*, 481; *Życie Warszawy*, no. 254 (4675), 23 October 1958, 4; Orlovskii and Ostrovich, *Erich Koch*, 90.

125 Black, *Ernst Kaltenbrunner*, 265.

126 *Trybuna Ludu*, no. 296 (3513), 23 October 1958, 1–2.

127 Ibid., no. 302 (3519), 29 October 1958, 2; no. 303 (3520), 30 October 1958, 1; *Życie Warszawy*, no. 259 (4680), 29 October 1958, 4.

128 *Trybuna Ludu*, no. 329 (3546), 25 November 1958, 1; no. 3 (3584), 3 January 1959, 3; *Życie Warszawy*, no. 4 (4738), 5 January 1959, 7; no. 35 (4769), 10 February 1959, 4.

129 *Trybuna Ludu*, no. 58 (3638), 27 February 1959, 2; no. 59 (3639), 28 February 1959, 3; *Życie Warszawy*, no. 51 (4785), 28 February 1959, 4.

130 IPN, trial of Erich Koch, GK 318/746, defence summation, 28 February 1959, n.pag.; Orlovskii and Ostrovich, *Erich Koch*, 81–3.

131 *Folks-shtime*, no. 38 (1932), 12 March 1959, 2.

132 *Trybuna Ludu*, no. 69 (3649), 10 March 1959, 1, 3; *Życie Warszawy*, no. 59 (4793), 10 March 1959, 1, 5.

133 IPN, trial of Erich Koch, GK 318/753, verdict, 9 March 1959, 56–61, 64.

134 Ibid., BU 1917/22, verdict, 9 March 1959, 591–6.

135 *Folks-shtime*, no. 38 (1932), 12 March 1959, 2.

136 IPN, trial of Erich Koch, GK 318/753, verdict, 9 March 1959, 102; Broszat, *Nationalsozialistische Polenpolitik*, 27–8.

137 Jędrzejewski, *Hitlerowska koncepcja*, 146–7.

138 IPN, trial of Erich Koch, GK 318/753, verdict, 9 March 1959, 95–6.

139 *Trybuna Ludu*, no. 345 (3562), 11 December 1958, 6; *Życie Warszawy*, no. 296 (4717), 11 December 1958, 5.

140 IPN, trial of Erich Koch, GK 318/760, testimony of Jakob Sporrenberg, 26 April 1952, 35–7.

141 Ibid., GK 318/742, indictment, 5 February 1955, 25; Broszat, *Nationalsozialistische Polenpolitik*, 64.

142 IPN, trial of Erich Koch, GK 318/742, indictment, 5 February 1955, 38.

143 Ibid., GK 318/758, protocol of evidence, 14 August 1950, 239–43.

144 Ibid., GK 318/753, verdict, 9 March 1959, 23; BU 1917/22, verdict, 9 March 1959, 549–51; Browning, *The Origins*, 107.

145 The Bialystok Ghetto was liquidated in August 1943.

146 IPN, trial of Erich Koch, GK 318/758, copy of the protocol from a conference in Berlin, 21 January 1943, 258–9; Gnatowski, "Nationalsozialistische Okkupationspolitik," 176.

147 IPN, trial of Erich Koch, GK318/753, verdict, 9 March 1959, pp. 111–12.

148 Gnatowski, "Nationalsozialistische Okkupationspolitik," 170.

149 IPN, trial of Erich Koch, GK318/742, indictment, 5 February 1955, 35–7; Meindl, *Ostpreussens Gauleiter*, 318–19; Gnatowski, Monkiewicz, and Kowalczyk, *Wieś białostocka*, 47.

150 IPN, trial of Erich Koch, GK 318/756, letter of a representative of the GKBZH, 24 July 1950, n.pag.; Meindl, *Ostpreussens Gauleiter*, 293.

151 *Trybuna Ludu*, no. 303 (3520), 30 October 1958, 3; no. 307 (3524), 3 November 1958, 4.

152 IPN, trial of Erich Koch, GK 318/742, indictment, 5 February 1955, 18.

153 Ibid., 16.

154 *Trybuna Ludu*, no. 295 (3512), 22 October 1958, 2; no. 16 (3596), 16 January 1959, 2; no. 17 (3597), 17 January 1959, 2; no. 49 (3629), 18 February 1959, 1.

155 Fuhrer and Schön, *Erich Koch*, 202.

156 *Trybuna Ludu*, no. 286 (3503), 13 October 1958, 2; no. 6 (3586), 6 January 1959, 8.

157 Orlovskii and Ostrovich, *Erich Koch*, 15–16.

158 IPN, trial of Erich Koch, BU 0678/274, "Notatka w sprawie Ericha Kocha," 2.

159 Ibid., 6.

160 Ibid., 4–6.

161 Ibid., 1, 4; Fuhrer and Schön, *Erich Koch*, 200.

162 IPN, trial of Erich Koch, BU 0 1917/22, note of the prison warden, 19[?] September 1968, 853–6.

163 Ibid., BU 0678/274, verbatim report of the meeting, 23 March 1973, 2–4.

164 See Scott-Clark and Levy, *The Amber Room*.

165 IPN, trial of Erich Koch, BU 0678/274, "Notatka w sprawie Ericha Kocha," 7–9.

166 "Dlaczego niemiecki zbrodniarz Erich Koch nie zginął? Plotka o Bursztynowej Komnacie była przykrywką dla akcji wywiadu," http://natemat.pl/94871 (accessed 29 May 2014).

167 IPN, trial of Erich Koch, BU 1917/22, conversation of three Polish intvestigators with Koch, 1 April 1976, 1007–9. Theodor Oberländer was Adenauer's minister for refugee affairs. During the war, he was a political

adviser to collaborationist formations in the Soviet Union. Reinhard Gehlen was an *Abwehr* officer and the chief of the West German intelligence service after the war.

168 Omiljanowicz, *Przed wyrokiem*, 74–8. Macholl had also previously confirmed this meeting. Aleksander Omiljanowicz (1923–2006) was a prisoner in German concentration camps. After the war, as a security service (UB) officer, he took part in combating anti-communist partisans. In the 1960s he turned to literary activities. In 2005 a Polish court sentenced Omiljanowicz to a prison term for crimes committed as an UB officer. Ironically, he served his term in the same prison in Barczewo (the Olsztyn District) as had Koch.

169 IPN, trial of Erich Koch, BU 0678/274, note regarding Koch's memoirs, 18 April 1973, 2–3.

170 Ibid., BU 1917/22, Koch's letter to the prison warden, 22 October 1964, 105; Fuhrer and Schön, *Erich Koch*, 217.

171 Fuhrer and Schön, *Erich Koch*, 217.

172 Meindl, *Ostpreussens Gauleiter*, 491.

173 Jacobs, "A Narrative of Justice," 135.

174 Markiewicz, "Materielle Ausdrucksformen," 201.

175 Fuhrer and Schön, *Erich Koch*, 108–9.

176 IPN, trial of Erich Koch, GK 318/753, verdict, 9 March 1959, 1698, 1764–7.

Epilogue

1 Dirks, *Die Verbrechen*, 330.

2 Ibid., 332.

3 On Nazi trials in East Germany, see, in addition to Dirks's book, Weinke, *Die Verfolgung*; idem, "'Allierter Angriff'," 37–93.

4 See Łuczak, "Szanse i trudności," 9–14.

5 Hirschfeld, *Nazi Rule*, 54. On the German occupation of the Netherlands, see also Warmbrunn, *The Dutch*; and the monumental study by de Jong, *Het Koninkrijk*.

6 Croes, "The Holocaust," 474–99. For general studies of the Holocaust in the Netherlands, see e.g. Presser, *Ashes*; Moore, *Victims*; Romijn, "The War," 296–335.

7 On the Dutch trials, see Belinfante, *In Plaats van Bijltjesdag*, esp. ch. 14; Fühner, *Nachspiel*, esp. 176–308; de Mildt and Meihuizen, "'Unser Land,'" 283–325. On the German perpetrators, see Presser, *Ashes*, esp. 336–48.

8 The discussion in this paragraph is inspired by Goldstein, "Framing Discipline," 364–81.

9 On the potential of testimony to help witnesses work through trauma, see Feldman, *The Juridical Unconscious*.

10 See Koźmińska-Frejlak and Finder, "Apart."

11 See Finder, "Introduction."

12 See Douglas, *The Memory*, ch. 6.

13 Ibid., 6 (emphasis in original).

14 Ibid.

Bibliography

Archival Collections

Archiwum Akt Nowych (AAN), Warsaw, Poland
  "Zeznania i relacje zbrodniarzy hitlerowskich dotyczące Powstania
  Warszawskiego," 1947, 203/X-47, 230/14, 230/15; 230/16.

Bundersarchiv-Ludwigsburg (BAL), Ludwigsburg, Germany
  II211 AR 178/71, "Ermittlungsverfahren gegen Ludwig Hahn."
  211 AR (Z) 1/1966, "Pawiak Komplex und KdS Warschau."

Goldstein-Goren Diaspora Research Center, Tel Aviv University, Tel Aviv, Israel
  Yosef Kermish, "Dray yor tetikayt fun Ts. Y. H. K. [Tsentrale Yidishe
  Historishe Komisye] un Yid[ishn] Hist[orishn] Institut in Polyn,"
  P 66/1217, n.d. [1947], 1–20.

*Instytut Pamięci Narodowej – Komisja Ścigania Zbrodni przeciwko Narodowi
Polskiemu (IPN), Warsaw, Poland*
  "Akta w sprawie Jürgena Stroopa, Franza Konrada i Hermana Höfla,"
  GK 317/874.
  "Akta w sprawie Paula Ottona Geibla," GK 317/890.
  "Akta w sprawie Ericha Kocha," GK 318/742, GK 318/753, GK 318/755,
  GK 318/756, GK 318/758, GK 318/759, GK 318/760, GK 318/762.
  "Biuro Udostępniania i Archiwizacji Dokumentów," 0678/274, 1917/22.
  [Filip] Friedman, 11 January 1946, "Międzynarodowy Tribunał Wojskowy w
  Norymberdze," Nor/2.
  "The Republic of Poland against the German War Criminals and Those
  Bodies and Organizations Indicted under Charge No. 1 before the

International Military Tribunal," 8 December 1945, KRN (Krajowa Rada
Narodowa) – National Council, Nor/1.

"Sprawozdanie delegacji Ministerstwa Sprawiedliwości z pobytu w Londynie
w sprawie przestępstw wojennych i procesu w Norymberdze," 30 October
1945, Główna Komisja Badania Zbrodni Hitlerowskich w Polsce
(GKBZHwP), 1048.

"Zbiór materiałów dotyczących zbrodni hitlerowskich w Polsce," 1100z/I,
1100z/II, 1100z/III.

National Archives and Records Administration (NARA), Washington, DC
Record Group-242, Series T-312, "Records of German Field Commands:
Armies."
Record Group-242, Series T-501, "Records of German Field Commands: Rear
Areas, Occupied Territories, and Others."

National Archives and Records Administration I, Berlin Documentation Center (BDC)
A-3343, SSO-053A, file of Ludwig Hahn.
A-3343, SSO-150A, file of Bronislav Kaminski.
A-3343, SSO-167B, file of Jürgen Stroop.

Simon Wiesenthal Archive (Vienna, Austria)
"Lemberg-Prozess," 20 December 1966, RG Lemberg 08, 2319–20.

United States Holocaust Memorial Museum (USHMM), Washington, DC
RG-15.084M, "Relacje ocalałych z Holocaustu = Holocaust Survivor
Testimonies."
RG-15.156M, "Sąd Okręgowy w Warszawie = District Court in Warsaw,
1945–1960."
RG-15.164M, "Sąd Okręgowy w Białymstoku = District Court in Białystok,
1945–69."
RG-15.165M, "Proces Ludwika Fischera et al. = Trial of Ludwig Fischer
et al."
RG-15.166M, "Proces Artura Greisera = Trial of Arthur Greiser."
RG-15.167M, "Proces Rudofa Hoessa = Trial of Rudolf Höss."
RG-15.169M, "Proces członków załogi Oświęcimia = Trial of the Staff of KL
Auschwitz-Birkenau."
RG-15.170M, "Proces Amona Goetha = Trial of Amon Göth."
RG-15.171M, "Proces Hansa Biebowa = Trial of Hans Biebow."
RG-15.174M, "Proces Józefa Bühlera = Trial of Josef Bühler."

Żydowski Instytut Historyczny (Jewish Historical Institute; ŻIH), Warsaw, Poland

[Filip Friedman], "Deutsche Verbrechen gegen die jüdische Bevölkerung in Polen," CŻKH 303/XX/272.

[Filip Friedman], "Die Motive des Verbrechens," CKŻP 303/XX/272.

"Odpis sprawozdania Głównej Komisji dla Zbadania Zbrodni Hitlerowskiej w Polsce o Treblince," CŻKH 303/XX/209.

Józef Kermisz, "W Treblince poraz drugi," CŻKH 303/XX/280.

"Protokoły posiedzeń pracowników CŻKH," CŻKH 330/XX/14.

Szymon Datner, memorandum, "Spuścizna Bernarda Marka," S/333/948.

Newspapers

Chłopski Sztandar (Warsaw)
Dos naje lebn **(Łódź and Warsaw)**
Dziennik Łódzki (Łódź)
Dziennik Ludowy (Warsaw)
Dziennik Zachodni (Katowice)
Folks-shtime **(Łódź and Warsaw)**
Gazeta Morska (Gdańsk)
Głos Ludu: Pismo Polskiej Partii Robotniczej (Warsaw)
Głos Wielkopolski (Poznań)
Nasze Słowo (Łódź and Warsaw)
Przekrój (Kraków)
Słowo Polskie: Bezpartyjny Dziennik Ziem Zachodnich (Wrocław)
Trybuna Ludu (Warsaw)
Tygodnik Powszechny (Kraków)
Życie Warszawy (Warsaw)

Document Collections

Cyprian, Tadeusz, Jerzy Sawicki, and Mieczysław Siewierski. *Głos ma procurator*. Warsaw: Iskry, 1962.

Dziennik Ustaw Rzeczypospolitej Polskiej no. 3, 31 March, 1943; no. 4, 31 August 1944; no. 4, 12 September 1944; no. 7, 16 February 1945; no. 69, 10 December 1946.

Kodeks karny. Prawo o wykroczeniach przepisy wprowadzające, związkowe i podatkowe. Edited by Lucjan Bekerman, Artur Miller, and Jan Gumiński. Warsaw: Nakładem Księgarni F. Hoesicka, 1932.

Konstytucja i podstawowe akty ustawodawcze Polskiej Rzeczypospolitej Ludowej.
Edited by Anna Grzybowska. Warsaw: Wydawnictwo Prawnicze, 1968.
Majdanek. Rozprawa sądowa przed Specjalnym Sądem Karnym w Lublinie. Krakow:
Spółdzielnia Wydawnicza "Czytelnik," 1945.
Mered geto varshah be'einei ha'oyev. Haduhot shel hageneral jirgn strop. 2nd ed.
Edited by Joseph Kermish. Jerusalem: Yad Vashem, 1966.
Metodologishe onvayzungen tsum oysforshn dem khurbn fun poylishn yidntum.
Edited by Tsentrale Yidishe Historishe Komisye baym tsentral-komitet fun
poylishe yidn. Łódź: 1945.
Powstanie Warszawskie 1944 w dokumentach z archiwów służb specjalnych. Edited
by Piotr Mierecki and Wasilij Christoforow. Warsaw: Instytut Pamięci
Narodowej-Komisja Ścigania Zbrodni przeciwko Narodowi Polskiemu, 2007.
Proces Hansa Biebowa. Zagłada getta łódzkiego. Akta i stenogramy sądowe.
Edited by Jerzy Lewiński. Warsaw: Glowna Komisja Badania Zbrodni
Hitlerowskich w Polsce; Instytut Pamięci Narodowi, 1987.
Proces ludobójcy Amona Leopolda Goetha przed Najwyższym Trybunałem Narodowym.
Warsaw and Kraków: Wydawnictwo Centralnej Żydowskiej Komisji
Historycznej w Polsce, 1947.
Raporty Ludwiga Fischera gubernatora dystryktu warszawskiego, 1939–1944. Warsaw:
Książka i Wiedza, 1987.
Sawicki, Jerzy. *Przed polskim prokuratorem. Dokumenty i komentarze.* Warsaw:
Iskry, 1958.
The Stroop Report: The Jewish Quarter of Warsaw Is No More! Translated by Sybil
Milton. New York: Pantheon Books, 1979.
*Trial of the Major War Criminals before the International Military Tribunal,
Nuremberg, 14 November 1945–1 October 1946.* 42 vols. Nuremberg:
International Military Tribunal, 1947.
United Nations War Crimes Commission. "Trial of Ulrich Greifelt and Others,
United States Military Tribunal, Nuremberg, 10th October, 1947–10th
March, 1948." In *Law Reports of Trials of War Criminals*, vol. 13, 1–69. London:
HMSO, 1949. 15 vols.
– "Trial of Wilhelm List and Others: United States Military Tribunal,
Nuremberg, 8th July 1947, to 19th February 1948 (The Hostages Trial)."
Law Reports of Trials of War Criminals, vol. 8, 34–92. London: HMSO, 1949.
15 vols.
The Warsaw Ghetto Revolt as Seen by the Enemy: General Jürgen Stroop's Reports,
2nd ed. Edited by Joseph Kermish. Jerusalem: Yad Vashem, 1966.
"Załącznik do protokołu z 4 posiedzenia Prezydium KRN w dniu 22 stycznia
1946 r." In *Protokoły posiedzeń Prezydium Krajowej Rady Narodowej 1944–1947*.

Edited by Jerzy Kochanowski. 280–96. Warsaw: Wydawnictwo Sejmowe, 1995.

"Załącznik do protokołu z 47 posiedzenia Prezydium KRN w dniu 26 sierpnia 1946 r." In *Protokoły posiedzeń Prezydium Krajowej Rady Narodowej 1944–1947*. Edited by Jerzy Kochanowski. 297–304. Warsaw: Wydawnictwo Sejmowe, 1995.

Zbior przepisow specjalnych przeciwko zbrodniarzom hitlerowskim i zdrajcom narodu, z komentarzem. Krakow: Czytelnik, 1945.

Zbrodnie okupanta na ludności cywilnej w czasie powstania warszawskiego w 1944 roku (w dokumentach). Edited by Szymon Datner and Kazimierz Leszczyński. Warsaw: Wydawnictwo Ministerstwa Obrony Narodowej, 1962.

Zburzenie Warszawy: zeznania generałów niemieckich przed polskim prokuratorem członkiem polskiej delegacji przy międzynarodowym trybunale wojennym w Norymberdze. Edited by Jerzy Sawicki. Katowice: Wydawnictwo AWIR, 1946.

Żydowska dzielnica mieszkaniowa w Warszawie już nie istnieje! Edited by Andrzej Żbikowski. Warsaw: Instytut Pamięci Narodowej i Żydowski Instytut Historyczny, 2009.

Monographs, Edited Collections, and Articles in Print

Abtahi, Hirad, and Philippa Webb, eds. *The Genocide Convention: The Travaux Préparatoires*. 2 vols. Leiden and Boston: Martinus Nijhoff, 2008.

Aleksiun, Natalia. "Organizing for Justice: Jewish Leadership in Poland and the Trial of the Nazi War Criminals at Nuremberg." In *Beyond Camps and Forced Labour: Current International Research on Survivors of Nazi Persecution: Proceedings of the International Conference, London, 11–13 January 2006*. Edited by Johannes-Dieter Steinert and Inge Weber-Newth. 184–94. Osnabrück: Secolo Verlag, 2007. CD-ROM.

– "The Central Jewish Historical Commission in Poland, 1944–1947." In *Making Holocaust Memory*. Edited by Gabriel N. Finder, Natalia Aleksiun, Antony Polonsky, and Jan Schwarz. 74–97. *Polin: Studies in Polish Jewry*, vol. 20. Oxford and Portland: Littman Library of Jewish Civilization, 2008.

Alexander, Leo. "War Crimes and Their Motivation: The Socio-Psychological Structure of the SS and the Criminalization of a Society." *Journal of Criminal Law and Criminology* 39, no. 3 (1948): 298–326.

Anders, Freia, Hauke-Hendrik Kutscher, and Katrin Stoll, eds. *Bialystok in Bielefeld. Nationalsozialistische Verbrechen vor dem Landgericht Bielefeld 1958 bis 1967*. Bielefeld: Verlag für Regionalgeschichte, 2003.

Arad, Yitzhak. *Belzec, Sobibor, Treblinka: The Operation Reinhard Death Camps.* Bloomington: Indiana University Press, 1999.

Arendt, Hannah. *Eichmann in Jerusalem: A Report on the Banality of Evil.* Introduction by Amos Elon. New York: Penguin Books, 2006.

Auerbach, Rachel. "In the Fields of Treblinka." In *The Death Camp Treblinka.* Edited by Alexander Donat. 17–74. New York: Holocaust Library, 1979.

– *Oyf di felder fun treblinke.* Warsaw, Łódź, and Kraków: Tsentrale yidishe historishe komisye baym ts. k. fun poylishe yidn, 1947.

Baird, Jay W., ed. *From Nuremberg to My Lai.* Lexington: D.C. Heath, 1972.

Banach, Jens. *Heydrichs Elite. Das Führerkorps der Sicherheitspolizei und des SD, 1936–1945.* Paderborn: Schöningh, 1998.

Bankier, David, and Dan Michman, eds. *Holocaust and Justice: Representation and Historiography of the Holocaust in Post-War Trials.* Jerusalem: Yad Vashem, 2010.

Barelkowski, Matthias. "Vom 'Schlagetot' zum 'Kronzeugen' nationalsozialistischer Verbrechen. Die Karriere des Erich von dem Bach-Zelewski." In *Der Warschauer Aufstand 1944. Ereignis und Wahrnehmung in Polen und Deutschland.* Edited by Hans-Jürgen Bömelburg, Eugeniusz Cezary Król, und Michael Thomae. 129–70. Im Auftrag des Militärgeschichtlichen Forschungsamtes, Potsdam, und des Zentrums für Historische Forschung der Polnischen Akademie der Wissenschaften, Berlin. Paderborn: Ferdinand Schöningh, 2011.

Barelkowski, Matthias, and Christoph Klessmann. "Die Wahrnehmung des Warschauer Aufstands in den deutschen Öffentlichkeiten." In *Der Warschauer Aufstand 1944. Ereignis und Wahrnehmung in Polen und Deutschland.* Edited by Hans-Jürgen Bömelburg, Eugeniusz Cezary Król, und Michael Thomae, 243–67. Im Auftrag des Militärgeschichtlichen Forschungsamtes, Potsdam, und des Zentrums für Historische Forschung der Polnischen Akademie der Wissenschaften, Berlin. Paderborn: Ferdinand Schöningh, 2011.

Bartoszewski, Władysław. *Prawda o von dem Bachu.* Warsaw: Wydawnictwo Zachodnie, 1961.

Basak, Adam. *Historia pewnej mistyfikacji. Zbrodnia katyńska przed Trybunałem Norymberskim.* Wrocław: Wydawnictwo Uniwersytetu Wrocławskiego, 1993.

– "Motywacje moralne w wyrokach na zbrodniarzy hitlerowskich." *Studia nad Faszyzmem i Zbrodniami Hitlerowskimi* 6 (1980): 247–75.

– "Zagadnienie ludobóstwa 'kulturalnego' w świetle wyroku Najwyższego Trybunału Narodowego na Artura Greisera." *Studia nad Faszyzmem i Zbrodniami Hitlerowskimi* 16, no. 1283 (1993): 277–319.

Bazyler, Michael J., and Frank M. Tuerkheimer. *Forgotten Trials of the Holocaust.* New York and London: NYU Press, 2014.

Belinfante, A.D. *In Plaats van Bijltjesdag. De Geschiedenis van de Bijzondere Rechtspleging na de Tweede Wereldoorlog*. Assen: Van Gorcum, 1978.

Belyaev, Vladimir. *Razoblachenie. Dokumental'nye ocherki i povesti*. L'viv: Knizhno-zhurnal'noe izdatel'stvo, 1960.

Berendt, Grzegorz. "Straty osobowe polskich Żydów w okresie II wojny światowej." In *Polska 1939–1945. Straty osobowe i ofiary represji pod dwiema okupacjami*. Edited by Wojciech Materski and Tomasz Szarota. 62–75. Warsaw: Instytut Pamięci Narodowej-Komisja Ścigania Zbrodni przeciwko Narodowi Polskiemu, 2009.

Biegański, Zdzisław. "Kara śmierci w orzecznictwie Specjalnych Sądów Karnych w Polsce (1944–1946)." *Echa Przeszłości* 5 (2004): 175–200.

Bieńczyk-Missala, Agnieszka, and Sławomir Dębski, eds. *Rafał Lemkin: A Hero of Humankind*. Warsaw: Polish Institute of International Affairs, 2010.

Birn, Ruth Bettina. "Heinrich Bergmann – eine deutsche Kriminalistenkarriere." In *Karrieren der Gewalt. Nationalsozialistische Täterbiographien*. Edited by Klaus-Michael Mallmann and Gerhard Paul. 47–55. Darmstadt: Wissenschaftliche Buchgesellschaft, 2004.

Black, Peter R. *Ernst Kaltenbrunner: Ideological Soldier of the Third Reich*. Princeton: Princeton University Press, 1984.

Bloxham, Donald. *Genocide on Trial: War Crimes Trials and the Formation of Holocaust History and Memory*. Oxford: Oxford University Press, 2001.

– "Jewish Witnesses in War Crimes Trials of the Postwar Era." In *Holocaust Historiography in Context: Emergences, Challenges, Polemics, and Achievements*. Edited by David Bankier and Dan Michman. 539–53. New York: Berghahn Books, 2008.

Blood, Philip W. *Hitler's Bandit Hunters: The SS and the Nazi Occupation of Europe*. Washington, D.C.: Potomac Books, 2006.

Borodziej, Włodzimierz. "'Hitlerische Verbrechen.' Die Ahndung deutscher Kriegs- und Besatzungsverbrechen in Polen." In *Transnationale Vergangenheitspolitik. Der Umgang mit deutschen Kriegsverbrechern in Europa nach dem Zweiten Weltkrieg*. Edited by Norbert Frei. 399–437. Göttingen: Wallstein Verlag, 2006.

– "Ściganie zbrodniarzy." In *Prawda, pamięć, odpowiedzialność. Powstanie Warszawskie w kontekście stosunków polsko-niemieckich*. Edited by Magda Cieszkowska et al. 115–29. Warsaw: Fundacja "Polsko-Niemieckie Pojednanie," 2010.

– "Widma przeszłości. Polacy o Niemcach i Niemczech 1945–1947." *Więź* 9 (1989): 43–56.

Breitman, Richard. "'Gegner Nummer eins.' Antisemitische Indoktrination in Himmlers Weltanschauung." In *Ausbildungsziel Judenmord?"Weltanschauliche*

Erziehung" von SS, Polizei und Waffen-SS im Rahmen der "Endlösung." Edited by Jürgen Matthäus, Konrad Kwiet, Jürgen Förster, and Richard Breitman. 21–34. Frankfurt am Main: Fischer Taschenbuch Verlag, 2003.

Broszat, Martin. *Nationalsozialistische Polenpolitik 1939–1945.* Frankfurt am Main und Hamburg: Fischer Bűcherei KG, 1961.

Browarek, Tomasz. "Próba periodyzacji polityki państwa polskiego wobec ludności niemieckiej po II wojnie światowej (1945–1989)." In *Władze komunistyczne wobec ludności niemieckiej w Polsce w latach 1945–1989.* Edited by Adam Dziurok, Piotr Madajczyk and Sebastian Rosenbaum. 233–44. Warsaw: Instytut Pamięci Narodowej – Komisja Ścigania Zbrodni przeciwko Narodowi Polskiemu, 2016.

Browder, George C. *Hitler's Enforcers: The Gestapo and the SS Security Service in the Nazi Revolution.* New York: Oxford University Press, 1996.

Browning, C.R. *Ordinary Men: Reserve Police Battalion 101 and the Final Solution in Poland.* New York: Harper Perennial, 1993.

– *The Origins of the Final Solution: The Evolution of Nazi Jewish Policy, September 1939–March 1942.* With contributions by Jürgen Matthäus. Lincoln: University of Nebraska Press, 2004.

Büchler, Yehoshua R. "'Unworthy Behavior': The Case of SS Officer Max Täubner." *Holocaust and Genocide Studies* 17, no. 3 (2003): 409–29.

Biuletyn Głównej Komisji Badania Zbrodni Niemieckich w Polsce, vol. 7. Warsaw: Wydawnictwo Ministerstwa Sprawiedliwości, 1951.

Chajn, Leon. "Próba bilansu." In *Wymiar sprawiedliwości w odrodzonej Polsce, 22. vii. 1944–22. vii. 1945.* 20–2. Warsaw: Ministerstwo Sprawiedliwości, 1945.

Chang, Iris. *The Rape of Nanking: The Forgotten Holocaust of World War II.* New York: Basic Books, 1997.

Cichopek, Anna. *Pogrom Żydów w Krakowie, 11 sierpnia 1945 r.* Warsaw: Żydowski Instytut Historyczny, 2000.

Cienciala, Anna M., Natalia S. Lebedeva, and Wojciech Materski, eds. *Katyn: A Crime without Punishment.* New Haven: Yale University Press, 2007.

Cohen, Boaz. *Hadorot haba'im – 'eykhekhah yelde'u: Leidato vehitpathuto shel heker hasho'ah hayisra'eli.* Jerusalem: Yad Vashem, 2010.

– "Holocaust Survivors and the Genesis of Holocaust Research." In *Beyond Camps and Forced Labour: Current International Research on Survivors of Nazi Persecution. Proceedings of the International Conference, 29–31 January 2003.* Edited by Johannes-Dieter Steinert and Inge Weber-Newth. 290–300. Osnabrück: Secolo Verlag, 2005. CD-ROM.

Conot, Robert E. *Justice at Nuremberg.* New York: Harper and Row, 1983.

Cooper, John. *Raphael Lemkin and the Struggle for the Genocide Convention.* New York: Palgrave Macmillan, 2007.

Croes, Marnix. "The Holocaust in the Netherlands and the Rate of Jewish Survival." *Holocaust and Genocide Studies* 20, no. 3 (2006): 474–99.

Cyprian, Tadeusz, and Jerzy Sawicki. *Ludzie i sprawy Norymbergi.* Poznań: Wydawnictwo Poznańskie, 1967.

– *Materiały norymberskie.* Warsaw: Spółdzielnia Wydawnicza "Książka," 1948.

– *Oskarżamy.* Kraków: Wydawnictwo Przełom, 1949.

– *Procesy wielkich zbrodniarzy wojennych w Polsce.* Warsaw: Spółdzielnia Wydawnicza-Oświatowa "Czytelnik," 1949.

– *Sprawy polskie w procesie norymberskim.* Poznań: Institut Zachodni, 1956.

Cyprian, Tadeusz, and Jerzy Sawicki, eds. *Siedem wyroków Najwyższego Trybunału Narodowego.* Poznań: Instytut Zachodni, 1962.

Datner, Szymon. "Niemiecki okupacyjny aparat bezpieczeństwa w Okręgu Białostockim (1941–1944) w świetle materiałów niemieckich (opracowania Waldemara Macholla)." *Biuletyn Głównej Komisji Badania Zbrodni Hitlerowskich w Polsce* 15 (1965): 1–30.

Dawidowicz, Lucy S. *The Holocaust and the Historians.* Cambridge, MA: Harvard University Press, 1981.

Deák, István. "A Fatal Compromise? The Debate over Collaboration and Resistance in Hungary." In *The Politics of Retribution in Europe: World War II and Its Aftermath.* Edited by István Deák, Jan T. Gross, and Tony Judt. 39–73. Princeton: Princeton University Press, 2000.

de Jong, L[ouis]. *Het Koninkrijk der Nederlanden in de Tweede Wereldoorlog.* 14 vols. The Hague: Nijhoff; SDU Uitgeverij, 1969–91.

de Mildt, Dirk, and Joggli Meihuizen, "'Unser Land muß tief gesunken sein …' Die Aburteilung deutscher Kriegsverbrecher in den Niederlanden." In *Transnationale Vergangenheitspolitik. Der Umgang mit deutschen Kriegsverbrechern in Europa nach dem Zweiten Weltkrieg.* Edited by Norbert Frei. 283–325. Göttingen: Wallstein Verlag, 2006.

Dirks, Christian. *Die Verbrechen der Anderen. Auschwitz und der Auschwitz-Prozeß der DDR. Das Verfahren gegen den KZ-Arzt Dr Horst Fischer.* Paderborn: Ferdinand Schöningh, 2006.

Dmitrów, Edmund. *Niemcy i okupacja hitlerowska w oczach Polaków: poglądy i opinie z lat 1945–1948.* Warsaw: Czytelnik, 1987.

Domańska, Regina. *Pawiak więzienie Gestapo. Kronika 1939–1944.* Warsaw: Książka i Wiedza, 1978.

Douglas, Lawrence. "The Didactic Trial: Filtering History and Memory in the Courtroom." *European Review* 14, no. 4 (2006): 513–22.

– *The Memory of Judgment: Making Law and History in the Trials of the Holocaust.* New Haven: Yale University Press, 2001.

Douglas, R.M. *Orderly and Humane: The Expulsion of the Germans after the Second World War.* New Haven: Yale University Press, 2012.

Drumbl, Mark A. "'Germans Are the Lords and Poles Are the Servants': The Trial of Arthur Greiser in Poland, 1946." In *The Hidden Histories of War Crimes Trials.* Edited by Kevin Jon Heller and Gerry Simpson. 411–29. Oxford: Oxford University Press, 2013.

– "The Supreme National Tribunal of Poland and the History of International Criminal Law." In *Historical Origins of International Criminal Law*, vol. 2. Edited by Morten Bergsmo, Cheah Wui Ling, and Yi Ping. 563–602. Brussels: Torkel Opsahl Academic EPublisher, 2014.

"Dziennik Iwana Waszenko," *Dzieje Najnowsze* 1, nos. 1–3/4 (1947): 324–35.

Epstein, Catherine. *Model Nazi: Arthur Greiser and the Occupation of Western Poland.* New York: Oxford University Press, 2010.

Feldman, Shoshana. *The Juridical Unconscious: Trials and Traumas in the Twentieth Century.* Cambridge, MA: Harvard University Press, 2002.

Puś, Wiesław, and Paweł Samuś, eds. *Fenomen getta łódzkiego 1940–1944.* Łódź: Wydawnictwo Uniwersytetu Łódzkiego, 2006.

Fest, Joachim C. *The Face of the Third Reich: Portraits of the Nazi Leadership.* Translated by Michael Bullock. New York: Pantheon Books, 1970.

Fijalkowski, Agata. "Politics, Law, and Justice in People's Poland: The Fieldorf File." *Slavic Review* 73, no. 1 (2014): 85–107.

Finder, Gabriel N. "Introduction." In *Making Holocaust Memory.* Polin: Studies in Polish Jewry, vol. 20. Edited by Gabriel N. Finder, Natalia Aleksiun, Antony Polonsky, and Jan Schwarz. 3–54. Oxford: Littman Library of Jewish Civilization, 2008.

– "The Politics of Retribution in Postwar Warsaw: In the Honor Court of the Central Committee of Polish Jews." In *Warsaw: The Jewish Metropolis: Essays in Honor of the 75th Birthday of Professor Antony Polonsky.* Edited by Glenn Dynner and François Guesnet. 539–61. Leiden and Boston: Brill, 2015.

– "The Trial of Shepsl Rotholc and the Politics of Retribution in the Aftermath of the Holocaust." *Gal-Ed: On the History and Culture of Polish Jewry*, vol. 20 (2006): 63–89 [English section].

Finder, Gabriel N., and Alexander V. Prusin. "Jewish Collaborators on Trial in Poland, 1944–1956." In *Making Holocaust Memory.* Polin: Studies in Polish Jewry, vol. 20. Edited by Gabriel N. Finder, Natalia Aleksiun, Antony Polonsky, and Jan Schwarz. 123–48. Oxford: Littman Library of Jewish Civilization, 2008.

Franecki, Jan, and Helena Kisiel. "Raporty i meldunki niemieckiej policji o Powstaniu Warszawskim 1944 roku." *Teki archiwalne* 17 (1978): 75–105.

Friedman, Filip. *Zagłada Żydów lwowskich*. Łódź: Centralna Żydowska Komisja Historyczna, 1945.

– "Zagłada Żydów polskich w latach 1939–1945." *Biuletyn Głównej Komisji Badania Zbrodni Niemieckich w Polsce* 1 (1946): 163–208.

Friedman, Jonathan. "Law and Politics in the Subsequent Nuremberg Trials, 1946–1949." In *Atrocities on Trial: Historical Perspectives on the Politics of Prosecuting War Crimes*. Edited by Patricia Heberer and Jürgen Matthäus. 75–102. Lincoln: University of Nebraska Press, 2008.

Friedman, Philip. "The Extermination of the Polish Jews during the German Occupation, 1939–1945." In *Roads to Extinction: Essays on the Holocaust*. Edited by Ada June Friedman. 211–43. New York and Philadelphia: Jewish Publication Society of America, 1980.

Friedman, Tuviah. *Sixty Years "Nazi Hunter," 1945–2005*. Edited and translated by David C. Gross. Haifa: Institute for the Documentation of Nazi War Crimes, 2006.

Frommer, Benjamin. *National Cleansing: Retribution against Nazi Collaborators in Postwar Czechoslovakia*. Cambridge: Cambridge University Press, 2005.

Führer, Harald. *Nachspiel: Die niederländische Politik und die Verfolgung von Kollaborateuren und NS-Verbrechern*. Münster and New York: Waxmann Verlag, 2005.

Fuhrer, Armin, and Heinz Schön. *Erich Koch, Hitler's braune Zar. Gauleiter von Ostpreussen und Reichskommissar der Ukraine*. Munich: Olzog, 2010.

Gawron, Edyta. "Amon Göth's Trial in Cracow: Its Impact on Holocaust Awareness in Poland." In *Holocaust and Justice: Representation and Historiography of the Holocaust in Post-War Trials*. Edited by David Bankier and Dan Michman. 281–98. Jerusalem: Yad Vashem, 2010.

Gerlach, Christian. "The Eichmann Interrogations in Holocaust Historiography." *Holocaust and Genocide Studies* 15, no. 3 (2001): 428–52.

Ginsburgs, George. *Moscow's Road to Nuremberg: The Soviet Background to the Trial*. The Hague, Boston, and London: Martinus Nijhoff, 1996.

Gnatowski, Michał. "Nationalsozialistische Okkupationspolitik im 'Bezirk Bialystok' 1941–1944." In *Bialystok in Bielefeld. Nationalsozialistische Verbrechen vor dem Landgericht Bielefeld 1958 bis 1967*. Edited by Freia Anders, Hauke-Hendrik Kutscher, and Katrin Stoll. 161–85. Bielefeld: Verlag für Regionalgeschichte, 2003.

Gnatowski, Michał, Waldemar Monkiewicz, and Józef Kowalczyk, eds. *Wieś białostocka oskarża: Ze studiów nad pacyfikacją wsi na Białostocczyźnie w latach wojny i okupacji hitlerowskiej*. Białystok: Okręgowa Komisja Badania Zbrodni Hitlerowskich-Ośrodek Badań Naukowych, 1981.

Goldhagen, Daniel Jonah. *Hitler's Willing Executioners: Ordinary Germans and the Holocaust*. New York: Random House, 1997.

Goldstein, Jan. "Framing Discipline with Law: Problems and Promises of the Liberal State." *American Historical Review* 98 (1993): 364–81.

Gondek, Leszek. *Polska karząca 1939–1945. Polski podziemny wymiar sprawiedliwości w okresie okupacji niemieckiej*. Warsaw: Instytut Wydawniczy Pax, 1988.

Grabowski, Waldemar. "Raport. Straty ludzkie poniesione przez Polskę w latach 1939–1945." In *Polska 1939–1945: Straty osobowe i ofiary represji pod dwiema okupacjami*. Edited by Wojciech Materski and Tomasz Szarota. 13–38. Warsaw: Instytut Pamięci Narodowej-Komisja Ścigania Zbrodni przeciwko Narodowi Polskiemu, 2009.

Greif, Gideon, ed. *We Wept without Tears: Testimonies of the Jewish Sonderkommando from Auschwitz*. Coral Gables: Sue and Leonard Miller Center for Contemporary Judaic Studies, University of Miami; New Haven: Yale University Press, 2005.

Grüss, Noe. *Rok pracy Centralnej Żydowskiej Komisji Historycznej*. Łódź: Wydawnictwa Centralnej Zydowskiej Komisji Historycznej przy C. K. Żydów Polskich, 1946.

Gumkowski, Janusz, and Tadeusz Kułakowski. *Zbrodniarze hitlerowscy przed Najwyższym Trybunałem Narodowym*. Warsaw: Wydawnictwo prawnicze, 1967.

Gutman, Israel. *The Jews of Warsaw, 1939–1943: Ghetto, Underground, Revolt*. Bloomington: Indiana University Press, 1989.

– *Resistance: The Warsaw Ghetto Uprising*. Boston and New York: Mariner Books, in association with the United States Holocaust Memorial Museum, 1994.

Gutman, Yisrael, and Michael Berenbaum, eds. *Anatomy of the Auschwitz Death Camp*. Bloomington: Indiana University Press, 1994.

Heberer, Patricia and Jürgen Matthäus, eds. *Atrocities on Trial: Historical Perspectives on the Politics of Prosecuting War Crimes*. Lincoln: University of Nebraska Press, 2008.

Heller, Kevin Jon, and Gerry Simpson, eds. *The Hidden Histories of War Crimes Trials*. Oxford, UK: Oxford University Press, 2013.

Henry, Patrick. *Jewish Resistance against the Nazis*. Washington, D.C.: Catholic University of America Press, 2014.

Hirsch, Francine. "The Soviets at Nuremberg: International Law, Propaganda, and the Making of the Postwar Order." *American Historical Review* 113, no. 3 (2008): 701–30.

Hirschfeld, Gerhard. *Nazi Rule and Dutch Collaboration: The Netherlands under German Occupation, 1940–1945.* Translated by Louise Willmot. Oxford, New York, and Hamburg: Berg Publishers, 1988.

Hölzl, Martin. "Walter Nord – Polizeisoldat und Weltanschauungenkrieger." In *Karrieren der Gewalt. Nationalsozialistische Täterbiographien.* Edited by Klaus-Michael Mallmann and Gerhard Paul. 166–75. Darmstadt: Wissenschaftliche Buchgesellschaft, 2004.

Höss, Rudolf. *Kommandant in Auschwitz: Autobiographische Aufzeichnungen.* Introduction and commentary by Martin Broszat. Stuttgart: Deutsche Verlags-Anstalt, 1958.

Huener, Jonathan. "Auschwitz 1945–1947: The Politics of Martyrdom and Memory." In *Making Holocaust Memory.* Polin: Studies in Polish Jewry, vol. 20. Edited by Gabriel N. Finder, Natalia Aleksiun, Antony Polonsky, and Jan Schwarz. 149–72. Oxford: Littman Library of Jewish Civilization, 2008.

– *Auschwitz, Poland, and the Politics of Commemoration, 1945–1979.* Athens: Ohio University Press, 2003.

Jacobs, Dov. "A Narrative of Justice and the (Re) Writing of History: Lessons Learned from World War II French Trials." In *The Hidden Histories of War Crimes Trials.* Edited by Kevin Jon Heller and Gerry Simpson. 122–36. Oxford: Oxford University Press, 2013.

Jakubowski, Grzegorz. *Sądownictwo powszechne w Polsce w latach 1944–1950.* Warsaw: Instytut Pamięci Narodowej-Komisja Ścigania Zbrodni przeciwko Narodowi Polskiemu, 2002.

Jankiewicz, Adam. "Przygotowania Rządu RP w latach II wojny światowej do procesu zbrodniarzy hitlerowskich. Dekret prezydenta Rzeczypospolitej o odpowiedzialności karnej za zbrodnie wojenne." *Pamięć i Sprawiedliwość* 40 (1997–8): 44–56.

Jasiński, Łukasz. "Zarys działalności Głównej Komisji Badania Zbrodni Niemieckich 1945–1949." In *Władze komunistyczne wobec ludności niemieckiej w Polsce w latach 1945–1989.* Edited by Adam Dziurok, Piotr Madajczyk, and Sebastian Rosenbaum. 39–47. Warsaw: Instytut Pamięci Narodowej-Komisja Ścigania Zbrodni przeciwko Narodowi Polskiemu, 2016.

Jędrzejewski, Edward. *Hitlerowska koncepcja administracji państwowej, 1933–1945. Studium polityczno-prawne.* Wrocław: Zakład Narodowy im. Ossolińskich, 1975.

Jockusch, Laura. *Collect and Record! Jewish Holocaust Documentation in Early Postwar Europe.* Oxford and New York: Oxford University Press, 2012.

– "Justice at Nuremberg? Jewish Responses to Nazi War-Crime Trials in Allied-Occupied Germany," *Jewish Social Studies* 19, no. 1 (Fall 2012): 107–47.

Kalicki, Włodzimierz. *Ostatni jeniec wielkiej wojny. Polacy i Niemcy po 1945 roku.*
Warsaw: Friedrich Ebert Stiftung; Wydawnictwo W.A.B., 2002.

Karski, Jan. *Story of a Secret State.* Boston: Houghton Mifflin, 1944.

Kassow, Samuel D. *Who Will Write Our History? Emanuel Ringelblum, the Warsaw
Ghetto, and the Oyneg Shabes Archive.* Bloomington: Indiana University Press,
2007.

[Kermish, Yosef]. "Metodologishe bamerkungen tsum historishn fregboygn."
In *Metodologishe onvayzungen tsum oysforshn dem khurbn fun poylishn yidntum.* Edited by Tsentrale yidishe historishe komisye baym tsentral-komitet
fun poylishe yidn. 1–7. Łódź: Tsentrale yidishe historishe komisye baym
tsentral-komitet fun poylishe yidn, 1945.

– "Rapport du Dr Jozef Kermisz. Trois années d'activité de la Commission
Centrale Historique Juive et de l'Institut Historique Juif auprès du Comité
Central des Juifs en Pologne." In Conférence européenne des commissions
historiques et des centres de documentation juifs, *Les juifs en Europe 1939–
1945: Rapports présentés à la première conference européenne des commissions
historiques et des centres de documentation juifs.* 140–4. Paris: Édition due
Centre, 1949.

– "Stroops teshuves oyf an ankete." *Bleter far geszichte* 1, nos. 3–4 (August–
December 1948): 166–94.

Kersten, Krystyna. *Narodziny systemu władzy. Polska 1943–1948.* Paris:
Wydawnictwo "Libella," 1986.

King, Henry T. "Personal Reflections on Nüremberg [sic]." *Case Western
Reserve Journal of International Law* 35, no. 2 (2003): 257–62.

Kiwerska, Jadwiga. "W atmosferze wrogości (1945–1970)." In *Polacy wobec
niemców. Z dziejów kultury politycznej Polski 1945–1989.* Edited by Anna
Wolff-Powęska. 45–3. Poznań: Instytut Zachodni, 1993.

Klein, Peter. *Die "Ghettoverwaltung Litzmannstadt" 1940 bis 1944. Eine Dienststelle
im Spannungsfeld von Kommunalbürokratie und staatlicher Verfolgungspolitik.*
Hamburg: Hamburger Edition, 2009.

Klimaszewski, Tadeusz. *Verbrennungskommando Warschau.* Warsaw: Czytelnik,
1984.

Kobierska-Motas, Elżbieta. *Ekstradycja przestępców wojennych do Polski z czterech
stref okupacyjnych Niemiec 1946–1950.* 2 vols. Warsaw: Główna Komisja
Badania Zbrodni przeciwko Narodowi Polskiemu – Instytut Pamięci
Narodowej, 1991–2.

– "Ściganie sprawców zbrodni hitlerowskich przez polski aparat wymiaru
sprawiedliwości w latach 1944–1950." In *W czterdziestolecie powołania
Najwyższego Trybunału Narodowego. Materiały z posiedzenia naukowego w*

dniu 20 stycznia 1986 r. 23–36. Warsaw: Główna Komisja Badania Zbrodni Hitlerowskich w Polsce – Instytut Pamięci Narodowej, 1986.

Kobylarz, Renata. *Walka o pamięć. Polityczne aspekty obchodów rocznicy powstania w getcie warszawskim 1944–1989.* Warsaw: Institut Pamieci Narodowej, 2009.

Kochanowski, Jerzy. *W polskiej niewoli. Niemieccy jeńcy wojenni w Polsce 1945–1950.* Warsaw: Wydawnictwo Neriton, 2001.

Kochanski, Halik. *The Eagle Unbound: Poland and the Poles in the Second World War.* Cambridge, MA: Harvard University Press, 2012.

Kochavi, Arieh J. *Prelude to Nuremberg: Allied War Crimes Policy and the Question of Punishment.* Chapel Hill: University of North Carolina Press, 1998.

Komorowski, Krzysztof. "Polityka PRL wobec sprawy Powstania Warszawskiego." In *Prawda, pamięć, odpowiedzialność. Powstanie Warszawskie w kontekście stosunków polsko-niemieckich.* Edited by Magda Cieszkowska et al. 193–206. Warsaw: Museum Powstania Warszawskiego, 2010.

Konrat, Marek. "Rafał Lemkin's Formative Years and the Beginning of International Career in Inter-War Poland (1918–1939)." In *Rafał Lemkin: A Hero of Humankind.* Edited by Agnieszka Bieńczyk-Missala and Sławomir Dębski. 59–74. Warsaw: Polish Institute of International Affairs, 2010.

Korey, William. "Lemkin's Passion: Origin and Fulfillment." In *Rafał Lemkin: A Hero of Humankind.* Edited by Agnieszka Bieńczyk-Missala and Sławomir Dębski. 75–98. Warsaw: Polish Institute of International Affairs, 2010.

Koźmińska-Frejlak, Ewa, and Gabriel N. Finder. "Apart: Polish-Jewish Relations in Communist Poland." *Gal-Ed: On the History and Culture of Polish Jewry* 25 (2017): 83–119 (English section).

Krakowski, Shmuel. "Josef Kermisz, 1907–2005." *Gal-Ed: On the History and Culture of Polish Jewry* 21 (2007): 161–3 (Hebrew section).

Kranz, Tomasz. "Die Erfassung der Todesfälle und die Häflingssterblichkeit im KZ Lublin." *Zeitschrift für Geschichtswissenschaft* 3 (2007): 220–44.

Krzepicki, Abraham. "Eighteen Days in Treblinka." In *The Death Camp Treblinka.* Edited by Alexander Donat. 77–145. New York: Holocaust Library, 1979.

Kubicki, Leszek. "Najwyższy Trybunał Narodowy. Próba bilansu orzecznictwa." In *W czterdziestolecie powołania Najwyższego Trybunału Narodowego: materiały z posiedzenia naukowego w dniu 20 stycznia 1986 r.* 9–22. Warsaw: Główna Komisja Badania Zbrodni Hitlerowskich w Polsce – Instytut Pamięci Narodowej, 1986.

– *Zbrodnie wojenne w świetle prawa polskiego.* Warsaw: Państwowe Wydawnictwo Naukowe, 1963.

Kułakowski, Tadeusz. "Proces Józefa Bühlera." In *Zbrodniarze hitlerowscy przed Najwyższym Trybunałem Narodowym.* Edited by Janusz Gumkowski and Tadeusz Kułakowski. 176–259. Warsaw: Wydawnictwo prawnicze, 1967.

Kulesza, Witold. "Der Beitrag der polnischen Nachkriegsjustiz zum europäischen Rechtskulturerbe am Beispiel zweier Prozesse wegen der Massenmorde im Warthegau (Posen, Kulmhof)." In *Gerechtigkeit nach Diktatur und Krieg. Transnational Justice 1945 bis heute – Strafverfaren und ihre Quellen*. Edited by Claudia Kuretsidis-Haider and Winfried R. Garscha. 115–29. Graz: CLIO, 2010.

Kunert, Andrzej Krzysztof. *Oskarżony. Kazimierz Moczarski*. Warsaw: Wydawnictwo Iskry, 2006.

Kuretsidis-Haider, Claudia, Irmgard Nöbauer, Winfried R. Garscha, Siegfried Sanwald, and Andrzej Selerowicz, eds. *Das KZ Lublin-Majdanek und die Justiz: Strafverfolgung und verweigerte Gerechtigkeit. Polen, Deutschland und Osterreich im Vergleich*. Graz: CLIO, 2011.

Lang, Berel. *Act and Idea in the Nazi Genocide*. Chicago: University of Chicago Press, 1990.

Langbein, Hermann. *People in Auschwitz*. Translated by Harry Zohn. Chapel Hill: University of North Carolina Press, published in association with the United States Holocaust Memorial Museum, 2004.

Lasik, Aleksander. "The Apprehension and Punishment of the Auschwitz Camp Staff." In *Auschwitz 1940–1945: Central Isues in the History of the Camp*. Vol 5. Edited by Danuta Czech, Stanisław Kłodziński, Aleksander Lasik, and Andrzej Strzelecki. 97–117. Oświęcim: Auschwitz-Birkenau State Museum, 2000.

Lebow, Richard Ned, Wulf Kansteiner, and Claudio Fogu, eds. *The Politics of Memory in Postwar Europe*. Durham: Duke University Press, 2006.

Lediakh, I.A., and F.M. Reshetnikov. "Kazhdyi natsistkii prestupnik dolzhen poniesti nakazanie." *Sovietskoe gosudarstvo i pravo* 2 (1965): 24–33.

Leszczyński, Kazimierz. *Heinz Reinefarth*. Poznań and Warsaw: Wydawnictwo Zachodnie, 1961.

Lewin, Abraham. *A Cup of Tears: A Diary of the Warsaw Ghetto*. Edited by Antony Polonsky. Oxford and New York: Basil Blackwell in association with the Institute for Polish-Jewish Studies, Oxford, 1988.

Liebman, Stuart. "Documenting the Liberation of the Camps: The Case of Aleksander Ford's Vernichtungslager Majdanek – Cmentarzysko Europy." *Lessons and Legacies VII: The Holocaust in International Perspective*. Edited by Dagmar Herzog. 333–51. Evanston: Northwestern University Press, 2006.

Lityński, Adam. "Criminal Law Legislation during the First Years of the People's Republic of Poland." In *Wojna domowa czy nowa okupacja? Polska po roku 1944*. Edited by Andrzej Ajnenkiel. 355–81. Warsaw: Światowy Związek Żołnierzy Armii Krajowej-Oficyna Wydawnicza RYTM, 2001.

Löw, Andrea. *Juden in Getto Litzmannstadt. Lebensbedingungen, Selbstwahrnehmung, Verhalten.* Göttingen: Wallstein Verlag, 2006.

Lower, Wendy. *Nazi Empire-Building and the Holocaust in Ukraine.* Chapel Hill: University of North Carolina Press, 2005.

Lubecka, Joanna. "Procesy zbrodniarzy niemieckich w Małopolsce w latach 1945–1950 ze szczególnym uwzględnieniem działalności Najwyższego Trybunału Narodowego." In *Władze komunistyczne wobec ludności niemieckiej w Polsce w latach 1945–1989.* Edited by Adam Dziurok, Piotr Madajczyk, and Sebastian Rosenbaum. 48–63. Warsaw: Instytut Pamięci Narodowej – Komisja Ścigania Zbrodni przeciwko Narodowi Polskiemu, 2016.

Łuczak, Czesław. "'Aktion Warschau.' Die Plünderung des polnischen Gutes im aufständischen Warschau." *Studia Historia Oeconomicae* 2 (1967): 201–7.

– *Polityka ludnościowa i ekonomiczna hitlerowskich Niemiec w okupowanej Polsce.* Poznań: Wydawnictwo Państwowe, 1979.

– "Szanse i trudności bilansu demograficznego Polski w latach 1939–1945. *Dzieje Najnowsze* 26, no. 2 (1994): 9–14.

Łukaszkiewicz, Zdzisław. *Obóz straceń w Treblince.* Warsaw: Państwowy Instytut Wydawniczy, 1946.

– "Obóz zagłady Treblinka." *Biuletyn Głównej Komisji Badania Zbrodni Niemieckich w Polsce* 1 (1946): 133–44.

– "The Treblinka Extermination Camp." In *German Crimes in Poland*, vol. 1. 93–106. Warsaw: Central Commission for Investigation of German Crimes in Poland, 1946.

Machcewicz, Anna. *Kazimierz Moczarski. Biografia.* Kraków: Wydawnictwo Znak, 2009.

Machnikowska, Anna. *Wymiar sprawiedliwości w Polsce w latach 1944–1950.* Gdańsk: Wydawnictwo Uniwersytetu Gdańskiego, 2008.

Madajczyk, Czesław. *Faszyzm i Okupacje 1938–1945. Wykonywanie okupacji przez Państwa Osi w Europie.* 2 vols. Poznań: Wydawnictwo Poznańskie, 1983.

– *Polityka III Rzeszy w okupowanej Polsce 1939–1945.* 2 vols. Warsaw: Państwowe Wydawnictwo Naukowe, 1970.

Madajczyk, Czesław, ed. *Ludność cywilna w powstaniu warszawskim.* 3 vols. Warsaw: Państwowy Instytut Wydawniczy, 1974.

Małcużyński, Karol. *Oskarżeni nie przyznają się do winy.* Warsaw: Interpress, 1971.

Mallmann, Klaus-Michael. "'Mensch, ich feiere heut' den tausenden Genickschuss.' Die Sicherheitspolizei und die Shoa in Westgalizien." In *Die Täter der Shoa. Fanatische National-Sozialisten oder ganz normale Deutsche?* Edited by Gerhard Paul. 109–36. Göttingen: Wallstein Verlag, 2002.

Mallmann, Klaus-Michael, Jochen Bühler, and Jürgen Matthäus, eds. *Einsatzgruppen in Polen. Darstellung und Dokumenation.* Darmstadt: Wissenschaftliche Buchgesellschaft, 2008.

Mark, Bernard. *Der oyfshtand in varshever geto. Naye dergentste oyflage und dokumentn-zamlung.* Warsaw: Farlag "Idisz-Buch," 1963.

– *Walka i zagłada warszawskiego getta.* Warsaw: Ministerstwo Obrony Narodowej, 1959.

Markiewicz, Tomasz. "Materielle Ausdrucksformen des Gedenkens in Polen und Deutschland." In *Der Warschauer Aufstand 1944. Ereignis und Wahrnehmung in Polen und Deutschland.* Edited by Hans-Jürgen Bömelburg, Eugeniusz Cezary Król, und Michael Thomae. 193–220. Im Auftrag des Militärgeschichtlichen Forschungsamtes, Potsdam, und des Zentrums für Historische Forschung der Polnischen Akademie der Wissenschaften, Berlin. Paderborn: Ferdinand Schöningh, 2011.

Marrus, Michael R. "The Holocaust at Nuremberg." *Yad Vashem Studies* 26 (1998): 5–41.

– *The Nuremberg Trial, 1945–1946: A Documentary History.* Boston and New York: Bedford Books, 1997.

Marti, Philipp. *Der Fall Reinefarth: Eine biografische Studie zum öffentlichen und juristischen Umgang mit den NS-Vergangenheit.* Neumünster-Hamburg: Wachholtz, 2014.

Materski, Wojciech, and Tomasz Szarota. *Polska 1939–1945. Straty osobowe i ofiary represji pod dwiema okupacjami.* Warsaw: Instytut Pamięci Narodowej-Komisja Ścigania Zbrodni przeciwko Narodowi Polskiemu, 2009.

Matthäus, Jürgen. "Die 'Judenfrage' als Schulungsthema von SS und Polizei. 'Innere Erlebnis' und Handlungslegitimation." In *Ausbildungsziel Judenmord? "Weltanschauliche Erziehung" von SS, Polizei und Waffen-SS im Rahmen der "Endlösung."* Edited by Jürgen Matthäus, Konrad Kwiet, Jürgen Förster, and Richard Breitman. 35–86. Frankfurt am Main: Fischer Teaschenbuch Verlag, 2003.

Matusiak, Tadeusz. "Zbrodniarze z obozu koncentracyjnego Stutthof przed sądami." *Komunikaty - Muzeum Stutthof w Sztutowie* 2 (1969): 1–10.

Meindl, Ralf. *Ostpreussens Gauleiter. Erich Koch – eine politische Biographie.* Osnabrück: Fibre Verlag, 2007.

Michaelis, Rolf. *Die SS-Sturmbrigade "Dirlewanger." Vom Warschauer Aufstand bis zum Kessel von Halbe.* Berlin: Michaelis-Verlag, 2003.

Micheels, Louis J. *Doctor #117641.* New Haven: Yale University Press, 1989.

Moczarski, Kaziemierz. *Conversations with an Executioner.* Englewood Cliffs: Prentice-Hall, 1981.

– *Rozmowy z katem.* Edited by Andrzej Krzysztof Kunert. Kraków: Wydawnictwo Znak, 2009.

Moore, Bob. *Victims and Survivors: The Nazi Persecution of the Jews in the Netherlands, 1940–1945.* London and New York: Arnold, 1997.

Motas, Mieczysław. "Delegacja polska w Norymberdze 1945–1946 (1947)." *Pamięć i Sprawiedliwość: Biuletyn Głównej Komisji Badania Zbrodni przeciwko Narodowi Polskiemu, Instytutu Pamięci Narodowej* 40 (1997–1998): 57–85.

Murzynowski, Andrzej, and Jan Rezler. *Wymiar sprawiedliwości w Polsce w latach 1944–1970. Ustawodawstwo, organizacja i działalność.* Warsaw: Wydawnictwo Uniwersytetu Warszawskiego, 1972.

Mushkat, M[arion]. "Yehudim betzeva'ot polin ha'amamit." *Lohamim yehudim bamilhamah neged hanatzim.* Edited by M[arion] Mushkat. 89–112. Tel Aviv: Sifriyat Po'alim, 5731 [1970–1].

Musial, Bogdan. "NS-Kriegsverbrecher vor polnischen Gerichten." *Vierteljahrshefte für Zeitgeschichte* 47 (1999): 25–56.

Nagorski, Andrew. *The Nazi Hunters.* New York: Simon and Schuster, 2016.

Naimark, Norman M. *Fires of Hatred: Ethnic Cleansing in Twentieth-Century Europe.* Cambridge, MA: Harvard University Press, 2001.

Neumann, Franz. *Behemoth: The Structure and Practice of National Socialism.* Toronto, New York, and London: Oxford University Press, 1942.

Omiljanowicz, Aleksander. *Cienie powracają.* Warsaw: Wydawnictwo Ministerstwa Obrony Narodowej, 1982.

– *Przed wyrokiem. Rozmowy z gestapowcem.* Białystok: Wydawnictwo "Łuk," 1998.

– *Zanikające echa.* Warsaw: Wydawnictwo Ministerstwa Obrony Narodowej, 1977.

Orla-Bukowska, Annamaria. "New Threads on an Old Loom: National Memory and Social Identity in Post-War and Post-Communist Poland." In *The Politics of Memory in Postwar Europe.* Edited by Richard Ned Lebow, Wulf Kansteiner, and Claudio Fogu. 177–209. Durham: Duke University Press, 2006.

Orlovskii, Slavomir, and Radoslav Ostrovich. *Erich Koch pered polskim sudom.* Moscow: Izdatel'stvo Mezhdunarodnykh otnoshenii, 1961.

Paczkowski, Andrzej. "Poland, the 'Enemy Nation.'" In *The Black Book of Communism: Crimes, Terror, Repression.* Edited by Stéphane Courtois et al. Translated by Jonathan Murphy and Mark Kramer. 363–93. Cambridge, MA: Harvard University Press, 1999.

Parrish, Michael. *The Lesser Terror: Soviet State Security, 1939–1953.* Westport: Praeger, 1996.

Pasek, Andrzej. *Przestępstwa okupacyjne w polskim prawie karnym z lat 1944–1956*. Wrocław: Wydawnictwo Uniwersytetu Wrocławskiego, 2002.

Patt, Avinoam. "Jewish Resistance in the Warsaw Ghetto." In *Jewish Resistance against the Nazis*. Edited by Patrick Henry. 393–425. Washington, D.C.: Catholic University of America Press, 2014.

Paul, Gerhard. "Von Psychopathen, Technokraten des Terrors und ganz 'gewöhnlichen' Deutschen. Die Täter der Shoa im Spiegel der Forschung." In *Die Täter der Shoa: Fanatische National-Sozialisten oder ganz normale Deutsche?* Edited by Gerhard Paul. 13–92. Göttingen: Wallstein Verlag, 2002.

Paul, Gerhard, and Klaus-Michael Mallmann. "Sozialisation, Milieu und Gewalt: Fortschritte und Probleme der neueren Täterforschung." In *Karrieren der Gewalt. Nationalsozialistische Täterbiographien*. Edited by Klaus-Michael Mallmann and Gerhard Paul. 1–32. Darmstadt: Wissenschaftliche Buchgesellschaft, 2004.

Pemper, Mietek, with Victoria Hertling, assisted by Marie Elisabeth Müller. *The Road to Rescue: The Untold Story of Schindler's List*. Translated by David Dollenmayer. New York: Other Press, 2008.

Pendas, Devin O. "Seeking Justice, Finding Law: Nazi Trials in Postwar Europe." *Journal of Modern History* 81, no. 2 (June 2009): 347–68.

Pendas, Devin O., Laura Jockusch, and Gabriel N. Finder. "Auschwitz Trials: The Jewish Dimension." *Yad Vashem Studies* 41, no. 2 (2013): 139–71.

Person, Katarzyna. "The Adventures of a Stamp Collector in the Warsaw Ghetto: Franz Konrad's Story." *Holocaust: Studies and Materials* (2013): 293–309.

– "Filatelisty w getcie warszawskim przypadki. Historia Franza Konrada." *Zagłada Żydów. Studia i Materiały* 7 (2011): 252–68.

– "Jürgen Stroop Speaks: The Trial of the Warsaw Ghetto Liquidator before the Warsaw Provincial Court." *Holocaust: Studies and Materials* (2013): 357–404.

– "Mówi Jürgen Stroop: Proces likwidatora powstania w getcie warszawskim przed Sądem Wojewodzkim w Warszawie." *Zagłada Żydów. Studia i Materiały* 9 (2013): 380–426.

Pietrzak, Jacek. "Hans Biebow–portret oprawcy." In *Fenomen getta łódzkiego 1940–1944*. Edited by Wiesław Puś and Paweł Samuś. 185–203. Łódź: Wydawnictwo Uniwersytetu Łódzkiego, 2006.

Pilichowski, Czesław, "Udział Polski w badaniu i ściganiu zbrodni hitlerowskich." In *Zbrodnie i sprawcy: Ludobójstwo hitlerowskie przed sądem ludzkości i historii*. Edited by Czesław Pilichowski. 23–87. Warsaw: Państwowe Wydawnictwo Naukowe, 1980.

Pilichowski, Czesław, ed. *Badanie i ściganie zbrodni hitlerowskich, 1944–1974.* Warsaw: Główna Komisja Badania Zbrodni Hitlerowskich w Polsce, 1975.
– *Ekspertyzy i orzeczenia przed Najwyższym Trybunałem Narodowym*, vol. 8. Warsaw: Ministerstwo Sprawiedliwości-Główna Komisja Badania Zbrodni Hitlerowskich w Polsce, 1982. 9 vols.
Piotrowski, Stanisław. *Dziennik Hansa Franka.* Warsaw: Wydawnictwo Prawnicze, 1956.
– *Dziennik Hansa Franka*, 2nd ed. Warsaw: Wydawnictwo Prawnicze, 1957.
– "Hans Frank – Der Mann und sein Werk. Der Generalgouverneur in seinen Tagebüchern." In *Proces Hansa Franka i dowody polskie przeciw SS.* Edited by Stanisław Piotrowski. 245–57. Warsaw: Wydawnictwo Prawnicze, 1970,
– *Sprawozdanie Juergena Stroopa.* Warsaw: Spódzielnia Wydawnicza "Książka," 1948.
Piper, Franciszek. "Auschwitz II-Birkenau Main Camp." *The United States Holocaust Memorial Museum Encyclopedia of Camps and Ghettos, 1933–1945*, vol. 1: *Early Camps, Youth Camps, and Concentration Camps under the SS-Business Administration Main Office (WVHA)*, pt A. Edited by Geoffrey P. Megargee. 209–14. Bloomington: Indiana University Press in association with the United States Holocaust Memorial Museum, 2009.
– "Estimating the Number of Deportees to and Victims of the Auschwitz-Birkenau Camp." *Yad Vashem Studies* 21 (1991): 49–103.
– "The Number of Victims." In *Anatomy of the Auschwitz Death Camp.* Edited by Yisrael Gutman and Michael Berenbaum. 61–76. Bloomington: Indiana University Press, 1994.
Piper, Franciszek, and Teresa Świebocka, eds. *Auschwitz. Nazistowski obóz śmierci.* Oświęcim-Brzezinka: Wydawnictwo Państwowego Muzeum Oświęcim-Brzezinka, 1993.
Plesch, Dan. *Human Rights after Hitler: The Lost History of Prosecuting Axis Crimes.* Washington, D.C.: Georgetown University Press, 2017.
Płoski, Stanisław, Zofia Połubiec, Danuta Dąbrowska, Lucjan Dobroszycki, and Mieczysław Tomala, eds. *Okupacja i ruch oporu w dzienniku Hansa Franka, 1939–1945.* Warsaw: Książka i Wiedza, 1970. 2 vols.
Pohl, Dieter. "Hans Krueger and the Murder of Jews in Stanislaw." *Yad Vashem Studies* 26 (1998): 239–65.
– *Nationalsozialistische Judenverfolgung in Ostgalizien 1941–1944. Organisation und Durchführung eines staatlichen Massenverbrechens.* Munich: R. Oldenbourg Verlag, 1996.
Polonsky, Antony. "Artur Eisenbach (1906–1992)." *Polin: Studies in Polish Jewry* 8 (1994): 423–6.

– "Foreword: Artur Eisenbach and Polish-Jewish History." In Artur Eisenbach, *The Emancipation of the Jews in Poland, 1780–1870*. Edited by Antony Polonsky. Translated by Janina Dorosz. xiii–xxvii. Oxford and Cambridge, MA: Basil Blackwell in association with the Institute for Polish-Jewish Studies, 1991.

– "Poles, Jews, and the Problems of Divided Memory." *Ab Imperio* 2 (2004): 125–47.

Porat, Dan. *The Boy*. New York: Hill and Wang, 2010.

Pospieszalski, K.M. "Nazi Terror in Poland 1939–1945." *Polish Western Affairs* 5, no. 1 (1964): 65–91.

Präg, Werner, and Wolfgang Jacobmeyer, eds. *Das Diensttagebuch des deutschen Generalgouverneurs in Polen 1939–1945*. Stuttgart: Deutsche Verlags-Anstalt, 1975.

Presser, Jacob. *Ashes in the Wind: The Destruction of Dutch Jewry*. Translated by Arnold Pomerans. London: Souvenir Press, 2010.

Prusin, Alexander V. "Poland's Nuremberg: The Seven Court Cases of the Supreme National Tribunal, 1946–1948." *Holocaust and Genocide Studies* 24, no. 1 (2010): 1–25.

Putrament, Jerzy. Pół wieku. Wojna. 9 vols. Warsaw: Czytelnik, 1962.

Radziwończyk, Kazimierz. "Rola i specyfika terroru fizycznego w hitlerowskim systemie walki z ruchem oporu na okupowanych ziemiach polskich w latach 1939–1945." In *Zbrodnie i sprawcy. Ludobójstwo hitlerowskie przed sądem ludzkości i historii*. Edited by Czesław Pilichowski. 238–56. Warsaw: Państwowe Wydawnictwo Naukowe, 1980.

Rappaport, Emil Stanisław. *Naród-zbrodniarz. Przestępstwa hitleryzmu a naród niemiecki. Szkic analityczny przestępczości i odpowiedzialności osobowo-zespołowej*. Łódź: Spółdzielnia dziennikarska "Prasa," 1945.

Reich-Ranicki, Marcel. *The Author of Himself: The Life of Marcel Reich-Ranicki*. Translated by Ewald Osers. Princeton: Princeton University Press, 2001.

Reitlinger, Gerald. "Last of the War Criminals: The Mystery of Erich Koch." *Commentary* 27, no. 1 (1959), 31–42.

"Relacja von dem Bacha o powstaniu Warszawskim." *Dzieje Najnowsze* 2, no. 1 (1947): 295–323.

Rojek, Wojciech. "The Government of the Republic of Poland in Exile, 1945–92." In *The Poles in Britain, 1940–2000*. Edited by Peter D. Stachura. 33–47. London and Portland: Frank Cass, 2004.

Rojowska, Elżbieta. "Wpływ dekretów radzieckich Rady Najwyższej ZSRR na polskie prawo karne dotyczące karania zbrodniarzy wojennych." *Studia Prawnoustrojowe* 15 (2012): 183–92.

Romijn, P[eter]. "The War, 1940–1945." In *The History of the Jews in the Netherlands.* Edited by J.C.H. Blom, R.G. Fuks-Mansfeld, and I. Schöffer. 296–335. Oxford: Littman Library of Jewish Civilization, 2002.

Roseman, Mark. "Beyond Conviction? Perpetrators, Ideas, and Action in the Holocaust in Historiographical Perspective." In *Conflict, Catastrophe, and Continuity: Essays on Modern German History.* Edited by Frank Biess, Mark Roseman, and Hanna Schissler. 83–103. New York and Oxford: Berghahn Books, 2007.

Roskies, David G. *Against the Apocalypse: Responses to Catastrophe in Modern Jewish Culture.* Cambridge, MA: Harvard University Press, 1984.

Rossino, Alexander B. *Hitler Strikes Poland: Blitzkrieg, Ideology, and Atrocity.* Lawrence: University Press of Kansas, 2003.

Rothberg, Michael. *Multidirectional Memory: Remembering the Holocaust in the Age of Decolonization.* Stanford: Stanford University Press, 2009.

Rozenberg-Rutkowski, A[dam]. "Działalność Żydowskiego Instytutu Historycznego w dziedzinie ścigania prezestępców wojennych i kolaboracjonistów." *Biuletyn Żydowskiego Instytutu Historycznego przy C.K. Żydów w Polsce* (March 1950): 15–16.

Rubenstein, Joshua. "The War and the Final Solution on the Russian Front." In *The Unknown Black Book: The Holocaust in German-Occupied Soviet Territories.* Edited by Joshua Rubenstein and Ilya Altman. 3–44. Bloomington: Indiana University Press in association with the United States Holocaust Memorial Museum, 2008.

Ruchniewicz, Krzysztof. *Warszawa–Berlin–Bonn. Stosunki polityczne 1949–1958.* Wrocław: Wydawnictwo Uniwersytetu Wrocławskiego, 2003.

Rzepliński, Andrzej. *Sądownictwo w PRL.* London: Polonia, 1989.

Sakson, Andrzej. "Niemcy w świadomości społecznej polaków." In *Polacy wobec niemców. Z dziejów kultury politycznej Polski 1945–1989.* Edited by Anna Wolff-Powęska, 408–29. Poznań: Instytut Zachodni, 1993.

Sands, Philippe. *East West Street: On the Origins of "Genocide" and "Crimes against Humanity."* New York: A.A. Knopf, 2016.

Sawicki, Jerzy. "O prawie sądów specjalnych." In *Wymiar sprawiedliwości w odrodzonej Polsce, 22. vii. 1944–22. vii. 1945,* 55–64. Warsaw: Ministerstwo Sprawiedliwości, 1945.

Sawicki, Tadeusz. *Rozkaz: zdławić powstanie. Siły zbrojne III Rzeszy w walce z Powstaniem Warszawskim 1944.* Warsaw: Dom Wydawniczy Bellona, 2001.

Schabas, William. *Genocide in International Law: The Crime of Crimes.* Cambridge and New York: Cambridge University Press, 2000.

Schenk, Dieter. *Hans Frank. Hitlers Kronjurist und Generalgouverneur.* Frankfurt am Main. S. Fischer Verlag, 2006.

– *Hitlers Mann in Danzig. Albert Forster und die NS-Verbrechen in Danzig-Westpreussen*. Bonn: J.H.W. Dietz, 2000.

Schilling, Donald G., ed. *Lessons and Legacies II: Teaching the Holocaust in a Changing World*. Evanston: Northwestern University Press, 1998.

Schwindt, Barbara. *Das Konzentrations- und Vernichtugslager Majdanek. Funktionswandel im Kontext der "Endlösung."* Würzburg: Könighauser & Neumann, 2005.

Scott-Clark, Catherine, and Adrian Levy. *The Amber Room: The Fate of the World's Greatest Lost Treasure*. New York: Walker Books, 2004.

Segev, Tom. *Simon Wiesenthal: The Life and Legend*. New York: Schocken Books, 2012.

Selerowicz, Andrzej, and Winfried R. Garscha. "Die strafrechtliche Ahndung in Polen." In *Das KZ Lublin-Majdanek und die Justiz. Strafverfolgung und verweigerte Gerechtigkeit: Polen, Deutschland und Osterreich im Vergleich*. Edited by Claudia Kuretsidis-Haider, Irmgard Nöbauer, Winfried R. Garscha, Siegfried Sanwald, and Andrzej Selerowicz. 53–115. Graz: CLIO, 2011.

Simonov, Constantin. *Un Camp d'Extermination 1944*. Moscow: Éditions Langues Étrangéres, 1944.

Snyder, Timothy. *Bloodlands: Europe between Hitler and Stalin*. New York: Basic Books, 2010.

Sosińska, Anna. "Powstanie i działalność Najwyższego Trybunału Narodowego." In *W czterdziestolecie powołania Najwyższego Trybunału Narodowego. Materiały z posiedzenia naukowego w dniu 20 stycznia 1986 r.* 37–47. Warsaw: Główna Komisja Badania Zbrodni Hitlerowskich w Polsce – Instytut Pamięci Narodowej, 1986.

Stach, Stefan. "Geschichtsschreibung und politische Vereinnahmungen. Das Jüdische Historische Institut in Warschau 1947–1968." *Jahrbuch des Simon-Dubnow-Instituts / Simon Dubnow Institute Yearbook* 7 (2008): 401–31.

– "'Praktische Geschichte.' Der Beitrag jüdischer Organisationen zur Verfolgung von NS-Verbrechern in Polen und Österreich in den späten 40er Jahren." In *Opfer als Akteure. Interventionen ehemaliger NS-Verfogter in der Nachkriegszeit*. Edited by Katharina Stengel and Werner Konitzer. 242–62. Frankfurt and New York: Campus Verlag in association with the Fritz Bauer Institute, 2008.

Staub, Ervin. *The Roots of Evil: The Origins of Genocide and Other Group Violence*. New York: Cambridge University Press, 1989.

Stauber, Roni. *Laying the Foundations for Holocaust Research: The Impact of the Historian Philip Friedman*. Jerusalem: Yad Vashem, 2009.

Szarota, Tomasz. *Niemcy i Polacy. Wzajemne postrzeganie i stereotypy*. Warsaw: Wydawnictwo Naukowe PWN, 1996.

Szczepański, Jan. *Dzienniki z lat 1945–1968*. Edited by Daniel Kadłubiec. Ustroń: Galeria "Na Gojach," 2013.

Szwagrzyk, Krzysztof. *Prawnicy czasu bezprawia. Sędziowie i prokuratorzy wojskowi w Polsce 1944–1956*. Kraków and Wrocław: Instytut Pamięci Narodowej-Komisja Ścigania Zbrodni przeciwko Narodowi Polskiemu, 2005.

Szyprowski, Bartłomiej. *Sąd kapturowy przy Komendzie Głównej Związku Walki Zbrojnej w Warszawie (sierpień 1940 r. – listopad 1941 r.). Podziemie w walce ze zdrajcami Rzeczypospolitej*. Warsaw: Historyczna, 2016.

Tippner, Anja. "Moczarskis Gespräche mit dem Henker. Zur Verschränkung von Opfer- und Täterdiskursen." In *Von Tätern und Opfern. Zur medialen Darstellung politisch und ethnisch motivierter Gewalt im 20./21. Jahrhundert*. Edited by Claudia Nickel and Silke Segler-Meßner. 41–59. Frankfurt am Main: Peter Lang Edition, 2013.

Tokarev, M. "V zamknutom kruge." In *Neotvratimoe vozmezdie. Po materialam sudebnykh protsessov nad izmennikami rodiny, fashistskimi palachami i agentami imperialisticheskikh razvedok*. Edited by S.S. Maksimov and M.E. Karyshev. 185–99. Moscow: Voennoe izdatel'stvo, 1987.

Tusa, Ann, and John Tusa. *The Nuremberg Trial*. New York: Atheneum, 1984.

Vogel, Thomas. "'Mann muss seine Augen und sein Herz verschliessen.' Der deutsche Hauptmann Wilm Hosenfeld als Augenzeuge des Warschauer Aufstand." In *Der Warschauer Aufstand 1944. Ereignis und Wahrnehmung in Polen und Deutschland*. Edited by Hans-Jürgen Bömelburg, Eugeniusz Cezary Król, und Michael Thomae. 231–42. Im Auftrag des Militärgeschichtlichen Forschungsamtes, Potsdam, und des Zentrums für Historische Forschung der Polnischen Akademie der Wissenschaften, Berlin. Paderborn: Ferdinand Schöningh, 2011.

Walden, Jesco von. *Und morgen die ganze Welt? Die Verschwörung der braunen Paladine*. Berlin: Kongress-Verlag, 1960.

Wardzyńska, Maria. *Był rok 1939. Operacja niemieckiej policji bezpieczeństwa w Polsce "Intelligenzaktion."* Warsaw: Instytut Pamięci Narodowej-Komisja Ścigania Zbrodni przeciwko Narodowi Polskiemu, 2009.

Warmbrunn, Werner. *The Dutch under German Occupation, 1940–1945*. Stanford: Stanford University Press, 1963.

W czterdziestolecie powołania Najwyższego Trybunału Narodowego, Materiały z posiedzenia naukowego w dniu 20 stycznia 1986 r. Warsaw: Główna Komisja Badania Zbrodni Hitlerowskich w Polsce – Instytut Pamięci Narodowej, 1986.

Weber, Jürgen, and Peter Steinbach, eds. *Vergangenheitsbewältigung durch Strafverfahren? NS-Prozesse in der Bundesrepublik Deutschland*. Munich: G. Olzog, 1984.

Weichert, Michał. *Zikhroynes*, vol. 4: *Nokhn khubn*. Tel Aviv: Orli, 1970.

Weinke, Annette. "'Allierter Angriff auf die nationale Souveränität'? Die Strafverfolgung von Kriegs- und NS-Verbrechen in der Bundesrepublik, der DDR, und Österreich." In *Transnationale Vergangenheitspolitik. Der Umgang mit deutschen Kriegsverbrechern in Europa nach dem Zweiten Weltkrieg.* Edited by Norbert Frei. 37–93. Göttingen: Wallstein Verlag, 2006.

– *Die Verfolgung von NS-Tätern im geteilten Deutschland. Vergangenheitsbewältigung 1949–1969 oder eine deutsch-deutsche Beziehungsgeschichte im Kalten Krieg.* Paderborn: Ferdinand Schöningh, 2002.

Werth, Alexander. *Russia at War, 1941–1945.* New York: Dutton, 1964.

Westermann, Edward B. *Hitler's Police Battalions: Enforcing Racial War in the East.* Lawrence: University Press of Kansas, 2005.

Wetzell, Richard F. *Inventing the Criminal: A History of German Criminology, 1881–1945.* Chapel Hill: University of North Carolina Press, 2000.

Wildt, Michael. *Generation des Unbedingten: Das Führungskorps des Reichssicherheitshauptamtes.* Hamburg: Hamburger Edition HIS, 2002.

Wirth, Andrzej. "Introduction." In *The Stroop Report: The Jewish Quarter of Warsaw Is No More!* Translated by Sybil Milton. n.pag. New York: Pantheon Books, 1979.

Wittmann, Rebecca. *Beyond Justice: The Auschwitz Trial.* Cambridge, MA: Harvard University Press, 2005.

Wojciechowska, Janina. *Przestępcy hitlerowscy przed Specjalnym Sądem Karnym w Toruniu, 1945–1946.* Toruń: Państwowe Wydawnictwo Naukowe, 1965.

Wspomnienia Rudolfa Hoessa komendanta obozu oświęcimskiego. Warsaw: Wydawnictwo Prawnicze, 1956.

Wulf, Joseph. *Das Dritte Reich und seine Vollstrecker.* Frankfurt am Main, Berlin, and Vienna: Ullstein, 1984.

Wymiar sprawiedliwości w odrodzonej Polsce, 22. vii. 1944–22. vii. 1945. Warsaw: Ministerstwo Sprawiedliwości, 1945.

Young, James E. *The Texture of Memory: Holocaust Memorials and Meaning.* New Haven: Yale University Press, 1993.

Zaborski, Marcin. "Czy bronić 'zdrajców Narodu,' 'zbrodniarzy faszystowsko-hitlerowskich,' i 'volksdeutschów'? Uchwała Naczelnej Rady Adwokackiej z dnia 25 maja 1946 r. w sprawie udziału adwokatów w procesach o zdradę narodu lub o rehabilitację wyłączonych ze społeczeństwa." *Palestra. Pismo Adwokatury Polskiej* 1–2, nos. 661–2 (2013): 234–47.

Załuski, Zbigniew. *Czterdziesty czwarty. Wydarzenia, obserwacje, refleksje.* Warsaw: Czytelnik, 1968.

Zamojski, Jan E. "The Social History of the Polish Exile (1939–1945): The Exile State and the Clandestine State: Society, Problems, and Reflections." In *Europe in Exile: European Exile Communities in Britain, 1940–1945.* Edited by Martin Conway and José Gotovitch, 183–211. New York and Oxford: Berghahn Books, 2001.

Zaremba, Marcin. *Wielka trwoga. Polska 1944–1947. Ludowa reakcja na kryzys.* Kraków and Warsaw: Społeczny Instytut Wydawniczy "Znak" – Instytut Studiów Politycznych Polskiej Akademii Nauk, 2012.

Żbikowski, Andrzej. "Wstęp." In Jürgen Stroop, *Żydowska dzielnica mieszkaniowa w Warszawie już nie istnieje!* Edited by Andrzej Żbikowski. 9–18. Warsaw: Instytut Pamięci Narodowej i Żydowski Instytut Historyczny, 2009.

Zillmer, Eric A., Molly Harrower, Barry A. Ritzler, and Robert P. Archer. *The Quest for Nazi Personality: A Psychological Investigation of Nazi War Criminals.* Hillsdale and Hove: Lawrence Erlbaum Associates, 1995.

Zimmerman, Joshua D. *The Polish Underground and the Jews, 1939–1945.* New York: Cambridge University Press, 2015.

Zuckerman, Yitzhak ("Antek"). *A Surplus of Memory: Chronicle of the Warsaw Ghetto Uprising.* Translated and edited by Barbara Harshav. Berkeley: University of California Press, 1993.

Encyclopedia

Crago, Laura. "Łódź." *The United States Holocaust Memorial Museum Encyclopedia of Camps and Ghettos, 1933–1945*, vol. 2: *Ghettos in German-Occupied Eastern Europe.* Edited by Martin Dean and Mel Hecker. 75–82. Bloomington: Indiana University Press in association with the United States Holocaust Memorial Museum, 2009.

"Cyprian, Tadeusz." *Wielka Encyklopedia Powszechna PWN*, vol. 2: 667. Warsaw: Państwowe Wydawnictwo Naukowe, 1963.

"Kurowski (Warszawski), Stefan." *Wielka Encyklopedia Powszechna PWN*, vol. 6: 314. Warsaw: Państwowe Wydawnictwo Naukowe, 1965.

Piper, Franciszek. "Auschwitz II–Birkenau Main Camp." *The United States Holocaust Memorial Museum Encyclopedia of Camps and Ghettos, 1933–1945*, vol. 1: *Early Camps, Youth Camps, and Concentration Camps under the SS-Business Administration Main Office (WVHA)*, pt A. Edited by Geoffrey P. Megargee. 209–14. Bloomington: Indiana University Press in association with the United States Holocaust Memorial Museum, 2009.

"Sawicki, Jerzy." *Wielka Encyklopedia Powszechna PWN*, vol. 10: 374. Warsaw: Państwowe Wydawnictwo Naukowe, 1967.

Sydnor, Charles. "Auschwitz I Main Camp." In *The United States Holocaust Memorial Museum Encyclopedia of Camps and Ghettos, 1933–1945*, vol. 1: *Early Camps, Youth Camps, and Concentration Camps under the SS-Business Administration Main Office (WVHA)*, pt A. Edited by Geoffrey P. Megargee.

204–8. Bloomington: Indiana University Press in association with the United States Holocaust Memorial Museum, 2009.

White, Elizabeth. "Lublin Main Camp [AKA Majdanek]." *The United States Holocaust Memorial Museum Encyclopedia of Camps and Ghettos, 1933–1945*, vol. 1: *Early Camps, Youth Camps, and Concentration Camps under the SS-Business Administration Main Office (WVHA)*, pt A.. Edited by Geoffrey P. Megargee. 875–9. Bloomington: Indiana University Press in association with the United States Holocaust Memorial Museum, 2009.

Interview

IPN archive director Dr Stanisław Biernacki, Warsaw, 21 July 1997.

Unpublished Source

Jasiński, Łukasz. "The Central Commission for the Investigation of German/Hitlerite Crimes in Poland as an Instrument of Postwar Retribution." Unpublished paper presented at "Beyond Camps and Forced Labour: Current International Research on Survivors of Nazi Persecution." Fifth International Multidisciplinary Conference, London, 7–9 January 2015.

Internet Sources

"Antoni Chmurski." https://pl.wikipedia.org/wiki/Antoni_Chmurski (accessed 25 July 2017).

"Dlaczego niemiecki zbrodniarz Erich Koch nie zginął? Plotka o Bursztynowej Komnacie była przykrywką dla akcji wywiadu." http://natemat.pl/94871, dlaczego-niemiecki-zbrodniarz-erich-koch-nie-zginal-plotka-o-bursztynowej-komnacie-byla-przykrywka-dla-akcji-wywiadu (accessed 29 May 2014).

Dobryszycka, Natalia. "Nazi gold train finders back up claims that £250m stolen from Russian Tsars by Hitler could be inside." *Mailonline*, 18 September 2015, http://www.dailymail.co.uk (accessed 28 October 2015).

Jandrić, Berislav. "Prijepori saveznika oko zahtjeva Jugoslavije za izručenjem osumnjičenih za ratne zločine iz savezničkih izbjegličkih logora u Italiji 1945. – 1947." *Časopis za suvremenu povijest* 38, no. 2 (December 2006): 457–98, http://hrcak.srce.hr/7736 (accessed 5 July 2017).

Kiwerska, Jadwiga. "Władysław Bartoszewski i dzieło porozumienia polsko-niemieckiego." *Biuletyn Instytutu Zachodniego*, no. 183, 4 May 2015, http://www.iz.poznan.pl/plik,pobierz,147,7905fc53d41d1dad319c4268ce4514ec/1157-Bartoszewski.pdf (accessed 24 July 2017).

Lemkin, Raphaël. "Les actes constituant un danger general (interétatique) consideres comme delites des droit des gens." In http://www.preventgenocide.org/fr/lemkin/madrid1933.htm (accessed 6 January 2013).

"Manfred Lachs." *Encyclopaedia Britannica Online*, http.www.britannica.com/biography/Manfred-Lachs (accessed 11 May 2016).

"Stanisław Hejmowski." http://wapedia.mobi/pl; also https://pl.wikipedia.org/wiki/Stanisław_Hejmowski (accessed 23 May 2017).

Rzepliński, Andrzej. "Ściganie zbrodni nazistowskich w Polsce w latach 1939–2004." http://absta.pl/andrzej-rzepliski-ciganie-zbrodni-nazistowskich-w-polsce-w-lat.html (accessed 29 December 2017).

"Wacław Barcikowski." http://encyclopedia.interia.pl (accessed 23 May 2017).

Wąsowicz, Marek. "Jerzy Sawicki." Internetowy Polski Słównik Biograficzny (iPSB), www.ipsb.nina.gov.pl/a/biografia/jerzy-sawicki (accessed 22 May 2017).

Index

German and European Studies

General Editor: Jennifer J. Jenkins